Soviet Policy in West Africa

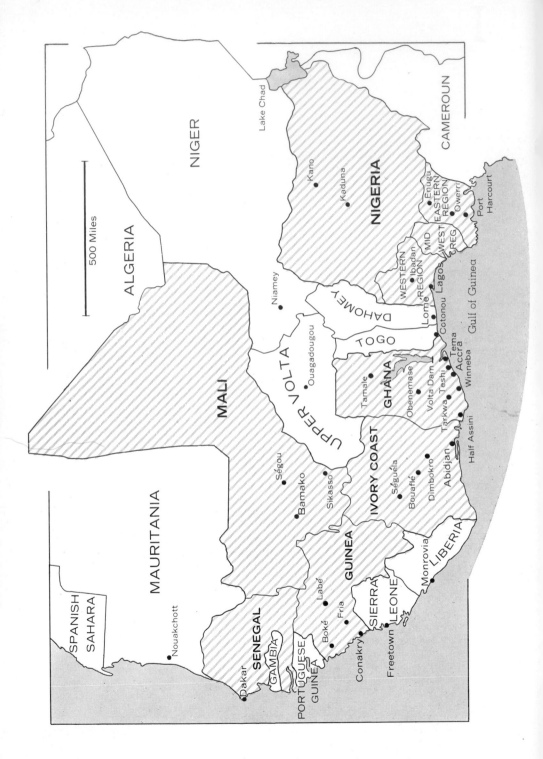

I

The Soviet Response to Colonial Africa

Black Africa did not become a serious concern of Soviet foreign policy until late in the 1950s. For the first forty years of Soviet history, a period sometimes marked by the most sweeping revolutionary expectations, this area stood on the outermost edge of Soviet consciousness. Never during this time, not even in those early fanciful years following the Revolution when Bolshevik leaders genuinely believed in the imminent uprising of oppressed peoples against colonial authority everywhere, did Black Africa receive more than fleeting notice. Even then, the small attention spared Africa was largely the result of the tie that directors of the Communist International saw between the problems of African and other, particularly American, blacks. After the Second World War, when the swift advance toward decolonization in South Asia kindled renewed interest in the "national liberation struggle," sub-Saharan Africa remained an uninspiring issue, an afterthought appended to considerations of the related but far more portentous problems of Indochina, India, the Middle East, and North Africa.

Inevitably Soviet aspirations in Africa, once aroused, were conditioned by the long period during which Soviet leaders knew or cared little about developments in this area. That failure to comprehend fully the social and political forces at work within Africa, the gratuitous expectations that policymakers held for Africa's part in the struggle against imperialism, and the occasional high-handedness of Soviet behavior were, in large part, an outcome of the years of neglect. Early Soviet policy in Africa ultimately stemmed as much from unfamiliarity as from the kind of political and diplomatic instruments available to policymakers; it owed as much to simple ignorance as to what Soviet writers call the correlation of historical forces of an epoch. These years of disregard, therefore, deserve careful summary. They compose the remarkably inauspicious prelude to the Soviet Union's clamorous entry into Africa a decade ago.

Policy before the Second World War

During the last years of World War I, as the prospects for revolution in Russia improved, Lenin dwelt increasingly on the role the colonial regions of Asia and Africa would play in the decisive assault which that revolution was to spark against the capitalist systems of Europe and America. He saw, as Marx had not, that the contest between oppressed and oppressor had been enlarged to include millions of people in the world's backward regions and that, if these auxiliary forces could be enlisted in the struggle, their revolt would fatally weaken European capitalism. In his single most important theoretical work, *Imperialism, the Highest Stage of Capitalism*—written little more than a year before the Bolshevik coup d'état—Lenin described how the modern class struggle had spread beyond capitalist societies to engulf Asian and African populations, how whole colonies had come to be transformed into the world's proletariat and European nations into its capitalists, and how—with the emergence of revolution in Russia—the upheaval of a Western proletariat and the struggle of colonial peoples would merge into a single revolutionary process directed against their common tormentors.[1]

After the revolution, the exigencies of the unconcluded war with Germany prevented Lenin and his collaborators from giving immediate form to this revolutionary alliance. Faced with the imminent prospect of military strangulation at the hands of the Kaiser's armies, they were compelled instead to concentrate their energies on efforts to invoke

---

1. This aspect of Lenin's thought has been analysed in many different places but nowhere better than in Alfred G. Meyer, *Leninism* (Cambridge: Harvard University Press, 1957), pp. 235–273.

the European revolution. Not until this danger had passed—relief purchased at a bitterly harsh price in the Brest-Litovsk Treaty of March 1918—did Soviet leaders dare leave the task of inciting Germany's workers and soldiers and begin to consider measures for fusing Asia's liberation movements with the impending proletarian revolution in Europe. By then the growing intervention of French, British, Japanese, and American forces in the north and far east of Russia raised a new danger made more vexing by a civil war in which these forces chose to meddle, and it gave Soviet leaders compelling reasons for summoning at once the exploited and toiling masses of colonial areas to join the struggle against Western imperialism. The East, as Stalin sought to remind his more Europe-oriented comrades, provided "inexhaustible reserves and is the most reliable rear base for world imperialism."[2] If these advantages could be denied Russia's newest assailants, if these regions could be set in turmoil, then the peril could be more easily and quickly surmounted.

Soviet leaders addressed their revolutionary exhortations to all colonial peoples, Africa's included. But from the very beginning the inclusion of Africa reflected mostly a desire to preserve symmetry in the appeal. In reality their expectations for revolutionary change in colonial and semicolonial areas depended almost wholly on their perceptions of the course of events in Asia and the Near East. For Soviet observers, these regions alone held the prospect of significant revolutionary development and, equally important, offered a chance for Soviet Russia to sustain and influence the colonial revolution. Geography placed Asia beside Russia and, as a consequence, the successful socialist revolution in Russia created a historic bridge linking the struggle of Asia with the more advanced proletarian struggle in West Europe. Africa remained remote and little known to Russia's new leaders.

The lack of interest was evident from the start. Africa sent few if any spokesmen to the Soviet-sponsored convocations of revolutionary nationalists; it figured to no significant degree in the discussions at these meetings; and it attracted little attention from the agencies established by these gatherings to strengthen revolutionary forces in colonial areas. When the Second Congress of the Comintern assembled in Moscow in July 1920, Turks, Persians, Chinese, Koreans, and even a Dutchman from Java were there to witness the famous exchange between Lenin and the prominent young Indian Communist M. N. Roy over the tactics

2. Joseph Stalin, *Sochineniya* (Works), IV (Moscow, 1947), 171.

to be pursued toward the bourgeois nationalists of dependent areas—but
no African was among them. Here for the first time Soviet Russia and
the newly formed Third Communist International attemped to come
to terms with the liberation movement Lenin had described as the natural
ally of the European revolution. But on the occasion no one paid attention to Africa. Later in the same year at Baku, the effort to rally colonial
peoples to form an alliance with Europe's proletariat continued, again
without significant African participation. Africa's absence this time, however, seems more important, for the convocation was expressly of "toilers
of the East," two thousand of them; and when Zinoviev moved the
exuberant delegates to a frenzy with a summons to wage a "holy war
against English imperialism," the presence of a handful of participants
claiming an attachment to Africa was scarcely noticed amid the din
of 235 Turks, 192 Persians, 156 Armenians, 100 Georgians, and the
others. To judge from the original appeal of the Comintern's executive
committee, no special effort had been made to attract African representatives: "We turn first of all to the workers and peasants of the Near
East [Persia, Armenia, Turkey], but we shall be glad to see among them
also delegates of the enslaved masses living farther from us—the representatives of India, and also the representatives of the Muslim peoples
living in free union with Soviet Russia."[3] Two months earlier, after
the Second Comintern Congress, an article in *Izvestiya* admitted that
it was clumsy to lump under the name of the East the peoples of Africa
and America as well as the peoples of Asia; yet apparently there was
little attempt to rectify the error at the Baku congress.[4]

To do so would have required more than an improvement in terminology, because the issue was essentially a matter of priorities. Not every
Bolshevik envisaged with the same ease as Lenin the convergence of the
socialist and colonial revolutions. Even in regions where revolution would
directly serve Soviet interests, the possibility of bringing socialism to
people still centuries away from extensive capitalist relationships seemed
preposterous to many. How much more unseemly—and irrelevant—
would any attempt be to match the revolutionary appeal casually extended to primitive African people with specific revolutionary efforts.
Lenin could show cause for manipulating the political unrest in nearby

3. *Izvestiya* (News), July 3, 1920, p. 1, quoted in Xenia Joukoff Eudin and
Robert C. North, eds., *Soviet Russia and the East, 1920–1927* (Stanford: Stanford
University Press, 1957), p. 80.
4. *Izvestiya,* August 11, 1920, p. 1, quoted in *ibid.,* p. 44.

colonial areas because revolution, even disturbances, in these areas struck at strategic points of British power. In fact in the Near East, Lenin was perfectly willing to ignore entirely the ideological issue and maneuver freely among such nationalist leaders as the Afghanistan emir, Amanullah Khan, his counterpart in Persia, Riza Khan, and in Turkey, Kemal Pasha, in order to weaken the British position where it had become the most vulnerable.[5] But what was to justify the staking of a substantial Soviet interest in Africa—this dark continent so unimaginably retarded in its social development, so inaccessible to Soviet influence, and so far from the principal theaters of great-power competition? There were in most regions of Africa no cadres from which to form local Communist parties, no substitute structures through which a revolutionary consciousness might be awakened among tribesmen, no revolutionary nationalists to organize the disaffection of the masses against colonial authority or to arouse even the first faint shudder beneath the weight of what Bolshevik writers called a "patriarchal-feudal" economic system.

In the circumstances Bolshevik leaders can scarcely be faulted for neglecting their revolutionary work in Africa. To men keenly aware of the limits imposed upon their action by the frailty of Soviet power and to men previously disinclined to sponsor pointless revolutionary initiatives, extending Comintern activity into Africa must have appeared a prodigal enterprise. As a direct consequence, agencies such as the Council for Propaganda and Action of the Peoples of the East, created by the Baku congress, placed sub-Saharan African conspicuously outside their sweep of attention. "In order to do more efficient and successful work in the East," ran one official proposal for improving the organization of the council,

the entire East will be divided into three separate spheres of influence [among departments of the council]: (1) The Near East, including Turkey, Arabia, Syria, Egypt, Armenia, Georgia, Persia, Azerbaijan, Daghestan, and Terek; (2) Middle Asia, including India, Afghanistan, Turkestan, Kirghizia, Bashkiria, West Chinese Turkestan, Kash-

5. A representative of Amanullah in Moscow in May 1919 declared: "I am not a communist or a socialist, but my political program has been so far that of driving the Britons from Asia. I am an irreconcilable foe of European capitalism in Asia, which is represented largely by the British. In this attitude I come close to the communists, and in that respect you and I are natural allies." *Izvestiya*, May 6, 1919, pp. 1–2, trans. in *ibid.*, p. 181. The sentiment reflected exactly the opportunity Soviet policy was most concerned to exploit.

mir, and Altai; and (3) the Far East, including China, Korea, Mongolia, Manchuria, Siberia, and Japan.[6]

Africa's exclusion from this division of labor within what was intended to be the Comintern's primary propaganda arm reflected the restrictions set upon Soviet involvement in national liberation struggles. From the vantage point of Soviet-African relations, it mattered little that the Council for Propaganda and Action expired within months of its formation or that the First Congress of Eastern Peoples was never followed by a second; Africa clearly had held no part in the Soviet calculation even while a commitment to militant revolutionary activity in colonial regions prevailed.

Soviet policy changed in 1921. It moved away from the unrestrained encouragement of revolution, which had been the mark of early idealism as well as a defensive reaction against the perils threatening the new regime, to a search for tentative accommodation with Western powers. The conventional requirements facing a nation-state, particularly the need for diplomatic acceptance and the benefits of economic cooperation, were beginning to impose themselves on the Soviet leadership. Immediately and without apparent self-consciousness, the propaganda assault on British imperialism eased; open efforts to foment revolt in the Middle East ceased; and growing ties, codified in a series of treaties signed over the early months of 1921, placed Soviet relations with Afghanistan, Persia, and Turkey on a circumspect intergovernmental basis. The New Economic Policy announced by Lenin in March 1921, depending as it did on the Soviet Union's ability to secure commodity credits and foreign investment capital, compelled Soviet leaders to reconceive the tactics of their policy toward Western countries and particularly toward Great Britain, the center of international finance.

A major point has already been made of the neglect Africa suffered during the initial period of revolutionary commitment to colonial areas. When Soviet tactics changed, reducing activity in these regions, it became even more unlikely that Africa would stimulate any prominent interest. The continued expansion of Comintern activity into the most far-flung regions of the world, evidence of the natural accumulation of duties and interests associated with any burgeoning instrument of foreign policy,

6. T. R. Tyskulov, "Komintern i rabota na Vostoke" (The Comintern and Work in the East), *Zhizn natsionalnostei* (Life of Nationalities), no. 46 (December 15, 1920), pp. 1–2, quoted in *ibid.*, p. 82.

did not alter the fact that the significance of world revolution had been subordinated to the imperatives of the Soviet revolution. Thus the attention eventually paid Black Africa was predictably the product of a moment free from imminent threats to the new regime's survival, when its leaders could explore secondary and tertiary interests as part of a more comprehensive international involvement. Having endured civil war and the intervention, salvaged the October Revolution, established priorities for foreign policy, and curtailed early revolutionary expectations, the Soviet leadership could now consider less pressing matters such as, one might assume, the task of promoting revolution in Africa. Even so throughout the 1920s Africa continued to receive paltry and curiously inappropriate notice.

In part the Soviet Union's retarded concern for developments within Africa stemmed from a near total inability to influence events taking place so far from home. Only one Communist party existed in all of Africa below the Sahara, and it was composed of white, not black, workers. The only Africans to attend the Third Comintern Congress in 1921 were white, and the first and only blacks present at the Fourth Comintern Congress in 1922 were Americans.[7] Literally, not more than a handful of black Africans had been actively enlisted in the work of the Comintern, and only a few more were ever recruited to study at the University for the Toilers of the East. Thus, even had Soviet leaders wished for a significantly larger role in formulating Africa's political course, they were, with South Africa excepted, deprived of indigenous structures and the necessary leaders.

Not so surprisingly, then, those in the Comintern responsible for the African phase of the national liberation struggle sought other channels through which to arouse, organize, and train African cadres. For them, the natural solution seemed to be the American black. He, more than the African, had been oppressed and degraded by capitalism and, once reached by the American Communist Party, he would help to implant Marxism not only in the United States but in Africa as well. The Negroes of North America, wrote one Comintern publicist, "can and must bring into being a Negro Communist literature and press, must establish training centers for agitators and propagandists who will carry on their work not only in the USA but in Africa itself by means of correspondence,

7. Roger Edward Kanet, "The Soviet Union and Sub-Saharan Africa: Communist Policy toward Africa, 1917–1965" (unpubl. diss., Princeton University, 1966), p. 101.

as well as by the dispatch of special emissaries to the various localities."[8] The author was elaborating an idea conceived by the Fourth Comintern Congress (1922), which had tacked to the report of a specially appointed Negro Commission a proposal to deploy American blacks as propagandists throughout Africa, underscoring their "important role in the liberation struggle of the entire African race."[9] Plans were made to infiltrate American Communists into black associations, particularly Marcus Garvey's back-to-Africa movement, and from these groups to draw blacks, who would be trained in Soviet Russia and dispatched to Africa, to stimulate the revolutionary consciousness of their African brothers.

But the American Communist Party found this a difficult task to carry out. The party succeeded only to a limited degree in penetrating the NAACP, Garvey's movement, and similar organizations, and it failed decisively to establish influence over their memberships. Relatively few blacks were converted to Communism, and those who did join the party frequently became victims of derisive, sometimes physical, attacks inflicted by the more fanatical followers of Garvey. Even the small group of American blacks attracted to the Soviet Union for study at Lenin University and the University of Toilers of the East disappointed their benefactors by choosing to return to the United States rather than evangelize African tribesmen. In Africa the effect of all this on the course of affairs was, inevitably, negligible. More than anything else, the tactical decision of the Fourth Comintern Congress to unite the African revolution and the American black's discontent demonstrates the helplessness of Soviet policymakers who sought progress in Africa.

The point is worth restating, however, that few if any among the new Soviet leaders found the overwhelming limits to Soviet influence in Africa particularly dismaying. Who among them cared? No member of the Commissariat of Foreign Affairs or the executive committee of the Comintern could have imagined, except by the greatest flight of fancy, that sub-Saharan Africa mattered in the slightest to men preoccupied with the immediate requirements of the New Economic Policy.

8. J. Steklov, "The Awakening of a Race," *International Press Correspondence,* II (November 24, 1922), 826.

9. Rose P. Stokes (pseud. "Sasha"), "Report and Resolution on the Negro Question," *International Press Correspondence,* III, no. 2 (1923), 21, quoted in Kanet, "The Soviet Union and Sub-Saharan Africa," p. 106.

It would have been idiocy to dream that Lenin, Bukharin, Zinoviev, or the Anglo-American Secretariat expected or wanted an African revolution.

What else explains the indifference of Soviet leaders, not to mention the Comintern, to events in the one sub-Saharan African country blessed with a functioning Communist party? South Africa, of course, was not representative of much of Black Africa; its large, intransigent non-African population dominated a far more highly developed economy, incorporating within its massive mining industry not hundreds but thousands of white laborers. Thus, in this sense, South Africa represented something more hopeful than the rest of Black Africa did, a society whose structure Marxist-Leninists could comprehend and whose development they could predict. Certainly if the new leaders of Russia had any interest in Africa, this country would have prompted more than passing reference in the context of the Comintern's concern for the American black.

Yet it received no more.[10] True, Comintern official considered the problem of the American black part of a larger world black problem (as they did the question of South Africa), but invariably their attitude toward America determined their approach to the general problem. From the Fourth Comintern Congress on, Comintern organizers left little doubt that the American black, not white South African Communists, spoke for the world's black people, even in Africa. It was a significant indication of the prevailing Comintern view that Sydney Bunting, the South African Communist Party's chief delegate to the congress, became a member of the special Negro Commission only because he asked to; and equally revealing that an American black delivered the Commission's report to the congress. Similarly, meetings of both the Comintern executive and the Red International of Labor Unions (Profintern), which raised from time to time the issue of international Communism's interest in the world Negro problem, made no attempt to involve the South Africans. As late as 1928 South African trade-union leaders were absent from the Fourth Congress of the Profintern and discussions dealing with the organization of black labor. American Negro Communists, on the

10. The following remarks about the South African Communist Party are based on information contained in an excellent and thorough study by Sheridan Waite Johns, III, "Marxism-Leninism in a Multi-Racial Environment: The Origins and Early History of the Communist Party of South Africa, 1914–1932" (unpubl. diss., Harvard University, 1965).

other hand, in nearly every instance contributed conspicuously, if not always significantly, to the dialogue staged at these conferences.[11]

In keeping with these priorities, specific efforts to organize black workers centered principally on the United States. Profintern officials thought it best to begin where the black appeared most easily organized and later, pending the results of experience in America, to extend these efforts elsewhere. So an American Negro Labor Congress was called by the American Communist Party for October 1925, to coordinate forces struggling to create a united black labor movement in the United States. A World Congress of Colored Workers planned for March 1926 in Brussels, supposedly to involve, in their turn, black workers from the Soudan, West Africa, and South Africa, never took place. Its fate, to a very great extent, symbolized the Soviet leadership's neglect of Africa generally and South Africa particularly. Time taught Communists in South Africa and their sympathizers in other parts of the continent to appreciate Bunting's lament in 1923 on his return from the Soviet Union:

> my chief regret is that during all the time I have been in Moscow, the 'Presidium,' *i.e.,* in effect this 'Big Five' have never found time to discuss South African affairs either with me or without me; not indeed, for want of interest, but because other matters are even more engrossing; delegates from countries with a bigger party and more immediate prospects are more important—Moscow soon takes the conceit out of a fellow![12]

Bunting must have been a generous man.

Perhaps Soviet leaders justified their lack of concern in terms of the difficulties confronting a Communist party in South Africa. These were indisputably discouraging. Founded by whites in 1921, the party, in guarding its original character, not only risked becoming a minority party of a minority group, it violated the basic Marxian notion of class solidarity. Yet to open the party to nonwhites raised the equally perilous prospect of driving away the more highly skilled and wealthy white cadre who were resentful of any improvement in the competitive position of the African worker. What was the party to say to striking workers

11. For an account of the American black's part in these sessions, see Theodore Draper, *American Communism and Soviet Russia* (New York: Viking Press, 1960).

12. *The International* (South Africa), January 19, 1923, quoted in Johns, "Marxism-Leninism in a Multi-Racial Environment," p. 413.

who marched under the banner: "Workers of the World, Fight and Unite for a white South Africa"?[13] On the other hand, how could it work with African organizations that were content to petition a bourgeois government for piecemeal improvements in the lot of the nonwhite worker and that betrayed at times unmistakable racist tendencies? To refuse an alliance with these parties, however, meant abdicating the advantages of affiliation with organizations extremely successful among black workers. And all of this existed before the sticky problem of what the party was to offer the vast portion of South Africa's population, the African peasantry. Perhaps these circumstances explained the Soviet Union's low enthusiasm for a party that, by its own estimation, had no more than four hundred members in January 1927.[14]

The answer is obscure, and the inclination exists to doubt whether it is even worth seeking. Certainly the effect was the same: South African and Soviet Communism proceeded along their separate courses, one stoutly impervious to the other's model, the second indifferent to the first's very existence. Indeed, for one period of more than three years from mid-1924 to late 1927, the two parties lost all direct contact. Supposedly only one South African visited the Soviet Union during this time and, needless to say, no Soviet official journeyed to South Africa. The South African Communist Party remained, as described by Sheridan Johns, merely "on the Comintern's mailing list."[15] It might be added that, in the familiar fashion of all victims of the addressograph, the party disregarded much of what was sent.

Are we then to accept the Soviet Union's continued isolation from developments within Africa as the perfectly comprehensible, even more the unavoidable, consequence of Africa's impenetrability? What more could the Soviet leadership have done to aid fellow revolutionaries in South Africa? Probably nothing, but that, as it turned out, was not the decisive issue. However massive were obstacles impeding the advance of Communism in Africa, Stalin, it appears, did not make his calculations on this basis.

At one time early in the history of Soviet policy, Soviet indifference could be read as a realistic adjustment to the problems posed by Africa.

13. Not only had white workers used this slogan during the historic 1922 Witwatersrand general strike, but before the strike was ended many of these workers had turned violently on black workers. See *ibid.*, p. 266.

14. *Ibid.*, p. 375.

15. *Ibid.*, p. 414.

In part, it was. But when late in the 1920s, without any basic transformation in Africa, the Soviet leadership suddenly took an interest in manipulating the South African Communist Party's program, it became evident that Soviet behavior depended on factors largely unrelated to the internal prospects of South African Communism. One of Stalin's important contributions to Soviet foreign policy was to prove that indifference to conditions in an area need not be passive; that a judicious disregard for the actual state of affairs in the area could justify the most active and resolute policy there. Stalin's disdain for local conditions in deciding what tactics a foreign Communist party would adopt, applying only the criteria of Soviet interests, represented a pioneering version of that peculiar perspective which would plague Soviet policy, distorting its underlying assumptions, well into the modern phase of Soviet involvement in Africa.

There is no contradiction between the contention that by 1928 Stalin assigned Africa a role betraying his complete insensitivity to the situation there and the argument that earlier the Soviet leadership's lack of interest in Africa derived from a keen awareness of its inability to influence African events. Both involved assessments of Soviet access to African politics, an issue somewhat removed from the actual outlook for socialism in Africa. Access, say through a fledgling Communist party, could have been exploited to accelerate a country's revolutionary preparation. Then, too, it could have been employed to serve immediate policy needs. Nothing, however, guaranteed that one objective would reinforce the other. Indeed, often they were viewed as competing. In Stalin's scheme of priorities, it was thoroughly inconceivable that the task of working for the reconstruction of other societies could take precedence over the least significant requirement of Soviet policy. Never was this plainer than in July 1928 when the Sixth Comintern Congress assembled to approve Stalin's new instructions to the international Communist movement.

To grasp the departures of what has been called the Comintern's Long Parliament (it met from July 17 to September 1), some of the most extraordinary of which related to South Africa, we should recall something of the atmosphere in the summer of 1928. The Soviet Union at the time was passing through the lingering phases of a mild war scare, which Soviet leaders either had themselves accepted or were consciously using for their own purposes. Allegedly the British, or some hostile neighbor sponsored by the British, stood ready to unleash an armed attack on the Soviet Union: witness the vilely provocative raids on the Soviet embassy in Peking on April 6, 1927, and the Soviet trade delegation and Arcos in London on May 12, 1927; the British government's decision to sever diplomatic relations; and then, as a desperate attempt to embitter Soviet-Polish relations, the assassination of the Soviet minister to Poland engineered by "agents of the Conservative Party" on June 7, 1927.[16] That no attack had been launched against the Soviet Union during the intervening year did not deter Soviet speakers at the Sixth Comintern Congress from vigorously insisting on the continuing likelihood of war—they referred constantly to "the approaching war"—if not war against the USSR, then war among capitalist powers, particularly the United States and Great Britain. In the circumstances a shift toward greater militancy in Comintern tactics should have surprised no one. The justification had already been established.

Unlike delegates to the congress, however, historians have the right to question whether "the struggle against the danger of imperialist war," as the main theses of the congress were entitled, fully explained the Comintern's bitter decision to intensify the assault on "social democracy." Or was the "adoption of sharper methods of struggle against the social-democratic parties"—borrowing Bukharin's phrase—inspired more by the specific apprehension that German social democrats wanted to accelerate Germany's growing rapprochement with France, thereby liquidating what remained of the post-Rapallo configuration of power in Europe?[17] Or possibly the attack on social-democratic parties reflected Soviet frustration and resentment over the continued vitality (Bukharin used this word) of an old foe, whose appeal to European workers would cut into Communist support at a moment when foreign enemies were huddling and when Soviet leaders were confronting the decision to embark upon the forced-draft industrialization of the Soviet economy. Or was it simply that Stalin was utilizing the specter of renewed intervention to eliminate domestic political competitors and to reconcile the Russian people to the burdens of the first Five-Year Plan?

Whatever its inspiration, the decision to throw over any alliance with

16. Stalin used the phrase, a reference to Stanley Baldwin's majority party, in an article on the war danger, July 28, 1927. Stalin, *Sochineniya*, IX, 322, trans. in Jane Degras, ed., *Soviet Documents on Foreign Policy*, II (London: Oxford University Press, 1952), 235.

17. From *Stenograficheski otchet VI Kongressa Kominterna* (Stenographic Report of the Sixth Comintern Congress), I (Moscow, 1929–1930), 27–28, trans. in Xenia J. Eudin and Robert M. Slusser, eds., *Soviet Foreign Policy, 1928–1934*, I (University Park: Pennsylvania State University Press, 1966), 118.

the European left echoed in the hostility declared against collaborating with national bourgeois movements in the Third World. June 1928 was but six months after the suppression of the Canton rising and the final humiliation of Stalin's strategy of cooperating with the Kuomintang. Twice in 1927 sections of the Kuomintang allied with the Chinese Communist Party had gone over to counterrevolution and each time the Chinese Communists had paid the human price for Stalin's political errors. Thus, Stalin had good reason, albeit embarrassing reason, for having bourgeois nationalists denounced before the Sixth Comintern Congress. Others must not repeat the "opportunistic" blunder of the Chinese Communist leadership, which had relied too completely on revolutionary-bourgeois nationalists and had overlooked signs of their impending treachery. As the carefully orchestrated congress warned, the risk of working with these elements was simply too great. " 'Worker-peasant parties,' no matter how revolutionary they may be at particular periods" could "too easily change into ordinary petty-bourgeois parties."[18]

The dissimulation was double: Stalin not only absolved himself from any blame for the tactical errors of the past half decade; he now adopted intact precisely the tactics Trotsky had been urging all along as an alternative to Stalin's. Trotsky had condemned the alliance between the Chinese Communist Party and the Wuhan left wing of the Kuomintang. He had demanded that the united front be abandoned before it was too late and encouragement be given to the increasingly radical actions of the peasantry. But Trotsky had been driven from the party at the Fifteenth Party Congress in December, and by the time the Sixth World Congress assembled he was already in flight from Moscow. Who, in June 1928, would have been insolent enough to point out that the new tactical line had been considered political heresy on Trotsky's lips only months earlier? Who, indeed, would soon be willing to challenge Stalin in any sphere? Reduced to its essence, the real importance of the Sixth Comintern Congress resided in the mute testimony it offered to the imposition of Stalin's iron control over the international Communist movement.

Africa had its small part to play in the coronation. As might be anticipated given the course of Soviet-African relations up to this point, its role turned out to be something less than gratifying. Every Communist

18. Excerpts from the theses on "The Revolutionary Movement in the Colonies and Semicolonies," adopted at the Sixth Congress of the Comintern, trans. in *ibid.*, p. 145.

party's reason for being, to understand the implications of the Sixth Comintern Congress, sprang from the service it could give the "only fatherland of socialism." In 1928, just as they girded for a monumental assault upon Russian society, Soviet leaders (supposedly) detected an alarming accumulation of forces threatening to disrupt the international environment. The very thought of war, a danger that within a few years would have real substance, started them fidgeting. The first priority of every other Communist party, therefore, automatically was to defend the Soviet Union against imperialist attack. Even the far-away South African Communist Party was wheeled into place. The party, according to instructions from the Comintern's executive, "must fight by all means against the help given to the military policy of Great Britain which found expression in the tacit support of the break of the British imperialists with the U.S.S.R."[19] In the coming months greater attention was to be paid to "antimilitarist work."

But this part of the directive told only a portion of the story. Other less explicit aspects of the new strategy far more fundamentally affected the condition and role of the party within its own milieu. A Communist party in a colonial region had more to do than simply bring to bear the tactics of public demonstration, strikes, and draft resistance; its whole strategy, its whole program, had to be calculated to strengthen Communism's position so that ultimately the Soviet Union's imperialist adversary could be effectively challenged, not merely harrassed. The strategy dictated to the South African Communist Party in 1928, no doubt, derived its inspiration from a genuine determination to enhance Communism in South Africa—if in a manner paralleling Soviet interests. But the more telling fact was that this strategy had originated in Moscow and that it had been imposed on a reluctant local Communist leadership. Moscow had decided, over the unhappy objections of South African delegates to the Sixth Congress, that if the party were to develop a mass appeal, it would have to focus on the black peasantry and that to do this it must advance immediately the slogan of "an independent native South African republic." South African protests, based on the conviction that neither white nor black would respond favorably—that the white would be frightened and angered by the prospect of black domination and that the black would be offended by a scheme he suspected was intended to preserve segregated communities—reverberated harmlessly

19. *Communist International,* VI (December 15, 1928), 53–56, in *ibid.,* p. 153.

within the carefully packed organs of the Comintern. Perhaps it was delusive to expect a completely impartial hearing from a committee comprising, in part, nine Russians, seven hand-picked American Communists, and one South African. Still, the refusal of the Negro Sub-Commission to listen at all to South African pleadings seems surprising. A disgruntled and distressed group of South African Communist leaders departed from the Soviet Union at the congress' conclusion and, in the months that followed, performed only with the greatest reluctance the tasks forced upon them by the Soviet leadership. Eventually the South African Communist Party was brought to heel as its disenchanted leaders were first rebuked and then expelled from the party they had founded a decade earlier.

In the next several years the combined failure of the tactics decreed by the Sixth Comintern Congress and the grim, overriding threat raised by Hitler's rise to power impelled Stalin again to revise the Comintern's direction. But the specific modification mattered little. It only served to confirm among a wider circle of black and African leaders Stalin's evident manipulation of the international Communist movement to reinforce his own policy objectives. For a man like George Padmore—the prominent, American-trained West Indian official of the Profintern—Stalin's latest turnabout was the last straw. With a good many other disgusted blacks, Padmore responded to instructions to muffle the emphasis on anticolonial struggle, lest the drive to build collective security in Europe be endangered, by severing his relationship with the Comintern.[20] No degree of recrimination against this highly respected leader of the Profintern sponsored International Trade Union Congress of Negro Workers could obscure the fact that Stalin's expediential approach to African Communism had alienated many black and white African Communists, not to mention revolutionary nationalists.

If more damage could have been done to the Soviet standing in colonial regions, it would have been difficult to imagine—that is, until Stalin accepted the Non-Aggression Pact with Germany in August 1939. African nationalists and Communists did not know it at the time, but in the fall of 1940 the Soviet Union had been willing to concede Central Africa to German colonial aspirations and to recognize Italy's conquest of Northeastern Africa in return for additional assurances concerning

20. An account more specific than any in Padmore's own writings is James R. Hooker, *Black Revolutionary: George Padmore's Path from Communism to Pan-Africanism* (London: Pall Mall Press, 1967), pp. 31–38.

Soviet Policy in West Africa

Soviet security.[21] Had they known, the Soviet leadership's reputation as the friend of the African national liberation struggle would no doubt have been further diminished. But by then Africa's fate had completely receded from Soviet thoughts. When Africa re-emerged as even a peripheral concern, the war was nearly over and the momentous process of decolonization was already underway.

The Decolonization of Africa

Many years after Stalin's rudely indifferent reaction to interwar developments within Africa, the Soviet Union's most prominent Africanist, the late Ivan Potekhin, remarked that "until the Second World War, Africa, particularly its huge, principal part south of the Sahara, stood, as it were, to the side of the high road of world history."[22] He was speaking generally about a circumstance, but the secondary judgment written into his comment characterized no country's perspective more perfectly than the Soviet Union's. Potekhin could hardly have been expected to blurt out that the Soviet Union, the epicenter of world revolution, had for two decades turned its back on developments within Africa, even less that the Soviet Union's jaundiced view of the world revolution partially accounted for this neglect. But he did give his reader some idea of those factors that in any circumstances would have discouraged Soviet interest in this area.

Until the war, Potekhin noted, there had been almost no "national political organization" in sub-Saharan Africa. The Kikuyu Central Association (KCA) in Kenya, according to him, had been an extremely

21. See Secret Protocol No. 1 (Draft) of "Agreement Between the States of the Three Power Pact, Germany, Italy and Japan, on the One Side, and the Soviet Union on the Other Side," in Raymond J. Sontag and James S. Biddie, eds., *Nazi-Soviet Relations, 1939–1941: Documents from the Archives of the German Foreign Office* (Washington: Government Printing Office, 1948), p. 257.

22. I. I. Potekhin, "Politicheskoe polozhenie v strankh Afriki" (The Political Situation in African Countries), *Sovetskoe vostokovedenie* (Soviet Orientology) no. 1 (1956), p. 22. A more recent remark by another commentator is also interesting: "The opportunities for direct contacts between young Soviet Russia and African countries were extremely limited; there was practically no intercourse. Consequently, only very few of the foreign policy actions of the Soviet Republic [were] directly concerned with Africa." Anatoly Gromyko, "Soviet Foreign Policy and Africa," *International Affairs*, no. 9 (1967), p. 23. Gromyko is the son of Foreign Minister Andrei Gromyko and, at the time, he was head of the international relations sector of the African Institute.

small organization, only "half legal" and incapable of more than the most feeble activity; the Nigerian National Democratic Party, incorporating the upper tier of the "colonial intelligentsia," had no influence beyond the city of Lagos; the West African National Congress in the Gold Coast had remained highly diffuse, without a clearly defined organizational program; and so the story went. Nowhere in Africa, outside Egypt, the Maghreb, and South Africa, had there appeared national organizations strong enough to guide the anti-imperialist movement.[23] It would miss the point to make an issue of Potekhin's inaccuracies: the KCA was not a " half legal" organization, faint-hearted and inept; it existed as a perfectly lawful organization from 1924 to 1940 during which time it attracted considerable membership (claimed at seven thousand by 1940), assumed a stubborn and significant role in colonial politics, and formed the basic political experience of a number of Kenyan leaders, including Jomo Kenyatta. Similarly the market women, tribal chieftans, and imams who comprised the core organization of the Nigerian NDP hardly constituted the "top strata of the colonial intelligentsia," though it was true that their influence through the party remained confined largely to the Lagos region; and the WANC, as comparisons go, represented one of the poorer specimens of political organization in the Gold Coast during the interwar period.[24] If Potekhin wanted to minimize the Gold Coast's strongest structures, he might have mentioned the more successful Aborigines' Rights Protection Society or, somewhat later, the National Democratic Party. But all of this is nitpicking and in the first place fails to challenge Potekin's major point that none of these political associations proved able to arouse and sustain national movements comparable to those of the postwar period. And, more important, it skips over the essential consideration that, whatever the facts were in the matter, the Soviet leadership undoubtedly saw the situation this way and acted accordingly. African colonies, Potekhin concluded, until the eve of the Second World War, could muster no more than "sporadic, local demonstrations" against the most intolerable aspects of colonial

23. Potekhin, "Politicheskoe polozhenie v stranakh Afriki," p. 24.

24. See Carl G. Rosberg, Jr., and John Nottingham, The Myth of "Mau Mau" Nationalism in Kenya (New York: Praeger, 1966), esp. pp. 71–104, 136–187; Donald L. Barnett and Karari Njama, Mau Mau from Within (New York: Monthly Review Press, 1966), pp. 37–39; Richard L. Sklar, Nigerian Political Parties (Princeton: Princeton University Press, 1963), pp. 46–48; David E. Apter, The Gold Coast in Transition (Princeton: Princeton University Press, 1955), pp. 35–36, 52–53.

rule, such as the expropriation of land, heavier tax levies, the imposition of forced labor, and the brutality of individual colonial administrators. The strong implication was that Africa afforded small revolutionary opportunity before the war.

The situation changed radically after 1945, Potekhin contended. "At once" in the majority of African countries "mass national organizations" appeared, proclaiming their determination to struggle for national liberation. There emerged in French West Africa the Rassemblement Démocratique Africain, a mass organization with a membership of nearly a million, sections in all fourteen French colonies, and the avowed purpose of achieving "national, economic, and social liberation." Counterpart organizations, such as the National Council of Nigeria and the Cameroons and the United Gold Coast Convention, sprang up in the British colonies of West Africa. And across Africa the process of forming political parties dedicated to the struggle against colonialism repeated itself again and again. The creation in so short a time of mass political organizations throughout the continent signaled, in Potekhin's words, "the beginning of a new historical stage in the life of African peoples."[25]

Potekhin was writing in 1956, however, and his enthusiasm over events in postwar Africa developed somewhat after the fact. Ten years earlier, when these parties began to form and the process of decolonization commenced, Potekhin had been far less sympathetic. It took Soviet commentators nearly a decade to decide that the nationalist movements of Africa were essentially progressive and deserved support. By then Soviet policymakers had to confront the first of the many new African states to achieve independence after the war. This transformation in attitudes, the shift from a vigorous hostility toward bourgeois African nationalists and the movements they led to their acceptance and even courtship, is the major concern of the remainder of this chapter. It constitutes the essential backdrop to the first Soviet involvement with independent Africa late in the fifties.

Potekhin himself personifies the evolution in the Soviet point of view. His work over this period provided clear landmarks at each turn of the shifting appraisal of the African situation. He lent continuity to the transition underway and because he so dominated the field of African studies, his estimation, no doubt schooled by what his party's leader expected of him, came to represent as nearly as possible the official

25. Potekhin, "Politicheskoe polozhenie v stranakh Afriki," p. 25.

assessment. Unlike his own teacher, the linguist D. A. Olderogge, Potekhin's writings were generally political, in an era when doing political research invariably meant reproducing rigid and hackneyed propaganda themes. Often his arguments appeared, with almost no change in wording, in several different articles, even sometimes in the work of other writers. Potekhin's interest in Africa stretched back to the first decade of Soviet power, by which time he was already busy with organizational tasks within the Bolshevik party. His graduate research on the South African Bantu was not published until 1955.[26] But long before the appearance of his first monograph, Potekhin had become deeply involved in shaping Soviet thought on Black Africa and, by his own admission, at times in implementing policy. He confessed, for example, to influencing the content of *The Negro Worker,* a publication of the International Trade Union Committee of Negro Workers launched in the early 1930s under the editorship of George Padmore and a handful of African and American blacks.[27] His precise role in the period before the war remains obscure, but by 1948 in a series of articles he had established his position as the Soviet Union's pre-eminent political commentator on sub-Saharan Africa.

During the first years after the war, Potekhin and a handful of other commentators argued unpersuasively, in part because they themselves seemed unpersuaded, that Black Africa had become an important part of the national liberation revolution. References to the awakening of the African masses, the mounting challenge to colonial rule, the growing cohesion of the proletariat, sounded rather hollow when made without supporting evidence, and the case advanced looked suspiciously like an attempt to slip Africa into the phalanxes of the decolonization movement by generalizing from the success of other areas. Frequent allusion to the impetus the war had given to the guerrilla movement in Southeast Asia, for example, was stretched to the limits of credibility when Potekhin contended in an early article on Nigeria that fear of losing the support of African colonial peoples during the war forced France, England, and

26. I. I. Potekhin, *Formirovanie natsionalnoi obshchnosti Yuzhnoafrikanskikh Bantu* (The Formation of a National Community of the South African Bantu; Moscow, 1955).

27. Rolf Italiaander, *Schwarze haut im roten Griff* (Dusseldorf–Vienna: Econ Verlag, 1962), p. 74, cited in Kanet, "The Soviet Union and Sub-Saharan Africa," p. 146. At the time, he was apparently working with the Comintern apparatus. For more biographical information see "Africana," *Mizan,* VI (October 1964), 5–6.

the United States to promise these areas freedom and independence.[28] It seemed similarly farfetched for another writer to maintain that the "mass pressure of local inhabitants" had compelled the French National Assembly to create the "Grand Councils" of French Equatorial and West Africa.[29] This point, however, emerges from a single short paragraph devoted to Black Africa in two hundred pages on the French colonial empire, and this is perhaps a better indication of the actual level of Soviet interest than the specific content of various *pro forma* endorsements. In any realistic order of priorities, Black Africa still ranked far behind Indochina, India, and even North Africa.

As a result, the arguments of Potekhin and others have a distinctly hollow ring. Either they were deceiving themselves (as, of course, they may well have been doing) or they were engaged in markedly disingenuous phrase mongering. Their analysis begins by emphasizing the peasantry's "principal" role in the "anti-imperialist movement"—after all it composed 95 percent of the population. Sheer mass made its participation "one of the chief factors in the development of this movement."[30] So Potekhin was encouraged by a series of incidents involving popular peasant revolt against "traditional leaders" who were considered too much the tool of British imperialism. In different villages of the Gold Coast, Sierra Leone, and Nigeria, the people had turned against their British-chosen chiefs, in some cases driving them from the region, and Potekhin took this to represent the heightening of revolutionary consciousness among the peasant masses.[31] He goes on to credit this progress to "the historic victory of the Socialist Countries over the forces of fascism" and, rather vaguely, to "the development of all postwar world events." Daily, he says, the peasants "are being drawn more decisively into the political life of the colonies."

But Potekhin's argument could be carried only up to a point; ulti-

28. I. I. Potekhin, "O'samobytnoi afrikanskoi' demokrati v Nigerii" (An "Original African" Democracy in Nigeria), *Sovetskaya etnografiya* (Soviet Ethnography), no. 4 (1947), p. 244.

29. F. N. Petrova, ed., "Frantsuzskaya kolonialnaya imperiya" (The French Colonial Empire), *Frantsiya i ee vladeniya* (France and Her Possessions; Moscow, 1948), p. 486.

30. I. I. Potekhin, "Manevry angliiskogo imperialisma v zapadnoi Afrike" (Maneuvers of English Imperialism in West Africa) in V. Ya. Vasileva, I. M. Lemin, and V. A. Maslennikov, eds., *Imperialisticheskaya borba za Afriky i osvoboditelnoe dvizhenie narodov* (Imperialist Struggle for Africa and the People's Liberation Movement; Moscow, 1953), p. 217.

31. *Ibid.*, p. 218.

mately he, like other writers, had to admit that the "peasant movement" in Africa "remained the weak part of the anti-imperialist front." However essential as the makeweight of revolution, the peasant was still part of an overwhelmingly shapeless stratum of society. He had no independent political organization. He was illiterate, "crushed by feudal customs," and untempered by the experience of political struggle. To say the least, the peasant had not yet generated any consistent opposition to the colonial policy of British imperialism.

What of his more revolutionary counterpart, the African worker, the bearer and beneficiary of the new socialist society? Was he likely to be a more reliable protagonist of the anticolonial struggle? Potekhin's argument at this point becomes almost wistful. The war had greatly accelerated the growth of an African proletariat, he contends. The European powers, to satisfy demands created by the military effort, had had no choice but to develop both small-scale manufacturing and the mining industry, and, in the process, they of course had given new impetus to the rising African proletariat. Moreover, the recruitment of African peasants into European armies had introduced those accustomed to a simple primitive existence to the world beyond the village, aroused new expectations, and, with demobilization, infused these transformed elements into the urban community. In French West Africa, noted one Soviet writer, the increase in the working class between 1935 and 1947 exceeded 30 percent.[32] Invariably writers of the period repeated at some point in every article the ritual tally of a growing proletariat. In the Gold Coast between 1947 and 1951 the number of workers grew from 277,000 to 306,000; in Nigeria by 1951 the number reached 274,000; in French West and Equatorial Africa the total approached 500,000; and so on. Oppressed by declining real wages, suffering severe unemployment (a figure of 30,000 was used for Nigeria), and forcibly prevented from doing anything to ease these problems, African workers resorted increasingly to mass strikes. When these were suppressed by colonial authorities, their alienation from the old order became complete. Already they had started to organize their forces by banding together in trade unions and, in some cases, trade-union federations. A conference of trade unions in British East Africa in 1948 had attracted "sixty" delegations

32. S. Datlin, "Borba narodov frantsuzskoi zapodnoi i ekvatorialnoi Afriki posle vtoroi mirovoi voiny" (The Struggle of the Peoples of French West and Equatorial Africa after the Second World War), in Vasileva et al., *Imperialisticheskaya borba za Afriky,* p. 238.

and was followed the next year by the formation of the militant East African Trades Union Congress; in Nigeria alone there were fifty-nine unions and, in Ghana, twenty.[33] Soviet writers tried to create the impression that the African proletariat was swiftly acquiring the strength to assume the revolutionary mission history had assigned it.

But the case for the African proletariat had been no more convincing than the deference paid to the African peasant. However much it pained the intellectuals of the world's leading proletarian state, workers were obviously not going to dominate the anti-imperialist struggle in Black Africa. They more than anyone (no one else would even have thought to raise the issue) knew that the proletariat was hopelessly insignificant in the African colonies. All the talk about the rapid expansion of the working class ended with the resigned admission that it represented no more than 2 percent of the population, and this, Potekhin conceded, explained why the proletariat "still had not become the leader of all democratic forces" in this region.[34] Furthermore, the vigor of even this small portion of society deserved to be regarded skeptically, for a high percentage of workers remained seasonal; thus when their work ended on the large farms they went back to the village, never quite freeing themselves from their traditional environment. A segment of the population other than the peasantry or the proletariat would have to take charge of the coalition against colonial power.

Inescapably this could only be the national bourgeoisie. The discomfort Soviet writers felt in the face of this fact is fairly obvious. The national bourgeoisie—it turned out that they were referring primarily to the évolués leading nationalist movements—were the principal movers of the liberation revolution and some kind of accommodation had to be reached with them. Still, these were unreliable, even treacherous, elements whose ultimate interests ensured that at some point they would betray the revolution and join the forces of imperialism. On what basis then could socialists accept African leaders and their bourgeois parties?

---

33. See I. Lemin, "Imperialisticheskoe sopernichestvo v Afrike i natsionalno-osvoboditelnoe dvizhenie afrikanskikh narodov" (Imperialist Competition in Africa and the National Liberation Movement of African Peoples), in V. A. Maslennikov, ed., *Uglublenie krizisa kolonialnoi sistemy imperialisma* (The Deepening Crisis of the Imperialist Colonial System; Moscow, 1953, p. 590, and Potekhin, "Manevry angliiskogo imperializma v zapodnoi Afrike," p. 220.

34. Potekhin, "Manevry angliiskogo imperializma v zapodnoi Afrike," p. 221. For a similar reference see Datlin, "Borba narodov frantsuzskoi zapodnoi i ekvatorial Afriki," p. 258.

Soviet attempts to resolve the dilemma became the outstanding feature of early Soviet interest in Africa, and more than any other determined the Soviet reaction to Africa. At this point it was the Soviet leadership's reluctance to accept the national bourgeoisie which inevitably produced the reserve in Soviet policy.

The Soviet view of the bourgeoisie in colonial regions had always been ambiguous, and that ambiguity was extended to the African bourgeoisie. Thus Soviet writers considered the *national* ("middle" or "liberal") bourgeoisie only a part of the whole bourgeoisie. They wrote as well of another group, the "comprador" (sometimes "big," sometimes "bureaucratic") bourgeoisie, an imprecise, though clearly opprobrious, category to which traders, "plantation owners," and native administrators were all at one time or another consigned. Already having thrown its lot in with the colonial master, this was a stratum of society beyond redemption. The difference between the national and the comprador bourgeoisie rested with the national bourgeoisie's temporary commitment to the struggle against imperialism. Thus, though eventually these people too would sell out the revolution, right now they might be counted upon to take part in the national liberation movement—a somewhat over-righteous formula since many whom Soviet writers labeled as the "national bourgeoisie" had fathered and now guided the only political organizations demanding independence.

But the shallowness and irrelevance of Soviet conceptions of political leadership in Africa generally characterized the way they responded to Africa during these early postwar years. Admittedly there was not much of a national bourgeoisie in the specific sense of the term; that is, there were very few local African capitalists since most enterprise, particularly the important mining industry, remained dominated by foreign capital. However, the small national bourgeoisie that had emerged, primarily in the agricultural and export sectors, allegedly resented the monopolistic economic position guarded by expatriates and wished to drive them from their colonies, if only to create opportunities for local capital. In any case, it was the "intelligentsia," to use the Soviet rubric closest to the truth, not shopkeepers or small manufacturers, who were making the African revolution and were therefore the ones Soviet writers primarily had in mind. To a degree they sensed the awkwardness of their classification and never firmly and clearly equated the intelligentsia with the national bourgeoisie. Yet, ultimately, the need to find an orthodox formulation to identify the new nationalists of Africa brought them to put Kwame Nkrumah in the same group as George Alfred Grant, one of the Gold Coast's wealthiest businessmen and the first president of the United Gold Coast Convention (UGCC). Nor can it be denied that in the last instance their terminology reflected the small difference they saw between these two men.

Say what you like about the restlessness of the national bourgeoisie, its growing resistance to colonial rule—and Soviet journals recounted in considerable detail its efforts to secure constitutions promising independence—it could not be trusted to carry the struggle to the end. Too soon it would accept the token concessions of the colonial administration and go over to the other side. Potekhin noted, for example, that the postwar Gold Coast party, the UGCC, originally rejected the 1946 constitution, the Burns Constitution, offered by the Labour government because, he contended, party leaders understood it as an attempt "to deceive the people with superficial reforms."[35] They had condemned its antidemocratic character, had taken a decision to boycott the legislative council established by the constitution, and later in 1948 had even turned to the increasingly impoverished masses, giving leadership to their amorphous pressures for relief against rising prices, "European speculators," and unemployment. "In order to weaken the growing anti-imperialist movement," for this had erupted in strikes and violence during 1948, British leaders then decided to make concessions to the national bourgeoisie by entrusting to it the drafting of a new constitution. Their maneuver succeeded: the moment of betrayal had arrived. The leadership of the Convention, "no less frightened than the English imperialists of the mass people's movement, readily took the bait."[36] Reproachfully but, one suspects, with a certain satisfaction, Potekhin elaborated the party's treason. The proof was in the pamphlet written by the leader of the party, J. B. Danquah, "Friendship and Empire," in which he "grovels before English imperialism, maintaining that England had changed its attitude toward the colonies and that therefore the previous slogan of the Convention, 'Independence in the Shortest Possible time' must be re-examined." The constitution produced (the Coussey Constitution) was, according to Potekhin, scarcely more democratic than former constitutions, leaving "English rule in complete inviolability" and granting the people "no rights." For a recognized role in carrying out this hoax, the United Gold Coast Convention had betrayed the masses.

35. *Ibid.*, p. 224.
36. *Ibid.*, p. 225.

But the compromise worked out between Danquah's party and the colonial administration had prompted Nkrumah to split with the UGCC and, in 1949, to form his own Convention People's Party committed to "self-government now." That Potekhin considered this new party hardly more commendable than Danquah's revealed with what suspicion the Soviet Union regarded even the most promising African nationalists. True, the new party had appealed to the "legitimate indignation of all democrats in the Gold Coast" over England's newest trick; it had organized "civil disobedience" to force London to grant dominion status; it had inspired the support of trade unions and "democratic youth organizations"; it had played a role in the general strike and the boycott of British trade in January 1950; its leaders had suffered police repression and as a result had gained stature among the masses. Despite all the intriguing of British agents, the party won overwhelmingly in the 1951 parliamentary elections, compelling the British to concede Nkrumah the post of "leader of Government business."[37] But in doing so, the British presented him with a test of conviction, which, of course, current Soviet theory insisted he would fail. And fail he did, emphasized Potekhin. "In coming to power the leader of the People's Party had turned suddenly to the right, toward collaboration with English imperialism."

> The old slogan of the Party, dominion status "now," used in the elections, gave way to another slogan, dominion status "in the future." If before the elections leaders of the People's Party criticized the constitution as undemocratic and, as a sign of protest, appealed for civil disobedience, then now Nkrumah praises the constitution and calls for "constructive action" on the basis of this constitution.[38]

If the Soviet Union considered West Africa the most important region of Black Africa in the early postwar period—and this seems to be the

37. *Ibid.*, pp. 226–227.
38. *Ibid.*, p. 228. As unfavorable as these references were, that Soviet writers had acknowledged Nkrumah's 1951 election victory at all represented an advance over the Soviet reaction at the time of the elections. Then, the Soviet press had not bothered even to make note of Nkrumah's triumph. Still on the whole it seems fair to say that Soviet leaders strongly disliked Nkrumah and shared the view expressed by Ben Bradley, the British Communist colonial expert, as late as April 1954. In a remark to the Conference of Commonwealth Communist Parties in London, Bradley noted that in the Sudan "the imperialists have not been able up to now to form a Nkrumah regime to stem the movement [national liberation movement] as in the Gold Coast." See George Padmore, *Pan-Africanism or Communism?* (New York: Roy Publishers, 1955), p. 341.

point of Soviet references to the more highly differentiated nature of class structures here than in, say, East Africa and to the greater strength of the national liberation movement—then among the West African colonies Soviet writers appeared to be watching most closely Nigeria. "Nigeria," said Potekhin, "is the most important of all the English colonies in Africa."[39] Nevertheless Potekhin and his colleagues treated Nigerian leaders no less harshly than they did other bourgeois nationalists.

Nigeria's most satisfactory party (in the Soviet view), the National Council of Nigeria and the Cameroons, an alliance of "two hundred political, trade union, youth, cultural, and other organizations," had turned its leadership over to the "bourgeoisie and intelligentsia grouped about Nnamdi Azikiwe," the son of a functionary in the colonial administration and the educational product of an American university. However much these leaders declared their determination to struggle for Nigerian self-determination, Potekhin for one remained skeptical. The slogan itself was "extremely imprecise" and subject to "the most diverse interpretations."[40] Furthermore Azikiwe struck Potekhin as an unsteady figure, who had already "changed his point of view on relations with the British Empire several times." He was unable to make up his mind, implied Potekhin: one time he would urge complete independence for Nigeria and its departure from the British Empire; the next time, Nigerian independence within the Empire. When striking miners at Enugu were shot in 1949, he pronounced himself in favor of peaceful methods in seeking independence. He, like Danquah and Nkrumah, had accepted the path of constitutional reform, and Soviet writers liked the constitutions given Nigeria no better than those bestowed upon the Gold Coast. Not much could be expected of these political leaders.

Even more dubious was the party of Western Nigeria, the Action Group. Potekhin in disgust calls it a party under the rule of "feudal, marionette princes of Yorubaland," committed to "monarchical institutions." Chief Obafemi Awolowo, a leader toward whom the Soviet view has softened considerably over the last ten years, appears as a wily individual who slandered his own people and despised their political innocence. The whole enterprise fell into the category of what Stalin had characterized as "feudal-monarchical nationalism."[41] The party of the North, the Northern People's Congress, Potekhin dismisses with a simple

39. *Ibid.*, p. 20. He was to preserve this view until as late as 1956. See Potekhin, "Politicheskoe polozhenie v stranakh Afriki," p. 29.
40. *Ibid.*, p. 229.
41. *Ibid.*, p. 230.

huff as a "reactionary organization." Nigeria might have been "on the eve of critical political events," as Potekhin stated, but it was clear he did not believe that any party existed capable of seeing Nigeria through.

As for the Rassemblement Démocratique Africain, Soviet writers charged its bourgeois leadership with acting only to "direct the people's movement along the channel of a struggle for reform which might speed the development of capitalist relations in the colonies and [which] would give the national bourgeoisie equal rights with French companies in the exploitation of the resources and population of these countries."[42] When in the fall of 1950 the RDA *parlementaires* renounced their parliamentary alliance with the French Communist Party and declared their support for the Pleven government, all the vilest things Soviet writers had ever thought about the African national bourgeoisie now seemed fully justified. After four years of parliamentary cooperation, after opposing together French policy in Vietnam and colonial policy in Africa, after having identified the fate of the colonial peoples with that of the French working class, after all the material aid extended by the French Communist Party, suddenly the *parlementaires* of the RDA tossed away the alliance for no more fundamental reason than that they found it tactically inconvenient. The issues originally producing the alliance remained the same, but Kwame Nkrumah was proving that independence could be more swiftly obtained by collaborating with the metropolitan government. This the *parlementaires* of the RDA now cynically acknowledged. What better evidence did Soviet analysts need of the ultimate treachery of the national bourgeoisie? With really outraged vigor they could now hate men like Félix Houphouet-Boigny, the RDA *parlementaire* ("unmasked at last") principally responsible for the split. The "shameful deal" between leaders of the RDA and the bloody repressors of popular democrats in Dimbokro, Bouaflé, Séguéla, and "hundreds" of other towns became the textbook case of national bourgeois faithlessness.[43] Who in 1950 could suggest working with so perfidious a group as this?

Yet how frustrating Soviet writers found their country's position: the only forces sufficiently cohesive and strong to wage the battle for inde-

42. Datlin, "Borba narodov frantsuzskoi zapodnoi i ekvatorial Afriki," p. 258.
43. The most thorough discussion of these events is in Datlin, pp. 258–263, but the betrayal is mentioned in nearly every article on Black Africa appearing in this period.

pendence turned out to be overwhelmingly distasteful. Those initial, half-hearted gestures toward recognizing the African national bourgeoisie as the firebrand of the anti-imperialist front ultimately collapsed. Soviet writers had no stomach for it, and in their helplessness they fell back on the mythical force of the African proletariat. They had already admitted that this class remained almost nonexistent, its few members disorganized, its character tradition-bound. Still, they returned faithfully to the ideological premise: "Events in Africa and the revolutionary experience of Asian countries, especially the Chinese experience, confirm that the national liberation movement can only triumph if it is headed by the working class, alone leading the masses."[44]

When this particular sample of Soviet fundamentalism appeared in late 1953, however, shortly after Stalin's death, events were already overtaking what had become for Soviet analysts an outmoded framework of thought. A re-evaluation of the role of important national bourgeois leaders could no longer be postponed. Enough had occurred in India, Indonesia, and the Middle East to move Stalin's successors to look again at the revolution effected by the Nehrus and Sukarnos of the world. They took less than a year to repudiate the traditional description of Nehru as a leader of "the counterrevolutionary bloc of Indian big bourgeoisie and landowners," and to do so by means of an extraordinary diplomatic and economic offensive, culminating in Nehru's remarkable, tumultuous reception in the Soviet Union in June 1955. Because Soviet attitudes toward Africa were now obviously a replica of the prevailing view toward the national bourgeoisie in more important regions, the exact transformation underway is of interest here. Potekhin not much later developed the new theme in his own work on Africa.

The temptation to see this reassessment of the national bourgeoisie as a sharp and baldly expediential departure from previous policy is difficult to resist, unless Stalin's view of the colonial bourgeoisie is examined more closely. Although indeed an important innovation in Soviet policy, the shift in approach, in fact, had important antecedents in Stalinist thought, and unless this is appreciated the absolutely crucial point of the evolution in Soviet perceptions of Africa will be lost.

Though not always for the same length of time or with the same intensity, postwar theory generally regarded significant nationalist leaders such as Gandhi, Nehru, Sukarno, Mossadeq, and Neguib to be untrust-

44. Lemin, "Imperialisticheskoe sopernichestvo v Afrike," p. 596.

worthy—in some instances already the tools of their imperialist masters—and their parties dangerous and impossible allies. Presumably they
put Nkrumah, Azikiwe, Senghor, d'Arboussier, and their colleagues in
the same category, though the failure ever to reject them unequivocally
no doubt indicates greater toleration of the African national bourgeois
leadership.[45] Since, however, Soviet writers unmistakably disliked the
idea of working with such leaders and expected them at any moment
to betray the anti-imperialist front, some explanation needs to be supplied
for a strategy which, long before Stalin's death, clearly required an alliance with the national bourgeoisie.[46]

As indicated before, Soviet writers did not see the indigenous colonial
bourgeoisie as a single, undifferentiated class; nor, as might be guessed,
did they offer to cooperate with groups that in another breath they
lustily condemned. They had consistently divided the bourgeoisie into
two basic groups—the big, including comprador, bourgeoisie, that group
in close collusion with the imperialists, and the national bourgeoisie, a
section of the bourgeoisie that still retained some independence from
imperialist domination. In most colonies, particularly in India and Indonesia, it was the first group that earned the virulent abhorrence of Soviet
analysts. Because, however, no major "exploited" segment of society—
neither the peasantry nor the proletariat—possessed the strength to
create the revolution by itself, the Soviet leadership sought additional
allies among other groups, including the liberal bourgeoisie.

Such an alliance became all the more attractive once Soviet leaders

45. After condemning the big bourgeoisie of India, Indonesia, the Philippines,
Egypt, and "many colonies and dependent countries," Potekhin (in a 1950 article)
went on to say: "The petty-bourgeois nationalist organizations and parties [he
was writing about Africa] have already shown their incapacity to limit themselves
to constitutional reforms, attaining a formal bourgeois democracy which cannot
provide a complete break from the system of imperialism—i.e., factual and not
formal independence." I. I. Potekhin, "Stalinskaya teoriya kolonialnoi revolutsii
i natsionalno-osvoboditelnoe dvizhenie v tropicheskoi i yuzhnoi Afrike" (Stalin's
Theory of Colonial Revolution and the National Liberation Movement in Tropical and South Africa), Sovetskaya etnografiya, no. 1 (1950), pp. 24–40, trans.
in Thomas Perry Thornton, ed., The Third World in Soviet Perspective (Princeton: Princeton University Press, 1964), p. 37.
46. John H. Kautsky has done this well in a series of articles reprinted in
his Communism and the Politics of Development (New York: John Wiley, 1968).
For two other excellent contributions see Charles B. McLane, Soviet Strategies
in Southeast Asia (Princeton: Princeton University Press, 1966), pp. 351–367;
and Donald S. Carlisle, "Stalin's Postwar Foreign Policy and the National Liberation Movement," Review of Politics, XXVII (July 1965), 334–363.

established American imperialism as the principal enemy. The struggle against American policy, rather than the conventional struggle to overthrow feudalism or capitalism, made it easier to embrace "progressive" capitalist forces. They need not have been anticapitalist, merely anti-American. Thus, by no means was it a simple coincidence that Soviet interest in the support of, so to speak, rank-and-file bourgeois elements intensified after Andrei Zhdanov, in his 1947 Cominform speech, sharply divided Europe and its allies into two camps—socialist and capitalist—a formulation that underscored the peril Soviet leaders saw in the extension of American influence and the growing power of the Western alliance. In order to combat this menace, Soviet leaders were now willing to encourage cooperation with some anti-Western capitalist elements in the colonies.

To locate the distinction between this and the strategy after Stalin's death, one must focus on the section of the bourgeoisie excluded from the original appeal to all anti-imperialist forces. When Soviet writers scored the big bourgeoisie, they had in mind the Kuomintang, the Indian Congress Party, the Moslem League, and bourgeois trade unions. In no circumstance should progressive forces seek to involve these groups in their anti-imperialist front. On the contrary, in order to undermine their influence and arouse the sympathy of more worthy sections of the national bourgeoisie, the Stalinist strategy envisaged a direct alliance with anti-imperialist capitalists, circumventing bourgeois parties and organizations—what is called a united front "from below." Whether they also meant to reject cooperation with national bourgeois parties in Africa is less clear. But since parties such as Nkrumah's CPP or Azikiwe's NCNC seemed generically the same as Nehru's Congress Party, until more conclusive evidence appears, we have reason to assume that these parties also shared the hearty disapproval of Soviet observers. The references from time to time to the leadership of these parties as the national bourgeoisie presumably illustrates John Kautsky's point that often the term "national bourgeoisie" meant no more than "native bourgeoisie."[47]

The change in strategy after Stalin's death, then, involved not a sudden turn toward the national bourgeoisie—as a social stratum, it was already an approved ally—but a new willingness to accept its leaders and parties. Stalin's heirs agreed to make peace with the same leaders bitterly condemned a few months earlier, in the interest of adding their independent

47. Kautsky, "The New Strategy of International Communism," *Communism*, p. 15.

and often disaffected voices to the resources of Soviet policy. By 1953 it was obvious to them that Indian and Pakistani independence signified more than that "both the Indian landlords and upper bourgeoisie represented by the National Congress, and the Muslim landlords and bourgeoisie whose interests are represented by the Muslim League, had openly gone over to the camp of imperialism and reaction;"[48] that not only did the transfer of power to local leaders spell a vast alteration in the status of these two countries, but that the new circumstances could be turned to excellent advantage for Soviet policy. And so Soviet language changed abruptly. Unfamiliar praise issued from the Soviet press for the "important part . . . India was playing in recent times in the international arena in favor of world peace and against imperialist warmongers."[49] Eventually even India's "progressive" contribution toward people's democracy and socialism received favorable mention.

African leaders also benefited from the change of Soviet heart. They were treated more gently in the Soviet press; credit was paid to their achievements in the struggle for independence and interest shown in the international role they would assume in the future—all presumably because Soviet writers included Africa in their new category of Third World "neutral" countries whose latent anti-Westernism was expected to offer fresh policy opportunities. Potekhin, for example, contributed a striking reappraisal of the Convention People's Party's 1951 election victory, which, it will be recalled, had been dismissed earlier as the beginning of collaboration with British imperialism. By 1955, however, he saw this election and the "creation of the first African colonial government headed by an African" as the "common victory" of all enslaved African peoples and equally as a "serious defeat for reactionary imperialist circles."[50] He quoted Margery Perham's comment that the "Gold Coast elections of February 1951 have sent a shock right through Africa . . . To white men who have made their home in the African continent the shock has come as a perhaps only half-formulated question: 'Is this the beginning of the end for us?' "[51] Despite Potekhin's rather large

48. J. M. MacKintosh, *Strategy and Tactics of Soviet Foreign Policy* (New York: Oxford University Press, 1963), p. 129.

49. Kautsky, "Indian Communist Party Strategy," *Communism*, p. 39.

50. I. I. Potekhin, "Antiimperialisticheskoe dvizhenie v kolonii Zolotoi Bereg" (The Anti-Imperialist Movement in the Gold Coast Colony), *Sovetskoe vostokovedenie*, no. 2 (1955), p. 68.

51. Margery Perham, "The British Problem in Africa," *Foreign Affairs*, XXIX (July 1951), 637.

scholarly debt to Dame Margery, this quotation had never previously been part of it. He went on to mark "the strengthening of the people's struggle, the creation of a Legislative Assembly, the chosen path of direct elections based on universal suffrage, the formation of a national government and the reform of local organs of authority" as a major blow against "British imperialist rule and the feudal leadership of the Gold Coast."[52] In another article published the next year, Potekhin made note of the concessions that Nigerian, Gold Coast, Sudanese, and other national leaders had wrung from colonial powers, concessions promising either to speed independence or, in Sudan's case, to strengthen independence already conceded.[53] He congratulated the Convention People's Party, described two years earlier as the "shield . . . for the dominion of British imperialism,"[54] for strengthening national forces and weakening the grasp of foreign imperialists. The tone of Soviet commentary on African leaders had definitely been modified. Signs of genuine respect for the accomplishments of the bourgeois nationalists replaced the visible disdain of the Stalin years. Without wincing as before, writers like Potekhin agreed that for the moment the national bourgeoisie "played an active, and in the majority of colonies, the leading role" in the national liberation movement.[55]

Yet despite the striking adjustment in Soviet attitudes toward Africa's nationalist leaders, the old suspicions of unreliability had not completely dissipated; nor had Soviet policymakers abandoned all their reservations over uniting with these forces. Scarcely had Potekhin completed his favorable reappraisal of Nkrumah's 1951 election triumph than he went on to credit his success to the "popular masses" and the trade unions— groups, he implied, that Nkrumah had let down in order to represent the interests of the local bourgeoisie. In the four years after 1951 he had done everything possible to strengthen the national bourgeoisie: he had founded a national bank, created a national cocoa-purchasing company, begun gradually to replace British administrators with members of the local intelligentsia, and so on. Certainly, said Potekhin, all those measures corresponded to the national interests of the Gold Coast, but they benefited first and primarily the national bourgeoisie. The govern-

52. Potekhin, "Antiimperialisticheskoe dvizhenie," p. 70.
53. Potekhin, "Politicheskoe polozhenie v stranakh Afriki," p. 28.
54. D. A. Olderogge and I. I. Potekhin, eds., *Narody Afriki* (The Peoples of Africa; Moscow, 1954), p. 345.
55. Potekhin, "Politicheskoe polozhenie v stranakh Afriki," p. 36.

ment, in contrast, had done nothing "to lighten the difficult situation of the popular masses." More ominously it had "begun to threaten with repression those who maintained left-wing opinions and had taken measures to weaken the trade unions with whose help it had come to power."[56] What is more, not only were Soviet writers sure that the colonial powers were trying to convert independence into "a mere formality," as Potekhin expressed it, they seemed deeply suspicious that bourgeois African leaders really were without the will to overcome such imperialist subterfuges and see to the achievement of full independence. These people were still far from the kind of political leaders to whom Soviet policymakers were willing to entrust Africa's revolutionary future. Though it would have been sheer stubbornness—of an unproductive variety—to deny the importance of nonproletarian nationalists in the struggle for independence, even the expectation that friendlier relations with the new leaders of Africa would strengthen the short-term requirements of Soviet policy could not dispel the apprehensions that a triumphant bourgeoisie raised in the Soviet mind. This stemmed partially from ignorance. Soviet leaders knew neither Africa nor its leaders very well.

Soviet unfamiliarity with Africa, I have been arguing, stemmed from the long period during which policymakers had paid only the briefest passing attention to African developments. Soviet leaders and political analysts had done almost nothing to learn about the nature of African society until the first wave of independent African states appeared right in front of them. Until this late hour they had been content to defer nearly complete responsibility for the cadre formation, tactical decisions, and propaganda work in African colonial territories to West European Communist parties. Admittedly, the decision to leave Africa's socialist future to the French, British, and other metropole Communist parties may have been justified by these parties' greater access to colonial politics. Yet, because the Soviet Union avoided involvement in the organization of radical African movements, it came to Africa without a reliable working knowledge of the political milieu there.

This is not to say that Soviet representatives had no contact with young African nationalists before independence. After World War II in the meetings of front organizations like the Prague-based World Federation of Trade Unions (WFTU), the World Federation of Democratic Youth (WFDY), and in the late 1940s the World Peace Movement,

56. Potekhin, "Antiimperialisticheskoe dvizhenie," p. 68.

Soviet delegates mixed with trade unionists, students, and the leaders of the pan-African movement. In fact a major impetus for forming such broadly based organizations derived from the Soviet desire to establish convenient points of assembly where its representatives might fraternize with nationalists from the colonial regions. Many Africans attending the Fifth Pan-African Congress, for example, were in Europe primarily to participate in the second conference of the WFTU scheduled for September 25–October 9, 1945, in Paris. The planners of the Pan-African Congress intentionally coordinated the dates of their meeting to take advantage of the delegates' presence.[57] Similarly, student groups such as the West African Students' Union, incorporating a substantial portion of the African students in England, affiliated their membership with the WFDY and the International Union of Students. In part through the intervention of either the WFTU or WFDY, a few Africans even undertook studies in East Europe and the Soviet Union. Still by any measure the number of Africans influenced directly through these mediums always remained insignificant.

Those Africans whose attitudes had been shaped by the ideas of Communism owed their training and involvement much more to the activity of European Communist parties. French Communists and their allies from the Confédération Générale du Travail took charge of whatever revolutionary preparation was possible in French-speaking Africa, and the British Communist party did the same in British colonies. In reality, the task of rousing the proletarian consciousness of local Africans and giving them the rudiments of organization fell to Communists who served in Africa as teachers and colonial administrators. In major French West African towns during the war, they formed the Groupes d'Etudes Communistes (GEC) where they could meet young African intellectuals, teach them the fundamentals of Marxism-Leninism (Soviet and French versions), and hammer out "a common strategy and tactics for fighting against colonialism within the mass organizations (political, trade union, cultural . . .) of the territory."[58] In such study circles a notable list of African leaders acquired an important part of their formative political

---

57. Padmore, *Pan-Africanism or Communism?*, pp. 154–155.

58. From mimeographed bylaws of the GEC of Dakar, quoted in Ruth Schachter Morgenthau, *Political Parties in French-Speaking West Africa* (Oxford: Oxford University Press, 1964), pp. 24–25. Although Mrs. Morgenthau's treatment of the GEC is very brief, it is the best available. For interesting evidence of the specific activities of GEC leaders in Bamako, see Frank Gregory Snyder, *One-Party Government in Mali* (New Haven: Yale University Press, 1965), pp. 41–42, 47–49.

training: men like Modibo Keita, the future president of Mali; Guinea's president, Sekou Touré; Idrissa Diarra, later secretary-general of Mali's dominant party, the Union Soudanaise; his predecessor and a founder of the party, Mamadou Konaté; Diallo Saifoulaye, secretary-general of the Parti Démocratique de Guinée; the list is much longer. It goes without saying that these intellectuals came no more from the proletariat than Lenin, Trotsky, or other Bolshevik leaders had. But that made little difference; circumstances in backward societies, in particular the low level of class differentiation, had always inevitably meant that *évolués*, the national bourgeoisie, formed the core of progressive organizations. Either they provided the leadership necessary to reach the masses or the masses remained sunken in their primitive mindless state.

In fact French Communists used these circumstances to justify their opposition to the creation of local Communist parties. They argued that in societies without much of a proletariat and where part of the national bourgeoisie had not yet defected to the imperialists, the immediate task was to help weld together a broad national front against imperialism.[59] When it became apparent, however, that even in the long-run French Communists had no intention of encouraging the formation of separate Communist parties, but instead "expected Africans and Europeans to continue within a single party, controlled from Paris," the more militant members of the GEC grew increasingly suspicious of their European benefactors.[60] Most Africans considered these Frenchmen rather insensitive to political realities on their continent in any case, and this narrowness together with the PCF's conspicuously equivocal support of African independence gradually eroded the party's revolutionary authority.[61] The behavior of French Communists during this era no doubt helped to reinforce the determination of African nationalists to remain at all times

59. *Ibid.*, p. 24.
60. *Ibid.*
61. At the PCF congress in Strasbourg, June 26, 1947, Etienne Fajon said: "The collapse of the French Union would bring upon you [the colonial peoples] an apparent independence, as the prelude to the pressing rule of the powers among whom the trusts rule as masters, among whom racist ideas are current, and by whom Negroes are lynched. Therefore, remain in the French Union with us. It will be what we together make of it and nothing can be strong enough to hinder the workers and republicans of France, in union with your democratic and national forces, from making out of it a real, brotherly and progressive Union." *L'Humanité,* June 27, 1947, quoted in Kanet, "The Soviet Union and Sub-Saharan Africa," pp. 210–221. Raymond Barbé, the PCF specialist on Africa, often repeated similar assurances.

their own men and perhaps made easier the decision of RDA *parlemen-taires* to break their alliance with the PCF in 1950.[62]

The Soviet Union's abdication of direct control over Communist organizations in sub-Saharan Africa had two consequences. First, given the reluctance of European Communist parties to see the creation of separate African Communist parties, these crucial formative years produced Communists without generating the structures that would give force to their presence. In a sense, European Communists applied to the problem of working-class and peasant organization the practices of colonialism, in particular the French policy of assimilation. Rather than encourage the development of indigenous Communist parties, European Communists preferred to incorporate African Communists into their own membership in much the same way that the French government made selected Africans citizens of France. African Communists who wanted to participate in local political structures joined mass parties spearheading the struggle for independence. After independence the Soviet Union discovered that the option of encouraging the formation of African Communist parties had been largely removed by the necessity of cooperating with bourgeois nationalist leaders. So, in effect, the fate of indigenous Communist organizations had been determined nearly a decade earlier.

Second, there can be little doubt that the Soviet Union's inactivity in Africa left its leadership ill prepared to cope with the new issues this area raised for its foreign policy. When finally the approach of independence moved Soviet policymakers to develop some competence in African affairs, they had little background on which to build. Their experience in Africa had been indirect and vicarious, conveyed primarily by West European Communist parties.

To compensate for this lack of direct experience, Soviet researchers could have significantly aided those left with the responsibility of composing policy had they been adequately motivated. Motivation for Soviet scholars is, of course, a complicated issue which encompasses far more than the preferences of the academic community, and it would be naive to assume that the neglect of African studies was singularly due to indifference on the part of Soviet researchers. We know that the party has made political demands of scholarship, frequently transforming it into little more than a tool for reinforcing and amplifying the current political line, and therefore it does not seem unreasonable to suspect that political

62. Fritz Schatten ably argues this point in "Africa: Nationalism and Communism," Walter Laqueur and Leopold Labedz, eds., *Polycentrism* (New York: Praeger, 1962), pp. 237–238.

agencies also set priorities for subjects and areas to be studied.[63] If this is the case, then the retarded condition of Soviet African studies in as late as 1957 reinforces the conclusion that Africa under colonialism aroused little interest among Soviet leaders.

Soviet African studies at the start of Soviet involvement in the area languished in an incontestably sorry state. Soviet administrators have said so themselves. In June 1957, Uzbek first secretary, N. A. Mukhitdinov, scolded the first All-Union Conference of Oriental Studies Specialists for "not studying all the Eastern countries to the same extent. Research on the countries of the huge African continent," he said "is especially inadequate."[64] Five years later Irina Yastrebova, the deputy director of the African Institute, lamented the fact that "the cadres [Africanists] already formed are slight in numbers and not sufficient to do research into all the problems with which they are presented."[65] In 1957 before the African Institute had been conceived and before intensive efforts were underway to develop trained Africanists, one Western journalist reported that only two Soviet African experts had ever seen Africa and few had ever met an African.[66] The feeling among outsiders that shortcomings prevailed, not only in the number of Soviet Africanists but in the organization of Soviet African studies, grew with the continuing subordination of African studies to the Institute of Orientology and with the dubious practice of lumping together Far Eastern and African studies. Looking at this arrangement it is easy to understand why Anastas Mikoyan rebuked the Institute of Orientology a year earlier at the Twentieth Congress of the Communist Party: "While the entire East has awakened in our time, this Institute has remained asleep."[67] Perhaps, however, the finger of censure had been unfairly pointed: it

63. For abundant evidence that this has also been the case in African studies, see David L. Morison, *The USSR and Africa* (London: Oxford University Press, 1964), pp. 59–72.

64. *Pravda,* June 14, 1957, pp. 4–5, trans. in *Current Digest of the Soviet Press,* IX (July 24, 1957), 11–13. A few months later Mukhitdinov was to become a member of both the party Presidium and the Secretariat.

65. *Vestnik Akademii nauk SSSR* (Herald of the Academy of Sciences of the USSR), no. 7 (1962), quoted in Morison, *The USSR and Africa,* p. 64. Yastrebova was speaking to the Third Coordinating Conference of Soviet Africanists in April 1962.

66. Pieter Lessing, in *Sunday Telegraph* (London), March 25, 1962.

67. "XX sezd Kommunisticheskoi Partii Sovetskogo Soyuza i zadachi izucheniya sovremennogo Vostoka" (Twentieth Congress of the Communist Party of the Soviet Union and the Tasks for the Study of the Contemporary East), *Sovremenny Vostok,* no. 1 (1956), p. 6.

might also have included political officials who, in the final analysis, provide direction for the institutes under the Academy of Sciences.

By 1956 the rapid approach of African independence had shaken Soviet leaders from their faithful indifference to this continent and caused them to begin preparing hastily for an active role in developments that were about to remake Africa's political character. But there remained a price to be paid for the years of disregard. The oversimplifications, the fanciful expectations, and the tactless behavior marking early Soviet policy toward independent Africa were the result of the decades that Stalin and his successors had either ignored Africa or considered it exclusively in terms of Soviet needs.

II

The First Contacts with Black Africa

Ghana's achievement of independence was the crucial event in postwar Africa. The swift, efficient, peaceful transfer of sovereignty from colonialist to colonial proved that the old order had expired and accelerated the process of decolonization elsewhere in Africa—disrupting previously set timetables and taxing the capacity of other European powers to adjust. An already doomed Fourth Republic hurried to preserve as much as possible of its crumbling African empire by offering increased autonomy to territories that were now eyeing more complete forms of independence.[1] Even the mechanism to which France resorted in making the accommodation betrayed the impact of developments in Ghana, for rather than endure the delays of normal, often paralysing, legislative procedures, the French National Assembly accepted a broad enabling act (Loi-Cadre) and left the executive with responsibility for getting

1. See William J. Foltz, *From French West Africa to the Mali Federation* (New Haven: Yale University Press, 1965), pp. 63–96; Morgenthau, *Political Parties in French-Speaking West Africa;* and Aristide R. Zolberg, *One-Party Government in the Ivory Coast* (Princeton: Princeton University Press, 1964), pp. 149–158, 170–183.

on with the details of the reform. In 1956, however, even swiftly granted concessions simply hastened the steady movement toward independence. Apparently it did not cross French minds that a defensive scheme based on the decentralization of empire would, in the circumstances, be a fatal modification. In 1958 it was France, indeed a reluctant France, which produced the Republic of Guinea, West Africa's second liberated colony.

The Soviet Union, too, failed to comprehend the full implications of Ghanaian independence. In fact it seemed less conscious than most of the significance of changes about to transform this continent. Stock references to the growing force of the anticolonial struggle in Africa neither identified those specific features of colonial politics which fired Soviet hopes nor gave evidence of genuine interest in the course of any specific country's struggle for independence. The extraordinary thing about Ghanaian events was that they evoked from the Soviet leadership so singular a display of apathy. The reaction in this case is particularly striking because Soviet leaders had already shown substantial interest in countries (such as India and Afghanistan) aspiring to a far less revolutionary position than Ghana and because within scarcely a year and half they would plunge enthusiastically into an elaborate relationship with Guinea.

One searches vainly for even a passing reference to Ghana in Foreign Minister Shepilov's semiannual foreign-policy review delivered to the Supreme Soviet just three weeks before Ghanaian independence.[2] To say that the press was uneffusive at this point scarcely communicates the full reality of its silence. Late in February very short notes in *Pravda* and *Izvestiya* mentioned the departure of a Soviet delegation to attend independence celebrations in Accra, the first and only acknowledgment in the six months prior to Ghanaian independence that something significant was about to happen in Black Africa.[3] In the same week *Pravda* devoted an entire page to the "growing struggle of peoples in colonial and dependent countries against the imperialist yoke."[4] There were articles entitled "Fulfill the Lawful Demands of the Indonesian People," "U.S. Monopolies Plunder Latin America," "For Reuniting Gao with India," "Colonizers Will Not Subjugate Algeria," and "Dirty War on Cyprus," but not one considering the implications of Ghanaian inde-

2. *Pravda,* February 13, 1957, pp. 3–5.
3. *Pravda,* February 25, 1957, p. 3, and *Izvestiya,* February 26, 1957, p. 3.
4. *Pravda,* February 22, 1957, p. 5.

pendence. Premier Bulganin's telegram to Nkrumah on independence day expressed "sincere congratulations on the occasion of this important date," but supplied no reason why his government thought it important.[5] An article in the *New Times* offered the incontestable observation that events in Ghana proved national independence had "spread to the very heart of the Dark Continent," but failed to say whether the specific form it had taken in Ghana was at all pleasing to the Soviet Union.[6] We may take it from *Pravda*'s correspondent in Accra that it was not. His article of March 3, 1957, celebrated the warm reception given the Soviet delegation by the Ghanaian people but expressed significant reservations over the condition of the country's basic economic structure:

> One cannot forget that the economy of the new African state thus far remains in the hands of foreign, primarily British and American, monopolies . . . The stranglehold of the foreign monopolies is obstructing the development of the national economy and the implementation of measures planned by the government to raise the material and cultural standards of the people.[7]

A few months later I. A. Benediktov, head of the Soviet delegation to Ghana's independence celebrations, shared his impressions with a group at Moscow's Polytechnical Museum, but *Pravda*'s account suggested that he limited himself to rather undramatic issues (such as the historical derivation of the state's new name).[8] Thus, after a brief and dubious gesture of recognition, the Soviet press lapsed into its traditional indifference toward Africa. This time, however, what came across as indifference corresponded to a genuine reserve in Soviet attitudes.

It is not difficult to guess what was so bothersome about the situation in Ghana, for Soviet writers were reasonably specific about the drawbacks they saw.[9] First, the 1957 constitution "was worked out and adopted

---

5. *Pravda*, March 7, 1957, p. 1.

6. "International Notes," *New Times*, no. 10 (1957), p. 19.

7. N. Pastukhov, in *Pravda*, March 3, 1957, p. 3. *Izvestiya*'s correspondent, L. Dybrvin, was slightly more complimentary, drawing attention to the measures taken since 1951 to develop a national economy and to improve the organization of education and health services. But he too noted the heavy foreign presence. Moreover, he added that Ghana remained within the Commonwealth and tolerated the English crown as head of state. *Izvestiya*, March 3, 1957, p. 5.

8. *Pravda*, May 17, 1957, p. 5.

9. Yu. A. Yudin, "Nekotorye problemy stanovleniya natsionalnoi gosudarstvennosti v nezavisimykh stranakh Afriki" (Problems in the Formation of the National State-Organization in the Independent Countries of Africa), *Sovetskoe gosudarstvo i pravo* (Soviet State and Law), no. 2 (1961), p. 42.

not by the parliament of Ghana, but by the English government . . .
The English Queen was recognized as the head of the new state and
represented by a governor-general." Second, the short supply of techni-
cally trained personnel forced the new government to retain a large
percentage of the "old foreign bureaucrats in its apparatus." Soviet apprehensions were well founded: expatriate advisers had stayed on to
man a wide range of critical positions within the bureaucracy, including
a sizable portion of the permanent secretaryships. Imagine how Soviet
policymakers regarded Nkrumah's congenial reliance on Sir Robert Jack-
son, his principal development adviser, or the great influence of
H. Millar-Craig within the Ministry of Finance, or the attention paid to
the economic advice of W. Arthur Lewis. Without looking further, Soviet
observers had uncovered enough to raise serious doubts about the quality
of Ghanaian independence. Potekhin, after a two-month visit to Ghana
at the end of 1957, listed still other shortcomings: the regime's unwillingness to abandon English as the state language, the continuing influence
of Christian missions on Ghanaian education, the survival of British
institutions, and the prevalent ignorance about the Soviet Union.[10]

Moreover, Nkrumah himself represented at best an unknown commodity. Although trained by British Marxists and given to Marxist expressions, his speech to the nation on Christmas Eve of 1957 was distinctly
non-Marxian: "Again and again I have emphasized that we welcome
foreign investment and will protect it. In our foreign relations we do
not forget that we are part of the Commonwealth."[11] Perhaps this was
no more than what David Williams has said: "Nkrumah was convinced
he would have to be the perfect 'neo-colonialist' leader to get Western
investment; the West would have to think him one of theirs. And he
had an image of exactly how he would have to behave to preserve
their support."[12] Perhaps so, but even had Soviet analysts been willing
to consider the possibility, they certainly could not have been sure. And
had Soviet analysts been perceptive and self-confident enough to believe
Nkrumah capable of this duplicity, they would then have been shrewd
enough to note the prominence of other Ghanaians urging, for quite

10. I. I. Potekhin, *Gana segodnya* (Ghana Today; Moscow, 1959), esp. pp.
73–77, 146–158. Note that Potekhin's account was not given to the press until
February 9, 1959, by which time the Soviet view was *less* critical.

11. Kwame Nkrumah, *I Speak of Freedom* (New York: Praeger, 1961),
p. 117.

12. Interview quoted in W. Scott Thompson, *Ghana's Foreign Policy,
1957–1966: Diplomacy, Ideology, and the New State* (Princeton: Princeton University Press, 1969) pp. 26–27. David Williams is editor of *West Africa*.

different reasons, the expansion of foreign investment in their country. Foremost were Nkrumah's old allies from the earliest pre-independence days: those who with him had created the Convention People's Party and placed it at the forefront of the independence movement, who had been his most constant and trusted advisers, and who now occupied the control posts of the new state—men like Komla Gbedemah, minister of finance, Kojo Botsio, minister for trade and industries, and Krobo Edusei, minister of interior. All advocated a substantial role for foreign investment and many of them had traveled widely, encouraging foreign investors to participate more extensively in Ghana's development. Most had important business interests of their own. T. R. Makonnen, the Marxist from British Guiana and one of Nkrumah's advisers, later recounted how cabinet members had disregarded his warnings against Western investment, distracted completely by their own personal stake in its growth.[13]

The foreign service constituted what from the Soviet point of view must have been another doubtful group in the shaping of Ghana's future course. Here was that perfectly fashioned tool of neocolonialism—elitist, intelligent, trained by the British Foreign Office, and firmly convinced of the need to strengthen Commonwealth ties and to secure considerable foreign investment.[14] One of the most promising among the original select group, Alex Quaison-Sackey, had written in a paper for the Institute of Commonwealth Studies in London that his government's politics would have to "inspire [that] confidence without which foreign assistance is impossible."[15] Anyone knowing Nkrumah well enough to suspect that he was capable of camouflaging his true feelings in order to secure the capital necessary for his country's development would also have been conscious of the nature of the regime on which he depended.

But Ghana's incorrigibly bourgeois governing class was not the only element close to Nkrumah which may have worried Soviet observers. Presumably they knew too that Nkrumah's most important foreign-affairs adviser was George Padmore, the West Indian leader who had bolted the Comintern in 1935 in protest against Stalin's sacrifice of colonial

13. *Ibid.*, p. 18. Thompson has described this situation in some detail. See his *Ghana's Foreign Policy*, pp. 17–18.

14. Thompson's book deals throughout with the Ghanaian foreign service. Pages 18–20, however, are specifically in this context.

15. Alex Quaison-Sackey, "The Foundations of Gold Coast's Foreign Policy: A Study of an Emergent Nation in the International Society," *Institute of Commonwealth Studies,* London, CW/55/8 (1955), quoted in Thompson, pp. 19–20.

revolution to the quest for collective security. Padmore never forgave the Soviet leadership for its insolent exploitation of the Comintern and affiliated organizations, and in the ensuing years he became one of the Soviet Union's angriest opponents. Though always a Marxist and committed to the thorough socialization of economic life, Padmore despised the form that the Soviet Union gave to the world revolution and defended his primary commitment to pan-Africanism largely in terms of the barrier it would establish against Communism.[16] He also mischievously made a point of drawing attention to the abuse Soviet commentators had once accorded Nkrumah as a typically unreliable bourgeois nationalist. Now Padmore was Nkrumah's most trusted foreign-policy adviser.[17]

These obstinate features of the political setup in Ghana detracted from the national liberation movement's first triumph in Black Africa. Soviet commentators had mistrusted Nkrumah for years, and little he said as leader of his newly independent state could have significantly reduced their distrust. His condemnation of "Great Power rivalry" as a "senseless fratricidal struggle to destroy the very substance of humanity" was hardly the kind of impartiality the Soviet Union expected of "nonaligned" leaders.[18] His conspicuous efforts to secure Western financing for Ghana's development and his filial references to the Commonwealth made his nonalignment even more suspect. Furthermore, what modest hopes Soviet leaders may have guarded that Nkrumah, like Nasser, would eventually turn on his old colonial masters must have been balanced against the reality of the influence possessed by major leaders and advisers, who firmly believed in continuing Ghana's close ties with Great Britain. Finally, it would have been hard for Soviet observers to ignore the presence in Accra of a large contingent of British civil servants and, even more so, the position of Padmore, the disaffected former ally of world socialism.

The dilatory way Soviet and Ghanaian leaders approached the question of exchanging embassies epitomizes the character of this early phase in Soviet-Ghanaian relations. The Soviet Union sent Minister of State Farms Ivan A. Benediktov to the March independence celebrations, with formal good wishes and instructions to explore the possibility of establish-

16. See Padmore, *Pan-Africanism or Communism?*
17. Thompson, *Ghana's Foreign Policy,* p. 22, and Hooker, *Black Revolutionary,* p. 136, make the same point.
18. Nkrumah, *I Speak of Freedom,* p. 116.

ing diplomatic relations.[19] Nkrumah said he would be delighted. But Nkrumah was saying a lot of things to a lot of people, and his momentary preoccupation with the favors of London and Washington made it doubtful that he would establish relations very soon. The Ghanaian civil service strongly opposed formal ties with the Soviet bloc, and its opposition, combined with the more subtle dissuasion of British advisers, left Nkrumah little freedom in the matter. He tried to convince Soviet representatives that he would agree to the exchange of diplomatic missions as soon as posssible.[20] But the agreement only to establish relations was delayed until January 1958; still another year would pass before the two countries agreed to open embassies. So successful were the civil service and expatriate advisers in postponing the formal entry of Soviet representatives, that the first Soviet ambassador to Ghana did not arrive until August 1959. And so, though the Soviet Union would probably have entered into diplomatic relations with Ghana soon after independence, its leaders must have kept carefully in mind the reasons Ghana could not.

A look at trade between the two countries in this early phase reinforces the impression that Soviet leaders felt no irrepressible urge to establish a special presence in Black Africa's vanguard state. In 1957 the Soviet Union made little effort or else failed to export to Ghana.[21] Thus, in this respect at least, nothing had changed from pre-independence days.

19. Benediktov's selection strikes one as odd, not only because a minister of agriculture represented something less than the diplomatic equivalent of the vice-president of the United States, the Duchess of Kent, and a head of state, but because he appears to have been an ally of Khrushchev's domestic opponents and slated for the earliest possible removal. Indeed he was dismissed two months later and then, in January 1958, demoted from his subsequent post as RSFSR minister of agriculture to deputy chairman of the RSFSR State Planning Committee. In 1959 he was appointed ambassador to India. See Robert Conquest, *Power and Policy in the USSR* (London: Macmillan, 1961); Wolfgang Leonhard, *The Kremlin since Stalin* (London: Oxford University Press, 1962); and Sidney Ploss, *Conflict and Decision-Making in Soviet Russia* (Princeton: Princeton University Press, 1965).

20. During the Commonwealth prime ministers' meeting in London (July 1957), Nkrumah reportedly met with Jakob Malik and assured him of how eager he was for the two countries to have official relations. (W. Scott Thompson told me this on the basis of his conversations with other members of the Ghanaian delegation at the London meeting.) *Izvestiya,* August 31, 1957, p. 3, reported his remark before Parliament that "Ghana has close ties with England, France and the USA, but we must as well maintain ties with the other two great powers of the world—the Soviet Union and China."

21. *Vneshnyaya torgovlya Soyuza SSR za 1955–59: Statisticheskii sbornik* (Foreign Trade of the USSR, 1955–1959; Moscow, 1961), pp. 14–15.

On the other hand, a large purchase of $18.7 million in cocoa beans (37.6 thousand tons) appeared at first to be a rather energetic attempt to ingratiate the Soviet Union with the new Ghanaian leadership. On closer examination, however, these sizable imports more probably reflected a decision to take advantage of low world market prices to build up stocks.[22] At least this would seem to be the case, since in the next year the Soviet Union virtually withdrew from the market, an action which, if Soviet leaders were actually trying to win favor through trade, strikes the outsider as conspicuously counterproductive.

But it was not trade figures alone which created the feeling that Soviet leaders harbored no great desire for vastly expanded economic ties between the two countries. The laggardly way the Soviet Union negotiated a trade agreement with Ghana contributes substantially to such a suspicion. Not until June 12, 1959, did Soviet and Ghanaian representatives agree to discuss a trade agreement; not until August 4, 1960, was a trade agreement actually concluded to become effective when ratified; and not until June 3, 1961, nearly two years after a formal accord had been first suggested, were ratifications exchanged. Soviet reluctance (or inability) to enter the Ghanaian market in the first years sharply contrasted with what happened earlier in Egypt and what would happen again in Guinea. A *Pravda* contributor was no doubt speaking with conviction when he wrote in February 1958 that "the forefront of the national liberation struggle [in Africa] is North Africa."[23]

Presumably, at this very early stage the Soviet Union confronted the decision whether to live quietly with a less than revolutionary situation or to intervene directly by encouraging the formation of a local Communist party. Admittedly, the choice was not clearcut given the near absence of a proletariat on which the party could be theoretically based, but, after all, this had seldom been an insuperable obstacle before. There were individual Ghanaians who fancied themselves Marxist-Leninists; so, hypothetically, had Soviet leaders wanted to harass Nkrumah's government they could have encouraged the formation of a Ghanaian Communist party and assigned it a militant role. Many of these people had found political refuge within the CPP and over the years, with Nkrumah's encouragement, had concentrated their attention on ideologi-

22. This is also the conclusion of the Economic Intelligence Unit, *Three-Monthly Economic Review of Ghana, Nigeria, Sierra Leone, Gambia,* no. 27 (August 1959), pp. 4–5.

23. S. Datlin, *Pravda,* February 17, 1958, p. 3.

cal work within the party. They were part of the National Association of Socialist Students' Organization, formed in the early days of the party's existence to safeguard ideological development.[24] From their editorial positions in Ghana's newspapers and radio and from their location in the Bureau of African Affairs[25] and the ideological apparatus of the party, they came to exercise exceptional influence over the country's opinion-forming institutions. Many among them, such as Kofi Batsaa, editor of *Spark* (after 1962), Kojo Addison, director of the Kwame Nkrumah Ideological Institute at Winneba (after 1961), and Kweku Akwei, ideological secretary of the CPP, professed a commitment to a rigorous socialist reorganization of society, used the idiom of Marxist-Leninism in their publications, and took as their inspiration the countries in the socialist camp. But their subservience to the Soviet Union or its proxy, the British Communist Party, was far from proven.

However that may have been, Soviet leaders apparently had little interest even in exploring the possibility and, to the extent of their authority, urged young Ghanaian Marxists to postpone the formal creation of a party and to join existing organizations in order to maximize their influence within the system. This is the advice credited to Potekhin by Ghanaian sources during his 1957 visit to Accra.[26] To have done otherwise would have been absurd, given the circumstances. Not only were "working-class organizations" exceedingly feeble but, in addition, those local dilettantes who professed Marxist-Leninist convictions clearly lacked the ideological training and personal discipline necessary for assuming the leadership of a Communist party. Moreover, they were pronounced opportunists who stood to lose too much by breaking with Nkrumah. Fundamentally, the Soviet leaders saw these people as unpre-

24. The best study of this group is Colin Legum, "Socialism in Ghana: A Political Interpretation," William H. Friedland and Carl G. Rosberg, Jr., eds., *African Socialism* (Stanford: Stanford University Press, 1964), pp. 131–159. For additional information see Apter, *The Gold Coast in Transition,* p. 209, and Thompson, *Ghana's Foreign Policy,* pp. 14–15. An interesting comment on the NASSO and its successor, the Study Group, is in the *Legon Observer* (Ghana), August 2, 1968, pp. 4–6.

25. See below, p. 162, 252.

26. Reported to Alexander Dallin, "The Soviet Union: Political Activity," Zbigniew Brzezinski, ed., *Africa and the Communist World* (Stanford: Stanford University Press, 1963), p. 24. Dallin also quotes A. B. Rosenthal in the *New York Times,* October 18, 1960, that "the indicated aim of the Soviet Union here is not to create a new Communist party, but to indoctrinate and influence enough leaders of Mr. Nkrumah's Convention People's Party so that a take-over of the existing authoritarian political machinery becomes relatively easy."

dictable, slightly frivolous, and generally incapable of providing reliable direction for a revolutionary movement.

Furthermore, if the Soviet Union had sponsored the creation of a Ghanaian Communist party, at the same time it would have antagonized Nkrumah, guaranteeing the early suppression of Communism in Ghana. Soviet leaders could not have misunderstood his position. In 1954 he had expelled trade-union leaders Anthony Woode and Turkson Ocran from the CPP for their continued association with the Soviet-dominated World Federation of Trade Unions.[27] He had told the Legislative Assembly on February 25, 1954, that the "Government will not tolerate the employment of public servants who have shown that their first loyalty is to an alien Power, or a foreign Agency which seeks to bring our country under its domination."[28] In the same period he had confiscated the party cards of Kofi Batsaa and others like him, for their ties with Communist-sponsored organizations. Some thought these actions were intended to reassure Great Britain, as it prepared to give the Gold Coast its independence, rather than being a reflection of his own preferences, but we should recall that in 1954 Soviet commentators were not likely to have suspected him of such insincerity. Though over the intervening years they had modified their estimation of Nkrumah, his remarks before the National Press Club in Washington on July 24, 1958, must have reinforced surviving suspicions. When a reporter asked him whether the establishment of a Communist party would be permitted, he replied that Ghana's "better institutions and the like . . . do not allow the ideology to have any fruitful setup in our country."[29] For Soviet listeners his response was only superficially evasive.

Therefore, because the Soviet leadership dared neither to trust local Communists nor to jeopardize Nkrumah's uncertain goodwill, an intermediate solution was settled upon. Ghana's proletarian leaders, bereft of their own viable organization, were encouraged to work within other functioning institutions. They were to pursue their objectives with partially borrowed structures. Soviet leaders for the first time had answered a question that was to reappear many times in the course of early Soviet-African relations.

27. Apter, *The Gold Coast in Transition*, p. 231.
28. *Legislative Assembly Debates, 1954* (Gold Coast), no. 1 (February 2–March 12, 1954), p. 981.
29. Appearance before the National Press Club, Washington, July 24, 1958, quoted in Nkrumah, *I Speak of Freedom*, p. 139.

At the same time, in Senegal a new party loyal to Marxism-Leninism proclaimed its existence. The Parti Africain de l'Indépendance (PAI), formed in September 1957, declared its intention to struggle for "scientific socialism" and against "repressive capitalism" and imperialism. It advocated socialization of the major economic sectors, collectivization of agriculture, and immediate Africanization of the bureaucracy.[30]

Despite a strong sympathy for the general Soviet point of view, local conditions rather than encouragement from Soviet officials prompted the creation of the PAI. It was an outgrowth of an earlier renegade section of the RDA, which for a period refused to disaffiliate from the Parti Communiste Français. When even this group broke with the French Communists, a wing of its most radical members, together with a number of students returning from Paris, formed the PAI. Although originally intended as a regional political grouping, its effective base would always be confined to Senegal. The PAI's formation, therefore, gives further evidence of the Soviet Union's reluctance, at this point, to sponsor Communist parties in Black Africa. The Soviet Union had very little, if anything, to do with the founding of the first Marxist-Leninist party in post-colonial West Africa.[31]

Thus Soviet leaders treated colonialism's initial retreat from West Africa with noticeable caution. Any inclination to fall in behind this new extension of the national liberation struggle faltered before a lingering distrust of Nkrumah and his revolution. Until it was certain that he meant to act independently of London, a large economic commitment must have seemed precipitous. There was not much point in placing a wedge in a door that opened into an empty room. A direct political approach shared the same difficulties and, in any case, would have been

30. See "Manifeste du Parti Africain de l'Indépendance," *Présence Africaine,* no. 16 (October–November 1957), pp. 190–198. For a speedy retreat before reality, see the much-revised program in Majhmout Diop's (secretary-general of the PAI) report to the African People's Conference (Accra, December 5–12, 1958) in *La Lutte* (PAI newspaper), no. 18 (March 1959). A superb study of the PAI is William J. Foltz's forthcoming "The Parti Africain de l'Indépendance: The Dilemmas of a Communist Movement in West Africa."

31. On this point see Morgenthau, *Political Parties in French-Speaking West Africa,* p. 160. The Soviet Union had very indirectly played a role by helping the most militant students within the Federation of Students from Black Africa in France (FEANF), and some of these returned to Senegal to participate in the formation of the PAI. Similarly, in 1954 Majhmout Diop, a principal founder of the PAI, worked full time for the International Union of Students in Bucharest. Foltz, "The Parti Africain de l'Indépendance," p. 4.

difficult to implement in the absence of an abrasive anti-Western issue to which the Soviet Union could rally. On the other hand, any attempt to apply political pressures through local Communists, even had this been possible, would have been premature. The Soviet attitude toward Ghana was suspicious, not hostile, and not without a certain degree of hope. In these circumstances the Soviet leadership apparently felt that the wisest action was inaction, for to act at all risked either strengthening British imperialism or generating antagonism where none was needed. The moment demanded patient watchfulness rather than impetuous activity. And so, during 1957, Soviet policymakers watched, waiting to receive some sign of the course that independent Ghana would follow.[32]

The Soviet Union, of course, established standards against which Ghana's "progress" could be measured, standards that either expressly or implicitly underlay a growing number of studies devoted to the postcolonial evolution of Ghana. Foremost among these criteria was the pursuit of "economic independence." Only as a precondition for economic independence did political independence take on significance. If economic independence—to be read as the destruction of economic relations with capitalist nations and of the local private sector and, simultaneously, as the establishment of close economic ties with socialist nations and noncapitalist development—did not follow the political revolution, both revolutions would fail. In the redefined language of Lenin, the struggle against neocolonialism succeeded the victory over colonialism, and as far as the Soviet Union was concerned Nkrumah had still to prove himself, not so much as capable of defeating neocolonialism as willing to wage the struggle.

Had words been enough, Nkrumah's often repeated warning, that "political independence is but an empty facade if economic freedom is not possible also," should have reassured Soviet observers.[33] But given colonialism's heritage and, more important, Nkrumah's untested intentions, they were wary of being deceived by sloganeering. First they needed

32. The restraint in Soviet policy toward sub-Saharan Africa in these years was only in part the result of a conservative assessment of conditions in Africa. It also depended to a great extent on the Soviet preoccupation with the Middle East. Events from Suez to Lebanon kept Soviet and American, not to mention Chinese and English, attention fixed on this region, largely to the exclusion of other sections of the Third World.

33. Kwame Nkrumah, "The Movement for Colonial Freedom," *Phylon,* XVI (fourth quarter 1955), 407.

to be convinced that Nkrumah really intended to secure Ghana's "economic freedom." After all, he still represented the interests of the national bourgeoisie. Although Soviet observers acknowledged that he deserved the respect of every Ghanaian for leading the Gold Coast to independence, they feared he might at any time cease to play a progressive role and go over to the side of the reactionary section of the bourgeoisie. There were indications that Nkrumah was already forgetting his debt to the working class, for in consolidating his power he had taken care to subdue organized labor and had even driven from the Convention People's Party labor leaders whose contact with the World Federation of Trade Unions he objected to. Moreover, Nkrumah in his autobiography, according to his Soviet reviewer, slighted the "important contribution of the working class to the struggle against imperialism."[34] On the other hand, Soviet commentators suggested, he was not in nearly so much a hurry to suppress foreign monopolies and to release Ghana from its dependence on imperialism. "This dependence means not only the further plundering of the country by foreign monopolies . . . it ties the hands of the government in carrying out social reforms and in pursuing an independent foreign policy."[35]

Giving Nkrumah the benefit of the doubt, Soviet writers attributed major responsibility for this state of affairs to "feudal elements," which opposed a "more democratic way of development."[36] Fearful of losing their privileges, feudal circles, primarily tribal chiefs, formed the United Party of Ghana to forestall the successful implementation of progressive reforms. That such feudal elements could survive at all, however, indicated how difficult the next phase of the revolution would be. A nation whose societal pattern is a "complicated mixture of capitalist, feudal, patriarchal-feudal and patriarchal-clan relations" moves only with considerable pain toward the "liquidation of the consequences of colonialism and the democratization of public life."[37]

All of these difficulties and limitations, including Nkrumah's frailties, Soviet leaders could have overlooked if Ghana's international behavior

---

34. D. K. Ponomarev, review of *Autobiography of Kwame Nkrumah,* in *Problemy vostokovedeniya,* no. 1 (1959), p. 190.

35. I. I. Potekhin, "V osvobozhdennoi Gane" (In Liberated Ghana), *Souremenny Vostok,* no. 3 (1958), p. 38.

36. V. Vavilov, "The Modern History of Ghana," *New Times,* no. 45 (1959), p. 18.

37. I. I. Potekhin, "Ethnographic Observations in Ghana," *Sovetskaya etnografiya,* no. 3 (1958), quoted in *Mizan,* II (December 1960), 19.

had struck them as particularly beneficial. From the very beginning, an African nation's foreign policy, not internal development, determined the reception accorded it by the Soviet Union. If a nation's pattern of development complemented a progressive foreign policy, this was a happy coincidence, enhancing that country's attractiveness. If not, then in certain circumstances a forward-looking foreign policy might compensate for domestic failings. The obverse of this consideration was that no state which advanced a "reactionary" foreign policy—that is, which remained unfriendly to the Soviet Union—could be capable of progressive reform. Presumably Marx would have turned this relationship around, but for Soviet policymakers such a stricture would have foreclosed short-term benefits to their own foreign policy. Again it was what Thomas P. Thornton has called the "primacy of politics over economics in Soviet analysis."

> Whether the matter under discussion is agricultural reform, the role of the state in the economy, the role of the military, the attitude toward local Communists, or whatever, the criterion applied is not the economic or social effect of a given act, but the presumed political auspices under which the act is performed. With very few exceptions, states that are not friendly to the Soviet Union are regarded as incapable of effective land reform, a rational industrialization policy, etc. Indeed the degree of this effectiveness is scaled in direct proportion to relative merit ascribed to the given country in the eyes of the Soviet leadership.[38]

None of this is to say that Ghana's foreign policy thoroughly distressed Soviet leaders—only that it did not justify any great enthusiasm. Publicly Soviet writers offered Ghana as "an example to other African nations in their struggle for national liberation."[39] They even went so far as to commend Ghana for "following a progressive foreign policy based on nonparticipation in military blocs and friendship for all countries irrespective of their social and political systems."[40]

Yet, clearly, these endorsements concealed serious reservations over

38. Thomas Perry Thornton, ed., *The Third World in Soviet Perspective* (Princeton: Princeton University Press, 1964), pp. 6–7.

39. "Ghana's First Birthday," *New Times,* no. 10 (March 1958), p. 20.

40. *Ibid.* Potekhin wrote on the first anniversary that the "People of Ghana have rendered the other people of tropical and South Africa a splendid example." See his article in *Izvestiya,* March 6, 1958, p. 4.

the foreign policy Nkrumah appeared likely to follow. He had an odd way of phrasing his policy statements which even his most sympathetic Soviet listener must have found rankling. No statement was ever a simple repudiation of imperialism, and no expression of anticolonial solidarity was without annoying qualifications. If, for example, he seemed ready to accept "other forms of economic aid from outside the United Nations," thereby inviting Soviet assistance, he added, "provided it does not compromise our independence."[41] If he cautioned Africa against the different forms that colonialism and imperialism can take, he clouded the issue by implying that the danger came not only from "old" imperialists employing "military means, economic penetration, and cultural assimilations," but from "new" imperialists as well, who depended on "ideological domination, psychological infiltration, and subversive activities."[42] Even his threat before the United States Council on Foreign Relations, on July 25, 1958, that "either we shall modernize with your interest and support—or we shall be compelled to turn elsewhere," could not have completely satisfied Soviet leaders, since it was clear to whom he had turned first.[43]

The Soviet Union responded in kind—on the one hand, praising Nkrumah publicly; on the other, leveling very thinly concealed criticism. Its reaction to the First All-African People's Conference held in Accra (December 1958) provides an excellent illustration of this technique. Ostensibly the Soviet Union welcomed the conference, "whose decisions rang out as a threatening warning to the imperialists."[44] Khrushchev wired a personal greeting to the participants who, according to him, were witnesses to the "growing solidarity among African peoples in their struggle against colonialism."[45] As a sign of the importance they attached to this meeting, Soviet leaders sent Potekhin and six other observers.

41. Speech to Accra conference, April 8–15, 1958, in Nkrumah, *I Speak of Freedom*, p. 129.

42. *Ibid.*, p. 128. Edwin S. Munger, "All-African People's Conference," *American Universities Field Staff Report*, West Africa Series, III (January 1959), 23, maintains that Nkrumah told him, when asked about another reference to colonialism and imperialism coming in a "different guise, not necessarily from Europe," that "you know which country I meant." Thompson, *Ghana's Foreign Policy*, p. 45, argues that Nkrumah may also have had the United States in mind, but Munger had no doubt about whom Nkrumah was speaking.

43. *Ibid.*, p. 145.

44. O. Orestov, "Gana: Na poroge tretego goda" (Ghana: On the Threshold of the Third Year), *Sovremenny Vostok*, no. 4 (1959), p. 47.

45. *Pravda*, December 5, 1958, p. 1.

Potekhin later admitted that the resolutions of the conference demonstrated considerable naiveté on the part of their authors. These resolutions, he lamented, "contained no hint of . . . dangerous imperialist maneuvers," specifically the imperialist tactic of accepting political independence in order to salvage "the rewards of neocolonialism."[46] He blamed these shortcomings on Tom Mboya (Kenya), the conference's chairman.[47] The striking thing, however, is the application these criticisms had to Nkrumah's own remarks, the more so because for every point he was the more celebrated spokesman.

Nkrumah hardly warmed his Soviet audience with his opening comment: "Some of us, I think, need reminding that Africa is a continent on its own. It is not an extension of Europe or any other continent."[48] One target of this remark was certainly the Soviet Union, which in league with China and Egypt appeared to him an unnecessary competitor in the struggle to free Africa. Nkrumah, who always lacked the grace to accept a genuine division of labor within the "African liberation movement," for many years looked upon the Afro-Asian Solidarity Council, sponsored by Moscow, Peking, and Cairo, as something of a rival to his own favorite organizational projects.[49] He made a point of inviting only the Egyptian member of the Solidarity Council to the Accra conference. Similarly, he was piqued by the council's "Quit Africa Day," which, he felt, detracted from his own "African Freedom Day." He made his feelings quite plain: "The liberation of Africa is the task of the Africans. We Africans alone can emancipate ourselves. We welcome the expressions of support from others," but the responsibility remained Africa's alone.[50]

The Soviet Union refused to tolerate a rebuff of this sort and retorted, "Colonialists and their agents tried to make the Accra Conference accept the idea of local struggle of the African peoples within the boundaries

46. I. I. Potekhin, "The African Peoples Forge Unity," *International Affairs,* no. 6 (1961), p. 80.

47. At least this is whom he said he was referring to. I. I. Potekhin, "Africa Throws Off Its Chains," *International Affairs,* no. 2 (1959), p. 118.

48. Munger, "All-African People's Conference," p. 23.

49. *Ibid.,* p. 10. According to another writer, Nkrumah confided his distaste for Afro-Asian solidarity organizations to King Mohammed V of Morocco and various African delegates. John K. Cooley, *East Wind over Africa* (New York: Walker and Company, 1965), p. 137. Thompson, *Ghana's Foreign Policy,* p. 50, citing an interview with Botsio, indicates that Nkrumah stayed clear of A-APSO "because of its external involvement" and because it was not his organization.

50. Munger, "All-African People's Conference," p. 23.

of their continent, fanning the nationalist passions. This move was . . . a flop."[51] Nor did it approve his emphasis on nonviolent techniques for liberating colonial peoples, an unnecessary concession from the Soviet point of view. The "call" to the conference had underscored the importance of the "Gandhian approach" to the independence struggle (it referred to the "ideology of the African nonviolent revolution"). Again the Russians responded: "In an effort to discourage the peoples of Africa, to suppress their determination to gain freedom and independence at all costs, the principle of nonviolence and nonresistance was put into play. But this trick of the colonialists failed completely."[52] Potekhin described the tactics of nonviolence as a "harmful illusion which the imperialists intentionally disseminate to prolong their rule in Africa."[53] The theory of nonresistance and nonviolence was, he said, "a dangerous error."

Since no one challenged Nkrumah as the leading proponent of political pan-Africanism, it was more difficult to disguise the object of Potekhin's remark that the pan-African idea contained many things "alien" to Communism.[54] At the very least, Nkrumah was guilty of defending causes generally condemned by the Soviet Union. Not until the end of 1958 did the Soviet Union find the authentic African revolutionary for whom it had been searching.

Guinean Independence

In French West Africa the progression from colonial status to independent nation-state followed a pattern somewhat different from Ghana's. Unlike leaders in the Gold Coast, French West African nationalists committed themselves to a series of intermediate objectives before ultimately accepting independence as the single acceptable one. They had long been eager to obtain a larger role in governing their own territories but did not fundamentally challenge the basic survival of a French union. Gradually their ambitions shifted toward transforming the union into a more genuinely equal federal system based on universal suffrage, the elimination of separate representation for Europeans and Africans in the governing institutions of the West African Federation

51. Kudryavtsev, in *Izvestiya*, December 16, 1958, p. 8.
52. *Ibid.*
53. I. I. Potekhin, "Istoricheski povorot" (Historic Turning Point), *Sovremenny Vostok*, no. 3 (1959), p. 9.
54. Potekhin, "Africa Throws Off Its Chains," p. 116.

(AOF), and territorial self-government. The Loi-Cadre reforms of 1956-57 recognized an important part of these aspirations (even providing for elected territorial executives and entrusting substantial power to their legislative assemblies) but did so in order to forestall the moment of independence. Moreover, this device frustrated the single other objective that most French African nationalists placed ahead of immediate independence—West African federation—thereby removing the last persuasive reason for the toleration of French tutelage. By decentralizing power to the territorial level and intentionally impeding the emergence of a stronger West African federation, the French reforms gave African leaders the incentive to press for independence sooner than they otherwise might have.

In the Gold Coast, where the colonial power found decolonization easier to contemplate, the transformation to independence was already far advanced. Each step of the way led swiftly and purposively to the next. After the CPP swept the 1951 elections, Nkrumah was released from jail and named Leader of Government Business, thus marking the first transfer of real power to the nationalists (together with the burden of responsibility). The equivalent step in French West Africa's evolution did not occur until the French National Assembly agreed in January 1957 to accept African leaders of government for each of the territories. Two years later the British government, in a "Motion of Destiny," projected the path to Gold Coast independence. The next year, in April 1954, a new constitution bestowed upon the colony internal self-government and full ministerial responsibility, and began to dismantle the authority of Britain's representative, the governor. From this point on, progress toward independence had London's blessing, pending the resolution of objections that Nkrumah's domestic opponents had to the form of state he planned to impose.

The circumstances in which the territories of French West Africa crept toward independence contrast markedly with this course of events. The Loi-Cadre reforms, created as the Gold Coast sped through the last phases of the preparations for independence, formally underscored the essential failure of France's original colonial policy of assimilation and, simultaneously, its inability to see the factors that would make independence the sole acceptable alternative for French-African nationalists. In this context "reformism" unwittingly provoked a critical challenge to France's basic colonial order. In February 1958, the leaders of virtually every party in French West and Equatorial Africa assembled in Paris and declared their intent to form "federations, democratically established by the territories on the bases of solidarity, equality, and voluntarily abandoned sovereignty"; these, in turn, might unite with metropolitan France "on the basis of free cooperation, absolute equality and the right to independence."[55] Perhaps even those who drew up the declaration did not realize it, but this had become an either/or proposition: either France would accept solidly constructed Black African federations as equal partners in a still larger federation or the fragmented portions of West and Equatorial Africa would seek complete independence. De Gaulle's return to power a few months later and the promulgation of the Fifth Republic's constitution merely postponed the dénouement. The continuing lure of French economic assistance, combined with the apprehension that independence at this stage would permanently destroy any chance of West African federation, constrained most of these leaders to approve de Gaulle's constitution (though it preserved under slightly different labels the essential features of the Loi-Cadre reforms). Nor should it be forgotten that most of these leaders believed de Gaulle perfectly capable of beating them in their own constituencies if they opposed the constitution.[56] In Guinea, however, where these imperatives were less compelling, local leaders seized the option de Gaulle offered and rejected membership in the projected French community.

It is true that, until the last weeks before the constitutional referendum, even Sekou Touré expressed interest in the preservation of a Franco-African community. His final decision to mobilize a no vote on the constitution was not taken until almost the last moment. Other leaders, when it came to a choice, were much more reluctant to cut their ties with the metropole. Thus, despite considerable ferment, the determination of the French government to make independence a difficult alternative prolonged the life of France's African colonial empire, but only by obscuring the force of events that were driving the territories relentlessly toward independence.

If the Soviet Union had not fully grasped the implications of the relatively straightforward transition to independence in Ghana, they were much more insensitive to the tortuous and ambiguous decolonization pro-

55. Morgenthau, *Political Parties in French-Speaking West Africa*, pp. 117–118.

56. William Foltz has indicated the considerable weight that Soudanese leaders attached to this consideration. (See Foltz, *From French West Africa to the Mali Federation*, p. 129.) Except in Guinea where the French did not have this kind of influence—to judge from Bakary Djibo's defeat in Niger, the fear was perfectly justified. See Morgenthau, *Political Parties in French-Speaking West Africa*, pp. 311–312.

cess in French West Africa. Soviet writers paid very little attention to developments there. They apparently considered the conflicting attitudes of Touré and Houphouet-Boigny toward the questions of federation and independence too insignificant to warrant comment. Throughout 1958, even into September, *Pravda* and *Izvestiya* completely ignored the rapidly culminating events in this area.

Touré's ambivalence toward the constitution can only partially explain this ponderously imperceptive response to what was happening in his country. Clearly they missed the significance of his petulant exchange with de Gaulle in Conakry a month before the referendum. The French leader was touring West Africa, canvassing support for the soon-to-be-announced constitution. Before arriving in Conakry he was apparently having considerable success; but matters changed in Guinea. In de Gaulle's presence, Touré testily insisted that the new constitution incorporate guarantees of the right to independence, of equal status with France in any federation, of a territorial regroupment, and of unrestricted internal self-government. De Gaulle was unwilling to make such concessions. He had already indicated that a no vote on the constitution would be a declaration of independence and now, for the benefit of the impertinent Guinean leader, he added that a country rejecting the constitution would have to "assume the consequences."[57] To everyone, except Soviet observers evidently, it became obvious that Guinea would vote no and that this act would provide another historical turning point in Black Africa's development. Less than two weeks before the referendum, the most that one Soviet journalist would say about the situation in French West Africa was that de Gaulle on his recent trip had been confronted with "one and the same demand—constitutional recognition of the *right* to independence for all parts of the French Union."[58] Since anything less than independence itself failed to impress Soviet leaders, presumably this did not excite them very much. When Guinea did ostentatiously opt for independence, they must have been surprised. But by the same token Guinean independence ended the casual indifference that had prevented Soviet policymakers from anticipating the startling events of 1958.

More than any other single event, it prompted a full Soviet commitment to Africa. It did so for several reasons. First, the isolation imposed

57. Sekou Touré, *Expérience guinéenne et unité africaine* (Paris: Présence Africaine, 1961), p. 88.
58. N. Gavrilov, "France and Dark Africa," *New Times*, no. 37 (1958), p. 16; emphasis added.

on Guinea by France after the 1958 referendum created a natural and irresistible target for Soviet attention. The Western nations had momentarily vacated an important arena of competition, and the Soviet Union gladly substituted its own presence. Guinea, unlike Ghana, had been undeniably, if involuntarily, freed from economic dependence on the West. Second, the Middle East, which over the previous two years had monopolized Soviet attention, lost some of its urgency when Nasser turned against local Syrian Communists and their foreign benefactors. The Soviet Union was pleased to discover a potential alternative ally in West Africa. Finally, China's nascent challenge to the Soviet Union's right to lead the revolution in Africa and Asia pushed Soviet leaders to secure their position in these areas of competition.

Turning to the first of these developments: Guinea, because of the circumstances in which it became independent, represented everything that Ghana had not. Independent Ghana remained economically tied to Great Britain, the United States and West Germany; Nkrumah, despite his frequent attacks on "neocolonialism," seemed content to tolerate this bane.[59] Guinea, on the other hand, achieved an unmistakable economic independence at the time of political independence. When de Gaulle warned Touré that any territory voting no would have to assume the consequences of its action, he was speaking of depriving the unruly territory of the economic benefits attached to membership in the French community. Within hours of Guinea's rebuff, de Gaulle began to inflict the sanctions he had promised. All French administrative, technical, and military advisers were recalled, along with doctors and educators. Their departure reduced Guinea's trained bureaucracy by 75 percent. Before leaving, they destroyed—partially in haste, partially in bitterness—virtually all records and all transportable capital equipment. What could not be burned was dumped into the ocean. De Gaulle was responding as much in anger as out of a need to contain the effects of Guinean defiance and to make credible France's policy in the remainder of its colonial possessions. He placed not only an economic blockade around Guinea but a diplomatic blockade as well, and he pressed the United States to join him in this policy.[60] A country as isolated as Guinea understandably seemed an attractive focus for Soviet policy.

59. Well over 85 percent of Ghana's trade was with the West. See *External Trade Statistics of Ghana*, IX (December 1959).

60. "Guinea after Five Years," *The World Today*, XX (March 1964), 113. Touré later said that in December 1958, through President Tubman of Liberia, he had asked Washington for military assistance. The request was never answered.

Moreover, Guinea's social structures posed fewer obstacles to "noncapitalist" development than those in Ghana. Unlike Ghana, Guinea suffered no feudal classes; its population was overwhelmingly peasant, the indigenous bourgeoisie almost nonexistent; and its single political party enjoyed, as a Soviet writer pointed out, the "mass support" of all Guineans.[61]

Finally, one may assume that Soviet leaders preferred Touré to Nkrumah. Twelve years earlier as a young man with only a primary-school education and holding a low rank in the civil service, he began his study of the Marxist classics in one of the Groupes d'Etudes Communiste. Soon after, he and other members of the GEC formed a new socialist political party that ultimately transformed itself into the Parti Démocratique de Guinée (PDG), the Guinean section of the Rassemblement Démocratique Africain. Finding his political career stymied by colonial administrators who considered him too sympathetic to the Communists, Touré turned to African labor, became the secretary-general of the coordinating committee of the AOF–Confédération Générale du Travail, and established his reputation as a "hero of the workers' movement."

Touré was not a Communist, and only the most fatuous Soviet observer would have thought him one. In fact he later led his labor group out of the CGT and the WFTU at a time when the RDA leadership was suppressing any lingering tie with the Communist movement. Nevertheless, it seems likely that he struck Soviet leaders first as a man of principle and, second, as a leader committed to socialism, even if a kind of his own definition. By contrast, they probably considered Nkrumah more the opportunist and therefore an undependable, if not dangerous, ally.

A second consideration sparking interest in Guinea related to developments in the Middle East. When in early 1958 Syria joined Egypt to form the United Arab Republic, Nasser immediately suppressed all competing political parties, including a promising Syrian Communist party. The Soviet leadership accepted Nasser's action regretfully but silently. They had little other choice. In July, however, their options increased

---

61. Yuri Bochkaryov, "The Guinean Experiment" *New Times,* no. 24 (June 1960), p. 29. Bochkaryov published a three-part report on Guinea that appeared in the *New Times,* nos. 24, 25, 29 (1960). Soviet writers were apparently aware that the PDG, in 1957 and 1958, while it still had the sympathy of the French bureaucracy, successfully destroyed the power of a very strong Fulani feudal class. See B. Ameillon, *La Guinée, bilan d'une indépendance* (Paris: François Maspero, 1954), pp. 13–35.

when a coup in Iraq brought Brigadier Abdel Karim Kassim to power. The new regime adopted a militant foreign policy, withdrew from the Baghdad Pact (leaving it without Baghdad), and legalized the Iraqi Communist Party, in pleasing contrast to Nasser's mounting attacks on Egyptian and Syrian Communists. Impressed with Kassim, the Soviet leadership felt less constrained to tolerate Nasser's anti-Communism. At the Twenty-First Party Congress (January 1959), not only did Khrushchev permit the Syrian Communist leader Khalid Bakdash to denounce Nasser; he himself took the opportunity to criticize the Egyptian leader. The Iraqi challenge to Egyptian pre-eminence in the Arab world, aggravated by Soviet and Chinese support for Kassim, gave Nasser additional reason to press his attack against Syrian and Egyptian Communists. The growing tension between these two countries erupted in open polemics in March 1959 when a pro-Communist demonstration in Mosul, Iraq, touched off a counter anti-Communist rebellion, which the Iraqi government blamed on Nasser. He retaliated by calling the Iraqi and Syrian Communist parties "agents of foreigners," subservient to orders from foreign Communist centers.

The Chinese responded with violent attacks on Nasser. Soviet officials, in contrast, again muted their criticism and sought to retain a certain level of cooperation. Yet things were not as they had been in 1956 or even a year earlier. The Chinese decided that Nasser could not be trusted and, as a result, began to look for revolutionary opportunities elsewhere. Their reaction reminded Soviet leaders that the problem had another dimension.

China's subsequent approach to Morocco in the spring of 1959 and its growing interest in the Algerian war coincided with an increasingly apparent divergence in Soviet and Chinese policy toward the Front de Libération Nationale. In October 1959 Khrushchev endorsed de Gaulle's proposals for a ceasefire in Algeria; the Chinese denounced the French proposal as "nothing but a sugar-coated poison pill."[62] This and other issues were, by late 1959, sending Soviet-Chinese relations careening toward the point of no return, thereby creating a critical new factor in Soviet relations with Africa.

Most fundamentally the dispute was becoming a question of who would direct the world revolutionary movement. Convinced that the Soviet Union had lost its revolution-making nerve, the Chinese advanced

62. New China News Agency, October 17, 1959, quoted in Richard Lowenthal, "China," in Brzezinski, *Africa and the Communist World*, p. 172.

their own revolutionary experience as a model for the colonial peoples of Asia and Africa. For the same reasons, they challenged Soviet priorities, demanding that the "struggle for national liberation" be given precedence over the "struggle for peace."[63] Their long-latent dispute over the proper strategy and tactics to be adopted in the Third World came out into the open in the fall of 1959, when China could no longer contain its disaffection over Soviet policy toward the Cameroun and Algerian rebel movements. Once China took the decision to come to the aid of these groups and perhaps any others that could be formed, Guinea attracted attention as the best possible control point in this part of Africa. Thus the moment the new Chinese ambassador to Morocco arrived at his post, in April 1959, he flew to Conakry with a gift of five thousand tons of rice. In October China and Guinea established diplomatic relations and concluded a cultural agreement. In the same month China initiated its foreign-language broadcasts to Africa. China was moving into Africa as a rival of the Soviet Union rather than as a collaborator, giving Soviet leaders their third reason for capitalizing on the emergence of independent Guinea.

The Soviet response engaged all possible diplomatic resources—public acclamation, political and cultural exchange, military assistance, trade agreements, and economic credits. Two days after the National Assembly formally proclaimed Guinea independent, the Soviet Union extended diplomatic recognition; in December 1958 Czechoslovakia offered Guinea an unconditional arms deal;[64] in February 1959 the Soviet Union negotiated a trade agreement with the new state; in August it granted economic credits; in September the CPSU sent representatives to the Fifth Congress of the PDG; in November Soviet leaders coaxed Touré to Moscow and secured his support for their approach to international problems; and in January 1960 Khrushchev accepted an invitation to visit Guinea.

The Soviet response to Guinea bears some obvious similarity to its policy toward Egypt in 1955, but in Guinea's case the Soviet Union enjoyed the advantage of operating in a free field. Like Egypt, Guinea also had turned to the United States with a request for military assistance

63. The best discussion of the emerging dispute is in Donald S. Zagoria, *The Sino-Soviet Conflict, 1956–1961* (Princeton: Princeton University Press, 1962), pp. 252–276.

64. Presumably the possibility was raised by a Soviet delegation arriving in Conakry on December 4, 1958.

and, as in the case of Egypt, the Soviet Union was happy to offer what could not be obtained in the West. Again the Soviet Union opened an area of influence through military assistance. This time, however, the arms came as a gift rather than as a sale. In March 1959 two shiploads of arms and armored cars arrived in Conakry, accompanied by an eighteen-member Czech military mission.[65]

Even before the ships reached Guinea, Soviet leaders, trading on the entrée offered by the arms promise, rushed a commercial delegation to Conakry. By the middle of February it had successfully negotiated a trade and payment agreement, the terms of which support the impression that the Soviet Union wished to establish as swiftly as possible a firmer foothold.[66] The agreement was to go into effect on the day it was signed (February 13, 1959), indicating the Russians' eagerness to launch commercial relations with Guinea. It took Ghana and the Soviet Union two and one half years to accomplish the same thing. The Soviet-Guinean trade agreement provided a swing credit (to cover deficits for either party) of $300,000, a sum increased to $600,000 in the next Soviet-Guinean trade agreement. The trade agreement with Ghana included none. Until Guinean independence, the two countries had exchanged no trade; in 1959, even before the trade agreement could have its full impact, the Soviet bloc supplied 9.3 percent of Guinea's imports and purchased 16.2 percent of its exports.[67]

The next phase in Soviet efforts to reinforce growing ties with Guinea occurred in late summer 1959, when Soviet authorities agreed to extend Touré's government $35 million in economic credits. In August Touré sent Saifoulaye Diallo, secretary-general of the PDG, and Ismael Touré, minister of public works, transportation, and communication, to Moscow to talk about the possibility of aid. Khrushchev's response was immediately favorable. Moreover, Khrushchev made sure the delegation was

65. All information on Soviet military aid during these early years is taken from the following sources: M. J. V. Bell, "Military Assistance to Independent African States," *Adelphi Papers*, no. 15 (December 1964), p. 11; Captain E. Hinterhoff, "The Soviet Military Aid and Its Implications," *Fifteen Nations* (February–March 1962), pp. 79–87; and a study by the Atlantic Research Corporation (Georgetown), June 1965. All of these studies agree on the statistics. The military grant was worth about $3 million.

66. The text of the agreement can be found in *SSSR i strany Afriki, 1946–1962* (The USSR and the Countries of Africa; Moscow, 1963), pp. 421–424.

67. Economist Intelligence Unit, *Three-Monthly Economic Review of French African Community*, no. 8 (March 1962), p. 16.

grandly feted, as befitted the first significant group of Black African leaders to visit the Soviet Union. After touring Baku, Kiev, Leningrad, and then Khrushchev's Crimean dacha, after public clamor, luncheons, effusive toasts, and an evening at the Bolshoi, Touré and Diallo returned to Conakry bearing Black Africa's first aid agreement with the Soviet Union. In the next month a Soviet delegation arrived in Guinea to attend the Fifth Congress of the PDG. There they joined the representatives of China.

In November Sekou Touré came to Moscow. His visit gave Soviet leaders their first opportunity to weigh the success of Soviet policy. Needless to say, the auspiciousness of the arrival of Africa's most celebrated revolutionary leader prompted considerable enthusiasm. Frol Kozlov, when he was not boasting of the miracle of Soviet industrialization, extolled Guinea's political course and explicitly pledged Soviet resources to continuing the struggle for Africa's liberation.[68] Touré was less fulsome. In speaking of his reasons for being in Moscow, he said: "We know there is the imperialist and there is the anti-imperialist. We are fighting imperialism and are therefore allies of the world that has chosen freedom and a place for all nations."[69] He was explaining that, to some degree, Guinea's isolation had created the bond drawing his country to the East. Had the West given him other recourse, Touré hinted, things might have been different. He continued, "We submit to the laws of no one else's doctrine or philosophy"; and more to the point, "Africa must choose not between the East and the West but between progress and colonialism, between peace and war."

As far as the Soviet Union was concerned, however, these minor qualifications detracted little from the full support Touré gave Soviet foreign policy in the joint communiqué, support viewed from the perspective of Khrushchev's October visit to Peking.[70] On three important questions with which the Chinese either were or would soon be openly disagreeing, Touré espoused the Soviet view. First, he agreed that Khrushchev's visit to the United States did much to promote an "atmosphere of genuine confidence and mutual understanding in international relations." Second, he noted that Guinea fully supported Khrushchev's proposals for "general and compelete disarmament." Finally, he expressed his confidence that resources released by disarmament would "raise the living

68. *Pravda,* November 27, 1959, pp. 1, 2.
69. *Ibid.*
70. For the communiqué see *ibid.,* p. 1.

standard in underdeveloped countries." Within a matter of months the Chinese would be opposing the Soviet position on each of these questions. Khrushchev must have been pleased with his first bid to secure African support for Soviet foreign policy.

Guinea's independence marked a turning point in Soviet relations with Black Africa. The opportunities that its existence opened for Soviet foreign policy excited the imagination of the Soviet leadership. Touré's backing for Khrushchev's approach to international problems, valuable not only in the competition with a traditional capitalist rival but now in the conflict with the Soviet Union's erstwhile Chinese ally, constituted but one of the benefits flowing from Soviet friendship with Guinea. Guinea also gave the Soviet Union access to the revolutionary movements of Africa, many of which had taken refuge in Conakry. Nor should it be forgotten that Guinea's abundant mineral resources, including some of the world's highest-grade bauxite, offered definite economic advantages to the nation aiding in their exploitation.[71]

Of far more fundamental importance, however, the shadow of major political and economic transformation that appeared to cross over Guinea promised an early arrival of the socialist revolution in Africa. Guinea and states to follow may have seemed, during the first moments of unspoiled Soviet optimism, a confirmation of an essential faith in Marxism-Leninism. For, even if Guinea were not soon to become a Communist state or a part of the socialist camp, the anti-Western orientation of its foreign policy and the radical course of its internal development strengthened what Soviet ideologists were beginning to call "the world revolutionary process." The phrase meant that the emerging nations of the world were defecting from the capitalist system, eschewing the capitalist path of development, and, within the international community, grouping behind the "progressive forces." These countries need not be Communist; it was sufficient under the strange political mercantilism of the cold war that one side lose and not that the other side win. In this somewhat limited sense, the Soviet Union grew confident that it could defeat the West in Africa. The search for other "Guineas" became the principal objective of the Soviet Union's African policy.

71. Soviet writers often emphasized the natural wealth of countries like Guinea ten years earlier, when condemning colonial powers for exploiting these resources so ruthlessly. Once the Soviet Union began developing economic relations with independent African states, less attention was drawn to the existence of these mineral reserves.

Soviet leaders believed that Western power could be rolled back by concentrating energies on those specific countries most susceptible to Soviet influence.

While newly independent Africa remained monochromatic, the Soviet Union could pursue these stakes with little diversion. In the following year, however, with the rapid influx of independent African states, the canvas grew immeasurably more complicated, confronting Soviet policy-makers with new responsibilities, new opportunities, and new difficulties.

III

The Era of Optimism, 1960

Ghana and Guinea opened the floodgates of independence. By the end of 1960 there were fifteen more new African nations, including the entire membership of what once had been Afrique Occidentale Française. After another year, in West Africa only the Gambia, Portuguese Guinea, and the islands of Fernando Po and São Tomé would remain under colonial sway. This rapid transfiguration of the African political map brought the Soviet Union into contact with a large number of new states, states whose political character and demeanor were often in great contrast. It was to be expected that Soviet leaders would see the differences among these states and that, as a result, preferences would require of policymakers some differentiation in designing their approach to Africa. Variety in itself would be a complicating factor.

Yet despite the distinctions that set these new nations apart—often most noticeably in their attitudes toward the former colonial metropole—the very process of decolonization endowed them, from the Soviet point of view, with a fundamentally common identity. The struggle for independence, accomplished however peacefully, automatically placed them among those revolutionary forces weakening the colonial system.

On this basis the Soviet Union could accept as allies most of the new African governments, and when it became difficult to overlook the "reactionary" qualities of some regimes, Soviet leaders framed their commitment more generally in terms of the "national liberation movement."

One of the preoccupations of the Soviet Union in 1960 was to entrench itself as the major spokesman and benefactor of this movement. In the United Nations, at executive sessions of both the World Peace Council and the World Federation of Trade Unions, and before the Second Conference of the Afro-Asian People's Solidarity Organization, the Soviet Union energetically sought the favor and endorsement of Africa. Soviet leaders exhorted Africa to consummate the revolution begun with self-government by determining to achieve economic independence. In this struggle they offered the lessons of Soviet experience and promised important material support. Increasingly the states of Africa understand, said Soviet commentators, the full range of tasks implicit in the national liberation revolution. Where previously there had been an "absence of agreement over the present and future for Africa," by 1960 Africa had united behind the single slogan, "Independence and Unity."[1] In discussing the Second All-African People's Conference which was held in Tunis on January 25–30, 1960, *Izvestiya's* African correspondent, Vladimir Kudryavtsev, underscored the transformation: "If at the Accra African People's Conference, 1958, they spoke about political independence while almost entirely forgetting about economic problems, then the situation was now fundamentally changed."[2]

Such Soviet optimism was general, reinforced by the momentum of events which seemed to generate expanded support for the "world revolutionary process." The process of decolonization appeared to Russian observers by its nature to damage the position of the Western countries in Africa and, therefore, to benefit the socialist revolution. Moreover, they were convinced that these new countries, faced with the imposing difficulties of modernizing their economies and determined to find for this transition a more effective mechanism than capitalism, would increasingly turn to radical economic solutions. The tension this trend would create between developing nations and capitalist nations promised to accelerate the alignment of the former with a sympathetic socialist camp. Countries such as Ghana and Guinea had already perceived the

1. V. Kudryavtsev, "Afrika shagaet vpered" (Africa Moves Forward), *Sovremenny Vostok,* no. 4 (1960), p. 45.
2. *Ibid.*

need to seek economic independence and, as the vanguard of the African revolution, were constantly warning their less perceptive neighbors against the wiles of Western neocolonialism. Kojo Botsio, leading the Ghanaian delegation to the Tunis All-African People's Conference, pointed to the "devilish new strategy" of colonial powers who retreated from open domination "to keep the African perpetually poor and dependent, even though politically free."[3] His Guinean colleague, Ismael Touré, reminded the conference of the "importance of combining the class struggle with the anticolonial struggle in Africa."[4] "Especially instructive," noted Soviet observers, was the eloquent example Guinea offered others in "breaking the trade and finance monopolies swindling her."[5]

Guinea: The Touchstone of Soviet Policy

In a period of revolutionary change, Guinea was clearly the most revolutionary African state. Proud and angry and confident, its leaders knew that their country was Africa's vanguard. Guinea had shown colonial Africa the path to dignity; now it would demonstrate how that dignity could be made secure through rapid, independent economic growth. No time would be lost in discarding the remnants of the old colonial economic structure; Guineans—that is, the PDG and the state it guided—planned to place severe restraints on expatriate involvement in their country's economic development. They preferred to submit instead to the discipline of comprehensive planning and to the leadership of the state in crucial economic sectors. President Touré's opening address to the Fifth National Congress of the PDG, on September 14, 1959 (a Soviet delegation was in his audience), promised that Guinea would soon establish an independent monetary system, eliminate parasitic importers and exporters, and circumscribe the freedom of foreign capital.[6] On March 1, 1960, Touré took his country out of the franc zone and announced the creation of a national bank to control the new Guinean

3. Kojo Botsio, speech to Second All-African People's Conference (Tunis) in *Afro-Asian Bulletin*, I (February–March 1960), 56.

4. "1960 god—god Afriki" (1960, Africa's Year), *Sovremenny Vostok*, no. 2 (1960), p. 9.

5. Kudryavtsev, "Afrika shagaet vpered," p. 46.

6. See Sekou Touré, "Ve Congrès national du Parti Démocratique de Guinée" (September 14–17, 1959), *Expérience guinéenne et unité africaine* (Paris: Présence Africaine, 1961), pp. 458–559.

franc. One month later a party conference at Kankan approved a three-year plan emphasizing the development of agriculture through producers' cooperatives, rural centers of modernization, and national centers for the production of pineapples, bananas, groundnuts, and rice (in effect, state plantations). The plan projected the formation and capitalization of five hundred producers' cooperatives. It strengthened a trade clearing-house, the Comptoir Guinéen de Commerce Extérieur, pointing toward an eventual state monopoly over external trade, and enhanced the powers of the newly established Comptoir Guinéen de Commerce Intérieur, an agency intended to undermine the position of private traders in retail commerce. The spirit of the new investment code, "not designed to attract foreign capital at any price, neither to discourage it en bloc," displayed a marked indifference to the role foreign capital might occupy in the plan's fulfillment.[7] Late in August the government placed extensive restrictions on local banks and, when French banks allegedly failed to comply, shut down all but the Banque d'Afrique Occidentale. In the first months of 1961 it nationalized the diamond industry and the two major public-utility companies for electricity and water. Guinea had embarked upon the radical reorganization of its economy and Soviet observers were delighted.

"Guinea will not take the road of capitalism or of bourgeois development," *Pravda* quoted N'Famara Keita, Guinean minister of planning, as saying.[8] Soviet leaders obviously expected a great deal. The new three-year development plan, they noted, provided for the extension of the state and cooperative sectors of the economy, and particularly for the establishment of more than "500 collective farms."[9] One of their enthusiastic analysts described the marketing cooperatives under the Mutual Aid Society for Rural Development as a system that "paved the way for producer cooperatives . . . and the collective cultivation of the land."[10] He credited the regime with removing a significant impediment to growth by establishing central control over external trade. By abolishing the "cantonal chieftaincy," it destroyed that "small section of the local population that lived by the direct exploitation of the peasantry."[11]

7. See Economist Intelligence Unit, *Three-Monthly Economic Review of French African Community,* no. 2 (June 1960), pp. 11–12.

8. *Pravda,* April 7, 1960, p. 3.

9. *Ibid.*

10. Yuri Bochkaryov, "The Guinean Experiment," *New Times,* no. 25 (June 1960), p. 24.

11. Bochkaryov, "The Guinean Experiment," no. 24, p. 24.

And most important, in abandoning the franc zone, it deprived French imperialism of a crucial "instrument for subordinating" the Guinean economy. In short, Guinea's leadership had "chosen a path of economic and political development that goes against the grain of the Western imperialists."[12]

In both social organization and pattern of development, Guinea represented for the Soviet Union the most advanced country in sub-Saharan Africa. In particular, the pace of economic reform distinguished it from such states as Ghana, which, though poised on the "threshold of the second revolution,"[13] hesitated to risk the dislocating effects of a major economic reorientation. Soviet commentators emphasized that Guinea had marked out a path of political and economic development "different from that followed by any of the other newly independent countries."[14] In discussing the political and social character of Guinea, Soviet writers set forth the qualities distinguishing it from other African countries: the mass character of the PDG; the "elimination of privately owned land"; the weakness of the local bourgeoisie; and the absence of a feudal class.[15] All of this inspired Soviet writers to stress as "the primary vital feature of the Republic the virtual absence of the basic exploiting classes."[16] By comparison they explicitly noted the survival of "basic exploiting elements" in Ghana; Potekhin described Ghanaian society as a "complicated mixture of capitalist, feudal, patriarchal-feudal and patriarchal-clan relations."[17]

Soviet confidence in Guinea's progress, however robust, was not unreserved. Persisting doubts reflected the general limits of Soviet hopes for any of the new African regimes. Thus, said Soviet analysts, although it was true that the Guinean bourgeoisie remained feeble, it was nevertheless growing. Similarly, although land had been "theoretically nationalized," in the communes individual peasant families continued to hold plots that "to all intents and purposes" they worked "as private

12. *Ibid.*

13. This was Nkrumah's expression used on the occasion of the tenth anniversary of the CPP in 1959. See Nkrumah, *I Speak of Freedom,* p. 163.

14. Bochkaryov, "The Guinean Experiment," no. 24, p. 23. At the time (June 1960) the number of independent African countries was still small, underscoring the applicability of this comparison to Ghana. Most other African states did not become independent until the second half of 1960.

15. *Ibid.,* no. 29, p. 29.

16. *Ibid.,* no. 24, p. 24.

17. I. I. Potekhin, "Ethnographic Observations in Ghana," *Sovetskaya etnografiya,* no. 3, quoted in *Mizan,* II (December 1960), 19.

owners."[18] And industry, where it existed, remained predominantly under the control of foreign monopoly capital.

Soviet policymakers might have agreed with the South African Communist publicist who argued that these shortcomings would persist so long as Guinean leaders refused to "arm the working classes and the masses of the people generally with the knowledge and understanding of Marxist-Leninist theory."[19] But they most certainly would have rejected his subsequent insinuation that the emergence of a strong Communist party constituted the appropriate antidote. Of course Soviet leaders assumed that before Guinea could achieve socialism, or even before Guinea would permanently close the door to the capitalist alternative, a Communist party had to take form, but this could occur, according to the Soviet view, only at a more advanced stage of industrialization. Soviet writers predicted that Guinea's economic plans would promote industrialization and, with it, the growth of a working class. "In these circumstances new social trends and *even organizations* may quite possibly arise."[20]

This was, in part, a realistic assessment of historical forces prevailing at the moment. It was equally a prudent appraisal of the limits to Sekou Touré's patience. In April 1960, the same month during which *The African Communist* hinted that what Guinea really needed was a Communist party, Touré announced that "if certain people wished to found a Guinean Communist party they should realize that the PDG would oppose them . . . for Communism was not the way for Africa."[21] If the Soviet Union had sponsored a Communist party in Guinea, not only would it have defied conditions which denied Communism a base there but, of more immediate concern, it would have sacrificed Touré's goodwill. This was an unreasonable price to pay for one African Communist party. For the time being, the advantages of cooperation with Touré far outweighed whatever limited instrumental utility a local Communist party may have offered the Soviet Union.

The advantages of cooperation with Guinea were twofold. As the temporary residence of Africa's most militant revolutionaries—Félix-Roland Moumié, Pierre Mulele, Antoine Gizenga, Mario Pinto de Andrade, and representatives of Sawaba and the Liberation Front for

18. *The African Communist* (April 1960), p. 26.
19. Bochkaryov, "The Guinean Experiment," no. 29, p. 30.
20. *Ibid.,* p. 29; emphasis added.
21. Walter Z. Laqueur, "Communism and Nationalism in Tropical Africa," *Foreign Affairs,* XXXIX (July 1961), 616.

the Ivory Coast—Guinea represented for the Soviets the control center of the national liberation movement in sub-Saharan Africa. It was the principal Black African member of the Afro-Asian People's Solidarity Organization, participating on the executive secretariat, serving as the permanent location for the A-APSO's Solidarity Fund, and, in April 1960, convening the second A-APSO conference. With the assistance of the World Federation of Trade Unions it organized in mid-1960 the Université Ouvrière Africaine, a training center for trade-union leaders from all parts of Africa. A school for African journalists founded in Conakry during this period received the support of the Prague-based International Journalists' Association. Through Guinea the Soviet Union had convenient access to the revolutionary movements of Africa, and from Conakry it could nurture those groups disposed to the socialist countries.

In addition, the general content of Guinean foreign policy corresponded with Soviet interests. Touré in his adamant hostility to the French, and consequently to the Western alliance system, condemned as vehemently as the Russians did the "intrigues of Western imperialism." Thus, according to *Pravda,* on his *second* visit to the Soviet Union, September 7–9, 1960, Touré made clear his scorn for "fifteen newly independent countries" which had signed "absurd agreements" receding to their former colonial masters the most fundamental features of their sovereignty.[22] These agreements, Touré scoffed, "permit colonial countries to maintain military bases on the territory of the new African states, to keep under their influence the military forces of these countries, to influence the economic development of these countries, to maintain control over telegraph communications and even to determine the policy . . . of these countries in international affairs." Khrushchev himself had never criticized more explicitly the arrangements countries such as Nigeria, Sierra Leone, Senegal, and the Entente states had reached with their former metropoles. The struggle to eliminate imperialism in whatever guise, Touré told his Soviet hosts, had arrived at a decisive stage, requiring a firm alliance between Guinea and "the forces of progress."

The alliance that Touré had in mind was primarily economic. Africa, he said, had undertaken to liberate itself culturally, politically, and economically, but Africa was weak and colonialism's heritage heavy; without substantial material assistance from the socialist countries, time threatened to deny the people of Africa their victory. Guinea, he continued,

22. *Pravda,* September 8, 1960, p. 2.

recognized that the huge progress attained by the socialist countries constituted a decisive factor in determining the balance of forces between imperialism and socialism and, as such, that it was of critical importance for the national liberation movement. He characterized the assistance already given Africa as of "immeasurable value," but implied that unless the flow of foreign aid quickened, the economic revolution in Africa would suffer delays enabling neocolonialists to re-establish their positions. Rarely in his public comments did Touré depart from this theme, and, duly impressed, the Soviet leadership responded by promising Guinea new credits totaling $21 million. Furthermore, in the final sentence of the joint communiqué signed at the close of Touré's visit, the Soviet government expressed readiness to participate in Guinea's grandiose plans for developing the Konkouré River.[23]

Coming only one year after the Soviet Union had first offered Guinea $35 million in economic assistance, the new aid agreement underscored the rapidly growing Soviet economic interest in this part of West Africa. Earlier in March, the two sides had signed a protocol specifying the projects to be financed under the previous aid agreement of August 24, 1959, and the list of a dozen undertakings ranged from geological surveys to a 25,000-seat stadium, from mechanical equipment for the port of Conakry to a polytechnical institute, and from a fruit and vegetable cannery to a shoe and leather tannery.[24] In August 1960 the economic offensive had been extended to Ghana, with the signature of a $40 million economic and technical cooperation agreement.

But the most remarkable index of mounting Soviet interest in Guinea appeared in trade statistics. By the end of 1960, Soviet exports accounted for 44.2 percent of all Guinean foreign purchasers, compared with 9.3 percent the previous year.[25] Sales to the Soviet Union increased from 16.2 percent of total Guinean exports in 1959 to 22.9 percent in 1960. Over the same period the exchange between Guinea and France collapsed from 57 percent of total Guinean exports to 28.7 percent and, in the case of imports, even more precipitously from 62.5 percent to 29 percent.[26] Trade with Ghana, despite that country's growing attraction for the Soviet Union as manifested in the August aid agreement, fell

23. *Pravda,* September 9, 1960, p. 1.
24. For the content of this agreement see *SSSR i strany Afriki, 1946–1962,* I, 580–584.
25. Economist Intelligence Unit, *Three-Monthly Economic Review of French African Community,* no. 5 (May 1961), p. 13.
26. Ken Post, *The New States of West Africa* (Baltimore: Penguin Books, 1964), p. 124.

far short of the tempo of commerce moving between the Soviet Union and Guinea. In 1960 Ghana exported 10 percent of its total sales to the Soviet Union, a noticeable increase over the 2 percent exported in 1959, but this increase was due primarily to the Soviet Union's fluctuating purchases of cocoa, which went down again the next year (and so, consequently, did the Soviet share of Ghana's total exports, to 4 percent).[27] Ghanaian imports from the Soviet Union were up in 1960 to 0.8 percent of total purchases.

One of the central issues of Touré's September discussions with Khrushchev, and presumably the principal reason he returned to the Soviet Union so soon after his original visit in 1959, was the Congo crisis. Both leaders were looking ahead to their forthcoming visits to the UN's Fifteenth General Assembly session, where the Congo question would surely be a major item on the agenda. With this in mind, Soviet leaders were particularly eager to explore the position that Touré might adopt.

The Congo

During 1960 and 1961, regimes outside West Africa heavily influenced Soviet relations with Ghana, Guinea, and Mali. One was in the Congo and the other in China. Both constituted major reference points for Soviet African policy and, therefore, now need to be introduced for the essential dimension they add to the story of Soviet relations with West Africa.

After July 1960 every African nation's external relations assumed a Congo dimension; that is, even the most remote bilateral relationship was affected by attitudes maintained on the Congo question. For a state like Guinea, the problem of the Congo virtually displaced other foreign-policy considerations and became the hinge of its relationship with the Soviet Union. Guinea and Ghana were both committed to an immediate and forceful suppression of the Katanga secession, but because they differed over who should apply the force, the Congo crisis produced conflicting attitudes toward the Soviet Union's role. These differences reflected Guinea's closer identification with the Soviet position.

Both Guinea and Ghana strongly supported the Lumumba government; both considered the Katanga secession the dangerous product of neocolonialist machinations; both desired a firm United Nations ini-

27. *Annual Report on External Trade in Ghana* (July 1962), pp. 23–25.

tiative and willingly contributed their own forces to the UN operation. But Nkrumah looked on the Congo crisis principally as a test of African unity and, as such, an invaluable opportunity for galvanizing support behind his pan-African aspirations. His priorities naturally militated against a major and direct role being assigned to the great powers, either West or East. Within the first days following the eruption of the Katanga revolt, Ghana announced its conviction "that the present difficulties in the Congo should be solved primarily through the efforts of the independent African States within the framework of the United Nations machinery. Intervention by Powers from outside the African continent, in the view of the Government of Ghana, is likely to increase rather than lessen tension."[28]

Touré, on the other hand, was more agitated by the nature of the situation in the Congo than by the opportunity to promote African unity. Seeing in the Congo another manifestation of colonialist intrigue, Touré reacted in rage, reminded no doubt of recent French policy toward his own government. For Touré the critical consideration centered on the search for an effective means to end the Belgian conspiracy sustaining the secession of Katanga and for some way to protect the government of a fellow revolutionary. If this could be accomplished by Africans within the United Nations framework, or even by a general UN initiative, he would have been quite satisfied. But when the United Nations appeared to be either incapable of or unwilling to end the Katanga secession and to restore the territorial integrity of the Congo, Touré predictably favored a more radical response, including direct Soviet involvement. Given his own relationship to the Soviet Union, Soviet intervention was not something from which he, in contrast to most other African leaders, drew back.

During August 1960, when the tone of Soviet pronouncements grew more violent, Guinea offered Lumumba what one expert observer has described as "the nearest thing to 'Communist' advice" that the Congolese leader received, advice that almost certainly inspired some of his most intransigent statements.[29] When Soviet diplomats began their public disagreement with the secretary-general of the UN, arguing in the Security Council on August 21, 1960, that he was wrong to deny

28. *Times,* July 14, 1960, p. 12.
29. Catherine Hoskyns, *The Congo since Independence, January 1960–December 1961* (London: Oxford University Press, 1965), p. 189. This is easily the most complete and responsible study of the Congo crisis yet to appear.

the United Nations' right to intervene actively to terminate the Katanga secession, the Guinean representative (given the opportunity to speak by the Soviet Union and Poland) strongly supported their interpretation. Four days later, when the Soviet Union first diverted transport lorries promised to the UN operation to Lumumba's forces and followed these with Ilyushin aircraft, the Guineans continued to encourage Lumumba in his course. In contrast, the Ghanaians in Leopoldville, particularly Andrew Djin and General Otu, warned the Congolese that an independent action could not possibly succeed and that the use of Soviet planes would have serious repercussions.[30]

Therefore Touré's visit to the Soviet Union in the first week of September occurred at a critical juncture in Soviet-Congolese relations. On September 5, the night before the Guinean leader arrived in Moscow, President Kasavubu dismissed Lumumba's government. Kasavubu's action brought the struggle between the two leaders into the open and altered the circumstances in which the Soviet Union had recently stepped up its direct involvement in this increasingly troubled country. Late in August, in collaboration with Lumumba, Soviet planes had begun ferrying Congolese troops into Kasai Province for an assault on Katanga, independent of the UN operation.[31] As but one indication of the Soviet Union's expanding role in the Congo, the airlift was bound to arouse misgivings among a number of African states. Khrushchev probably feared that a challenge on this issue at the General Assembly session would detract from his bid to rally the Afro-Asian movement behind Soviet policy. He quite likely concluded, therefore, that a sympathetic spokesman could usefully be recruited from within the Afro-Asian group. Judging from his general position on the Congo question, Touré must have seemed a likely candidate.

If this is what Khrushchev had in mind, then presumably he found Touré's response somewhat disappointing. His speeches ignored Khrushchev's angry denunciation of the imperialist conspiracy in the Congo.[32] No mention was made of the material assistance being supplied directly to Lumumba's government, despite the fact that two days later Khrushchev felt compelled to defend this action in a letter to the secretary-general.[33] And although the joint communiqué referred to a "unity of

30. *Ibid.*, p. 190.
31. *Ibid.*
32. *Pravda*, September 8, 1960, p. 1.
33. *Pravda*, September 11, 1960, p. 5. Khrushchev was under pressure to explain Soviet intervention after the secretary-general's note of September 5.

views" concerning the situation produced by imperialist aggression against the independence and territorial integrity of the Congo Republic, it contained no criticism of the UN operation or of the secretary-general.[34] Still, in all other pronouncements, Soviet officials made plain their hostility both to the UN operation and to the secretary-general. A lengthy statement appearing in *Pravda* the day following Touré's departure censured Hammarskjöld for failing to "display the minimum of objectivity demanded of him in very complicated circumstances."[35] Touré's evident reluctance to align Guinea's position firmly with that of the Soviet Union owed to his primary allegiance to the Afro-Asian group, and the Afro-Asian group at this point was unwilling to turn on the secretary-general.

Before Touré rejoined Khrushchev in New York, however, it became apparent that Lumumba had been outmaneuvered by Kasavubu in the jockeying that followed his dismissal on September 5—outmaneuvered with the connivance of UN representatives and Western diplomats in Leopoldville.[36] Not just in Conakry, but in Accra and Cairo, the explosion of anger more than matched the report heard in Moscow. Touré immediately threatened to withdraw the Guinean contingent from the UN Congo forces. Nkrumah, particularly embarrassed by the use of Ghanaian troops to keep the radio station out of Lumumba's hands on September 11, indicated that he might also withdraw his forces if Lumumba were not allowed full use of the radio station. The *Ghanaian Times* in an editorial wrote that "the UN itself is not at fault; its agents are astonishingly at fault."[37]

It was at this point that the Soviet Union unleashed an unrestrained, bitter personal attack on Hammarskjöld and, simultaneously, tabled plans to reorganize the Secretariat on the "troika" basis. Significantly, Ghana refused to go along. Concerned as Ghanaians were over what seemed to be the questionable impartiality of UN officials in the Congo and antagonistic toward the Belgians, their representative to the UN pointedly praised the secretary-general and appealed to the Security Council to refrain from personal attacks. On the question of Soviet aid to Lumumba, he stated that the assistance given Katanga by the Belgians made it hard to condemn the Soviet Union, but that "in princi-

34. *Pravda*, September 9, 1960, p. 1.
35. *Pravda*, September 10, 1960, p. 1.
36. For a discussion of this point see Hoskyns, *The Congo since Independence*, pp. 207–225, and Conor Cruise O'Brien, *To Katanga and Back* (London: Hutchinson and Co., 1962), pp. 93–97.
37. *Ghanaian Times*, September 14, 1960.

ple all aid should be channeled through the UN."[38] A resolution introduced by nine Afro-Asian states during the fourth emergency session of the General Assembly and ultimately adopted (with the Soviet Union abstaining) provided in part:

> The General Assembly . . . without prejudice to the sovereign rights of the Republic of the Congo, *calls upon* all States to refrain from the direct and indirect provision of arms or other material of war and military personnel . . . except upon the request of the United Nations through the Secretary General.[39]

A Ghanaian who participated in the Afro-Asian meeting that drew up this resolution recalled that the Guineans strongly resisted such a restriction and that the phrase, "without prejudice to the sovereign rights of the Republic of the Congo," was included to mollify them.[40] From this point on, however, events in the Congo served to draw Guinea, Ghana, and Mali closer together. Embittered by the obstructions they felt had been thrown up before effective UN intervention (except when directed against Lumumba's government), they grew increasingly hostile toward both the UN operation and the Western powers, and at the same time drifted closer to the extreme position maintained by the Soviet Union.

Competition with China

The Congo crisis was only one of the problems preoccupying Soviet leaders in 1960. In addition to developments in the Congo, the Soviet Union found more and more diverting the undisguised Chinese challenge to the Soviet position in Africa. Unlike the Congolese problem, the rift with the Chinese menaced the Soviet relationship with progressive African regimes and therefore created a bothersome distraction. In 1960 China not only leveled the rudest indictment yet against Soviet theory, strategy, and tactics; it also launched an open attempt to incite the developing countries against Soviet policy at international conferences attended by the Afro-Asian group. The burgeoning dispute with the Chinese compelled the Soviet Union to account for its activity in Africa under the curious gaze of its revolutionary allies, to establish the doctrinal

38. Hoskyns, *The Congo since Independence*, p. 230.
39. Resolution adopted by the Fourth Emergency Session of the General Assembly on September 20, 1960, A/ES/1474/REV. 1. (ES-IV).
40. Interview with Alex Quaison-Sackey, July 1966.

validity of its policy (at best a humiliating duty for the acknowledged "head of the socialist camp"), and most significantly to expend considerable energy in competing for approval and influence within the Third World. To either side the Soviet Union faced competition: on the one hand, with capitalist powers possessing the advantages of large economic resources and a long-established presence in the developing nations and, on the other, with the Chinese, who could offer the impatient nationalists of Asia and Africa a more revolutionary approach to the problem of decolonization and the tasks of political and economic modernization. This dual competition inevitably reduced the Soviet Union's maneuverability.

To an important degree the disagreement between the Soviet Union and China involved two opposing assessments of prevailing revolutionary opportunities. These led, in turn, to a conflict over strategy and tactics. But the implication of this conflict was not simply that one side urged violence to capitalize on favorable revolutionary opportunities while the other side cautioned inactivity until circumstances became more promising. On the contrary, if anything, the Soviet position reflected greater optimism because of its prudence; and Chinese enthusiasm for revolution making recalled the essential uncertainty often characterizing earlier periods in the evolution of Marxism-Leninism. Soviet leaders disavowed a strategy founded primarily on the overt promotion of revolution because they remained convinced that the weight of events underway in Africa and other emerging areas had shifted in their favor and that ultimately the African revolution and its counterpart on other continents would lead to the socialist revolution. To the Chinese, depriving the revolutionary process of direct stimulation and guidance was tantamount to *khvostizm* (*khvost* is the Russian word for tail, hence "tailism"), the charge Lenin leveled against the Mensheviks, who he said had turned the party (the engine of revolution) into the tail of the proletarian masses (the disordered revolutionary process). Soviet leaders, on the other hand, believed in the "consciousness" of the new African nations which, they maintained, was leading these societies in the right direction and which would draw them over to the Soviet side. The example of Guinea, and to a lesser extent Ghana, reinforced Soviet confidence in the eventual alignment of Africa with the socialist countries.

However, it is not only that Soviet leaders placed their faith in the peaceful triumph of socialism in Africa and elsewhere; they feared that if an alternative approach were adopted, based on indiscriminate encouragement for revolutionary action, the natural evolution of this process would be seriously retarded. Apart from whatever impact this support for armed struggle might have had on Soviet efforts to establish a détente with the West, it risked provoking the United States and its allies to intervene and hence endangered the revolutionary struggle.

The Chinese, on the other hand, argued that the Soviet nuclear deterrent should be deployed as a shield from behind which revolutionary action could be fomented. In reply, Soviet ideologists contended that Soviet military power would protect the underdeveloped countries from Western interference, allowing their revolutions to mature unharmed, only so long as the socialist countries did not stimulate this interference by intervening first.

The Soviet position did not, of course, commit the Soviet Union to abstain from all participation in national liberation struggles, but just as the Soviet role in the Congo in August and September 1960 demonstrated a Soviet willingness to indulge in "direct action," the response to the Algerian crisis indicated under which conditions and to what extent direct action would be undertaken. Soviet priorities rated support for armed struggle secondary to measures designed to weaken the Western alliance. Since, short of a direct confrontation with the West, intervention in the Congo did not contravene these priorities, the Soviet Union felt free to paddle about in troubled Congolese waters. To take the part of the Algerian rebels wholeheartedly, however, would have violated priorities, because in this case Soviet leaders believed it of greater advantage to split France from the NATO alliance. Heavy support for the Algerian national liberation front would have made this more difficult to achieve.

It was the limitation on Soviet backing for the national liberation revolution which the Chinese sought to exploit. Thus, when Mikoyan was asked by an Iraqi news reporter during his April visit to Baghdad why, if the Soviet Union was the staunchest defender of the Algerian people's struggle for freedom, it had failed to recognize the Algerian government in exile even though "other countries" had done so, he betrayed distinct sensitivities in replying: "We are giving the greatest possible support to Algeria, even more so than some of the countries which have recognized the Algerian government."[41] The obvious target of his remark had just made the Soviet position more uncomfortable by proposing to the Second Afro-Asian People's Solidarity Conference (Conakry, April 11–15) that an "Afro-Asian volunteer army" be sent

41. Moscow radio (home service), April 18, 1960, quoted in Zagoria, *The Sino-Soviet Conflict,* p. 274.

to Algeria.[42] When the reporter pressed the matter by demanding whether the Soviet Union planned to contribute volunteers to such an army, Mikoyan exploded in anger: "Do you understand what this would mean? When you think about it you will understand that you asked this question to no purpose. Some people who heard your question will hasten to declare that the Bolsheviks want to occupy Algeria by volunteers and make it [their] colony."[43]

To remind the developing nations of the nature of Soviet priorities, Chinese leaders consistently juxtaposed the "struggle for peace" and "the national liberation struggle." They handled the issue most deftly. Accusing the Soviet Union of subordinating the national liberation struggle to the struggle for peace, they opened a multifaceted campaign to attract the support of the Afro-Asian movement, individual revolutionary groups, and the radical governments of Africa. Chinese spokesmen circulated with increasing abandon the innuendo that the Soviet policy of peaceful coexistence required oppressed nations to accept colonial domination. When Khrushchev touted disarmament both as a means to pave the way for a lasting peace and to provide funds for aiding the developing countries, they called his proposals "illusory" and, what was worse, a scheme to deceive the leaders of the Afro-Asian movement. The Chinese implied that, with as untrustworthy an ally as the Soviet Union, the countries of Asia and Africa would be wise to emphasize Afro-Asian solidarity and self-reliance.

Unquestionably the sensitive manipulation of the peace-versus-revolution issue made an impression on some African leaders. In an address to the General Assembly the previous autumn, Sekou Touré stressed the "necessity of considering the fight against misery as equally important as the struggle to maintain the world peace."[44] To make his point more emphatic, he added: "We consider the struggle against imperialism in Africa a determining factor in the world's struggle for peace." Later the Chinese press fully reported a similar comment included by the Guinean president in his opening speech before the second A-APSO conference (Conakry, April 1960).[45]

By this time the Chinese had decided to press the struggle against

42. *Times,* November 12, 1964, p. 15.
43. Zagoria, *The Sino-Soviet Conflict,* pp. 274–275.
44. Sekou Touré's speech to the Fourteenth General Assembly in *Afro-Asian Bulletin,* I (February–March 1960), 8.
45. Renmin Ribao, editorial reprinted in *Peking Review,* III (April 19, 1960), 14.

the Soviet Union in public. In April, the month of the Conakry A-APSO conference, the Chinese released a series of articles comprising the most comprehensive and caustic attack yet staged against Soviet theory and policy. The culminating article entitled "Long Live Leninism," appearing in the Chinese Communist party journal, *Hung ch'i,* on the ninetieth anniversary of Lenin's birth, contained a lengthy assault upon Khrushchev's revisions of Leninist thought and reasserted the basic rapport between revolution and progress.

Simultaneously the Chinese launched what one Soviet observer later described as "their first open attempt to gain control of the Afro-Asian People's Solidarity Organization."[46] The speeches delivered by Chinese delegates to the second A-APSO conference served as open evidence that China intended to discredit the current revolutionary contribution of the Soviet Union. Before long it would be trying to exclude the Soviet Union from all organizations of the national liberation movement. Not only was an initial reference to the victory won by the Afro-Asians over imperialist intervention in Egypt, Iraq, Lebanon, and Jordan "with the help of other peoples of the world" an uncharitable snub—made by the leader of the Chinese delegation, Liao Cheng-chih—it was an early indication that the Chinese considered their Soviet allies unworthy members of the Afro-Asian movement.[47] Lest anyone miss the point, Liao added that "thanks to the support of the people of a large part of the world" the Chinese had succeeded in frustrating the American armed provocation in the Taiwan Straits. The Chinese were beginning to complain among friends outside the Communist movement that the Soviet Union had reneged on its commitment to the national liberation revolution.

To weaken Soviet control over the Afro-Asian Solidarity Organization, the Chinese delegation advocated the transfer of the secretariat from Cairo to Conakry.[48] When this maneuver failed, they tried to replace the organization's general secretary, Youssef as'Sibai (UAR), with someone more sympathetic to the Chinese position.[49] Nor, according to Lev

46. Lev Stepanov, "Afro-Asian Solidarity and 'Exclusiveness,'" *New Times,* no. 39 (October 2, 1963), p. 10.

47. *Survey of China Mainland Press,* no. 2242 (April 22, 1960), p. 26; hereafter cited as *SCMP.*

48. Kurt Mueller, "Der Ostblock und die Entwicklungsländer," in *Das Parlament* (Bonn), July 12, 1961, and G. Zinke, *Aus der internationalen Arbeiterbewegung,* October 1960, cited in Brzezinski, ed., *Africa and the Communist World,* p. 177.

49. Nicholas Lang, "La première conférence de solidarité des peuples d'Asie, d'Afrique et d'Amérique latine à la Havane," *Est et Ouest,* no. 352 (December 1–15, 1965), p. 5.

Stepanov, was this the end of Chinese mischief. Liao Cheng-chih and his colleagues were

> determined to make the Conference accept the Peking position which already at the time was a challenge to the position of the Soviet Union and other Socialist states. In the committees drafting the reso- lutions they fought tooth and nail against including disarmament . demands. In the lobbies we saw them working assiduously on mem- bers of other delegations. At the committee meetings, speakers urging support for general disarmament were promptly accused by the Chinese of "preaching illusions" and "disorienting the Afro-Asian peoples."[50]

Two months later at the general council meeting of the World Federa- tion of Trade Unions in Peking (June 5–9), attended by a number of African delegates, the Chinese were even more acrimonious in their attacks. Their speeches ridiculed the possibility of eliminating atomic war and the hope of achieving disarmament while imperialism existed. Outside the conference hall they lobbied intensively for support among the Afro-Asian and Communist delegates, often openly disparaging Khrushchev's policies. The discussion centered on theory but the issue remained Soviet priorities. To think that after disarmament imperialism would use funds devoted to war for the welfare of the laboring masses and for assisting underdeveloped countries was, the Chinese delegate said, "downright whitewashing and embellishing imperialism, and indeed this was helping imperialism headed by the U.S. to dupe the people throughout the world."[51] Chinese intransigence impressed some delegates, including several from Africa, but not sufficiently to endanger the ma- jority still commanded by the Soviet Union on key questions. The general resolution of the Conference commended the peace policy of the socialist camp, in particular, of the Soviet Union, which made it "really possible to avoid the menace of an atomic war" and to impose disarmament on the imperialists, releasing "enormous resources . . . for the economic, social and cultural progress of all the peoples."[52]

During these months, despite mounting vehemence from Peking, the largest number of Afro-Asian delegates at meetings of the WFTU and World Peace Council remained loyal to the Soviet point of view. When the Chinese next challenged the Soviet position before an Afro-Asian

50. Stepanov, "Afro-Asian Solidarity and 'Exclusiveness,' " p. 10.
51. *Peking Review*, III (June 14, 1960), 14.
52. *Ibid.*, p. 17.

audience, at a WPC bureau meeting in Stockholm (July 9–11), their spokesman was again Liao Cheng-chih, chairman of the Chinese Committee for Afro-Asian Solidarity. His efforts notwithstanding, a separate meeting of the Afro-Asian delegates produced a declaration fully endorsing "honest attempts at general and complete disarmament."[53] The declaration congratulated the Soviet Union and its premier for endeavoring to bring "the Great Powers of the world to an agreement on this all-important question," and appealed to all African and Asian peoples to back the campaign for disarmament launched by the bureau of the WPC.

China also sought the support of a number of radical African trade unions, liberation fronts, and the Parti Africain de l'Indépendance. Symptomatically, however, the more significant the group, the less success the Chinese had. If we look at the various delegations visiting China over this period, it is clear that the more militant the group, the more support it gave the Chinese view, but the more irrelevant it was to the politics of its country. Thus Assi Camille Adam—chairman of the National Liberation Committee of the Ivory Coast, a small and rather insignificant band of Ivoiriens isolated in Conakry—fully endorsed Peking's positions. Leader of a group dedicated to revolutionary struggle, Adam praised China's foreign policy, agreed that United States imperialism was "enemy number one," reaffirmed China's claim to the territory of Taiwan, and lauded Chinese achievements under the "great leap forward."[54] Like Adam, radical trade-union leaders from the Mali Federation and Guinea denounced the continued independent existence of Taiwan and expressed admiration for the great leap forward, but unlike him they conspicuously refrained from sanctioning China's revolutionary approach to international problems.[55]

West Africa's only significant Communist party, the PAI in Senegal, manifested even less desire to support the Chinese. A letter sent by the central committee of the PAI to the Twenty-First Congress of the Communist Party of the Soviet Union praised the "intransigence" of

53. *Ibid.*

54. *SCMP*, no. 2292 (July 8, 1960), pp. 33, 34.

55. Led by Mamadou N'Dao, vice-general-secretary of the Secular Educational United Trade Union of Senegal, and administrative and economic secretary of the National Confederation of Trade Unions of the Mali Federation, a delegation of trade unions from the Mali Federation was in China in May. See *SCMP*, no. 2263 (May 23, 1960), pp. 45, 46. N'Dao returned with another delegation in September. See *SCMP*, no. 2347 (September 28, 1960), pp. 21, 22. Ousmane Keita, secretary of the Veterinarians' Trade Union, led a delegation of Guinean trade unionists to China in May. *SCMP*, no. 2264 (May 24, 1960), p. 35.

the CPSU in the "struggle against dogmatism and revisionism."[56] A series of articles appearing in *La Lutte*, following Babacar Niang's visit to China in February 1960, carefully avoided any mention of the Chinese position in the Sino-Soviet conflict, focusing on traditional Chinese hospitality and recent economic progress.[57] Tidiane Baidy Ly, a member of the PAI central committee, during a May visit to China, ignored the great leap forward and exhortations for armed struggle.[58] But it was Majhmout Diop, the party's secretary-general, who gave the most explicit evidence of the PAI's loyalties. In January a Soviet periodical quoted his description of Khrushchev's "historic mission" to the United States as "the greatest of the events on the eve of the new decade."[59] The Chinese were seriously distressed by Khrushchev's trip to the United States. Diop went on to say that "together with . . . the Soviet Union's victories in scientific and technical areas" this visit initiated "a new stage in the development toward the peaceful coexistence of the two systems, peaceful competition and the flowering of science."

In its African dimension, however, the Sino-Soviet dispute was principally a contest to win the favor of independent governments, and, from the contestants' point of view, Guinea's was the most worth winning. The intrusion of Chinese competition into Soviet relations with Africa made Touré's September visit to China particularly interesting. During his stay in Moscow, judging from the joint communiqué issued at the close of talks, Soviet leaders had succeeded in securing Touré's general agreement on world problems, including the defense of peace, disarmament, and prohibition of nuclear tests.[60] But until he went to Peking, the extent to which Touré actually supported the Soviet leadership in its dispute with the Chinese remained unclear.[61]

56. "Message du comité central du PAI au XXIe Congrès du Parti Communiste de l'Union Soviétique," *La Lutte*, no. 17, January 1959.

57. For coverage of this visit see *SCMP*, no. 2205 (February 29, 1960), p. 36, and *SCMP*, no. 2216 (March 15, 1960), p. 43. Niang was second secretary of the PAI central committee and political director of *La Lutte*. See *La Lutte* beginning with no. 5, May 1960.

58. *SCMP*, no. 2267 (May 27, 1960), p. 31.

59. Majhmout Diop, "U poroga velikikh sversheni" (On the Threshold of Great Progress, *Sovremenny Vostok*, no. 1 (1960), p. 19.

60. *Pravda*, September 9, 1960, p. 1.

61. To say that Touré or any other African leader supported either the Soviet or Chinese position does not mean, of course, that he intentionally took one side against the other. Although it seems unlikely that an African leader would be completely oblivious to the bias of his remarks, I am only saying what a good Marxist would say: that *objectively* his position paralleled that of one side or the other.

Touré's arrival in China inspired an extremely enthusiastic reception, evidence that Chinese leaders considered his presence of special significance. When the Guinean president stepped from his plane, Premier Chou En-lai along with Chief of State Liu Shao-chi awaited him, and behind them "numerous bands" played, firecrackers exploded, drums and cymbals sounded, and flower-laden crowds cheered.[62] He was greeted as a "national hero who had led the Guinean people to independence." To give the visit a pleasant start, Liu Shao-chi assured his guest that China stood for the peaceful settlement of international disputes and "always supported Soviet proposals for disarmament and the prohibition of nuclear weapons." To warm the Guinean president even more, the Chinese extended his country an interest-free loan of $25 million, their first to a sub-Saharan country.

Touré was effusive in praising Chinese economic progress, but more evasive when discussing specific political issues. At points his remarks (as well as his omissions) were critical. Although Mayor Peng Chen mentioned the great leap forward during a Peking rally, Touré avoided any reference to the subject.[63] At no time did he refer explicitly to China's rights to Taiwan. When Liu Shao-chi insisted "that the facts clearly show that U.S. imperialism is the most dangerous enemy of the Asian, African and Latin American people . . . as well as . . . all of the peace loving countries," a formula the Soviet Union rejected, Touré responded, "It has no hate, this Africa, against any nation, against any people."[64] For the remainder of the week, the formula designating the United States "enemy number one" disappeared from the public comments of Chinese speakers and failed to make a reappearance in the joint Sino-Guinean communiqué signed at the end of Touré's visit. In one of the few comments that could have generally satisfied his Chinese hosts, Touré said that although Guinea would defend the objectives of peaceful coexistence and disarmament, "for peace to be achieved, true peace, *which is not that by a few statesmen*, but a peace by the people united in fraternity and solidarity, it is necessary that justice triumph."[65] Despite this admonition, in a joint communiqué noticeably devoid of concessions to the Chinese point of view, the two parties expressed "their support without reservations for all actions in favor of general disarmament and with the prohibition of nuclear weapons, which

62. See *SCMP,* no. 2338 (September 15, 1960), p. 34.
63. *SCMP,* no. 2340 (September 19, 1960), p. 18.
64. *SCMP,* no. 2339 (September 16, 1960), p. 33.
65. *Ibid.;* emphasis added.

are inseparable from the liberation struggle."[66] In the communiqué the government of Guinea assured the government of China that it would "continue to pursue its foreign policy of peace and positive neutralism," and China expressed "full respect for the policy of peace and neutrality pursued by the Republic of Guinea." The mild tone of the Sino-Guinean communiqué reflected not only Guinea's reluctance to identify itself with the Chinese position, but the concessions that China would make to be identified with Guinean support.

For Russian accountants tabulating Soviet advances in Africa in 1960, Touré's performance in Peking represented their most tangible and precise success. Of more lasting importance, however, it was part of the general shift seen in the Third World's foreign policy. Not only were states such as Guinea and Ghana identifying increasingly with Soviet foreign policy, but their internal development, the ultimate determinant of foreign policy, foreshadowed fundamental changes. Although much in the revolutionary program of these leaders remained promise rather than reality, the Soviet leadership was beginning to allow its optimism to be buoyed by their fervent declarations of intent. Confidence grew when a Senegalese coup d'état divided the Mali Federation on August 20, 1960.

Mali, the New Revolutionary State

Guinea's was by no means the only leadership impatient with the transformation of France's West African empire. Modibo Keita and his colleagues in Soudan shared Touré's commitment to independence. They too viewed this commitment as the integral first phase in an implacable struggle against colonialism. But they hesitated to enter the fray directly without first doing everything possible to strengthen their African base. To them West African unity deserved prior attention. This, for the time being, put them closer to Senegal's nonrevolutionary leadership than to Touré and his allies. Thus, having managed a yes vote on the Fifth Republic's constitution, it was natural that Soudan and Senegal should set about building up this unity. Within six months of the referendum, their efforts produced the Mali Federation, a truncated version

---

66. *SCMP,* no. 2341 (September 20, 1960), p. 25. This is one of those instances where a comma changes the meaning of a sentence. If the comma had been omitted, Sino-Guinean support would have been reserved to only those actions in favor of disarmament which promoted the national liberation struggle, a position generally supported by the Chinese. As it was, the phrase tended to identify the interests of the national liberation struggle with the achievement of disarmament, a position generally opposed by the Chinese.

of the original plan to weld together Senegal, Soudan, Upper Volta, and Dahomey.[67] The other two states immediately abandoned the project under pressure from France and federalism's most forceful opponent, the Ivory Coast. Later that year, in September, Malian leaders persuaded de Gaulle to grant the Federation independence within the French community. It became independent on June 20, 1960. Two months later it disintegrated.

The undeniable impetus toward unity—deriving from a genuine commitment to federation on the part of both leaderships and the economic imperatives of a land-locked Soudan—simply proved weaker than the divisive factors. As Keita later said, "There was a contradiction between the economic, political, and social systems to which the leaderships of Mali and Senegal belonged."[68] The two leaderships maintained basically incompatible views of socialism (Soudan's was more rigorous), the nature of the Federation (Soudan wanted a strong, centralized state; Senegal, a more loosely organized arrangement), and the Federation's relationship with France (Soudan was less willing to modulate the militancy of its foreign policy, say on the Algerian question, in order to share in French beneficence). Once Mali's leaders began to exploit their considerable popularity among the young and more militant members of Senghor's party to build up influence throughout the Federation, the partnership became intolerable and the Senegalese abruptly withdrew.

The union between Senegal and Soudan had never inspired excessive Soviet enthusiasm, and from its inception the general tone of Soviet commentary was unfavorable. One year before independence a Soviet writer allowed that the formation of the Mali Federation had originally aroused fears among colonialists that the new union would "stimulate the national-liberation movement in the Soudan and Senegal," but he concluded, "whatever the final results, it is clear that the community set up almost a year ago, January 1959, does not satisfy the African peoples," for "what they want is genuine independence."[69] When independence did come in June 1960 the Soviet press paid it scant notice

67. For the history of this period see Foltz, *From French West Africa to the Mali Federation*.

68. *Le Mali en marche* (publication of the Secrétariat d'Etat à l'Information, 1962), p. 17, quoted in French in Thomas Hodgkin and Ruth Schachter Morgenthau, "Mali," in James S. Coleman and Carl G. Rosberg, Jr., eds., *Political Parties and National Integration in Tropical Africa* (Berkeley: University of California Press, 1964), p. 243.

69. "The Mali Decision," *New Times*, no. 50 (December 1959), p. 23.

and the Soviet radio remained openly suspicious, characterizing Malian independence as "only the first step towards real freedom and independence." It described the "unequal agreements" concluded with France as an "obstacle to economic independence."[70] According to Jean Suret-Canale, writing in *International Affairs* (Moscow), by these agreements France retained its military bases and, through them, "strategic control" over this country; it kept its monetary and economic privileges, a preferential customs system, and exclusive control over essential strategic materials such as lithium, beryllium, and helium; and it continued to supervise and administer the country's higher educational system.[71]

There can be no confusion over which side had Soviet sympathy when the Federation split apart. Senegal's sudden withdrawal received the full-throated condemnation of Soviet publicists, who treated it as a new colonialist maneuver designed to reinforce fading French influence.[72] Although first Soviet accounts of the coup d'état were ambivalent in evaluating the exact French role, none doubted collusion—a possibility augmented by the broad Soviet definition of French collusion. Soviet commentators did not distinguish very precisely between the activity of official France, expatriate Frenchmen living and working in former colonial territories, and "agents of French imperialism" (African leaders such as Léopold Senghor and Mamadou Dia, who lacked Soviet favor). Within this framework, one Soviet commentator concluded that "the coup was carried out with the assistance of foreign imperialist forces."[73] In another journal, he contended that French colonials, disconcerted by their diminishing influence in the Federation, "decided to tear Senegal from it," and "acting through their agents . . . they produced a coup in Dakar."[74] Correctly assigning a crucial role in the crisis to French officers and gendarmery serving in the Federation's military forces, Soviet reporters hinted darkly at overt French participation in the "revolution." Nor was any good drawn from the fact that Mamadou Dia and Léopold Senghor, "men who are known for their links with French circles," had recently visited Paris.[75]

70. Radio broadcasts, quoted in *Mizan*, II (July–August 1960), 17.

71. J. Suret-Canale, "The French Community at the Hour of African Independence," *International Affairs*, no. 1 (1961), p. 34.

72. For a Western interpretation of the coup see Foltz, *From West Africa to the Mali Federation*, pp. 166–184.

73. S. Volk, "The Mali Coup," *New Times*, no. 36 (September 1960), p. 18.

74. S. Volk, "Nasledniki velikogo Mali" (Heirs of Great Mali), *Sovremenny Vostok*, no. 12 (1960), p. 18.

75. V. Maevsky, in *Pravda*, August 22, 1960, p. 4.

According to these observers, France and its agents had many reasons
for wanting to destroy the Mali Federation. To begin with, Senegalese
leaders who had cast in their lot with the former colonial master "were
afraid of losing their privileges in the event Mali began to develop
according to the model of the Guinean Republic."[76] Second, the internal
and external policies of the leaders of the Union Soudanaise (the dominant party in Soudan) "rapidly won authority and popularity not only
in Soudan but among the wide masses in Senegal"; because these policies
stipulated the "liquidation of French economic domination" and support
for national liberation struggles like the one underway in Algeria, this
course of events "inspired anxiety in imperialist circles in Paris."[77] Moreover, as one Soviet writer reported, the French military began to fear
that Modibo Keita in his sympathy for the Algerian National Liberation Front might, at some point, insist on the neutralization or abolition
of French bases in Mali. "That is why, from a military point of view,
it was important for the levers of government in Mali to be in the
hands of Francophiles, such as most Senegalese leaders are."[78] As a general
conclusion Soviet commentators expressed the conviction that France,
threatened by the complete loss of control over the Mali Federation
once the influence of the Soudanese leaders predominated, staged the
coup to salvage at least part of its former empire.[79]

Mali's (Soudan's) addition to the group of developing countries committed to a revolutionary approach to modernization accentuated the
hopeful progressive course Africa appeared to be following. The rapid
changes promised in Guinea, the sudden emergence of the Mali Republic,
as well as the liberation struggles being waged in Algeria and the Congo,
embodied the rapid pace and quality of change remaking the character
of African politics. These countries were, from the Soviet point of view,
the vanguard of the African nations, hewing a path along which others
would surely follow. Guinea, not the Ivory Coast, seemed to Soviet observers to personify the spirit of an African revolution which would
ultimately catch up the entire continent.

The large group of newly independent states waiting in the foyers

76. Volk, "Nasledniki velikogo Mali," p. 17.

77. Volk, "The Mali Coup," p. 19.

78. *Ibid.* This is not an altogether compelling explanation for the coup d'état
since Keita did exactly this and with particular haste after the coup.

79. In addition to the above authors, see A. M. Sivolobov, *Natsionalnoe
osvoboditelnoe dvizhenie v Afrike* (National Liberation Movement in Africa;
Moscow, 1961), pp. 13–14.

of the Fifteenth General Assembly session represented the first phase of this monumental transition. The thought of becoming their patron was exhilarating to Khrushchev. It gave him further reason for going personally to the United Nations to launch the appeal to these "downtrodden" peoples. There he took the lead in urging a declaration demanding complete decolonization by 1962.

The First Response to Diversity

Up to this point, the effect that the rapid appearance of independent African states had on Soviet policy has only been hinted at. Before 1960 the Soviet Union could limit its concern to a handful of sub-Saharan countries, most of which espoused more or less acceptable foreign policies and pursued essentially "progressive" developmental plans. A large group of states attaining independence in 1960, however, were not nearly so hostile to their former colonial masters and not nearly so ready to reject the capitalist path. Not all of these new states were readily disposed to accept the Soviet Union's revolutionary example.

Thus, despite the Soviet Union's rather mystical attachment to the Afro-Asian liberation struggle, there remained the practical problem of state-to-state relations in instances where African states hesitated to develop significant ties with the socialist countries. Typical is the case of Nigeria.

There is a good deal of evidence that Nigeria's new coalition government was reluctant to become involved with the Soviet Union; that it delayed the establishment of diplomatic relations; that it later restricted the size of the Soviet mission in Lagos; that it obstructed travel to the Soviet bloc, particularly for study; that it refused to permit academicians from East European countries to teach in Nigerian institutions; that it frustrated attempts to make use of Soviet-bloc aid and trade; and that it blocked the importation of Communist materials. In these circumstances a certain reserve in the Soviet attitude was to be anticipated.

Yet the Soviet leadership was not willing to turn its back completely on this country when events might force a change in leadership or orientation. At the time of Nigerian independence *Pravda* announced that the Soviet government, "in accordance with its policy of friendship and cooperation with all countries whatever their social and political system," recognized Nigeria's independence and wished to establish diplomatic relations; what was more, the Soviet government hoped that "friendly relations based on mutual understanding and close cooperation would be established between both countries and peoples."[80] In the same issue, *Pravda*'s special West African correspondent, Oleg Orestov, noted that the inclusion of President Azikiwe's NCNC party in Nigeria's coalition government had exerted a positive influence on the government's foreign policy. Commentators underscored Azikiwe's publicly expressed intention to establish diplomatic relations with the USSR after independence.[81] They made a point of repeating Premier Balewa's assurance that his government did not want to join any bloc and was ready to accept aid from any country prepared to give it.[82] In an obvious attempt to exhort through flattery, Orestov ridiculed so-called British attempts to portray Nigerian independence as a gift of the crown which would change little in the relationship between the two countries. He said that "the popular masses and the younger generation" were determined their independence would be "real and complete" and that "foreign influence would have no place in Nigeria."

Soviet theorists, however, could not ignore the predominance of the conservative Northern People's Congress in the coalition government. They regarded the Party's effective leader, the Sardauna of Sokoto, as "the most influential and most reactionary figure on the contemporary Nigerian political stage."[83] As for the party itself, V. Rybakov said, it "expresses the interest of the Hausa feudalists."[84]

The general tenor of Nigerian politics at this juncture was far less militant than was the case in Ghana. Nigerian leaders made no pretense of repudiating all entanglements with their former colonial master. On the contrary, they assumed that Nigeria would continue to depend heavily on Great Britain. Soviet observers knew that this was so. Rybakov, for instance, noted that Chief Awolowo, leader of the Western Region's principal party, the Action Group, had "more than once openly declared that his party intended to bind Nigeria firmly to the Western bloc."[85]

80. *Pravda,* October 1, 1960, p. 1.

81. V. Rybakov, "Nigeriya na poroge nezavisimosti" (Nigeria on the Threshold of Independence), *Mirovaya ekonomika i mezhdunarodnye otnosheniya,* no. 2 (1960), p. 85.

82 *Pravda,* October 1, 1960, p. 1.

83. O. Orestov, "Vseobshchie vybory v Nigerii" (General Elections in Nigeria), *Sovremenny Vostok,* no. 4 (1960), p. 50.

84. Rybakov, "Nigeriya na poroge nezavisimosti," p. 85. Hausa emirs were the dominant social and political force in the largest and most populous region in Nigeria.

85. *Ibid.;* and Orestov, "Vseobshchie vybory v Nigerii," p. 50.

Awolowo told the Sixth Annual Conference of the Action Group on September 11, 1959: "In the present world contest, when atheistic materialism is threatening to destroy or stifle all that is best and noblest in man, neutrality in international affairs, whether passive, positive or independent, is an unmitigated disservice to humanity."[86]

The more moderate stand of the NCNC, the party of the Eastern Region and of the Ibo, understandably held greater appeal to Soviet observers. The day following Awolowo's address, Azikiwe retorted that while Nigerians would bind themselves "closer to the United Kingdom and the United States . . . it would be foolhardy to align with the Western democracies as a whole in the way the Action Group suggests."[87] Party spokesmen contended that despite their commitment to Fabian socialism (a philosophy "stoutly opposed to Communism as a way of life"), they did not believe that "anti-Communism in and of itself is a sufficient basis for a foreign policy."[88]

Soviet writers rewarded this hint of restraint by treating the NCNC as the most progressive party in Nigeria, the party most closely resembling Nkrumah's CPP. Although it, like the CPP, preferred to remain within the Commonwealth, it nevertheless sought "peace and friendship with all nations."[89] According to Soviet accounts, colonialists had opposed the NCNC because of its more progressive policies and had tried to obstruct its success. In contrast they accused the Action Group of inviting Western intervention in the 1959 federal parliamentary elections by hiring American advertising firms to run its campaign. This party, they sniffed, "represents the upper strata of the bourgeoisie in the Western Region and the Yoruba feudalists."[90] Adding to the insult, they recalled that the Action Group's appearance ten years earlier had "led to the weakening of the NCNC, disintegrating the united national front and momentarily strengthening the position of the colonialists."[91]

But Nigerian politics were more volatile and less doctrinaire than some. Thus when the Action Group lost the critical pre-independence elections in 1959 and abandoned its former political programs for a

86. *Daily Service,* September 12, 1959, quoted in Claude S. Phillips, Jr., *The Development of Nigerian Foreign Policy* (Evanston: Northwestern University Press, 1964), p. 16.

87. *Daily Times,* September 12, 1959, quoted in *ibid.,* p. 17.

88. *Daily Times,* October 23, 1959, quoted in *ibid.,* p. 20.

89. Orestov, "Vseobshchie vybory v Nigerii," p. 50.

90. Rybakov, "Nigeriya na poroge nezavisimosti," p. 85.

91. L. Pribytkovsky, "Nigeriya: Nezavisimost zavoevana v borbe" (Nigeria: Independence Won in Struggle), *Sovremenny Vostok,* no. 1 (1960), p. 23.

more militant line, Soviet commentators found themselves in the mildly ridiculous position of defending a party that they had previously considered reactionary. Now Awolowo's party insisted that the Nigerian government support Lumumba, that it more actively oppose the regime in South Africa, and that it invigorate its commitment to pan-Africanism. Moreover, Awolowo told the Nigerian parliament in November that the government had· no right "to discriminate against the countries of the Eastern bloc," especially in the field of technological education.[92] He urged that students be allowed to study in both the United States and the Soviet Union. And he vigorously attacked the proposed defense pact with England.

Before independence Nigeria had agreed to grant Britain tropicalization testing, overflying, and air-staging facilities in exchange for military personnel and training. Neither side was obligated to intervene directly in the defense of the other, and there was no provision for granting Britain Nigerian bases.[93] Yet the Soviet Union assumed the worst possible and was no doubt impressed when Awolowo warned parliament that the treaty concealed other commitments. They must have approved when he decried the "pact" for drawing Nigeria into military alignment and involvement with Britain. After parliament approved the defense agreement, *Pravda* called it a decision arousing "profound indignation on the part of the country's public," and quietly went over to praising Awolowo's position.[94] Two weeks earlier the Soviet press congratulated him for "speaking out in defense of Nigerianization" of the Nigerian bureaucracy and quoted his accusation that "Great Britain is waging a rear-guard battle to preserve its solid influence in independent Nigeria" by stifling "the legitimate desire of qualified Nigerians to occupy responsible positions in their own government."[95]

Thus Soviet commentators moved nimbly to maintain stride during this sudden turn in Nigerian politics. Both to explain what was now occurring and to anticipate what might occur in the future, they began to identify contradictions within each of the Nigerian parties. Even the

92. House of Representatives debates (Nigeria), November session, 1960, p. 202, quoted in Phillips, *The Development of Nigerian Foreign Policy*, p. 63.

93. Although the commitment in the mutual-aid provision of the treaty ("to afford to the other such assistance as may be necessary for mutual defense") was much less precise than, say, Article 5 of the NATO treaty, in the circumstances of British-Nigerian relations it could be construed very broadly. It was, in any case, less innocuous than the government pretended.

94. *Pravda,* December 1, 1960, p. 3.

95. O. Orestov, in *Pravda,* November 16, 1960, p. 5.

hopelessly archaic NPC contained progressive elements concerned with Nigeria's neutrality.[96] On the other hand, right-wing leaders within the NCNC were said to be resisting the progressive orientation of the party's left wing. Soviet publications frequently reprinted the demands of young NCNC intellectuals that the government "replace all heads of state institutions with Nigerians" and that the prime minister prove "his government has a friendly attitude toward the Soviet Union and the Soviet people."[97] "Some of us might not like Communism," one article was supposed to have gone, "but this does not mean that we have nothing to gain from the country that has sent a rocket to the moon. We want Soviet diplomatic representation in Lagos."[98] Voices of the "popular masses" emerged for Soviet observers as the fulcrum of Nigerian politics, "correcting [their government's] mistakes with healthy criticism."[99] In 1960 the trade-union movement split, and its "most advanced" section, the Nigerian Trade Union Congress, pressed the government to "pursue a policy of nonadherence to blocs" and to forbid the creation of any foreign military bases on its territory.[100] The confederation of Nigerian youth groups, the National Union of Nigerian Students, passed resolutions opposing passport restriction on travel to the Eastern countries, asking the government to call for volunteers to fight in Algeria, defending the Lumumba government, and advocating a unitary form of government for Nigeria—resolutions in many ways too lenient to satisfy the even more radical Nigerian Youth Congress. *Pravda* piously observed that Prime Minister Balewa answered this "friendly criticism in rather rude tones . . . The good will of the public has met no response from the government leaders."[101]

In retrospect, until deliberations of the Fifteenth General Assembly exposed the unsatisfactory character of Nigerian foreign policy and that of states like it, the uncomfortable premonition that these countries would diverge from the revolutionary tack set by other new states, such as Guinea, Ghana, and now Mali, remained partially hidden beneath the Soviet Union's general and idealized faith in the world revolutionary process. Whatever Soviet reservations were over Nigeria's likely foreign-

96. V. Pulavsky, "Nigeria," *New Times,* no. 40 (September 1960) pp. 29–30.
97. V. Larin, in *Izvestiya,* November 15, 1960, p. 2, and Orestov, p. 5.
98. Orestov, p. 5.
99. *Ibid.*
100. *Izvestiya,* October 3, 1960, p. 1.
101. Orestov, p. 5.

policy orientation and despite the recriminations against Senegal for destroying the Mali Federation, until positions on questions such as the Congo, Algeria, and disarmament were officially asserted, the Soviet Union continued to seek African friendship, hoping that the views of the newest nations could be squared with those of more radical members within the Afro-Asian group. Events within the United Nations in the fall of 1960 revealed these hopes to be illusory, for war in the Congo and Algeria served to damage rather than promote African unity. When African governments divided on these isssues at the United Nations and then created blocs embodying this division, Soviet policymakers were compelled to make choices. Africa in reality was again less malleable than they had anticipated.

IV

Africa Divided

The conflict among African states late in 1960 over the Congo destroyed any thought Soviet leaders may have had that Africa could be united against imperialism and neocolonialism. By the time the Fifteenth General Assembly convened, Africa was already deeply divided over the role the United Nations had assumed in the Congo. Those who expected speedy UN intervention to suppress Katanga's secession resented what they considered to be excessive tolerance on the part of their more patient colleagues. The so-called moderate African states, in turn, mistrusted the passion of their angry neighbors, feeling that their more emotional response would make the contending forces irreconcilable. Kasavubu's dismissal of Lumumba in September deepened the rift between African states on one side and the other, and in November the two groups collided openly when Touré initiated a move to seat the Lumumba delegation in the General Assembly. Other African states responded by backing a successful countermove to give Kasavubu's delegation the Congo seat.

Conflict over the Congo, however, represented only one issue dividing African leaders. They also differed over policy toward the Algerian war, particularly on the question of recognizing the FLN, and over the wisest response to French nuclear testing in the Sahara. Moreover, these disagreements were but symbols for the real source of antagonism: basically conflicting judgments about the proper relation between newly independent states and former colonial powers. These differences impelled each group to withdraw into ever narrower convocations, reduced to governments generally agreed on such issues as the Congo, Algeria, and colonialism. This development, manifest in the 1960-61 meetings at Abidjan, Brazzaville, Monrovia, and Casablanca, accentuated the divided mind of Africa and made it more difficult for powers outside the continent to remain free of the dispute. The Soviet Union's growing involvement with certain African states inevitably forced its leaders to clarify their preferences. Soviet predilections, of course, were by this time well formed, but organized differences in Africa accelerated their evolution and in the process induced the Soviet Union to elaborate the criteria by which it classified African states.

The fragmentation of Africa's continental politics stirred a predictable Soviet response. Commentators immediately deputized the Casablanca grouping (Algeria, Ghana, Guinea, Mali, Morocco, and the UAR) as an important organization in the African phase of the struggle against imperialism and endorsed its members as Africa's only genuine revolutionaries. Their competitors in the Brazzaville group were left with the well-worn mantle of "splitters" and "imperialism's collaborators," who, rather than attending the Casablanca meeting, had created their own special conference at Brazzaville where they could "spread the myth" about the positive aspects of neocolonialism.[1] These were leaders who were said to have "entered compromises with their old colonial masters," expecting to receive "some kind of bribe for their treachery." According to Potekhin, President Houphouet-Boigny had openly confessed that "the twelve countries [taking] part in the Brazzaville conference selected the West, while another group of African states selected the East."[2] The Afro-Malagasy Union, which grew out of subsequent meetings of the

---

1. Valiev, "Osnovy edinstva Afrikanskikh gosudarstv" (Foundations of African Unity), *Sovremenny Vostok*, no. 2 (1961), p. 58. The twelve members of the Brazzaville group were Cameroun, Central African Republic, Congo-Brazzaville, Ivory Coast, Dahomey, Gabon, Upper Volta, Madagascar, Mauritania, Niger, Senegal, and Chad.

2. I. Potekhin, "Afrika: Itogi i perspektivy antiimperialisticheskoi revolyutsii" (Africa: The Results and the Perspectives of the Anti-Imperialist Revolution), *Aziya i Afrika segodnya* (Asia and Africa Today), no. 9 (1961), p. 13.

Brazzaville group, preferred "unity with imperialists to the unity of African countries," Potekhin said.

In the spring at a conference in Monrovia, when Nigeria and Liberia's attempt failed to heal the division left over from Brazzaville and Casablanca and instead ended with the enlargement of the so-called moderate group, Soviet comment continued to be hostile. As one Soviet observer remarked, the absence of the "most consistently anti-imperialist countries" determined the bias of the Monrovia conference and guaranteed an agenda "evading the most acute problems in the struggle against imperialism."[3] The conference, it was said, refused to defend Algeria; it did not denounce imperialism or speak of the need to abolish colonialism and to fight neocolonialist tendencies; it reaffirmed confidence in the United Nations' Congo operation; but it said nothing about neutrality and avoided the question of military bases and foreign troops in African countries. Understandably, this same source concluded, the imperialist press praised the conference as a "stage in the 'anti-Communist struggle' in Africa."[4] The Monrovia conference, argued another writer, was "called as a reply to the Casablanca Conference . . . not without the collaboration of the imperialists."[5] Most of the states attending were subservient in matters of either foreign or internal policy; the countries of the Afro-Malagasy Union "were linked with France by military and economic agreements"; Liberia, "as is well known, is dependent on American capital"; and Nigeria and Sierra Leone "still have to keep a close eye on the City."[6] Again in January 1962, after Prime Minister Balewa had worked without success to include members of the Casablanca group in a heads-of-state conference at Lagos, the Soviet press re-emphasized its disapproval of the Monrovian powers. These countries, particularly the Brazzaville group, it said, continued to bend to the dictates of the French. Paris had insisted that the Algerian Provisional Government be denied an invitation to the conference, and those countries "which have not yet liquidated their dependence" on France complied.[7] In the same way, by refusing to adopt a resolution fixing 1970 as the final date for the abolition of colonialism in Africa, this conference

3. "The Monrovian Group of African States," *International Affairs,* no. 10 (1962), p. 114.

4. *Ibid.*

5. Galov, in *Trud,* February 2, 1962, quoted in *Mizan,* IV (February 1962), 19.

6. *Ibid.*

7. N. Khokhlov, in *Izvestiya,* January 27, 1962, p. 2.

had revealed again its unwillingness to support the national liberation movement.[8]

But because the Brazzaville-Monrovian group constituted no more than the sum of its parts, Soviet theorists directed their most pointed criticism against individual countries. Placed beside the progressive and independent governments of Guinea, Ghana, and Mali, the governments of Senegal, Nigeria, and the Ivory Coast appeared all the more sub-servient to Western neocolonialism. Each group of leaders promoted capitalist development, preserved colonial influence by subordinating major political institutions to foreign control, and persecuted "democratic organizations."

The Hardening of Categories

Not only did Soviet analysts now begin to distinguish more sharply between groups of African states, but they differentiated more carefully among individual states within a group. Their distinctions were most evident in the case of the Monrovia states. The worst of these from the Soviet Union's vantage point was the Ivory Coast, but a state like Senegal was scarcely more acceptable. (Nigeria was something slightly different and it is treated separately later.)

In any ranking, Soviet commentators invariably consigned the Ivory Coast to the low rung and reserved for President Houphouet-Boigny their liveliest contempt. By their accounts, the Ivory Coast was becoming a capitalist state, and its leaders protagonists of the free-enterprise sys-tem.[9] The problem of creating a state sector, which was "on the agenda of so many young African states, is of little interest to local ruling circles," who preferred the " 'advantages' of private initiative." In a place no more commendable than Senegal, leaders allegedly served foreign capital and reaped the benefits of their service, but their transgressions seemed less infamous than those of the Ivoiriens. Even Senghor as an agent or collaborator of colonialism appeared to rank higher (or lower) among those condemned by Soviet analysts than Houphouet-Boigny, a "black capitalist" and "an African [only] by the color of his skin."[10] Was the implication that Houphouet-Boigny had sold his soul while Senghor had

8. "The Monrovian Group of States," *International Affairs*, p. 114.
9. M. Azembski, "Report on the Ivory Coast," *New Times*, no. 40 (October 4, 1961), p. 28.
10. *Ibid*.

only mortgaged his? Houphouet-Boigny was, said Kudryavtsev in one exuberant attack on the Ivory Coast leader, a "troubadour of neocolonialism."[11]

Not surprisingly, Soviet–Ivory Coast relations reflected these unflattering assessments. Neither side made a move to establish diplomatic relations and, when a reporter raised the question in June 1962, nearly two years after Ivory Coast independence, at a time when other members of the Brazzaville group had decided to increase contacts with the Soviet Union, Houphouet responded merely that the possibility was under study. To the irritation of Soviet reporters, he added that his government would consider the issue of economic agreements when cooperation appeared possible without inviting interference in his country's internal affairs.[12] Retorted *Izvestiya*, since the president of the Ivory Coast could not be unaware that noninterference was a cardinal principle of Soviet foreign policy, obviously he had "again made it his business to please certain circles in the West."[13]

Exchanges like this were becoming a dominant feature of the frail and abrasive dialogue between these two countries. Soviet officials had despised Houphouet from the day he led the RDA out of its alliance with the French Communist Party; now they considered him the moving spirit behind the "reactionary" Brazzaville grouping. In March 1961 after one of the president's press conferences, a Soviet writer rebuked him for adopting "the hackneyed terminology of anti-Communist propaganda."[14] He was displeased because Houphouet had recently warned that China and the Communist world lurked behind the neutrality of the Bandung Afro-Asian bloc and that Africa independent from the West would become prey to Chinese or Russian Communism. During a June visit to France another of Houphouet's remarks, this time on the Algerian question, spurred a Soviet commentator to say: "He delighted his colonialist hosts by expressing on African lips the program of neocolonialism."[15] This particular report concluded by denouncing Houphouet as a "big plantation owner enriched through the exploitation

11. V. Kudryavtsev, in *Izvestiya*, June 14, 1961, p. 2.

12. V. Silantyev, in *Izvestiya*, June 10, 1962, p. 2. It would not be worth mentioning that the two countries exchanged virtually no trade in 1961 and 1962 if the Soviet Union had not, in 1960, while it could still purchase through France, imported just short of $3 million worth of goods from the Ivory Coast.

13. *Ibid.*

14. Yu. Gavrilov, in *Pravda*, March 19, 1961, p. 6.

15. Kudryavtsev, in *Izvestiya*, June 14, 1961, p. 2.

of underpaid African labor." In general, according to the Soviet press, the president of the Ivory Coast had proven himself a reliable ally of the colonialists; he had supported the French atomic tests in the Sahara and colonialist aggression in the Congo; he had committed his government to the pro-imperialist Brazzaville group; and he had, under the April 1961 agreements with France, seriously compromised his country's sovereignty.[16]

Senegal, the Ivory Coast's partner in the Brazzaville grouping, generated scarcely more enthusiasm. According to the Soviet view, it was a country independent in name only. Business, "plantations," the army, and police all remained under the control of Frenchmen.[17] President Senghor and Prime Minister Dia had distinguished themselves primarily as servants of French imperialism, subverting the Mali Federation on French bidding, giving license to plots against neighboring Guinea, and repressing local patriots (the PAI).[18] Soviet writers described the trial of PAI members, following violence occasioned by the July 1960 Senegalese elections, as an artifice, staged without substantive evidence and over popular opposition. "The progressive people of Africa and many countries of the world are distressed by the reprisals of colonialism's agents against progressive fighters for African independence."[19] To "justify in the eyes of the masses their collaboration with colonialism," Senegalese leaders were said to have evolved a "bogus theory of 'African socialism.'"[20] And as for Senegal's new four-year plan, Soviet commentators predicted that Senghor's government would have difficulty arousing support for a scheme "which in effect meant giving foreign monopolies control of Senegal's economy."[21]

The indictment continued with an allegation that the Senegalese leadership had subordinated "the elite Red Guard" as well as the entire

16. V. Sidenko, "Gde bivni slona?" (Where Are the Tusks of the Elephant?), *Aziya i Afrika segodnya,* no. 8 (1961), p. 38.

17. S. Zykov, in *Izvestiya,* May 17, 1961, p. 5.

18. See Chapter Three; also Sivolobov, *Natsionalnoe osvoboditelnoe dvizhenie v Afrike,* pp. 13–14. *Krasnaya zvezda* (Red Star), January 3, 1961, quoted in *Mizan,* III (January 1961), 29. See I. Plyshevsky, "Some Problems of the Independence Struggle in Africa," *World Marxist Review,* IV (July 1961), 34. Plyshevsky was *Pravda*'s editor for Asian and African affairs and an adviser to the foreign ministry.

19. S. Volk, "Sudilishche v Senegale" (Trial in Senegal), *Aziya i Afrika segodnya,* no. 8 (1961), p. 54.

20. S. Zykov, in *Izvestiya,* May 24, 1961, p. 5.

21. *Ibid.*

Senegalese army to French command and, in concluding military agreements with France, turned Dakar into "NATO's major stronghold in this part of the African continent."[22] "It rejects the policy of nonalignment and supports Senegal's participation in the French-sponsored Afro-Malagasy Union which is counterposed to the independent African states of the Casablanca group."[23]

Soviet commentators, of course, had been critical of the regimes in Senegal and the Ivory Coast before the formation of the Brazzaville group and the Afro-Malagasy Union but, after December and January 1961, the volume and vehemence of their criticism rose conspicuously. It is hard not to find a correlation between the harsher cast of Soviet commentary and changes occurring within Africa. The division after Brazzaville and Casablanca involved the Soviet Union in Africa's antagonisms, underlined distinctions in different African foreign and domestic policies, and as a result accentuated the Soviet Union's already well-developed inclination to condemn the leaderships in Senegal, the Ivory Coast, and Nigeria. On the other hand, it is an oversimplification to make Soviet policy appear so neatly bifurcated. A growing divergence in the public analysis devoted to states within the two groupings did clearly emerge in the Soviet press and, to the extent that the remarks of political commentators as well as the speeches of political leaders mirror official attitudes, Soviet policy had become less tolerant of Senegal, the Ivory Coast, and Nigeria. Yet the optimism motivating Soviet policy in this period tended to soften Soviet hostility. The Soviet Union saw at work in Africa historical anticolonialist forces whose momentum promised to push aside leaders resisting its sweep.

In the meantime, the Soviet Union hesitated to sever ties with any African people; long-term expectations restrained short-run impatience. Thus in March 1961 the Soviet Union dispatched a delegation of the Soviet-African Friendship Society, headed by the eminent professor, D. A. Olderogge, to meet with President Senghor.[24] The next month, when Senegal celebrated the first anniversary of its independence, a Soviet delegation, including Deputy Foreign Minister Jakob Malik, brought congratulations and good wishes from the Soviet government and Premier

22. V. Sidenko, "Dakar," *New Times*, no. 35 (August 30, 1961), p. 29.
23. *Mezhdunarodnaya zhizn*, no. 10 (1961), quoted in *Mizan*, IV (May 1962), 34.
24. Dakar radio (domestic service in French), 8.00 Greenwich Mean Time (GMT), March 6, 1961.

Khrushchev.[25] In September 1961 the Soviet government invited Prime Minister Dia to pay an official visit to the USSR, a matter of months after an important Soviet spokesman had publicly classified him as "an inveterate supporter of the French colonialists . . . who [urged] African countries voluntarily to abridge their freedom and ally themselves with their former colonial rulers."[26]

Soviet ambivalence stemmed from the conviction that these leaders would ultimately alter their course or be removed by the masses. "It must be borne in mind," exclaimed one Soviet author, "that these states were the product of the mighty upsurge of the national liberation movement in Asia and Africa . . . There is no doubt that in these countries too the movement will advance to full independence."[27] Voicing his confidence in the people of one such country, the French Communist, Jean Suret-Canale, wrote:

> The opportunities open to neo-colonialism in Senegal should not be overestimated. The desire for independence is as strong there as elsewhere and it is not very likely that the national pride of the Senegalese, which was dealt a blow during the Mali Federation crisis, will reconcile itself to Senegal remaining at the tail of the political evolution of the West African countries.[28]

A similar optimism pervaded Soviet commentary on Nigeria. Soviet spokesmen wrote that although the Nigerian government was pursuing a policy designed to steer the country toward capialism, as in other instances, "it would . . . be incorrect to assume that these nations have already made their final choice in this respect."[29]

In general, rigid categorization was ill suited to the Nigerian case. If Soviet observers had looked only at the internal structure of Nigeria,

25. *Times,* April 3, 1961, p. 7. *Izvestiya,* April 4, 1961, p. 2, and S. Zykov, in *Izvestiya,* April 5, 1961, p. 2.

26. Plyshevsky, "Some Problems of the Independence Struggle in Africa," pp. 34–35. *Pravda,* September 5, 1961, p. 1, carried a report of the invitation.

27. S. Voskov, "The Collapse of Colonialism and New Trends in International Relations," *International Affairs,* no. 9 (1961), p. 13.

28. J. Suret-Canale, "The French Community at the Hour of African Independence," *International Affairs,* no. 2 (1961), p. 25. Suret-Canale is a prominent French economist and historian, who in this period headed the National Institute of Research and Documentation in Conakry. He has returned to France and is a prominent member of the Communist Party.

29. I. Potekhin, "Some Aspects of the National Question in Africa," *World Marxist Review,* IV (November 1961), 45–46.

they could have, without difficulty, placed it among Africa's unprogressive states. Dependent on Western investment, Western advisers, and Western trade, Nigeria was in form and spirit no better than the Ivory Coast or Senegal. Potekhin, for one, noted that "the whole economy of the country, including foreign trade, is controlled by foreign, principally British, capital."[30] Constantly Soviet observers argued that Nigeria's independence had been impaired by the presence of British advisers, the defense pact with Great Britain, and the ubiquitous British businessman.

Nevertheless, a nation's foreign policy has generally weighed more heavily in the Soviet estimation than the nature of that country's political and economic system, and on this basis Nigeria differed from most of its partners in the Monrovian grouping. Soviet leaders were hardly confusing Nigerian policy with the progressive orientation of the Casablanca members, but neither were they ignoring Nigeria's early attempts to play a moderating role between the Brazzaville and Casablanca groups. At the United Nations and on the African diplomatic front, Nigeria sought a middle ground where the two competing groups could reassemble on questions such as the Congo and Algeria.

Moreover, in some areas Nigerian policy was clearly more progressive than the policies of the Brazzaville countries. Nigerian leaders had often declared their opposition to the existence of power blocs and had earlier sworn off involvement with any bloc. In the United Nations Nigeria had voted for the inclusion of the question of China's admission on the General Assembly's agenda, had supported efforts to enlarge the Security Council, and had sponsored a resolution for the liquidation of colonialism. It had severed relations with France over the question of French nuclear tests in the Sahara (an issue on which Soviet sanctions were noticeably less zealous). During the spring of 1961, it consented to exchange diplomatic missions with the Soviet Union and in December accepted the credentials of the first Soviet ambassador.[31] Earlier in June, Nigeria sent a high-level economic mission, headed by the minister of finance, Chief Festus Okotie-Eboh, to Moscow to explore the possibility of increasing economic ties between the two countries. The visit yielded both a decision to "conclude a trade and cultural agreement in the near future" and a tentative Soviet promise to render economic and

30. I. I. Potekhin, ed., *Afrika, 1956–1961* (Moscow, 1961), quoted in *Mizan,* IV (May 1962), 30.

31. *Pravda,* April 3, 1961, p. 1.

technical aid in organizing certain agricultural projects, in building plants for processing agricultural products, and in establishing centers for training personnel for industry and agriculture.[32]

Finally, the appearance not only of opposition parties but of opposition elements within the dominant parties made Nigeria seem less hopelessly monolithic in its commitment to reactionary programs and policies. Unlike the situation in Senegal and the Ivory Coast, where the regimes confronted little effective opposition, the nature of Nigerian politics always preserved the possibility that other policies might be forced upon the government.[33]

It is characteristic of policy in this period, however, that on balance the Soviet Union continued to criticize Nigeria. Having failed to conciliate the Casablanca and Brazzaville groups, it had aligned itself with the expanded Monrovian grouping and had more and more assumed a hostile position on international questions. If Nigerian foreign policy seemed moderately progressive when compared with the foreign policy of Senegal and the Ivory Coast, then its shortcomings were equally obvious when compared with the foreign policy of Guinea, Ghana, and Mali, not to mention its own earlier promises. Before independence, both Balewa and Azikiwe had declared their opposition to blocs; but in practice, according to Soviet writers, their government had participated fully in the NATO alliance by concluding a defense pact with Great Britain. They had obstructed a termination to nuclear testing by opposing Soviet proposals before the Fifteenth General Assembly and then had openly supported the American decision to resume nuclear tests. They had "expressed a negative view" of the Soviet proposal to reorganize the UN Secretariat on a troika basis, and they had rejected Khrushchev's suggestion to hold a summit meeting on the issue of disarmament, a proposal for which he sought their support as members of the eighteen-member UN disarmament committee.[34] They continued to back the aggression of the United Nations in the Congo. They had permitted the establishment of a secret NATO radio station and an American Mercury tracking station in the country. And they had refused to attend the Belgrade Non-Aligned Congress.

Nor, ultimately, did the semicompetitive character of Nigeria's internal politics induce Soviet commentators to moderate their criticism of Ni-

32. *Pravda,* June 10, 1961, p. 1.

33. Soviet authorities harbored no illusions about the significance of the PAI, particularly after its suppression in August 1960.

34. *Sunday Express,* February 25, 1962, quoted in Phillips, *The Development of Nigerian Foreign Policy,* p. 96.

gerian policy. For if the existence of local political critics appeared to introduce flexibility into the political system, it was at the moment highlighting the many aspects of policy which Soviet leaders disliked. In 1961 the public discontent of radical members of the NCNC and Awolowo's Action Group became a crucial feature of Nigerian politics.

The All-Nigerian People's Conference held in Lagos, in August 1961, exemplified their opposition. Organized by K. O. Mbadiwe, a personal adviser to the prime minister, and attended by the angry young men in the NCNC and the Action Group, the conference approved recommendations to: (1) counter the dangers of neocolonialism by restricting the number of agencies such as the Peace Corps and Operation Crossroads; (2) give the Soviet Union diplomatic accommodations equal to that of any other country; (3) invite Khrushchev as well as Nkrumah to Nigeria; (4) desist from Communist witch hunting; (5) recognize East Germany; and (6) repudiate the European Economic Community.[35] Simultaneously Chief Awolowo denounced the Monrovian conference for inviting the financial support of "certain Western powers," and he urged Nigeria to join the Guinea-Ghana-Mali Union.[36] Because of military and economic ties "forced upon them by the European metropoles," he contended, the "ostensibly independent" Monrovian countries were not free at all. In September, Awolowo accused Balewa of complete subordination to Prime Minister Macmillan.[37] As part of the same speech, delivered before Nigerian students in London, he alleged that "every obstacle is . . . being placed in the way" of the Soviet embassy's being opened in Nigeria, and he ridiculed the government for letting the fear of driving away foreign investment deter it from the path of true socialism.

Awolowo's speech received generous coverage in the Soviet press. *Pravda* particularly noted his attacks on the Anglo-Nigerian defense agreement and his call for its immediate abrogation.[38] Throughout this period the defense agreement served as a touchstone for discontent over Nigeria's close dependence on Britain, and Awolowo, as the agreement's most stentorian critic, harvested both the loyalty of the regime's radical opponents and the praise of the Soviet press.[39] But there were other

35. *Ibid.*, pp. 57–58.
36. *Ibid.*, p. 63.
37. *Daily Express*, September 12–14, 1961, quoted in *ibid.*
38. *Pravda*, September 6, 1961, p. 5.
39. L. Kim "Pervy god nezavisimosti Nigerii" (Nigeria's First Year of Independence) *Mirovaya ekonomika i mezhdunarodnye otnosheniya*, no. 8. (1961), p. 97.

of Awolowo's actions which had strong Soviet support; among the many problems "on which the opinions of the broad public and of the Nigerian Government differ sharply," Oleg Orestov (*Pravda* correspondent) credited Awolowo with leading the campaign to Africanize the Nigerian administrative apparatus, and he quoted approvingly Awolowo's statement that "the sky would not fall if all the British left Nigeria at once."[40] Soviet commentators said that Awolowo and the left wing of the NCNC had also urged the nationalization of foreign undertakings, but that less progressive leaders within the NCNC, such as Michael Okpara, premier of the Eastern Region, had resisted their demands.[41] And Soviet writers talked generally about the progressive section of the Nigerian national bourgeoisie who valued the useful example provided by the Soviet Union and who, in building up their own economy, wanted to make use of its experience.[42]

But invidious comparisons between so-called progressive elements within major political parties and the governing leadership cannot be attributed solely to the impact of the Casablanca-Brazzaville (Monrovian) rift. They were just as much a reflection of political changes within Nigeria that would have influenced Soviet policy even had the division in Africa never occurred. Nevertheless, in a few instances—for example, when Nigeria repudiated its defense agreement with Britain in January 1962—the Soviet reaction appeared particularly influenced by an atmosphere of exaggerated suspicion and criticism. Soviet commentators belittled an action that would have normally stirred approval as a "paper gesture" which would not in effect change the situation.[43] Soviet preference rested with the Casablanca nations.

The Casablanca Grouping

After the emergence of African blocs, the Soviet Union placed particular emphasis on developing its ties with the Black African members of the Casablanca group—the most promising among the Casablanca participants. As a result, Soviet interest—until 1961, largely focused on Guinea—was now extended to Ghana and the newly created Mali Republic. Subsequently Soviet leaders brought to these countries the

40. Orestov, in *Pravda*, November 16, 1960, p. 5.

41. Kim, "Pervy god nezavisimosti Nigerii," p. 98.

42. Orestov, p. 5.

43. See, for example, *Trud*, January 23, 1962, in *Mizan*, IV (February 1962), 27.

economic and diplomatic offensive already flourishing in Guinea. For Mali its growing alliance with the Soviet Union followed a course set from the start. For Ghana, however, the sudden advance in its relations with the Soviet Union clearly represented a turning point. Yet despite the Soviet Union's increasingly enthusiastic commitment to Black Africa's most progressive states, the period also produced the first major setback for Soviet policy—the expulsion of the Soviet ambassador from Guinea.

Before examining these developments, a word needs to be said about the theory underlying Soviet policy toward the advanced states of Black Africa. Justification for developing relations with Guinea, Ghana, and Mali derived from the concept of national democracy, worked out at the November 1960 meeting of eighty-one Communist parties. The idea was a Soviet invention, intended as a further accommodation with the forces of nationalism. It gave a place within the ideological pantheon to newly independent nations that, though lacking the prerequisites for the immediate transition to socialism, maintained progressive foreign and domestic policies. More than that, it prescribed the basis for cooperation among local Communist parties, the Soviet Union, and these young regimes. (Although the concept did not require the hegemony of local Communist parties, it clearly assumed their survival or emergence.) In foreign policy, according to the model, the national democratic state struggled against imperialism and strengthened its independence by abstaining from military blocs and by denying military bases to imperialist powers. At home, the government minimized Western economic influence, reinforced the state sector of the economy, and guaranteed the liberties of "democratic forces," such as indigenous Communist parties. In turn, local Communists were to enlist in national democratic fronts to aid in completing these tasks.

Originally the theory was intended for countries like Cuba, but soon after its promulgation the Cubans made it plain that the whole notion seriously underestimated the achievements of their revolution. Consequently in May 1962, Soviet theoreticians announced that Cuba "had embarked on the path of building socialism," leaving national democracy to the nascent and potential revolutionary states of Africa and Asia.

This posed problems, however, for the theoretical reconciliation reached with non-Communist bourgeois nationalists assumed the safeguard of a local Communist party. Without local Communist parties Soviet leaders were constrained to trust bourgeois leaders to guide their new nations toward socialism, a concession they hesitated to make publicly. These difficulties—the absence of Communist parties in Africa, the marginal importance of the African proletariat, and the not altogether certain direction selected by new African governments—Soviet analysts discussed in their journals in the months following the November 1960 meeting.[44] Judging from their imprecise and often evasive commentary, they could arrive at no easy solution. Nevertheless, nations such as Guinea, Ghana, and Mali had set goals that largely paralleled those of the national democratic model and their foreign policy complemented that of the socialist countries. The Soviet Union, therefore, felt the need to give its relationship with these states theoretical legitimacy.

Significantly, for the response revealed the limits of Soviet expectations, the theory of national democracy was first used to supply these countries with a goal, rather than to describe their achievements. Throughout 1961, references to Guinea, Ghana, and Mali recognized them only as candidates for national democracy. Brezhnev's comment in Guinea during his February 1961 visit is typical: "The first years of independence for Guinea have demonstrated that your people are capable of transforming your country into a most flourshing national democratic state."[45] Stated more pointedly, Soviet leaders thought it possible for Guinea, as the most revolutionary country in sub-Saharan Africa, to embark on the national democratic course, but they denied that Guinea had yet done so.

In 1962, when the Soviet Union changed its mind and specifically listed Guinea, Ghana, and Mali as national democratic states, the concept had been noticeably altered. As Mikoyan expressed it in his election speech on March 14, 1962, Africa was pioneering "new forms of national

44. See "Proekt programmy KPSS i nekotorye problemy natsionalno-osvobodi-telnogo dvizheniya narodov Azii i Afriki" (The Draft Program of the CPSU and Some Problems of the National Liberation Movement in Asia and Africa), *Narody Azii i Afriki* (Peoples of Asia and Africa), no. 5 (1961), pp. 3–14.

45. *Izvestiya*, February 17, 1961, p. 2. In the first major commentary on the theory of national democracy, Boris Ponomarev was ambiguous about its application. (See his "O gosudarstve natsionalnoi demokratii" (On the National Democratic State), *Kommunist*, no. 8 [1961], pp. 33–48.) Cuba had just declared its transition to socialist construction and Ponomarev appeared to be left defending a model which, for the moment, remained largely theoretical. He avoided any specific identification of the five leading candidates—Cuba, Guinea, Ghana, Mali, and Indonesia—as national democratic states. Instead, he concluded: "It is not a matter of lining up all states that have won freedom and stating: 'These belong to this category, and these to a second or third category.' Such an approach would be schematic and harmful . . . The peoples themselves will decide what country will take the path of national democracy." (p. 43)

democracy."[46] These new forms no longer led the developing nation directly to socialism, but instead "created the conditions for the transition of the countries liberated from the colonial chains to the road of non-capitalist development."[47] According to the descriptions of another commentator, the "non-capitalist path of development" represented a *further* "transitional form of political and economic development" during which the "conditions for undertaking the task of socialist revolution and the establishment of the dictatorship of the proletariat are created."[48] Rather than bestow unearned legitimacy on these African regimes, the theory of national democracy was made to retreat one stage, to a point preceding the preparation for the actual transition to socialism. Soviet writers now carefully stated what had formerly been implied: the state of national democracy was not a socialist type of state; the first, they underscored, "does not undertake to implement socialist tasks." "Its purpose is to complete the general democratic, anti-imperialist, anti-feudal revolution."[49] Notably, the anticapitalist phase, the process of extirpating whatever remnants of capitalism survived in former colonies, was postponed until these countries entered on the noncapitalist path. In effect Soviet ideologists were restating their conviction that even the most progressive bourgeois nationalist leaders would falter prior to the achievement of socialism, and that in the last stages of the transition to socialism sturdier forces from the working class would have to grasp leadership. In the present epoch, Potekhin wrote, there was every possibility for independent African territories, "after uprooting colonialism," to avoid the path of normal capitalist development and to take instead a noncapitalist road to progress and prosperity. But this line of development is possible only "when the leading role in the broad national front is taken by the working class."[50]

A comparable restraint characterized the Soviet response to the theories

46. *Pravda,* March 15, 1962, quoted in William T. Shinn, Jr., "The 'National Democratic State,' " *World Politics,* XV (April 1963), 384.

47. G. Mirsky, "Whither the Newly Independent Countries," *International Affairs,* no. 12 (1962), p. 27.

48. B. Dimitrov, *Filosofska misul* [Bulgarian-language magazine], no. 4 (1962), pp. 91–102; trans. in Joint Publications Research Service (JPRS), 16–17, November 14, 1962, p. 7.

49. Mirsky, "Whither the Newly Independent Countries," p. 27.

50. I. Potekhin, "The Future of Africa and the African Working Class," *International Affairs,* no. 2 (1962), p. 100. See also "Natsionalno-osvoboditelnoe dvizhenie na sovremennom etape" (The Current Stage of the National Liberation Movement), *Kommunist,* no. 13 (September 1962), pp. 89–109.

advocated by African leaders, particularly their various versions of African socialism. From the outset, Soviet commentators disparaged the notion that Africa had created a "third way" to socialism based on ideas and structures adapted to Africa's own peculiar conditions. For them there existed no third way between capitalism and socialism, and no socialism other than "scientific socialism." They denounced Africans who argued that their countries, unlike developed societies, could reach socialism without class struggle, that African socialism rested firmly on traditional African religion, and that Communism had no place in Africa. Said one Soviet writer: "Pro-imperialist circles hiding behind talk about 'real African socialism,' are attempting to castrate the class content of proletarian struggle and to force the African working class to betray the principles of proletarian internationalism."[51] He predicted, "the day is not far off when the all-conquering teachings of scientific socialism will triumph on the African continent." Potekhin contended that "the theory of 'African socialism' is being used to deceive the toiling masses in the interest of the capitalist development."[52] *Sovremenny Vostok* reprinted an abusive attack by Majhmout Diop, the secretary-general of the PAI, on the "miserable arguments" of the supporters of purely African socialism or "socialism based on the belief in God."[53] To make the condemnation official, the 1961 party program specifically repudiated "socialism of the national type." It said that this "petty-bourgeois illusion of socialism" misleads the people, hampers the development of the national liberation movement, and imperils its gains.[54] Ostensibly Soviet criticism was directed against the kind of socialism espoused by moderate African leaders, particularly Léopold Senghor, Mamadou Dia, and Nnamdi Azikiwe. Thus an early article classified Senghor, Keita (written before the Federation split), and Dia as the "champions of the so-called African way to socialism," a notion having a "marked petty-bourgeois and reformist character."[55]

Soviet writers no doubt drew a distinction between the socialism of

51. Yuri Popov, "Zhizn oprovergaet" (Life Refutes), *Aziya i Afrika segodnya,* no. 12 (1961), p. 11.

52. I. Potekhin, "Nekotorye problemy afrikanistiki v svete resheni XXII sezda KPSS" (Some Problems of Africanistics in Light of the Decisions of the Twenty-Second Congress of the CPSU), *Narody Azii i Afriki,* no. 1 (1962), p. 15.

53. N. Gavrilov, "Istoriya Afriki v novom svete" (African History in a New Light), *Sovremenny Vostok,* no. 4 (1960), p. 55.

54. "Program of the Communist Party of the Soviet Union," *New Times,* no. 48 (November 29, 1961), p. 24.

55. Y. Abet, "Federatsiya Mali" (The Mali Federation), *Mirovaya ekonomika i mezhdunarodnye otnosheniya,* no. 5 (1960), p. 106.

Senghor, and others like him, and that advanced by Touré, Nkrumah, and eventually Keita. They carefully exempted these so-called progressive leaders from explicit, pejorative references to right-wing socialists, pro-imperialist elements, and antipopular circles. On the other hand, Nkrumah, Touré, and Keita claimed equally that their socialism incorporated features from several systems, not only Marxism-Leninism, that it conformed uniquely to African conditions, and that it obviated the class struggle. Although Soviet leaders have argued before the proposition that evil is the doer and not the act, it seems unlikely that they meant to exclude Touré's "communocracy" or "Nkrumaism" from criticism directed generally against African socialism. As a matter of fact, the language of Khrushchev's celebrated warning to African socialists delivered in Sofia on May 19, 1962, left the impression that he was speaking particularly to these leaders.[56] His opening reference to "fine people ready to devote all their energies to the fight for freedom and happiness of their peoples" was not the current Soviet description of Senghor and similar leaders. These people (the "fine people"), he said, "are trying to pursue a kind of fence-sitting policy, are trying to ignore the class structure of society and the class struggle, which are matters of fact in their countries." He went on: "One can only rejoice [when] they say . . . they are building socialism . . . But what kind of socialism do they have in mind?" On which forces will they rely? Those leaders who really have the "best interests of the people, the working masses, at heart" will sooner or later have to realize that only by leaning on the working class can "the victory be achieved and correct solutions found to vital social problems." If not, Khrushchev threatened, "other people would come after them who would better understand the demands of life." Part of his impatience may have been due to Guinea's recent expulsion of the Soviet ambassador, but it seems more likely that he expressed the genuine reservation of Soviet leaders toward the philosophy of Africa's radicals. However much Soviet leaders may have approved their foreign policy and the revolution they proclaimed, whatever their optimism over the inexorable march of events generated by African liberation, at this moment they rejected the ideology of Africa's most progressive leaders. Understanding the importance of ideology in Soviet society, this rejection signifies the limits of the Soviet commitment.

Already in 1962, however, modest appeals for a more lenient appraisal of "socialism of a national type" were gently intruded into Soviet publications. In an early discussion, published in the spring issue of *Mirovaya*

56. *Pravda,* May 20, 1962, p. 2.

ekonomika i mezhdunarodnye otnosheniya, members of the Institute of World Economics and International Relations urged that a more supple attitude be assumed toward this question. One prominent participant, Victor Tyagunenko, recalled the party program's condemnation of socialism of a national type, but emphasized that many who defend this doctrine were "sincerely seeking the most efficient means to solve economic and social problems in present international and internal circumstances."[57] Measures of economic and social transformation instituted by leaders such as Touré, Keita, and Nkrumah, he noted, were already steps toward the noncapitalist path. In these circumstances "a real possibility [existed] of the most far-sighted representatives of nonproletarian elements going over to the positions of the working class." A few months later, Vladimir Kudryavtsev, *Izvestiya*'s correspondent, argued in much the same way that just because Africans saw their socialism in abstract rather than scientific terms, Soviet observers should not therefore "reject it out of hand."[58] He concluded, "We must not throw the baby out with the bathwater. We must accept all of its positive elements, everything that takes a given African country forward, bearing in mind that one step often leads to another." Understandably, given the tradition-ridden experience of Africans, socialism gets caught up in religious and social custom, but this must be tolerated until these societies attain "general literacy and higher cultural standards." He suggested, for example, that anyone who denied that socialism could be built with the "hands of religious people because it is a scientific outlook which is only consistent with atheism" was himself following the abstract approach. Unlike the liberal view of academician Yuri Zhukov, expressed two years earlier in *Pravda*, Kudryavtsev justified his argument with an essentially optimistic assessment of African socialism. Zhukov, for reasons that sound closely connected with the interests of Soviet foreign policy, had asserted that a "haughty attitude towards anti-imperialist actions" maintained by nonproletarian elements represented a dangerous sectarianism "leading to self-isolation."[59] Kudryavtsev, in somewhat different fashion, argued that

57. V. Tyagunenko, "Tendentsii obshchestvennogo razvitiya osvobodivshikhsya stran v sovremennuu epokhu" (Current Tendencies of Social Development in the Liberated Countries), *Mirovaya ekonomika i mezhdunarodnye otnosheniya,* no. 3 (1962), p. 23.

58. V. Kudryavtsev, "Fighting Africa's Daily Round," *International Affairs,* no. 10 (1962), p. 53.

59. Y. Zhukov, *Pravda,* August 26, 1960, pp. 3, 4. *Mizan,* VI (July–August 1962), 14–15, comments on this article.

African socialism might in fact set a country on the way to socialism. "This may be determined not so much by the wishes of a leader . . . ," he said, "as by the pressure of the masses who do not acquire their taste for socialism from treatises . . . but from the hard facts of life." Let them "taste the fruits of socialism," even of counterfeit African socialism, and they "will see what and who hinders their progress." Then they would be able to decide for themselves "whether socialist construction is compatible with religious prejudice." Echoing more orthodox views Kudryavtsev added that the people "will draw the necessary conclusions, [but] naturally with the assistance of an organizing political force in the form of working people's parties."

In 1961, though, even before this tentative reassessment, basic doubts over the ideological underpinning of favored African regimes were obscured by the amiable tone of Soviet public diplomacy. If the Soviet Union had misgivings about specific features of the Guinean, Ghanaian, or Malian political systems, these seemed insignificant amid the general praise for internal reform and foreign policy. References to the continuing presence of foreign investment in Ghana, the flow of trade to the West, or the appearance of a petty-bourgeois element appeared unimportant beside approving accounts of Nkrumah's plans for socialism (a rapid expansion of the state sector and the establishment of controls over private capital) or beside exaltations of Ghana's energetic contribution to the struggle against imperialism.

Guinea: Climax and Retreat

Most praised was Guinea. "Guinea has already achieved economic independence," Soviet journals reported.[60] Through the nationalization of external trade, the limitation on foreign monopolies, and the strengthening of internal trade, Guinea had thwarted neocolonialism and marked out a path of independent economic development. As proof of the people's support for this program and for the party's foreign policy of "positive neutrality" as well as the "development of friendly relations with the socialist countries," elections had recently given President Touré "more than 99 percent of the vote."[61] His overwhelming victory was due in large part to the single-party system in Guinea, which in turn Soviet writers described as a *union* of parties produced by the struggle

60. Lotar Kilmer, "Strana planov i sversheni" (Country of Plans and Progress), *Aziya i Afrika segodnya,* no. 3 (1961), p. 36.
61. O. Orestov, in *Pravda,* February 12, 1961, p. 4.

for independence. They went on to say that it is "difficult to speak about antagonistic classes in a country where more than 90 percent of the population are peasants and where a national bourgeoisie does not exist."[62] A commentator as important as Boris Ponomarev, the Central Committee secretary responsible for relations with nonruling Communist parties, drew attention to Guinea as a country carrying out major transformations.[63] By comparison, he said Ghana had introduced substantial measures aimed only at "strengthening political independence." As a further indication of its esteem, the Soviet Union selected Touré over Keita or Nkrumah to receive the 1961 Lenin Prize "for strengthening peace between peoples."[64]

President Brezhnev's official visit to Guinea in early 1961 illuminated the reasons for Soviet enthusiasm. Neither Soviet nor Guinean officials made any effort to explain why Brezhnev came to Guinea in February, and one is left to conjecture. Most likely, however, Brezhnev as chief of state was fulfilling Khrushchev's broken promise of 1960 to honor Guinea with a state visit. He may also have been following up policy initiatives undertaken during Touré's September visit to Moscow and continued at the United Nations later that month, particularly since with the disappearance of Lumumba the Congo was rapidly reaching a new crisis point. Always the Soviet leadership was seeking reassurance in its growing conflict with the Chinese, and in February it was probably bothered by the effect this dispute might have on the newly formed Afro-Asian Solidarity Fund. The Fund, a creation of the Conakry A-APSO conference (April 1960), represented the most significant conduit for Communist aid to Africa's liberation movements, and both the Soviet Union and China had subscribed heavily; both had representatives sitting on the Fund's controlling committee. A further reason for Brezhnev's visit may have been to mollify Guineans who had begun to complain of tardiness in Soviet trade and aid deliveries. I. F. Semichastnov, deputy minister of foreign trade, and A. I. Alikhanov, deputy chairman of the State Committee for Foreign Economic Relations, accompanied Brezhnev, and in a joint communiqué they pledged their government's readiness to increase deliveries of machinery and equipment, oil products, and food and consumer goods.[65]

62. Article from *L'Humanité* reprinted in *Sovremenny Vostok*, no. 5 (1960), p. 43.
63. Ponomarev, "O gosudarstve natsionalnoi demokratii," p. 37.
64. *Pravda*, May 1, 1961, p. 2.
65. *Pravda*, February 17, 1961, p. 1.

Two days before Brezhnev arrived in Conakry, the convergence of Soviet-Guinean policy toward the Congo advanced another step when, as *Pravda* noted, the people of Conakry turned out to welcome the first battalion of Guinean troops recalled from the Congo.[66] Touré refused to subdue his anger any longer. He withdrew the Guinean troops from the Congo operation just as he had said he would early in the fifteenth session of the General Assembly and just as he had urged others to do at the Casablanca meeting. Then, as reported by one Western source, it was Nkrumah who struggled alone against abandoning the UN operation and who, after "a serious clash" with Sekou Touré, persuaded the Casablanca group not to commit themselves to a specific withdrawal date.[67] Later when other Casablanca participants, including Mali, withdrew their forces from the UN command, only Nkrumah refused.[68]

While Brezhnev was still in Conakry, Moise Tshombe's minister of interior, Godefroid Munongo, announced what everyone had already guessed, that the arrested Lumumba had been murdered. In a chorus of rage Touré and Brezhnev thundered against "imperialism masked under the flag of the United Nations" and condemned the secretary-general together with the colonialist government of Belgium and its allies for this "hideous crime."[69] The two governments in their joint communiqué transferred "resolute and complete support" to Lumumba's dauphin, Antoine Gizenga, who, they maintained, was leader of the "only legal government in the Congo." The next day Touré addressed a letter to the UN Secretariat demanding the dismissal of Hammarskjöld and his chief colleagues.[70] In contrast to the condemnation contained in the public documents of Brezhnev's Guinean visit, the joint statement issued at the close of his stay in Ghana blamed no one for the murder of Lumumba, said nothing about support for Gizenga, and noted only that "the intrigues of colonialists and their stooges are not preventing the Congolese people from taking their fate into their own hands."[71]

The Congo crisis was not, however, the only issue on which Touré's

66. O. Orestov, in *Pravda,* February 12, 1961, p. 4.

67. *Guardian,* January 13, 1961, p. 12.

68. Potekhin later wrote, "Not all the African states who sent contingents to the Congo recalled them when it became clear that the UN Command was employing them against the interests of the Congolese people." "The African Peoples Forge Unity," *International Affairs,* no. 6 (1961) p. 81.

69. See Soviet-Guinean joint communiqué in *Pravda,* February 17, 1961, p. 1.

70. This was reported in *Pravda,* February 18, 1961, p. 4.

71. *Pravda,* February 21, 1961, p. 1.

views resembled those of Soviet leaders. In one major speech before a Conakry audience of twenty thousand, he gratified his Soviet listeners with the following series of endorsements: (1) "We are decisively opposed to the creation and maintenance of strategic bases and the deployment of troops in Africa"; (2) "We praise the moral, political and material assistance your government and your people have given the Algerian FLN"; (3) We "will with every means support the [Soviet] policy of general disarmament"; and (4) "We approve the Soviet policy of peaceful coexistence."[72] In sum, according to the joint communiqué, discussions between the two parties "revealed a complete unity of views on the most important international problems." (The Soviet-Ghanaian statement evoked no issue other than the Congo and said only that "the exchange of opinion . . . revealed viewpoints held in common on the most important questions of international politics."[73])

But one should be careful not to make too much of appearances or to overdraw Guinea's identification with Soviet policy (just as one must guard against overdrawing Ghana's resistance to Soviet policy). Undeniably Guinean leaders held points of view which in a number of cases closely paralleled Soviet policy. And indeed, with the emergence of the Casablanca grouping and the death of Lumumba, Guinea drew nearer to the Soviet bloc than ever before. Economic relations were extremely close. Nearly fifteen hundred technicians and other personnel from the Soviet Union, East Europe, and China had come to Guinea to help with projects utilizing funds from the more than $100 million promised. Guinea's imports from the socialist countries exceeded three quarters of its entire purchases. But these figures, the emphasis on the similarity between Soviet and Guinean policy, and praise-filled Soviet accounts tended to conceal Guinea's uncompromising desire to keep its independence intact. Considerations of this sort obscured the effect of John Kennedy's election on US-Guinean relations. And just as important, they concealed the impact of a series of abrasive incidents which jarred Guinea's relationship with Soviet Union in 1961. In short, they left the innocent observer unprepared for Touré's November confrontation with the Soviet ambassador and the sudden ensuing adjustment in Soviet-Guinean amity.

"Guineans are not Communists," Touré said to Brezhnev and a

72. *Pravda*, February 14, 1961, pp. 5, 6.
73. *Pravda*, February 21, 1961, p. 1.

Guinean audience; "the PDG is not a Communist party, the Guinean state is not the organizational appendage of any people or military clan."[74] Those who portrayed his remark as the meaningless trappings of Guinea's nonalignment also represented Touré's extensive ties with the socialist countries as a personal inclination toward Communism and a willingness to guide his country into the socialist camp. Thus they mistakenly assumed that the common interests Touré shared with the Soviet Union were joint interests. The distinction is an important one. In the Congo, for example, Guinea and the Soviet Union had a common interest in seeing Tshombe's regime crushed, Belgian colonialists and their allies driven out, and a Lumumbist government installed. But they did not share these interests for the same reasons—that is, to influence the East-West power balance by depriving the Western alliance of influence in a strategic area of sub-Saharan Africa or to prepare the ground for a regime that might support close relations with the socialist camp and perhaps adopt an orthodox Marxist-Leninist approach to development.

Moreover, these same pessimists disregarded the external factors that from the outset propelled Touré toward the socialist countries. Although the close common cause that Touré found with the Soviet leadership would have existed in any case, it clearly prospered under the isolation that France imposed on Guinea. More important, without Western hostility—or, at least, aloofness—extensive economic ties with the socialist countries would have been missing and the apparent influence wielded by the Soviet Union would not have seemed so great. When these external conditions changed, then, the impulse toward a firm alignment with the socialist countries weakened. The election of John Kennedy inserted an alternative into a relationship where dependence had earlier supplemented desire. Arthur Schlesinger and others have told how Kennedy resolved to approach Africa's angry nationalists and how, subsequently, unusual personal friendships grew, affecting the relations between countries.[75] Touré's friendship with Kennedy became one of the most celebrated.

The Guinean leader first met Kennedy in a privately arranged and

74. *Pravda,* February 14, 1961, p. 5.
75. Arthur M. Schlesinger, Jr., *A Thousand Days* (Boston: Houghton-Mifflin, 1965), pp. 567–570. The former American ambassador to Guinea, William Attwood, supported the same point in his memoirs of those years. See William Attwood, *The Reds and the Blacks* (New York: Harper and Row, 1967).

little publicized interview at Disneyland during his fall 1959 visit to
the United States. John Morrow, President Eisenhower's ambassador
to Guinea and Touré's companion on this tour, later noted the profoundly
favorable impression the young senator made on the visiting president.[76]
The Kennedy manner—the youthfulness and vigor—struck an especially
responsive chord in Africa's famous radical. Touré had been interested
in Kennedy's outspoken advocacy of Algerian independence (at the time
he was chairman of the foreign relations subcommittee on Africa) and
during their interview had congratulated him for his stand. But it was
clear that he was responding far more basically to a personality. There
was no question of whom Touré wished to see win the 1960 election.
It is worth noting, therefore, that the beginnings of the special relationship
between these two leaders occurred before the deterioration of Soviet-
Guinean relations in the fall of 1961. Kennedy's ambassador to Guinea,
William Attwood, worked very hard to convince Touré that new toleration had been infused into American policy, that the president sympa-
thized with his country's problems, and that the United States would
be willing to help in solving them. By May 1961 Western reporters
sensed Touré's increasing interest in American aid, and they viewed
Ambassador Attwood's return to Washington following "extended conversations" with the Guinean president as a move to secure that help.
They were right.[77] In Washington Attwood vigorously lobbied for a sizable aid offer to develop Guinean industry. Washington was in no mood
to underwrite Touré's dream of a huge Konkouré Dam (it was at the
moment even balking at official participation in Ghana's Volta Dam
project, something to which it had long ago given tentative support),
but it did consent to a $25 million aid package providing for a small
dam and power station, six small plants for processing consumer goods,
a turbine and generator, a vocational training program for Guinean
workers, and so on.[78] The process of "retrieving Guinea from the Soviet
orbit" continued with Sargent Shriver's highly successful visit to Conakry
in June.

Touré's readiness to accept the alternative American aid offer reflected
his willingness to admit that Guinea's original development plans had
been overambitious. In August he reported to a PDG conference, called

76. John H. Morrow, *First American Ambassador to Guinea* (New Brunswick:
Rutgers University Press, 1968), pp. 107–108.
77. See Courtney Sheldon, in *Christian Science Monitor,* May 26, 1961, p. 3.
78. Attwood, *The Reds and the Blacks,* pp. 37–41.

to review progress on the three-year plan, that achievements had been less than expected and that Guinea would temporarily forget about the massive Konkouré Dam project, settling instead for a series of small hydroelectric dams. By this time it was generally apparent (presumably to Soviet diplomats as well) that Guinea's economic revolution was bumping along rather unhappily. In March Touré had complained that the state trading system had broken down, victim of "appalling inefficiency," corruption, insufficient distribution facilities, black marketeering, and illegal foreign trade. The two comptoirs were disbanded and later replaced by a series of state trading corporations which, it was soon obvious, were faring no better. The new currency had deteriorated disastrously, exchanging in some West African capitals for one third of its official value. The balance of payments was in heavy imbalance and consumer goods increasingly in short supply.

Meanwhile in April the government signed an agreement with an international consortium, Consafrique, for the prospecting and exploitation of the Nimba-Simandou iron-ore deposits based on fifty-year concession rights. Other plans were afoot to make similar arrangements with Western firms for the further exploitation of Guinea's bauxite reserves. Guinea clearly had not given itself over totally to the socialist option. As a matter of fact, in 1960–61, the period when Guinea's trade with the socialist countries mounted so substantially, it was West Germany that became its single most important trading partner. No doubt the West Germans were profiting from a 20 DM million loan given Guinea earlier together with export credit guarantees, but the Guineans also valued the high-quality goods and excellent technical service supplied by the Germans.[79]

They were not nearly so happy with Eastern bloc trade. Their growing disenchantment over this aspect of Soviet-Guinean cooperation was to figure importantly in events during the months before Touré's confrontation with the Soviet ambassador. By late 1961 rumors freely circulated that Guineans were complaining about tardy deliveries under the trade agreement and about delays in implementing aid promises. When the goods arrived, the Guineans criticized their quality. Socialist sugar was too hard or the grains too large; socialist matches "just would not light";

79. In March 1960 West Germany's angry response to the establishment of diplomatic relations with the GDR forced Touré to retreat hastily. The world was told that Guinea's ambassador to the Soviet Union had never presented his credentials to the East German president, though the event was recorded on a news film and announced by the East German news agency.

electrical goods wore out too rapidly; movie projectors "burned out instantaneously"; typewriters collapsed—the list was long. If goods were not late or of inferior quality then they were in the wrong quantity, in the wrong place, or without accompanying parts. Western reporters recounted stories of thousands of toilet bowls without seats, water tanks, or fittings stacked up along the route from the airport into Conakry, or of the famous snowplows sitting conspicuously on Conakry's docks under the tropical sun.[80] People referred to the public-address system the East Germans had supplied the president for his capital but which, because of faulty wiring, had never worked. And so did they talk of the hundred-kilowatt radio transmitter switched on in late September without result because it had been constructed atop one of Guinea's more substantial veins of iron ore. A Soviet-aided seven-thousand-hectare state rice farm at La Fie had soaked up the better part of 3,000 million Guinean francs, but because of poor equipment or equipment unsuited to climatic conditions it had yet to produce. Nor allegedly did the Guineans sympathize with the difficulties and unavoidable delays involved in constructing a stadium or hotel in an underdeveloped country. The insufficient selflessness of eighteen Soviet diamond engineers, who were sent to aid Guinea's nationalized diamond industry but who in August were arrested for smuggling diamonds off to the Soviet Union, did little to increase confidence in Soviet assistance.[81]

Soviet officials in turn responded with a series of their own complaints. To Guinean leaders they protested the inefficient planning that frequently kept Soviet ships out of the port for weeks and then sent them back to the Soviet Union only one third loaded with Guinean bananas. When given a chance, Soviet representatives had their own explanation for discontinuities in the exchange of trade. Similarly they resented the ingratitude of Guineans who criticized their aid, and they blamed them for obstructing the efficient completion of Soviet projects. Even Soviet Ambassador Solod reportedly grumbled in private that the Guineans

80. Marshall I. Goldman, "A Balance Sheet of Soviet Foreign Aid," *Foreign Affairs,* XLII (January 1965), 355, reported that the snowplow incident was a case of mistaken identity; that the Soviet Union had really delivered winterized tractors. Other equally fair-minded witnesses, who swore they saw snowplows, explained that the Soviet factory preparing such shipments received a request for two complete road-building outfits to be sent to Guinea, and in the Soviet Union each complete road-building unit includes a snowplow.

81. "Solod's Retreat from Conakry," Radio Free Europe (RFE) Research and Evaluation Department, December 22, 1961.

"did not want to work, were ruining Soviet equipment and were not to be taken seriously."[82] If Solod actually made this remark—and the recurrent testimony of people who observed the ambassador during this period makes it seem likely—then he underestimated the Guineans. For "not taking the Guineans seriously," in less than two months Solod found himself Moscow-bound as the former ambassador to Guinea.

On December 13 the Soviet ambassador had turned out with the rest of the diplomatic corps to receive Nigeria's visting prime minister, Sir Abubakar Tafawa Balewa. Scarcely had he arrived than Guinea's chief of protocol told him that he would not be permitted to receive the Nigerian leader.[83] Three days later he and Mrs. Solod were on a plane home. He had been sent away from Guinea for "personal reasons" and had been told not to wait for the weekly Czech flight, which would have made his unhappy return at least more convenient. Solod had snapped President Touré's patience by carelessly and indiscreetly meddling in a domestic quarrel between the regime and its teachers and students.

To a confident, sometimes arrogant ambassador and the government he represented, this expulsion was a particularly serious rebuff. Solod had arrived in Guinea in 1960, already a well-known diplomat and at that moment deputy head of the Near Eastern department of the Soviet foreign office. His appointment indicated the importance assigned to Soviet-Guinean relations. In the immediate postwar years Solod had headed Soviet missions in Syria and Lebanon, returning to the Soviet Union in 1950 to become a member of the ministry's executive staff. Appointed ambassador to Egypt in 1954 (while holding his previous position), Solod earned his reputation as the official who successfully shepherded Soviet-Egyptian relations in this early period. No one could have misunderstood that he had been sent to Conakry to enhance Soviet influence south of the desert and that his responsibilities extended far beyond the frontiers of Guinea.

Solod's problems began in early 1961, when the executive committee

82. *France-Soir*, October 26, 1961.

83. See Philippe DeCraene, in *Le Monde*, December 30, 1961, p. 1. *Daily Worker* (London), December 21, 1961, reported the expulsion of the Soviet ambassador. Guinea's ambassador to France, Tibou Tounkara, took pains to assure reporters that Solod had been asked to leave for personal reasons and that he had not been expelled—no doubt a *legally* accurate distinction. For further detail see Attwood, *The Reds and the Blacks*, p. 63.

of the Guinean teachers' union distributed a memorandum criticizing government policies and "making demands considered to be of a nature to incite a section of workers against the Guinean revolution."[84] According to government spokesmen, Eastern embassies had received this memorandum, although it had not been cleared with the PDG leadership. On November 16 Touré denounced the leadership of the teachers' union before the Confédération Nationale du Travail Guinéen and insisted on the expulsion of Keita Koumandian, one of Touré's old rivals from pre-independence days and the man thought to be behind the memorandum. Three days later five members of the executive committee of the teachers' union were tried before the Haute Cour de Justice and harshly sentenced. Two of those sentenced, Koumandian and Ray Autra, were "known for their Communist tendencies" and for their opposition to Guinea's nonaligned posture.[85] In the next few days a series of incidents erupted in Labé and Conakry. On November 24 the schools went on strike and the students began organizing demonstrations against Touré's government.

Whatever had been the Soviet role up to this point, it seems fairly conclusive that Soviet diplomats encouraged the students to protest and, more than that, attempted to give their demonstrations a particular direction. During the demonstrations leaflets appeared, some say from out of unmarked Soviet embassy cars, which asked the question, "How can a country be neutral, neither aligned with East or West?" and supplied the answer, "We must belong to one bloc or the other."[86] On December 5 Touré delivered a speech denouncing the imperialist plot against his government supported by foreign enemies, blaming in particular "Eastern embassies."[87] In the next several days Guinean police arrested more people, including a representative of the Guinean press agency named Diallo Alpha Ibrahima Diawara whom Guinean radio accused of being "the damned soul of the plot" and a militant Communist who engaged in "systematic economic espionage" for Eastern embassies. On December 11 at another public rally Touré charged the plotters with passing information to Eastern embassies and with aiding "a secret Communist organization" located at Labé, a town 550 kilome-

84. Leopoldville radio (domestic service in French), 10.45 GMT, December 27, 1961.

85. DeCraene, p. 4.

86. One published account appeared in an article by Colin Legum, *The Observer*, March 25, 1962, p. 10.

87. DeCraene, in *Le Monde*, December 29, 1961, p. 4.

ters north of Conakry.[88] He alleged that investigations of the student riots revealed a subversive network reaching out to Dakar, Paris, and "an Eastern bloc embassy." On December 15, the Guinean president summoned the heads of Communist-bloc diplomatic missions to his office. The next morning Solod left Guinea.[89]

To compound the awkwardness of their situation, Soviet leaders next sanctioned, or perhaps instigated, public demands by Guinean students in the USSR that Solod be allowed to return to Guinea. When Touré asked for their repatriation, the Soviet government at first refused but soon relented when he promised that otherwise they would be the last Guineans to study in the Soviet Union. Touré added, "We don't need misguided propagandists here."[90]

If developments up to this point are less than perfectly comprehensible, then what followed obscures the situation even more. On the heels of Solod's departure, Touré sent the foreign ministry's young principal secretary, Diallo Alpha, to Moscow to speak with Khrushchev. The Soviet press gave no hint of what their talks were about, but presumably Touré was eager both to underscore his unwillingness to tolerate interference in Guinea's internal affairs and, at the same time, to reassure the Soviet leader that this incident should not be considered a fatal blow to Soviet-Guinean friendship. It may be that Khrushchev sought to persuade Diallo that the real culprit in this whole affair was France— of which Touré was generally easily persuaded. Whether it was Khrushchev's doing or not, a week later Touré told a party conference at Labé that France was the "leading element in the plot."[91] The French embassy in Conakry, he said, had permitted the conspirators to use the diplomatic pouch to communicate with "the Guinean antiparty group in Paris and Moscow."[92] In Moscow supposedly the French ambassador had served as the intermediary for passing documents on to the students. Nevertheless this last-minute attempt to inculpate the French did not seriously detract from Touré's firm insistence that the November disturbances were the work "of a Marxist-Leninist group whose Machiavellian plan was to unleash a Marxist revolution in Guinea." Nor did it compensate

88. *Le Monde,* December 13, 1961, p. 2. See also *New York Times,* December 13, 1961, p. 14.
89. Touré later told Attwood that "we caught him redhanded." Attwood, *The Reds and the Blacks,* p. 63.
90. Legum, in *The Observer,* March 25, 1962, p. 10.
91. See *Le Monde,* December 30, 1961, p. 2.
92. *Le Monde,* December 28, 1961, p. 4.

for the fact that it was the Soviet ambassador who had been disgraced. A chagrined Soviet leadership hurried to announce that Anastas Mikoyan would visit Guinea early the next month to discuss "various problems of further cooperation between the two countries."[93]

Observers seeking an explanation for the Guinean president's violent reaction to Soviet interference in the student disturbances have generally concluded that it represented the culminating incident in a deteriorating relationship. They point to the frictions arising over Soviet foreign aid and trade. Even (or perhaps particularly) the Yugoslavs noted that Soviet foreign aid had been below expectations—most projects had fallen behind schedule, were costing more than planned, including the expense of foreign technicians, and the training of Guineans in technical work was lagging.[94] Others add that Touré had become concerned over the Soviet Union and its Eastern allies' increasing presence and, when confronted with this bold attempt to exert influence over his country's affairs, that he seized the moment to readjust the balance. Walter Kolarz in one radio broadcast mused that possibly Nasser had warned Touré against Communist intrigue during his visit to the UAR in May.[95] At least Kolarz thought that might explain the timely Conakry radio broadcast linking the Syrian plot against Egyptian leaders (which tore Syria from the UAR, with Soviet blessings) to the "recent subversive activities in Guinea."[96]

Such speculation sounds plausible and it does impute to Touré's actions the firm foundation of long-term provocations. The magnitude of the challenge when formulated in this way seems to justify his abrupt shift away from a stout friendship with the Soviet Union. As a watershed event in Soviet relations with sub-Saharan Africa, the whole affair appears suitably prepared and the moral sufficiently evident. The Soviet Union had allowed optimism to exceed prudence. In their optimism Soviet officials had been heavy-footed and insolent. Officials would have to pay more attention to their manners in the future—a future whose benefits no longer seemed either imminent or ready-made. But this is

93. Moscow radio, evening of December 27, as reported in the *New York Times*, December 28, 1961, p. 2. *Pravda*'s report the next day was less precise. It said Mikoyan was going to Guinea for important discussions intended to strengthen cooperation between the two countries.

94. Belgrade radio, 12.00 GMT, January 4, 1962.

95. Walter Kolarz, Central Research Unit (BBC overseas service), talk no. 2230, December 14, 1961.

96. There is even an unconfirmed report that Touré sent Saifoulaye Diallo to warn Nkrumah against Soviet intrigue and himself went to Bamako.

the nature of international politics, and Soviet leaders knew from previous experience that bilateral relationships would from time to time whirl off in the wrong direction.

On the other hand, if Touré had acted in a moment of fury, and contrary to any previous inclination, to undo an elaborate and presumably durable friendship, then Soviet leaders must have been all the more startled. Subsequently the unpredictability of African behavior, favorable as well as unfavorable, would leave Soviet policymakers gun-shy and suspicious. To judge by Touré's behavior in this case, and more than once afterward, he was capable of acting impetuously.[97] Before the student disturbances he had betrayed no discontent over the course of Soviet-Guinean relations and, with the exception of the chronic complaints over economic ties, nothing suggests that Guinea wished to upset its relationship with the Soviet Union. (This is not to say, however, that Guinea did not also hope to increase ties with the United States.) Without thoroughly discounting the impact of these broader problems, it would be interesting to know whether Soviet leaders themselves concluded that Touré had reacted more out of pique and momentary fright than out of deep and general concern.

What happened to Soviet-Guinean relations after Solod's expulsion and what specific imprint this confrontation left on future Soviet activity throughout Africa are questions more conveniently treated in the next chapter. For the moment it is worth noting that it may be Touré's loss of temper which most impressed Soviet leaders. The damage done to Soviet prestige in Africa and the disturbing realization that the socialist revolution was not at hand contributed to Soviet disappointment, but the lasting impact of this incident was to convince Soviet leaders of the unpredictability of African personalities and events.

The Shift of Priorities to Ghana

In December, when Soviet relations with Guinea were buffeted so suddenly and uncongenially, an entirely different situation prevailed in

---

97. Touré again demonstrated a reflexive anger in 1964 when he tossed out French diplomats and broke relations that had only recently and with considerable strain been established; and in June 1966, when unleashing a violent attack against Senegal on the basis of a planted rumor, he quashed friendly relations that had only two weeks earlier been re-established after a long estrangement; he sheltered the deposed Nkrumah; and again in October–November 1966, he placed under house arrest the American ambassador for complicity in the detention of Guinea's foreign minister and delegation by the Ghanaian government.

Ghana and Mali. Throughout 1961 contact between these two countries and the Soviet Union had grown, producing by the end of the year a field of opportunity that was fundamentally changed from a year earlier. Ghana, particularly, was moving through a critical period in the evolution of both its foreign and its domestic policies. By 1960 most expatriate Englishmen had relinquished their posts in the bureaucracy to Ghanaians. Freed of their restraining influence, Nkrumah had determined to go ahead with his internal revolution. Outside Ghana the course of events, especially in the Congo, had embittered Nkrumah against the United States and its European allies. Nkrumah's domestic ambitions and his disillusionment in foreign affairs converged to turn Ghana's face eastward.[98]

While they remained in Ghana, British advisers had delayed the establishment of relations with the Soviet Union and the arrival of a Soviet ambassador; they had postponed Nkrumah's opportunity to make the acquaintance of the socialist countries and had stood as a palpable reminder that Ghana's destiny still rested with the countries of the West. More than anything else they symbolized an order inherited from a colonial past calling into question the revolutionary ambitions of Ghana's new leadership. Until their departure, the "second Ghanaian revolution" had to wait.

With the notable exception of Nkrumah's chief of staff, most of these people were gone from their posts by 1961. With their departure and, in 1960, with the establishment of Ghana as a republic and Nkrumah as president (no longer was the Queen head of state), the country prepared to embark on a radical new course. The 1960 constitution gave the president considerably reinforced authority, enabling him to implement a number of reforms designed to centralize political power. Organized political opposition virtually disappeared with Nkrumah's triumph over J. B. Danquah in the 1960 plebiscite. In April 1961 Nkrumah announced the subordination of all major voluntary associations—the Trade Union Congress, the United Ghana Farmers' Council, the National Cooperative Council, and the National Council of Ghana Women—to his Convention People's Party. According to the president, the central committee of the CPP had even decided to eliminate separate membership cards for these organizations and, in all regional head-

98. Thompson argues that indeed foreign affairs, most especially the failure of Nkrumah's continental aspirations, led him to increase the pace of domestic revolution. See Thompson, *Ghana's Foreign Policy*, p. 361.

quarters, to house their executives in the same building with the party organization.[99] An exhortation of his delivered before the 1960 plebiscite, that "the Convention People's Party is Ghana, and Ghana is the Convention People's Party," turned out to be more than simply campaign oratory.

The press, radio, and other communications media became the exclusive instrument of Ghana's single political party, under the direction of party radicals who were taken with the need to indoctrinate the reading and listening masses in "Nkrumaism." A new press-censorship regulation in August 1960 guaranteed that only their voices would reach the people. Within the president's own circle, influence fell to a fresh group of expatriate advisers who shared few of the views of the old British civil servants; some were or had been affiliated with the British or South African Communist parties. From their offices within the presidential residence, they sustained the ideological fervor of the regime and eventually became Nkrumah's closest advisers, forming a personal cabinet usurping the powers of parliamentary ministers. Between February and June 1961, Nkrumah himself assumed leadership of a new program in "ideological education" aimed at reinforcing the influence of the party and galvanizing the people behind efforts to promote economic and political development.[100]

The transformation Nkrumah seemed to be preparing took as its obvious point of departure the experience of the socialist countries. Admittedly his revolution was cast substantially in his own image, ill defined as a commitment to Nkrumaism, but neither the egocentrism of his program nor its ambiguity concealed the inspiration provided by Marxism-Leninism. The Soviet leadership may have thought Nkrumah a fuzzy thinker who understood little about scientific socialism, but this had small relation to Nkrumah's own estimation. By 1961 his long-nurtured attachment to Marxism and Leninism, developed as a student and latent in many of his pronouncements from 1948 to 1957, clearly emerged as the backdrop for his regime. "The Convention People's Party is, above all, a dynamic Party with a clear-cut social goal and political ideology to guide it," he said in an address on the tenth anniversary of the party. "We aim at creating in Ghana a socialist society in which each will give according to his ability and receive according to his needs."[101]

99. Nkrumah, *I Speak of Freedom,* p. 207.
100. Legum, "Socialism in Ghana, p. 144.
101. Nkrumah, *I Speak of Freedom,* p. 165.

Ideologically, Nkrumah's affinity remained with nineteenth-century Marxism "adapted to Africa's conditions." This, of course, the Soviet Union rejected. Organizationally, however, Nkrumah selected Leninism as his model, emphasizing the need to employ a select group to stir the consciousness of the masses. He proclaimed "democratic centralism" to be the organizational principle of the CPP, sounding more than a little like Lenin when he said to party members: "All are free to express their views. But once a majority decision is taken, we expect such a decision to be loyally executed, even by those who might have opposed that decision."[102] He advocated that not only branch secretaries of the party but even ministers, parliamentary secretaries, and members of parliament attend courses at a party school. "In fact the Central Committee intends making such a course of study in Party ideology obligatory upon them."[103] Members of the party, called "Vanguard Activists," drawn from the "most politically educated section of the Party," were to be trained in special courses to explain the objectives of the CPP to the masses.

All of this, however, probably overstates the clarity of Nkrumah's vision and the consistency of his actions. There is the risk in briefly summarizing Nkrumah's statements of giving them greater coherence and bite than they really possessed. He was far less committed to an immediate assault upon the status quo than his speeches implied. He was far more the eminently usable creature of confidants who now sought to advance their own confused revolutionary notions.[104] But Nkrumah had his preferences, and Tawia Adamafio and the other radicals in the CPP succeeded to the extent that they cultivated (and manipulated) his sense of revolution. He unquestionably harbored a fascination for the political structures of the socialist countries. This too they sought to turn to good account.

Over the first half of 1961 a number of Ghanaian delegations began traveling to the Soviet Union to learn firsthand how that society was organized and to study its techniques of propaganda and education. In January 1961 a group of ten leaders from the Ghana Young Pioneers was sent to the Soviet Union for six months to study the techniques of youth organization. A second group of twenty-seven followed in December 1961. Earlier, in the fall of 1960, eighteen Ghanaians left to

102. *Ibid.*, p. 164.
103. *Ibid.*, p. 165.
104. On this point see Thompson, *Ghana's Foreign Policy*, pp. 198–262.

enroll in a two-year course at the Moscow Cooperative Institute to study cooperative farming. In the spring of 1961 a Ghanaian military delegation led by Brigadier S. J. A. Otu visited the USSR to discuss the organization of Ghana's armed forces. Thus the undisguised ascendence of a Marxian program, prompted by the problems of political and economic development, together with Nkrumah's growing interest in highly controlled political institutions, stimulated a natural curiosity about the solutions of the Soviet system.

The frustrations of Nkrumah's foreign policy also pushed Ghana toward the Soviet Union or, more accurately, away from the United States and its NATO allies. Angered by events in the Congo, particularly the death of Lumumba, Nkrumah took fewer pains to validate his frequently proclaimed policy of nonalignment. In 1960 he had signed a secret agreement with Lumumba providing for the eventual union of the Congo with Ghana, and when this prospect collapsed with the murder of Lumumba, thereby endangering Nkrumah's dearest dream of pan-African unity, the Ghanaian president lashed out against the Western alliance. For the moment he resisted attacking the United Nations directly and instead selected as his culprit the United States, presumably because that country was the most influential member of the Western alliance. Soon after the arrest of Lumumba, the Ghanaian press began a campaign to excoriate American policy in the Congo. These attacks the Soviet press happily aired: "Ghana, by virtue of its non-alignment and positive neutralism reserves the right to condemn this betrayal of the African people and the Charter of Human Rights by the government of the United States of America . . . America appears to have emerged concretely as a big apologist of colonialism—in fact, much more than that— the big God-father of the colony-owning imperialists."[105] The indictment was meant to be applied to American policy toward Africa in general and not merely the Congo. When Francis Russell, the new United States ambassador, arrived in Ghana in January 1961, the *Ghanaian Times* underlined the fundamental divergences existing between the United States and Ghana: "We detest their role in the Congo; we reject their assiduous attempts to subject the people of other countries to the dollar; and we find it objectionable that they sacrifice what is right to preserve peace within the NATO alliance."[106] The editorial concluded this less

105. *Evening News* (Ghana), undated, quoted in V. Goncharov, "In the Republic of Ghana," *New Times,* no. 1 (January 1961), p. 29.
106. *Pravda,* January 7, 1961, p. 4.

than cordial greeting with a recommendation that, if he expected to accomplish anything in Ghana, Russell would first have to seek in Washington "a more progressive and truly good-willed policy not only with respect to Africa but on many problems which confront the world." Similarly when the State Department reportedly issued one of the first accounts of an attempted coup d'état in Ethiopia in late 1960, the Ghanaian press implied that the Americans had good reason to know in advance these details. "It is a secret to no one that the USA has been displeased with Haile Selassie's expressions of willingness to accept unconditional aid from the socialist countries."[107]

The obverse of Ghana's growing alienation from the United States and Western Europe was its rapprochement with the Soviet Union and Eastern Europe. In a speech on October 18, 1960, Nkrumah reportedly maintained that no decisive successes in securing world peace would be possible until the Western powers became "less fanatical towards Communism and towards everything that happens in Russia."[108] And he added that from his talks with Premier Khrushchev in New York during the UN General Assembly session he was convinced "Russia wanted peace more than anything in the world."

By then Ghana had already begun forging closer ties with the Soviet Union. Nkrumah secured Ghana's first Soviet credits in August 1960, at the time two of his closest collaborators, Tawia Adamafio and John Tettegah, chairman of the Trade Union Congress, were in Moscow for talks with Soviet leaders. The initial credit totaled nearly $40 million, to be used for a variety of projects, including industrial enterprises, a geological survey, a hydroelectric dam complex, fishing equipment, and so on. Before the end of October a group of Soviet technicians— geologists, electrical engineers, civil engineers, architects, and agricultural and fishery experts—arrived in Ghana to initiate the first of these projects.[109] In February 1961, obviously playing on Nkrumah's predilection for grandiose schemes, the Soviet Union agreed to design and supply equipment, fuel, and necessary materials for an atomic reactor, to assist in constructing a laboratory for the production of isotopes, and to prepare Ghanaian cadres in the peaceful exploitation of atomic energy.[110] A few days later Orestov in *Pravda* announced that Ghana

107. *Ghanaian Times,* undated, quoted in *Pravda,* December 19, 1960, p. 3.
108. *Kommunist Tadzhikistana,* October 22, 1960, quoted in *Mizan,* II (November 1960), 26.
109. *Krasnaya zvezda,* October 30, 1960, in *ibid.,* p. 28.
110. The agreement is reproduced in *SSSR i strany Afriki,* II, 223–225.

Airways had recently purchased four Ilyushin-18 aircraft and that pilots were already being trained in the USSR.[111] Orestov's article reviewed for *Pravda* readers the rapid advances in Soviet-Ghanaian cooperation, citing the number of Ghanaian students now attending Friendship University, the Moscow Cooperative Institute, and other universities; the arrival of Ghanaians to study Soviet cotton and corn production and the Soviet fishing industry; the presence of Soviet health experts in Ghana working to solve the problem of malaria; the imminent prospect of a Soviet cultural center in Accra; and the recently opened showroom for Soviet merchandise located in central Accra. In June the Ghanaians established a high-level Committee for Economic Cooperation with the Eastern Countries, charged with "expediting economic arrangements" between Ghana and the socialist bloc.[112] Increasing contact between Ghana and the Soviet Union reflected a mounting mutual interest in the other side's foreign policy and internal development. Perhaps curiosity would be more accurate because at this point neither party was sure that it fully understood or could trust the program and promises of the other country.

In this sense the critical event in early Soviet-Ghanaian relations occurred when Nkrumah visited the Soviet Union in July 1961.[113] From this visit one can date Nkrumah's conscious attempts to emulate the Soviet approach to political modernization. Now he bound his ambitions at home and his policies abroad more closely to those of the socialist countries. Soviet leaders, for their part, were no less impressed by Nkrumah's qualities as a revolutionary leader, with his usefulness as an ally, and, one can speculate, with his susceptibility to Soviet influence.

After a four-year delay caused by the presence of British advisers, by the requirements of economic development—for example, the need to secure Western support for the Upper Volta River project—and by the uncertainty of the 1960 national elections, Nkrumah arrived in Moscow ebullient and, as he himself said, ready to see "the great achievements of the Soviet people which we have heard so much about, the glorious results of the Communist Revolution and reconstruction."[114] From all accounts Nkrumah came away deeply impressed. His speeches

111. O. Orestov, in *Pravda,* March 6, 1961, p. 3.

112. MFA to Ghana/Moscow, June 2, 1961, CFA-10, in Thompson, *Ghana's Foreign Policy,* p. 186.

113. *Ibid.,* pp. 173–177, provides a detailed account of Nkrumah's Eastern pilgrimage.

114. *Pravda,* July 11, 1961, p. 2.

praised at greater length than those of any previous African leader the Soviet Union's revolutionary achievements in science and culture, in industry and agriculture, and in education and national unification.[115] In all spheres (including agriculture) he commended the Soviet example not only to Ghana but to all of Africa. Ghanaians who look back on the visit recall that his enthusiasm was genuine, far more than the polite response of a visiting African. He returned to Ghana fired with visions of new means to accelerate Ghana's economic and political development and filled with fresh schemes for political and military reorganization. Within weeks plans were underway for introducing state farms into Ghanaian agriculture, with the assistance of Soviet experts. The president projected a new seven-year plan and called upon the Hungarian economist, Joseph Bognor, to help with its formulation. He announced the expansion of workers' brigades and the compulsory establishment of graduated levels of youth organizations in every school from kindergarten to the university. Ten days after his return from the Soviet Union and East Europe, he summoned Major-General H. T. Alexander, Ghana's British chief of staff, and instructed him to turn over command that hour to Brigadier Otu.[116] Other British officers were to do the same on the day following. While Nkrumah was in the Soviet Union, Alexander had received orders to send four hundred candidate officers to Moscow for military training and to see to their departure within a fortnight.[117] Through the minister of defense, C. de Graft Dickson, Nkrumah even told Alexander that he wanted the President's Own Guard Regiment to be taught the Russian goosestep and outfitted in Russian-type jackboots.[118]

These changes—taking, if not Soviet advice, then pages from the Soviet organizational manual—of course received warm approval from the Russians. They particularly mentioned Nkrumah's decision to dismiss Alexander and noted with satisfaction that this and his decision to assume personal command over the armed forces had caused "great irritation" in Washington.[119] But Nkrumah's position on international questions, expressed in Moscow and later at the Belgrade conference of nonaligned

115. See his speeches in *Pravda,* July 12, 1961, p. 2, and July 25, 1961, p. 1.
116. H. T. Alexander, *African Tightrope* (London: Pall Mall Press, 1965), p. 94.
117. *Ibid.,* p. 91.
118. *Ibid.,* p. 102.
119. See *Izvestiya,* September 27, 1961, p. 4, and *Pravda,* October 3, 1961, p. 5.

nations, pleased them more. On each key problem—disarmament, Algeria, reorganization of the United Nations, French intervention in Tunisia over Bizerta, the European Economic Community, the Sino-Soviet conflict, Germany, the Congo—Nkrumah rallied to the Soviet side. In one of the most detailed communiqués an African leader had signed with the Soviet Union, the Ghanaian president joined Soviet leaders in condemning French policy in Algeria and Tunisia. He assailed attempts by the EEC to "tie African countries to European imperialism, to prevent African countries from conducting an independent, neutral policy, to obstruct the restoration of mutually advantageous economic ties among these countries, and to retain the African countries as raw material suppliers for the imperialist powers."[120] Although the Congo crisis lost some of its urgency that month with the Lovanium compromise between Gizenga and Adoula, and although Nkrumah still refused to repudiate the secretary-general, he did condemn "imperialist aggression in the Congo" and affirm public support for the Congo's "only legal government," headed by Antoine Gizenga. (The last was conspicuously missing from the communiqué signed at the close of Brezhnev's February visit to Ghana and may have represented a new concession on Nkrumah's part.) Of significance in its dispute with the Chinese, Nkrumah supported the Soviet leadership's dedication to complete and general disarmament (including the view that these resources could be used for economic development in Asia and Africa), the policy of peaceful coexistence, Khrushchev's Vienna meeting with Kennedy, and the Soviet Union's role in the national liberation struggle. He also gave the Soviet propaganda apparatus what must be the most frequently quoted endorsement in all of Soviet-African relations: "If it were not for the Soviet Union, the movement for liberation from the colonial yoke in Africa would experience the full force of brutal and crude suppression."[121]

In July 1961, however, Soviet policymakers were preoccupied with their successful efforts to reheat the German question to a boiling point, an enterprise touching Soviet relations with Africa as well as with Europe and the United States. A year earlier, when the Soviet Union sought a spokesman among the Afro-Asian group to defend Soviet Congo policy in the General Assembly, it chose Touré. Now the focal issue was the Soviet ultimatum on Berlin, the forum, the Belgrade nonaligned conference scheduled for September, and the candidate for devil's advocate,

120. *Pravda,* July 26, 1961, p. 1, 2.
121. *Pravda,* July 25, 1961, p. 1.

Nkrumah. He responded sympathetically or, in the words of the joint communiqué, he received Soviet proposals for a resolution to the Berlin problem "with understanding."[122] Contrasted with his subsequent stance at the Belgrade conference this represented more than a mild understatement. There Nkrumah proposed that the conference call upon the great powers to sign a German peace treaty without delay and, to the consternation of his West German suitors, urged that the "only sensible solution was to recognize the existence of two sovereign states, West Germany and East Germany."[123] He assured his listeners that free access to West Berlin would not be a problem for the present boundaries, after sixteen years, "are inviolable." "Why," he asked, "should the peace be shattered because of a problem to which a solution is entirely possible?"

There was in Nkrumah's statements a double return to Soviet policy. First, the Soviet government obviously benefited from his direct support for what was basically its position on the German question. In addition, his behavior angered the United States and West Germany, who then pointedly feigned to review their foreign-aid programs, in turn increasing Nkrumah's irritation with the Western countries. The Soviet press diligently reminded Nkrumah that his exercise in independence had provoked economic and political retaliation from capitalist countries. *Pravda* alleged, with reason known best to Nkrumah, that the United States was using economic assistance as a means of pressure; specifically, because the State Department disliked Nkrumah's "recent statements on international issues," it had postponed an agreement on aid for the critical Volta River project.[124] But Nkrumah needed no one to ginger his emotions at this point. He never forgot these attempts to twist his arm, and five years later, when Ghana celebrated the completion of this

122. *Pravda,* July 26, 1961, p. 1. Thompson reports an interesting and probably disingenuous bit of confusion among the Ghanaians over this portion of the communiqué. The Ghanaian text used the phrase, "The Government of Ghana *appreciated* the proposals of the Soviet Government concerning . . . " According to Thompson, Ako Adjei, Ghanaian foreign minister, later tried to explain to Dean Rusk "that the key word, *appreciate,* was used in its strict sense, derived from Latin, to establish that Ghana had taken note of the Russian position." (See Thompson, *Ghana's Foreign Policy,* p. 175.) Be that as it may, the Russian version of the communiqué used the phrase *s ponimaniem,* which Soviet officials clearly understood to mean "with understanding."

123. V. Maevsky and B. Tarasov, in *Pravda,* September 3, 1961, p. 4.

124. See *Pravda,* September 26, 1961, p. 6, and Leonid Paramov, "Washington and Ghana," *New Times,* no. 41 (1961), p. 21.

mammoth project (January 22, 1966), Nkrumah flashed his scarcely concealed bitterness: "My faith in it [the Volta project] never faltered, in spite of the disappointments and frustrations created by the difficult and intricate financial negotiations." President Kennedy despite opposition forces both in his cabinet and in congress continued to support the idea of American involvement. "Indeed," said Nkrumah, "at one time [Kennedy] stood alone in his cabinet on this matter."[125]

Nkrumah's visit to the Soviet Union also opened the way for more extensive economic cooperation between the two countries. The two sides agreed to toss aside their standing trade agreement, so lethargically negotiated and so unexceptional in content, although it had come into force only the previous month, and to replace it with an agreement more accurately reflecting their eagerness to trade.[126] When negotiated in November, the new agreement and an accompanying payment agreement were to come into temporary force immediately after signature (unlike the former agreement, which remained in legal limbo for nearly two years). Moreover, unlike the previous agreement the new accord provided for a sizable swing credit of $11 million.[127] A set of protocols (not legally binding) reflected the Soviet Union's intention to purchase annually a specified quantity of cocoa beans, increasing to 60,000 tons in five years, and to pay for these purchases partially in a freely convertible currency, decreasing annually from 55 percent of the first year's purchases.

Those planning Nkrumah's trip to the Soviet Union in the rarefied atmosphere of early 1961 envisaged asking Soviet leaders for $280 million in new credits, to which they never doubted their hosts would happily agree. Nkrumah did not make the request, however. As he said at a Kremlin breakfast: "We came here not for assistance but in order to study ways and means to improve trade relations between us."[128] Nevertheless a very satisfied Soviet leadership offered him additional credits totaling $42 million. According to the terms of a second economic and technical cooperation agreement signed on November 4, 1961, the new

125. See *Ghanaian Times*, January 23, 1966, p. 4.

126. See Chapter Two.

127. *1961 Ghana Treaty Series*, IV (October 19–December 20), Ministry of Foreign Affairs, pp. 59–61.

128. *Pravda*, July 12, 1961, p. 2. Why the Ghanaians did not press for the aid is not quite clear, though it may have been Nkrumah who did not want to seem a beggar on his first triumphal visit to the Soviet Union.

aid was to finance, in addition to the projects already agreed upon, a plant for the production of large reinforced-concrete panels, a paper mill, a textile mill, a machine-tool plant, and so on.[129]

To keep these matters in perspective, however, it should be pointed out that few specific project contracts were ever signed and, as we shall see later, even fewer credits were ever drawn down. Trade between the two countries, despite an increase in Soviet imports, actually declined over 1961, and even at the end of 1962 commercial exchange remained smaller than in 1960 when no trade agreement was in force.[130] In both economic assistance and trade the laggard party appears to have been Ghana, not the Soviet Union. Soviet leaders, it is true, soon lost their enthusiasm for projects like the Bui Dam, but generally it was Ghana's economic administrators and planners who applied bureaucratic constraints to Nkrumah's plans for utilizing Soviet aid. In the case of trade, private importers, uncontrolled by a national import organization, rejected Soviet export items in favor of familiar British products.

None of these factors, however, diminished Ghana's growing attractiveness to the Soviet Union, especially in the months following Solod's expulsion from Guinea. Deputy Premier Mikoyan's trip to West Africa in January 1962 indicated the changes taking place. He came primarily to calm Guinea's very angry president, but it was an awkward mission and he no doubt looked forward more to the other stops on his itinerary. According to witnesses, Mikoyan's hasty peace mission received a "glacial" reception in Conakry. Attwood said that Touré refused even to receive him, joining him only at a public ceremony.[131] In his comments

129. *SSSR i strany Afriki, 1946–1962,* II, 441–443.

130. *Annual Report on External Trade in Ghana,* I (July 1962), 23–25. Soviet figures for the same period are somewhat misleading because they include in the trade summary all goods shipped to Ghana under suppliers' credits (for aid projects) as well as the normal commercial exchange. Ghanaian figures show a substantial favorable balance of trade each year in Ghana's favor; that is, the balance was against the Soviet Union in the clearing account. Soviet figures indicate that the Soviet Union had a very large favorable balance of trade with Ghana. Therefore, not only do Soviet statistics fail to indicate the state of the swing credit, they seriously overestimate the Soviet Union's ability to penetrate the local market.

131. Attwood, *The Reds and the Blacks,* p. 65. *Le Monde's* correspondent reported that Mikoyan was scheduled to pay a courtesy call on the president on Saturday, January 6, before the two of them attended the Soviet trade exhibition. (See *Le Monde,* January 7–8, 1962, p. 2.) *Le Monde* the next day implied that that call had been made, but Attwood may know what actually happened in the presidential residence. Later in the week Touré did give a reception for his Soviet visitor.

the Soviet leader trod lightly. Together the two sounded like estranged lovers, one repentant, the other still agitated, making small, impersonal talk about things that had once animated their relationship—imperialism, neocolonialism, and the struggle to achieve economic independence. At one point, however, Touré referred to the trouble between their countries: "The spirit of [our] cooperation must of course be based on the idea of the equality of states, noninterference in the internal affairs of each, and on reciprocal loyalty and friendship, the more so since our people rejects any relations of inequality."[132] And Mikoyan responded as presumably he had been sent to respond: "In supporting the Guinean people in their struggle to consolidate their independence the Soviet Union seeks no profit for itself, poses no political or other conditions; it has no intention of interfering in the internal affairs of your country or any other, or of imposing its ideology."[133] This reassurance given, he boarded a plane for Accra.

In Accra his reception was particularly warm, and throughout the visit Soviet newspapers continued to report the enthusiasm of the Ghanaian people for friendship with the Soviet Union. (They had not done this while Mikoyan was in Guinea.) Nkrumah chatted about vacationing in the Crimea, vaunted the splendor of Soviet achievements, and spoke enthusiastically of Soviet-Ghanaian cooperation.[134] But his excitement appeared modest beside the exuberance displayed by his Soviet guest.

Mikoyan praised the "splendid understanding" of international politics which Nkrumah demonstrated at the Belgrade conference as "clear and profound," and he acclaimed Ghana's contribution to the struggle against colonialism in Africa.[135] He went further and in one startling burst of flattery allowed that Ghana "had made great progress in building socialism." "Our parties operate under different conditions," he said; "they have a different history and different tasks," but we are brought nearer to each other by "your effort to build socialism." "Your party has assumed the task of stirring all people to attain and build socialism under African conditions." Mikoyan's remarks, because they were isolated and unconnected to prevailing theory, undoubtedly belong to that genre of praise designed primarily to please the listener's ear. Nevertheless, the

132. *Pravda,* January 9, 1962, p. 3.
133. Conakry radio (domestic service in French), 20.00 GMT, January 10, 1962.
134. *Pravda,* January 14, 1962, p. 4.
135. *Pravda,* January 13, 1962, p. 3.

simple fact that he was willing to make this remark in Accra (and not in Guinea) not only indicated a shift in preferences but, most important, the Soviet Union's special interest in Ghana. In April it was Nkrumah's turn to receive the Lenin Peace Prize.

Strengthening Ties with Mali

From Ghana, Mikoyan traveled next to Mali, the third West African member of the Casablanca grouping. Relations between the Soviet Union and Mali had burgeoned after the failure of the Mali Federation in August 1960, so that by the time Mikoyan arrived in Bamako in January 1962, the country was enjoying considerable Soviet political and material support.

Soviet leaders had strongly approved Mali's first demonstrations of independence—the abrogation of all treaties and agreements with France in October 1960, recognition of the Algerian Provisional Government and the Gizenga regime in February 1961, and the liquidation of French military bases in March—and they had moved quickly to entrench their influence in this country. They took the side of Malian leaders in condemning the Senegalese coup d'état, at times exceeding the Malians in the violence of their attack. In March they extended Mali $44 million in credits to assist with a broad range of development projects and created the basis for closer commercial relations by negotiating a trade agreement, leading to the immediate sale of five Ilyushin aircraft and several more Antonov-24s to Mali Airways.

As Guinea's most consistent ally within the Casablanca group, Mali rapidly acquired the reputation of being tropical Africa's second most revolutionary state, inspiring the Soviet Union to draw even more sharply the contrast between Mali and its erstwhile political partner, now a leader in the Brazzaville group. One Soviet visitor, for example, compared life in Senegal, a "semicolony" in the French community, to life in Mali, a country that had selected the path of "building a truly independent state."[136] In one, rich Europeans, living in luxurious, segregated quarters in Dakar, oppressed "poverty-stricken, disease-ridden" Africans. In the other, a "hard-working, frugal people enthusiastically participated in the building of the country."

Paradoxically Mali, like Guinea, seemed to the Soviet Union the most

136. V. Kuznetsov, "Dve Afrikanskie respubliki" (Two African Republics), *Aziya i Afrika segodnya*, no. 11 (1961), pp. 32–33, 47.

capable of making a direct transition to socialism because of its extreme backwardness. The absence of industry, which on the one hand retarded Mali's economic modernization, on the other, delayed significant class differentiation. Soviet analysts constantly stressed that the weakness of the bourgeoisie could facilitate Mali's escape from the capitalist phase of development. This advantage combined with a communal social pattern in the villages, undermining the concept of private property and strengthening modern cooperative structures, was thought to reduce the barriers to noncapitalist development and eventually to socialism.[137]

The "progressive" nature of the Malian government raised further Soviet expectations. Determined to achieve economic development through socialism, the regime, according to Soviet commentators, had already implemented measures intended to curb the influence of foreign monopolies, to expand the state sector, and to promote the spread of cooperative organization in agriculture. The creation of a national currency, an independent national bank, and a national transport executive, the subordination of external trade to government control, the augmentation of cooperative farming, and the institution of a five-year plan all "permit one to say that Mali is taking some steps in the direction of noncapitalist development."[138] These "democratic reforms" might one day "lead to a transition to socialism in the Marxist-Leninist sense."[139]

Significantly, however, Soviet descriptions insisted that Mali had not yet embarked on the noncapitalist path. This assessment, of course, fitted fully with the current, conservative appraisal of African socialism, even its most progressive strains. Yet because Mali's leadership boasted more than others about a program to build socialism, Soviet ideologists may have caused a certain irritation by contradicting its well-advertised claims. When President Keita proclaimed Mali's dedication to socialism during Mikoyan's January visit, his guest replied that the distance separating the two countries was great but that friendship drew them to-

137. See N. I. Gavrilov, "Respublika Mali—Molodoe nezavisimoe gosudarstvo Afriki" (The Republic of Mali—Young Independent African State), *Narody Azii i Afriki,* no. 4 (1961), p. 33; and Y. P. Dementyev, "Kooperirovanie v Maliskom derevne" (Cooperation in the Mali Countryside), *Mirovaya ekonomika i mezhdunarodnye otnosheniya,* no. 7 (1961), pp. 109–111. Dementyev was also the author of a short book on Mali, *Respublika Mali,* published in 1962.

138. Gavrilov, "Respublika Mali," p. 35.

139. G. Starushenko, "Cherez obshchedemokraticheskie preobrazovaniya k sotsialisticheskim" (Through Social Democratic Transformation to the Socialist), *Kommunist,* no. 13 (1962), p. 109.

gether.[140] When Keita stepped from his plane in Moscow in May 1962, and expressed his delight to be in the country first to undertake the construction of socialism, "which as you know, the government and people of Mali have selected as their own path," Khrushchev twice wished the Malian people success in "constructing a new life" but said nothing about socialism.[141] When Keita persisted, saying in another speech that Mali had chosen socialism over social inequality and human exploitation, Khrushchev politely responded that the "Soviet people can only welcome such a decision" but: "It would be wrong to think that it is enough to proclaim the slogan, 'We are for socialism' and then lie in the shade of a tree waiting for everything to arrange itself. No, great energy, persistence and labor are demanded of a people building socialism . . . We would like our Malian friends to see and understand the complexity of the tasks which arise in the building of a new society."[142] Scarcely a week earlier in Sofia, Khrushchev had delivered his sharp rebuke to "well-intentioned" African socialists who guarded the myth of class harmony and a middle road to socialism.

The Soviet Union was perfectly willing to accept Mali as an ally in the struggle against imperialism but not as a partner in socialism. Keita, like Touré and Nkrumah, had closely identified Mali's foreign policy with the foreign policy of the Soviet Union—supporting in their joint communiqué the Soviet approach to disarmament, peaceful coexistence, and the national liberation movement.[143] At one point he had gone beyond the endorsement of either Touré or Nkrumah to express the conviction that "So long as there are in the world two forces, victory will in the end be to the force that is the more dynamic. And this powerful idea will triumph, despite the attacks to which socialism is subjected by imperialism."[144] Comfort of this kind entitled Mali to reciprocal praise from the Soviet leadership and to a definite revolutionary status. It did not, though, overcome the Russians' reluctance to accept the Malian regime's view of itself.

The era of optimism had entered a new phase, disciplined largely by the course of events in Africa and not by the initiative of Kremlin policymakers. The expectations that Soviet leaders held for the future

140. *Pravda,* January 19, 1962, p. 4.
141. *Pravda,* May 22, 1962, p. 1.
142. *Pravda,* May 31, 1962, p. 1.
143. *Pravda,* June 1, 1962, p. 2.
144. *Pravda,* May 23, 1962, p. 1.

in Ghana, Guinea, and Mali—if, as we have seen, not without reservation—now provoked impatience toward the other countries of West Africa. No longer did these inspire tolerance, as they had in Africa's first year of independence. The emergence of a division in African politics redirected Soviet optimism. Vague hopes and spontaneous emotions snagged on specific political problems and the complications of events within Africa. No doubt Soviet writers would have become less gracious in their descriptions of Nigeria, and more critical of Senegal and the Ivory Coast, had there never emerged the Casablanca alternative, simply because the position adopted by these governments on a number of specific international questions disappointed, without altogether surprising, Soviet leaders. The existence of the Casablanca group, however, underscored the unsupportable quality of the "moderate" position. And the reality of antagonism between the two groups moved the Soviet Union to an exaggerated defense of its friends.

This argument, however, is based on the words of Soviet spokesmen, not on their deeds. Consequently the distinctions drawn among different African states, to the extent that they possess significance, relate more to Soviet attitudes than to Soviet activity. Not that the actions of Soviet diplomats, the foreign ministry, or the State Committee for Foreign Economic Relations seriously contradicted these attitudes. The feeble diplomatic connection between the Soviet Union and the states of the Monrovian group faithfully reflects the low position they occupied in Soviet estimations. On the other hand, no one could argue that the speeches of Khrushchev, Brezhnev, and Mikoyan embodied only private reactions rather than the substance of Soviet diplomatic activity. In looking at the process of policy formation—assessment and response—it is not easy to establish precise demarcations dividing one step from the next. Nor can the problem be skirted by arguing that the content of policy is essentially the exchange of parliamentary delegations, the work of an embassy first secretary, or the conclusion of a new agreement on economic cooperation—forgetting a *Pravda* article on the single-party system in Guinea, a radio broadcast to Africa on the Ivory Coast's collaboration with imperialism, or a special remark made by Khrushchev on African socialism.[145]

The fact that Soviet diplomacy merely betrayed preferences, whereas the public forum communicated hostility toward some African states, would not attract notice were it not for a further qualification. At the

145. See Note on Methodology.

same time that Soviet commentators were denigrating the political system and foreign policy of the so-called moderates, Soviet diplomats were gently pressing to increase diplomatic ties with these countries and even to expand economic and cultural relations. These countries, not Moscow, primarily obstructed the establishment and promotion of relations. The Soviet initiative was modest, hardly on a scale to make hypocrites of Soviet writers, and no more than a remnant of the early assumption that any African country, however conservative, belonged to the Afro-Asian movement. As a patron of this group, the Soviet Union believed that it should have diplomatic ties with all of its members.

V

Policy in Transition, 1962–1963

By the middle of 1962, considerations behind Soviet policy in Africa had changed significantly. The Algerian war was ended. The era of opportunity in the Congo had temporarily closed, if, as a Soviet diplomat might have dolefully wondered, it had ever existed. Once these crises passed from view, old jealousies and differences within the Casablanca group had prompted renewed interest in broader African unity, undercutting the reason for a sharp differentiation in Soviet policy toward African states. The vanguard nation in the African revolution, Guinea, had rebuffed its Soviet mentor and was now seeking new contacts with the West, in particular, the United States. China for the first time had generated more than nebulous sympathy among African members of the Afro-Asian People's Solidarity Organization. And the Common Market, which to the Soviet Union suddenly seemed a genuine peril, had begun to manifest greater interest in such crucial African countries as Nigeria.

Confronted with this combination of adverse developments, Soviet optimism gave way to a realism freed from the earlier illusions of short-term revolutionary gains. As seen from Moscow, the period of revolutionary change in Africa expired after 1961 and over the next year or so a gradual deflation in Soviet spirits set in. New realism reduced the former exuberance of Soviet comment to constraint and, at times, disappointment.

The Growing Effect of Chinese Competition

One of the Soviet Union's most galling preoccupations between 1961 and 1963 was the remarkably contemptuous challenge thrown down by China. Over the three years following the first public Chinese attacks on Soviet strategy and tactics, the dispute had degenerated into a bitter, open feud that engulfed all of Soviet relations, most particularly those with the countries of Asia and Africa. By 1963 even the practice of attacking the other side indirectly (the Soviet Union condemned Albania, and China, Yugoslavia) had been abandoned, and both parties, in a series of particularly vehement public manifestos, began to assail the other by name.

Month by month, the Chinese denounced more furiously the priorities of Soviet foreign policy. They carped about the Soviet Union's faithless betrayal of the national liberation revolution, maintaining that the Soviet Union wished to subordinate the legitimate struggle of oppressed peoples in Asia, Africa, and Latin America to the struggle for peace. Conjuring up the image of collusion between the Soviet leadership and imperialists, the Chinese charged that Soviet policymakers, with little compunction, were sacrificing the interests of Afro-Asia to this primary purpose. Soviet priorities, the Chinese suggested, accounted for the fright caused Soviet leaders by the prospect of "just" local wars. Soviet leaders were afraid that the "revolutionary storm" in colonial territories (say Algeria) would disrupt their efforts to curry favor with imperialist powers (say France). For this reason, said the Chinese, the Soviet Union peddled the struggle for peace and fostered the illusion that the imperialists might soon disarm.

By the end of 1961 Chinese dissension began to have a serious effect among the more militant leaders of Africa. Not all of Chinese policy toward Africa and not all points in the Chinese indictment of Soviet preferences were received sympathetically by African leaders. But from the Soviet point of view, the developing tendency of African friends to echo Chinese criticism of its policy priorities, and particularly the resistance they offered to the idea that the Soviet Union deserved an integral role in the Afro-Asian movement, must have been discomforting. That the Chinese challenge had impressed African leaders was evident late in 1961 at two important international conferences: the Fifth Congress of the WFTU (Moscow, December 4–15) and the World Peace Council meeting in Stockholm (December 16–19). At both conferences the issue of priorities—the peace struggle versus the national liberation struggle—dominated discussions. Although the large majority of participants at each meeting accepted the Soviet view that the struggle for peace and disarmament constituted the day's overriding priority, China found several of its most important allies among the African delegates. Where the controversy was most relevant, at the conference of the World Peace Council, Guinea spoke for the small cluster of disaffected African states. Addressing the conference a matter of days after Solod's expulsion, the Guinean delegate, Seydou Diallo, contended that the struggle for peace was inseparable from the struggle for freedom and independence. "Some say that the main content of our epoch is disarmament," he continued; "I say that the main content of our epoch is anti-imperialism, anti-colonialism and anti-racial discrimination."[1] Reversing Touré's previous support for Soviet efforts to achieve disarmament, he insisted that this "definitely should not be listed as the most important question" facing the world peace movement. With the energetic backing of the Chinese, Diallo tried to insert into the proposed agenda of a forthcoming peace congress the topic of independence. His initiative failed by a very sizable margin, but the support coming from other African delegates indicated that on this issue the Chinese enjoyed considerable sympathy among the African delegations. At the Moshi conference of A-APSO (February 4–11, 1963) the Guinean delegate, Mamadou Camara, continued the attack on Soviet priorities, insisting that the struggle for national liberation represented a critical aspect of the struggle for peace.[2] To the extent that African leaders were distracted by the problems of their own continent, it was natural that they should resent the apparent willingness of the Soviet Union to sacrifice these interests rather than jeopardize its own priorities in Western Europe.

Chinese leaders ridiculed the Soviet notion that the national liberation movement had entered a new stage whose principal characteristic was the struggle for economic independence. The national liberation movement had indeed reached a new stage, said the Chinese, "but this

1. Peking radio, New China News Agency (in English to Asia), 19.51 GMT, December 21, 1961.
2. Peking NCNA (in English to Asia and Europe), 15.03 GMT, February 13, 1963, and Accra radio (in English to Africa), 14.45 GMT, February 6, 1963.

is by no means the kind of 'new stage' described by the CPSU leader-ship."[3] Instead, in this new stage the political consciousness of oppressed people had risen higher than ever, demanding the equal development in political, economic, military, cultural, ideological, and other spheres of the struggle against imperialism. In fact, continued the Chinese, "the struggles in all these spheres still find their most concentrated expression in political struggle, which often unavoidably develops into armed strug-gle when the imperialists resort to direct or indirect armed suppression." Allegedly the Soviet Union had abandoned the real struggle against imperialism and colonialism, advocating instead economic development as the principal task of the national liberation movement.

Here, however, Chinese criticism evoked less sympathy. This part of the argument appealed little to African leaders, who themselves had set economic development as their primary goal. They accepted the Soviet position that efforts to achieve economic independence constituted the most important means for weakening neocolonialism, now the princi-pal obstacle to national liberation. Moreover, they suspected that in this instance the Chinese objected to Soviet priorities for other than purely ideological reasons. Because the Chinese lacked the economic resources to compete with the Soviet aid program, they presumably sought to depreciate the economic phase of the struggle against "imperialism, old and new colonialism and their lackeys." Betraying the disadvantage they felt, the Chinese directly assailed the Soviet program of economic as-sistance as a so-called "nostrum for all the ills of the oppressed nations." To speak plainly, said the Chinese, the policy and purpose of Soviet foreign aid should be questioned. In giving aid Soviet leaders "often take an attitude of great-power chauvinism and national egoism"; they attach conditions which "harm the economic and political interests of the receiving countries"; and they extend aid for "ulterior motives," as in the case of aid to India which was given "to encourage the Nehru government in its policies directed against Communism, against the peo-ple."[4] And to all this evidence the Chinese added the final incriminating fact that the Soviet government "openly proposes cooperating with the

3. Peking NCNA (in English to Asia and Europe), 15.03 GMT, October 21, 1963. This was the fourth in a series of comments on the July 1963 CPSU "open letter" and appeared in the *People's Daily* and *Red Flag,* October 21, 1963, under the title "Apologists of Neocolonialism." It represented the most explicit attack on Soviet strategy and tactics in the underdeveloped regions of the world to that date.

4. *Ibid.*

United States" in aiding the backward nations. Rather than depend on this kind of pernicious support, the Chinese urged the countries of Asia, Africa, and Latin America to rely on their own forces.

Despite these attempts to downgrade the importance of economic development, the Chinese leadership realized that the aspiration to modernize moved a larger number of Africans than did the hue and cry against colonialism, and that therefore they had no choice in the end but to compete with the Soviet program of economic assistance. In sub-Saharan Africa the Chinese had first reacted to the pressure of economic competition with an aid promise to Guinea during Touré's September 1960 visit. The next year, during a similar visit by Nkrumah, the Chinese increased their aid offensive with new credits to Ghana totaling $19.5 million and, one month later in September 1961, promised an identical sum to a Malian delegation led by Mali's minister of defense, Madeira Keita. In each case Chinese assistance clearly invited invidious comparison with already established Soviet programs. Chinese credits in every instance were longer-term, interest-free, and with a more generous period of grace.[5]

At the same time, the Chinese started an interesting, though not notably successful, push to enlarge the level of cooperation with West African moderates, particularly Nigeria. In early April 1961, Vice-Minister of Foreign Trade Lu Hsu-chang brought a delegation to Lagos to explore the possibility of establishing diplomatic relations and improving economic and cultural relations between the two countries. Two months later, the Nigerian government dispatched an important twenty-five-member economic delegation and the Minister of Finance Okotie-Eboh to China to discuss the matter further. A joint communiqué signed by the two sides agreed that the establishment of diplomatic relations would promote cooperation and friendship and that trade and cultural relations should be developed.[6] In the previous month Peking had sent a delegation from the Chinese-African Peoples' Friendship Association, headed by Liao Chang-sheng, to Senegal and several of the Entente states

5. Perhaps with Solod's experience in mind, on September 27, 1963, the Chinese press published the following comment: "Talking to the correspondents the Chinese gave unstinting praise to the hardworking intelligent Guinean workers who they said took pride in the work of building up a modern industry for their beloved country . . . They mastered their trades surprisingly fast. They have exploded the lie spread by those upholders of white supremacy that Guinean workers are lazy and stupid." Peking NCNA (in English to Asia and Europe), 15.36 GMT, September 27, 1963.
6. *Survey of the China Mainland Press,* no. 2523, June 23, 1961, pp. 34–35.

(Dahomey, Niger, and Upper Volta). The conversations between the delegation and the heads of state in most of these countries, however, presumably related more to the Chinese interest in supplanting the diplomatic presence of Nationalist China than to any thought of improving relations with members of the Brazzaville group before the Soviet Union had a chance to do the same.

None of these initiatives yielded a tangible success—either the opening of formal diplomatic relations or an increase in economic cooperation. The Nigerians did nothing to follow up their first contacts with the Chinese, not even toward establishing diplomatic relations. And in the case of the Entente states, the Chinese delegation had scarcely left than all traces of its visit vanished.

Nor did China's more extensive economic relations with Guinea, Ghana, and Mali permit it to displace the predominant Soviet influence in these countries. By the end of 1963, Soviet credits extended Guinea, Ghana, and Mali exceeded Chinese promises by $100 million. And if in the Soviet case less than 50 percent had actually been drawn down, the same figure for the Chinese hardly exceeded 15 percent. Between 1961 and 1963 Chinese imports from these three countries failed to reach one third of the level of Soviet imports, and Chinese exports remained even more feeble at one quarter of the level of Soviet exports. Obviously, then, China's decision to enter into competition with the Soviet aid program had not yet endangered the Soviet Union's advantage in West Africa. It was in other areas that the Chinese challenge to Soviet policy achieved success.

As a part of the attempt to belittle general Soviet policy, the Chinese also launched an effort to exclude the Soviet Union and its allied organizations from meetings of the Afro-Asian movement, an effort based ultimately on the appeal to race. This, as it turned out, became the most noisome aspect of the threat posed by the Chinese in the Third World. By the end of 1961 and the first months of 1962, the Chinese had moved beyond arguing with the Soviet viewpoint at A-APSO meetings to seeking the Soviet Union's exclusion from the organization. In December 1961 during an executive committee meeting of A-APSO at Gaza, UAR, the Chinese criticized Soviet participation in the controlling organs of the A-APSO and resisted the further development of relations between the WPC and Afro-Asian movement.[7] At the Cairo Afro-Asian

7. Lang, "La première conférence de solidarité des peuples d'Asie, d'Afrique et d'Amérique latine à la Havane," p. 5.

writers' conference held in February 1962, the Chinese began to tell Africans that "these Europeans are all the same . . . we non-whites must hold together."[8] By February 1963, at the third conference of A-APSO (Moshi, Tanganyika), the garish application of the race issue had become a permanent feature of Afro-Asian solidarity meetings.

To the distress of Soviet representatives, it was not merely that the Chinese raised the issue of race in the lobbies of the conference but, more seriously, that several delegations from Asia and Africa seemed to agree with the point, or so the Soviet Union thought. *Izvestiya*'s commentator, Vladimir Kudryavtsev, after attending the Moshi conference, bemoaned the determination of the "more chauvinistically-inclined" Afro-Asian leaders "to direct the solidarity movement not against imperialism, colonialism and its agents, but against all white people."[9]

It is, of course, conceivable that Kudryavtsev did not really believe that African leaders had weakened in their disdain for racist tactics and that he sought instead to discredit opposition to heavy Soviet involvement in Afro-Asian affairs—based not on racial grounds but on reasons of history and level of development—by attaching the stigma of racism to those responsible. That is, a number of African delegations believed that the Soviet Union, despite its pretensions to be an Asian nation, belonged essentially to Europe and that it therefore lacked the qualifications for membership in Afro-Asian organizations. These were feelings founded not on a sense of racial exclusiveness, but on the conviction that the geographical notion of Asia and Africa delineated areas facing common problems and thus offered the basis for common identification. (They had no difficulty, for example, in projecting the extension of the Afro-Asian movement to include the white countries of Latin America.) The Soviet Union, however, saw in this attitude the repugnant signs of racism. "They pretend," wrote Kudryavtsev, "that the liberation of Asia, Africa, and Latin America is possible even without the participation of progressive organizations [front organizations such as the WPC, WFDY, and WFTU controlled by the Soviet Union] . . . without those white people who because of their views actively fight against imperialism and its colonial attributes."[10]

8. *Daily Nation* (Nairobi), March 12, 1962, quoted in W.A.C. Adie, "China, Russia and the Third World," *China Quarterly*, no. 11 (July–September 1962), p. 208.
9. V. Kudryavtsev, "Problems of Afro-Asian Solidarity," *International Affairs*, no. 5 (1962), p. 52.
10. *Ibid.*

For their part, the Chinese left no doubt that the effort to exclude the Soviet Union and East Europe from Afro-Asian organizations rested on an appeal for racial unity. At both the preparatory session in Cairo and the Moshi conference, the Chinese worked to bar representatives from East Europe and from Soviet-dominated front organizations, saying, according to the Soviet open letter in July, that "the whites have nothing to do here."[11] During the same period, at a planning meeting for the Afro-Asian journalists' conference, the Chinese succeeded in reducing Soviet participation to observer status, and at the conference itself (April in Djakarta) when Outer Mongolia urged admitting Soviet representatives as full delegates, its proposal failed by an overwhelming margin.[12] The Soviet Union must have been rankled by the apparent willingness of Guinea and Ghana to accept the Chinese argument that it had no business being part of Afro-Asian solidarity organizations. Guinea, for example, openly backed Chinese proposals to circumscribe Soviet participation at Moshi and later meetings of the Afro-Asian movement. Foreign Minister Louis-Lansana Beavogui told a plenary session of the Djakarta preparatory meeting for the Second Afro-Asian Conference (April 10–14, 1964) that despite the Soviet Union's "excellent relations with Africa," it was nevertheless a European country. "If it were said that part of the Soviet Union lay in Asia, the same might be said of the USA with Hawaii, Puerto Rico, etc."[13]

More than this restrictive definition of Afro-Asia, the Soviet leadership resented insinuations by prominent, and otherwise sympathetic, African leaders that Soviet policy actually injured the interests of Africa. At Moshi, Julius Nyerere, the host president—and, by Soviet description, "one of the outstanding leaders of the new Africa"—startled the conference by accusing the Soviet Union of taking part in "a second invasion of Africa . . . more dangerous than the first."[14] He contended that the rich capitalist states and the "rich socialist countries" were using their wealth not to wipe out poverty but to "gain might and prestige" and

11. *Pravda,* July 14, 1963, reprinted in trans. in William E. Griffith, *The Sino-Soviet Rift* (Cambridge: MIT Press, 1964), p. 296.

12. Griffith, *The Sino-Soviet Rift,* pp. 125–126.

13. See Proceedings of the Meeting of Ministers in Preparation of the Second African-Asian Conference, April 10–14, 1964 (Djakarta; mimeo), p. 41. For the more ambiguous, and only slightly more reassuring, position of the Ghanaian delegation, see *ibid.,* pp. 53, 58. Interestingly, the Soviet press strongly condemned China and Pakistan for their behavior at this meeting without mentioning either Guinea or Ghana. *Pravda,* April 25, 1964, p. 3.

14. Kudryavtsev, "Problems of Afro-Asian Solidarity," p. 55.

that to do this they were both willing to disunite the African people by inciting country against country. Africa's inability to distinguish between friends and enemies puzzled Soviet spokesmen, and they concluded that statements such as Nyerere's were the "product not of African 'originality,' but of the subtle, corrupting propaganda of the neo-colonialists."[15] Nevertheless, warned Khrushchev, "this confused thinking pollutes the minds of the liberated peoples and makes it easier for the colonialists to preserve their positions in the young independent countries."[16]

Both the thought that Soviet policy might injure the objectives of Afro-Asian nations and that formal Soviet involvement in the Afro-Asian movement was not legitimate revealed again the collision between nationalism in the Third World and the interests of Soviet policy. By 1963 the policy of nonalignment no longer appeared invariably to be an aid to Soviet strategy, and the satisfaction this development gave to China heightened Soviet discouragement. Understating the way Soviet leaders felt, Kudryavtsev remarked that the atmosphere at conferences of A-APSO had changed since 1957 and "not all these changes have been for the better."[17]

Guinea's Retrenchment

No less than China's furious and partially successful attack on the Soviet position in the Third World, Guinea's swift turn toward the West accentuated Russia's disappointment. Only days after Solod departed from Conakry and Guinean students returned from the Soviet Union, Guinea veered unmistakably toward a restoration of economic relations with Western Europe and the United States. Over a period when Soviet trade with Guinea plummeted to scarcly half of its previous level, Touré concluded a series of new economic arrangements with the West. First West Germany's president Heinrich Lübke arrived in January to offer a $12 million aid program, and then in May Guinea and the United States signed an aid agreement for $12.5 million. In the time between these agreements Guinea applied for membership to both the International Monetary Fund and the World Bank, institutions previously denounced as instruments of imperialism.[18] In March after the Evian Ac-

15. *Ibid.*, p. 56.
16. *Ibid.*
17. *Ibid.*, p. 51.
18. Touré had been sympathetic to Attwood's recommendation that Guinea re-examine its attitude toward the IMF and the Bank before December 1961. See Attwood, *The Reds and the Blacks*, p. 41.

cords between France and Algeria, Touré announced that Guinea was "modifying its line of conduct" toward France and a few months later embarked on negotiations to settle financial responsibilities left over from the 1958 break.[19] The two countries reached a tentative agreement in May 1963 on their mutual debts, including pensions that France owed Guinean veterans of the French army and claims the French had against the Guinean government.[20] In addition, France agreed to resume its technical assistance program. Nothing came of these settlements, but at the time they appeared to underscore Guinea's shifting orientation. In April 1962, the Guinean government announced a more liberal investment code and several months later began discussions with a number of British, French, and American Aluminum companies (Harvey and Alcan) to develop Guinea's rich bauxite reserves in the Boké area. Over this same period, trade between Guinea and the Soviet Union fell from $31.1 million in 1961 to $22.4 million in 1962 to $16.3 million in 1963.[21]

Guinea had not, of course, repudiated its close economic relationship with the Soviet Union. Soviet technicians remained to continue construction on the Polytechnic Institute, a new sawmill, and prefabricated housing; Soviet geologists continued their survey of national resources; Soviet teachers still taught in the schools; and plans went ahead for a new Soviet-supported stadium, hotel, power plant, and so on. But Touré's glance to the West lent increased credibility to his public assurance that Guinea did not belong to the "east, the west, the north, the south, [only] to . . . progressive humanity."[22] Guinea, he said, had no desire to align itself blindly with any of the power blocs.[23] "The reality which dominates the life of our people, the thought which mobilizes our people,

19. Reuter dispatch from Conakry, Radio Free Europe (Munich), November 11, 1962.

20. *International Financial News Survey,* XV (June 7, 1963), 200. See also Georges Chaffard, *Les carnets secrets de la décolonisation,* II (Paris: Calmann-Lévy, 1967), 254–256.

21. *Vneshnyaya torgovlya SSSR za 1963 god* (Moscow, 1964), p. 239. Guinea's statistics for this period are not reliable. The Soviet statistics include, as mentioned earlier, all deliveries under suppliers' credits, as well as the normal commercial exchange, and so in one sense do not reflect the precise decline in trade, although in another sense they do indicate the slowdown in deliveries for Soviet aid projects—most of which were only getting underway in this period.

22. Touré's closing address to the Sixth Congress of the PDG, Conakry radio (domestic service in French), 20.00 GMT, December 31, 1962.

23. Touré's address to the inaugural session of the Sixth Congress of the PDG, Conakry radio (domestic service in French), 20.00 GMT, December 27, 1962.

is the ardent desire to *restore* the ties of cooperation with all countries of the world."[24]

In politics as well as economics, Touré manifested his spirited determination to remain independent of Soviet policy. This became particularly evident during the 1962 Cuban missile crisis. Less than two weeks before the crisis, Touré had been in Washington for talks with President Kennedy, held in an atmosphere described as "unusually cordial."[25] Touré praised Kennedy, saying that thanks to people like the president most of the African nations were today independent, and he invited Washington to expand its aid and economic cooperation programs in Guinea. During the missile crisis itself Touré denied permission to Soviet aircraft bound for the Carribbean to land on an airstrip that the Soviet Union had just lengthened to accommodate jet traffic.[26] According to former Ambassador Attwood: "On October 24 the Acting Foreign Minister, Alpha Diallo, confirmed to me that the Russians had requested landing rights in Conakry for long-range jets. But he told me not to worry; the government agreed with our stand on the missiles build-up, and Touré himself had made the decision to refuse the Soviet request."[27] Although the National Political Bureau of the PDG on November 6 condemned all foreign bases on Cuban soil, Touré reportedly asked Chester Bowles to convey to Kennedy his "general support for [the United States'] strong position regarding the missile bases in Cuba" together with his warmest regards.[28]

The Soviet Union never publicly responded to these actions; in fact, no part of Guinea's shift stirred overt criticism. From time to time an article appeared, reminding the Guineans that it was the Soviet Union who stood by them when France and its allies had tried to subvert their independence.[29] But Soviet commentators quietly dropped Guinea from their list of Africa's most progressive states. It was typical of the Soviet reaction that when in the fall of 1963 Guinea reorganized its internal retail trade, returning a large segment to the private sector

24. Touré's closing address to the Sixth Congress of the PDG, Conakry radio (domestic service in French), 20.00 GMT, December 21, 1962; emphasis added.

25. See *New York Times,* October 11, 1962, p. 1.

26. See *Afrique Express,* November 25, 1962; *Christian Science Monitor,* February 9, 1965, p. 3.

27. Attwood, *The Reds and the Blacks,* p. 109.

28. See *Horoya* (Guinea), November 11, 1962, and Reuter dispatch from Conakry, RFE (Munich), November 11, 1962.

29. See I. Vasilev, "Gvineya: Proshloe i budushchee" (Guinea: The Past and the Future), *Aziya i Afrika segodnya,* no. 10 (1963), pp. 3–10.

along with diamond prospecting, the Soviet press abstained from any comment. In general, Soviet leaders seemed eager not to worsen the friction already generated.

Mikoyan during his healing mission in January 1962 brought, in addition to conciliatory assurances that the Soviet Union would not meddle again, a new aid offer of $13 million. With him came Ambassador Solod's successor, Dimitri Degtyar, the former deputy chairman of the State Committee for Foreign Economic Relations. The old man seemed to his contemporaries in Conakry what one would have expected of a bureaucrat trained and expended in the application of foreign aid. They described him as kind but lackluster and befuddled by Africa. His principal task, so far as they could discern, was to oversee the completion of Soviet projects and, at a low key, to begin restoring Touré's spent confidence. Unlike his overweening and interfering predecessor or his cautious but active successor, Degtyar made no effort to ingratiate himself with the Guinean president, let alone give direction to Guinean politics or policy.[30]

Nevertheless, Degtyar found his commission a difficult one. For one reason or another, Soviet projects had fallen far behind schedule and Soviet officials were showing increasing uneasiness over this blot on their aid-giving record. Projects such as the polytechnic institute, refrigerated abattoir, and the power station scheduled for completion in 1963 or early 1964 were by 1963 barely underway. A primary reason for these delays, it was said, was Guinea's tardiness in finishing preparatory and auxiliary work—clearing land, opening access routes, supplying local material, and such. An even more serious obstacle stemmed from Guinea's decision to retain the supervision of actual construction, compounding normal delays with administrative inefficiency. To expedite matters, in June 1963, Soviet leaders sent Degtyar's old superior, Semen Skachkov, chairman of the State Committee for Foreign Economic Relations, to Guinea. He persuaded the Guinean government to transfer to Soviet officials the administrative control over the implementation of Soviet aid.

30. In one case Degtyar's embassy did complicate its existence by trying to smuggle out of the country a Soviet teacher of mathematics, who according to her own account had been "fraternizing socially with Guineans." She told a passport officer that she was being forced to leave by those accompanying her and he insisted that she be permitted to stay. Later she appeared similarly escorted without a passport but in an air hostess' uniform. She and her escort were arrested. *New York Herald Tribune*, February 7, 1963. The London *Daily Telegraph*, February 14, 1963, reported that Degtyar had been called in to the presidential residence, reprimanded, and reminded of his predecessor's fate. For full details of the affair see Attwood, *The Reds and the Blacks*, pp. 120–122.

(According to the protocol: "To increase the effectiveness of Soviet aid and technical assistance a Soviet construction organization will be responsible for the completion of works on schedule and for their quality."[31])

Thus after 1961 Soviet interests in West Africa had suffered a series of setbacks, most important being Guinea's defection from its firm alignment with Soviet policy and China's partial success in rallying the Afro-Asian solidarity movement against the Soviet Union. Add to this the unhappy turn of events in the Congo after Lumumba's defeat in September 1960, together with two successive "reactionary" coups d'état in Syria and Iraq during 1963 that led to the violent harassment of local Communists, and it is no wonder that Soviet enthusiasm for the national liberation revolution declined.

Response to the Frustrations of 1961–62

The Soviet Union reacted to these reverses by downgrading the importance it attached to the role of the developing countries in international affairs. In their July 14 open letter, Soviet leaders accused the Chinese of trying to win cheap popularity among the peoples of Asia, Africa, and Latin America by peddling the myth that the decisive force in the struggle against imperialism was not the world system of socialism, not the struggle of the international working class, but the national liberation movement.[32] This "new theory," argued Soviet ideologists, contradicted Leninism, for though it "goes without saying" that the national liberation movement constituted a great force in the world revolutionary process, "it is not the main arena of the international class struggle."[33] The most powerful forces of the world socialist revolution were concentrated elsewhere in "the revolutionary movement of the working class in the capitalist countries." The Chinese aimed, said another Soviet writer, to shift the center of the world revolution to the zone of the national liberation movement in an effort "to disparage the role of the Soviet Union, to discredit the socialist camp . . . by re-

31. Conakry radio (domestic service in French), 20.00 GMT, June 27, 1963.
32. Open letter in Griffith, *The Sino-Soviet Rift*, p. 316.
33. See the presentation of V. G. Korionov, "The Ideological Struggle and Present International Relations," *International Affairs*, no. 8 (1963), p. 13, given to a conference organized in July under the auspices of the agitprop section of the Moscow City Committee of the CPSU, the Institute of World Economics and International Relations, and the editorial board of *International Affairs*.

garding it (and particularly the industrially developed socialist countries) merely as an instrument of the national-liberation movement and a source of aid to the young national states rather than as the main force of the revolutionary transformation of *all* human society."[34] As another eminent Soviet commentator wrote, in practice the Chinese seek to "counterpose the Afro-Asian solidarity movement to the other progressive anti-imperialist movements of our times."[35] Being neither proletarian nor class-conscious, but "contradictory and heterogeneous in composition," the national liberation movement could hardly be the single decisive force in the world revolution. To think that the national liberation movement alone could cause the downfall of imperialism was simply to present under a different name the old bourgeois notion of the "chosen people" or "special people superior to the white race," substituting the " 'unity' of certain races and nations" for "proletarian solidarity."

The frustrations of 1962 and 1963 contributed to a second shift in the Soviet attitude toward the national liberation movement, a shift that was to be of far greater consequence and far more permanent than the depreciation of the role of Afro-Asia. Left without active revolutionary situations once the Algerian and Congo crises expired, and dispirited by the course of events in Guinea, Iraq, and the Afro-Asian solidarity movement, the Soviet leadership altered considerably its pledge to the revolutionary leaders of the Third World. By implication it publicly abandoned the possibility of intervening directly to salvage "democratic revolutions." Promises born of optimism and inspired by the prospect of early revolutionary advances were obsolete by 1962.

Often during the previous three years Khrushchev and his colleagues had assured nations "struggling for independence" that if the United Nations remained ineffective, as in the case of the Congo, the "peace-loving states" would act on their behalf. Although Soviet leaders took care not to disrupt their priorities in and outside Africa by giving injudicious support to subversion, and although they as a rule advertised their commitment to peaceful revolution, they had maintained a secondary commitment to "direct action," in non-Marxist terms, to direct or indirect intervention. From the Congo to Laos, the Soviet Union had provided material encouragement for insurrection, over and again

34. A. Chernyayev, *Pravda,* August 3, 1963, quoted in Griffith,. *The Sino-Soviet Rift,* p. 163. See also *Pravda,* August 4, 1963, for a similar statement by the Soviet government.
35. G. Mirsky, in *Izvestiya,* July 16, 1963, p. 2.

repeating its willingness to do even more. Whatever Chinese accusations were concerning Soviet betrayal of popular uprisings and wars of liberation, Khrushchev, in his tough public pronouncements of early 1961, convinced at least President Kennedy of the Soviet Union's enduring faith in victory through rebellion, subversion, and guerrilla warfare.[36] The airlift of arms and ammunition to the Pathet Lao, the trucks and aircraft supplied to the Lumumbists, the Soviet weapons funneled into Latin America through Cuba, demonstrated that the Soviet leadership had no wish to eschew the promotion of revolution where it promised to hasten the triumph of favorable regimes. And in Angola, the Congo, Portuguese Guinea, not to mention countries in Southeast Asia, the Middle East, Central America, and South America, guerrilla war still seemed to the Soviet Union an attractive investment.

West Africa's role, as the Soviet leadership evidently envisaged it, was to serve as a depot for materials going to countries where the torch of insurrection had already been fired, and in some cases to train freedom fighters for these ventures. The Soviet Union was less interested in sponsoring subversion against stable, independent regimes in the Ivory Coast, Nigeria, Liberia, Sierra Leone, and the other countries of this area, despite their disagreeable internal politics and external policies. Little evidence exists to prove that Soviet representatives ever gave more than living allowances and organizing funds to groups such as the National Liberation Committee for the Ivory Coast and the PAI. The ill-equipped and poorly planned (perhaps spontaneous) attempt by the PAI to disrupt Senegal's 1960 elections indicates, if anything, that the Soviet Union refused to make a heavy material commitment to this kind of activity. On the other hand, shipments of military equipment, sizable by African standards, flowed into Guinea, Mali, and Ghana between 1959 and 1961. One study, for example, said that Guinea had received eight thousand rifles for its two-thousand-man army and speculated that the extra rifles may have been intended for re-export to other parts of Africa.[37] London newspapers reported that Ghana was running Soviet and Czech guns into Angola, and General Alexander mentions a consignment of arms from the East unloaded at Takoradi port which Nkrumah hinted to him were promised to Gizenga.[38]

36. Schlesinger, *A Thousand Days*, p. 303.
37. Study of the Atlantic Research Corporation.
38. *Sunday Telegraph*, May 14, 1961, and Alexander, *African Tightrope*, pp. 99–100.

In addition, the Soviet Union extended token assistance to early proto-types of Nkrumah's future subversion camps. These were administered by the Bureau of African Affairs, an institutional ploy developed by Nkrumah in 1960 to circumvent the foreign ministry in the conduct of relations with other African countries.[39] Established outside the control of the ministry and under the immediate direction of A. K. Barden (by everyone's account, an irresponsible opportunist), the bureau eventually became the operations center for the less public features of Nkrumah's African policy. During his July 1961 visit to the Soviet Union, Nkrumah had arranged for Soviet participation in these camps—organized to train so-called freedom fighters from still colonially oppressed territories. (The problem was that Nkrumah defined "freedom fighters" rather broadly and from the start included a number from neighboring independent states.) When the first camp opened in December 1961 at Mampong, the Soviet Union contributed two of the teaching staff.[40] They remained for only one six-month "term," however, and then departed. Significantly, they were not replaced. Not only were Soviet officials disconcerted by a totally inept operation, but they found this kind of activity generally of diminishing value.

By the middle of 1962, the Soviet commitment to subversion and guerrilla warfare had largely dissolved, and only ritualistic incantations of support for the struggle of oppressed peoples echoed from the Kremlin. Soviet advisers left Nkrumah's camp before June,[41] and over 1962 and 1963 Soviet military assistance to Mali, Guinea, and Ghana virtually ceased.[42] Simultaneously Soviet spokesmen issued a significantly revised guarantee to those fighting for national independence. No longer did they speak of the Soviet Union's determination to intervene directly to rescue besieged democratic revolutions (as during the Congo crisis), nor did they repeat Khrushchev's bellicose endorsement of subversion and guerrilla warfare. They promised instead "broad moral, political,

39. See Thompson, *Ghana's Foreign Policy*, p. 107.

40. *Communist Influence in Nkrumah's Ghana* (May 1966), p. 25, published by *African Review*. See also *ibid.*, p. 226.

41. Private comments by a former highly placed official in the Bureau of African Affairs. This official was seconded to the BAA in June 1962, by which time the Soviet participants had departed.

42. Bell, "Military Assistance to Independent African States," pp. 10–13. Similarly, "after the July 1962 Geneva accords on Laos, Khrushchev had decided to abandon any active policy in Southeast Asia and had therefore refused to increase Soviet military and economic aid to Hanoi." William E. Griffith, *Sino-Soviet Relations, 1964–1965* (Cambridge: MIT Press, 1967), p. 67.

and material support" to the national liberation movement.[43] In areas where people were battling openly for national independence, "this support takes the form of constant diplomatic struggle, the unmasking of the colonialists and the mobilization of public opinion in defense of the oppressed peoples." In areas "fighting for economic independence . . . the support of the socialist camp also takes the form of extensive economic aid."[44] Moreover, the Soviet Union left no doubt that it assigned primary importance to this second storm center of the national liberation movement. If, as the Chinese comrades asserted, the only effective weapons of revolution were firearms, challenged one writer in *Pravda*, "how are they to be used to solve the basic problem of the modern national liberation movement, which is to bring about the liquidation of economic backwardness and to achieve economic independence?"[45] At the close of the era of optimism, revolution making seemed increasingly a risky and diverting enterprise. It was, moreover, a factor that obstructed the Soviet Union's impending effort to expand connections with the so-called moderate states of Africa.

Effects of the Waning Casablanca-Monrovian Division

During 1962 and 1963 Soviet policy toward West Africa was changing in still another significant respect. On the one hand, events in Guinea and the support of some African leaders for aspects of the Chinese position moved the Soviet leadership to downgrade the national liberation movement and to modify the kind of backing it was willing to give the liberation struggle. On the other hand, the simultaneous weakening of the Casablanca-Monrovian split softened Soviet attitudes toward the less militant neighbors of Guinea, Ghana, and Mali. Once problems inspiring the rupture between these two groups of states receded, the underlying desire for broader African unity re-emerged. Working settlements in the Congo and Algeria, reached during 1961 and 1962, reduced the bitterness that had held each group together and both groups apart. Without this restraint, differences within the Casablanca group—between Nkrumah and Nasser and between Nkrumah and Touré—reappeared,

43. Editorial in *Kommunist*, no. 2 (January 1962), p. 18. See also Y. Dolgopolov, "National Liberation Wars in the Present Epoch," *International Affairs*, no. 2 (1962), pp. 17–21, and V. Matveyev, "Wars of Liberation and Diplomacy," *International Affairs*, no. 3 (1963), pp. 69–72.

44. *Ibid.*, p. 19.

45. L. Stepanov, in *Pravda*, July 18, 1963, p. 3.

further destroying the group's cohesion. Thus more than a year before Africa's independent states met at Addis Ababa to form the Organization of African Unity, two interrelated developments were set in motion which caused a substantial modification in Soviet policy toward Africa. The growing commitment to African unity and emerging frictions within the Casablanca group undermined the basis for a sharp differentiation in the Soviet approach.

When the Cairo conference of the Casablanca nations adjourned in June 1962, its noticeably moderate communiqué contained pleas for greater unity and a proposal to form an association of African states.[46] That same month in Moscow, Senegal's prime minister, Mamadou Dia, spoke of the need to build bridges between the Monrovia and Casablanca groups.[47] And in Africa Sekou Touré and the Emperor of Ethiopia had already agreed to work toward the consolidation of the two groups.[48] The change in atmosphere could not be missed. Six months earlier, the lingering influence of the Algerian problem, together with Nkrumah's intrigues, had wrecked Nigeria's attempt to bring together heads of state from the two groups at a conference in Lagos. But now the tensions were easing.

The movement toward unity tended to blur the distinctions in various African foreign policies and hence tended to remove the basis for the Soviet Union's classification of states. The process was accentuated by telltale irritations arising within the Casablanca group. No doubt Soviet leaders were attuned to the differences emerging among the Casablanca powers, particularly the deterioration in relations between Ghana and Guinea. Touré's relationship with Nkrumah had never been a particularly fond one, despite their common membership in the Casablanca group, their political union with Mali, and Ghana's significant economic aid to Guinea following the 1958 referendum. The two leaders had clashed bitterly over what position should be adopted in the Congo crisis and, in particular, toward the UN operation. Following President Olympio's assassination in January 1963, an affair that many African leaders whispered had involved Nkrumah, Touré wired the Ghanaian president condemning his government's hasty recognition of the new Togolese government.[49] Nkrumah's entourage had for several weeks been

46. *Guardian,* June 19, 1962, p. 9.
47. *Pravda,* June 15, 1962, p. 4.
48. Thompson, *Ghana's Foreign Policy,* p. 220.
49. Ken Post, *The New States of West Africa* (Baltimore: Penguin Books, 1964), p. 173.

delivering intemperate threats against the Togolese government, and though it seems unlikely that Ghana actually played a role in Olympio's murder, Touré was sufficiently enraged to demand an international investigation of the whole affair.[50] Touré later joined efforts with the Nigerian prime minister to keep the new Togolese regime from attending the Addis Ababa conference, since neither of their countries yet recognized the Togolese government. Moreover, less than a month before Addis Ababa during Touré's visit to Nigeria, after "considering the recent events which disturbed African political life," the two leaders signed a joint communiqué reaffirming the "strict necessity of noninterference in the internal affairs of other states" and the necessity of searching for measures to prevent subversion in Africa.[51]

Touré's disaffection with Nkrumah involved more than an aversion to his ally's apparent willingness to subvert governments unamenable to Ghanaian influence; he objected as well to Nkrumah's program for Africa's political development. When Nkrumah circulated to a pre-summit meeting of foreign ministers a draft plan for African unity, calling for an elaborate political union with a single foreign policy, a common set of diplomatic representatives, and a common economic and industrial plan, Touré denounced the idea as an attempt on Nkrumah's part to promote his own ambitions.[52] Already Touré had attacked Nkrumah's conception of African unity before the United Nations, dismissing it as a "doctrinal theory" impeding "honest cooperation."[53] At the Addis Ababa conference in May 1963, Touré joined Balewa, Haile Selassie, and a number of other African leaders, both moderate and radical, who firmly rejected political integration and urged instead a functional approach to unity founded on economic and cultural cooperation.

The shift in Soviet attitude toward moderate African states no doubt received further reinforcement from the course of events in Guinea. Before, when Guinea's pattern of development promised an early arrival of the socialist revolution in Africa, any nation whose political course ran contrary to this vision was treated with considerable suspicion and hostility. When Guinea's progress turned out to be illusory, Soviet leaders could not be so confident that the path followed by Senegal, the Ivory Coast, and other such countries was imminently doomed. No longer

50. Thompson, *Ghana's Foreign Policy*, p. 313.
51. Conakry radio (domestic service in French), 07.00 GMT, April 30, 1963.
52. *New York Times,* May 20, 1963, p. 7.
53. Thompson, *Ghana's Foreign Policy,* p. 307.

was indifference an adequate guideline for policy. Thus both the passing of the formal rift between the Casablanca and the Monrovian nations and the demise of Soviet-Guinean solidarity combined to promote renewed interest in broader contact with Africa.

By the middle of 1962 the Soviet Union had good reasons for wanting to increase relations with a wider range of African countries. All that seemed to stand in the way was the lingering wariness of moderate African leaders toward increased involvement with the Soviet Union. In June, an editorial in *New Times* underscored the Soviet Union's desire to develop "good relations" with the Brazzaville countries.[54] The Soviet Union was one of the first great powers to recognize the independence of these countries and to propose diplomatic relations, recounted the editorial, "but cooperation and friendship is a two-way street." Quoting Khrushchev's remark that "you cannot clap with one hand," the editorial contended that "it was not the Soviet hand that was wanting."[55] Nevertheless, the editorialist expressed his confidence that diplomatic relations recently established with Dahomey heralded a new readiness to deal with the Soviet Union.

And indeed there were signs that the reluctance of many African leaders to open diplomatic relations with the Soviet Union had dwindled. The visit of Senegal's prime minister, Mamadou Dia, to the Soviet Union from June 5 to June 15 reflected a willingness to undertake increased relations with the Soviet Union—together with the limitations attached to this willingness.

In welcoming the prime minister to the Soviet Union, Khrushchev stressed his country's desire to develop good relations with the African states, based on complete equality, noninterference, and respect for the other's sovereignty.[56] Khrushchev made clear the nature of the relationship he had in mind: "We are in favor of developing businesslike and useful cooperation and strengthening trust and friendship between all peoples and countries." Dia, in turn, referred to Senegal's eagerness to receive all ideas and all people with the single condition that "these people respect [its] independence and its individuality."[57] With memorable candor, he told his hosts that Senegal had selected socialism as

54. "The Soviet Union and Africa," *New Times*, no. 25 (June 20, 1962), p. 2.
55. *Ibid.*, p. 3.
56. *Pravda*, June 6, 1962, p. 1.
57. *Ibid.*

its path of development, but socialism proceeding from Senegal's natural economic and social conditions, not from theoretical schemes. "We say at the same time that we do not want to be dogmatists. And I want to say to you, since I am bound to be frank here, that we do not pretend to be Marxist-Leninists. We are above all, people of good will, concerned over the future of our country and greatly determined to master the lessons of history." His theme was that Senegal stood ready to do more than simply coexist with the Soviet Union, that it wished to cooperate with the Soviet Union and to learn from its experience. On his return to Senegal Dia said: "I repeat that I am not coming back as a convert to Communism, but I am convinced that what is happening over there is extremely important and that countries like ours cannot ignore it. A new world and even a new humanism is being created."[58] While in the Soviet Union, Dia had signed a trade agreement, an agreement on economic and technical cooperation, a convention on cultural cooperation, and an agreement to exchange diplomatic representation at the embassy level.

But Dia had also stressed that Senegalese-Soviet cooperation was conditionally founded on the good behavior of Soviet representatives. Initially the atmosphere of his conversations with Khrushchev had been uneasy, held taut by the Soviet leader's grotesquely playful approach to diplomacy. On their first working encounter, Khrushchev had startled his guest by saying, "I don't know if you are aware or not that I am a Leninist Communist: Perhaps you knew that? I have a little secret to confide to you, Comrade Gromyko here is also a Communist . . . there are a number of communists in the world, you know."[59] Khrushchev rolled on: without the theory of Marxism-Leninism a country was like a man blindfolded, advancing without knowing where he was going. He would butt his head against the wall again and again, but eventually he would come around to socialism, for he could not escape history. "You will see," he said. As his guests stirred, Khrushchev turned to his subordinates for agreement, adding, "You are not of our Party. You are not Communists. Not yet."[60] Agitated, Dia interrupted Khrushchev with the admonition, "I don't think you really expect that of me," and

58. Paris Agence France Presse (in French to Africa and Madagascar), 10.25 GMT, June 27, 1962.

59. Joseph Ma Thiam (Senegalese Commissaire Adjoint au Plan), *L'Unité Africaine* (Senegal), July 10, 1962, p. 6. Thiam was a member of the Senegalese delegation.

60. *Ibid.*, p. 7.

Khrushchev smiled and replied, "Oh no, I only expect cooperation and peace." When the first Soviet chargé arrived in Dakar four months later, Senegal's foreign minister, Doudou Thiam, drew careful attention to two principles of his country's foreign policy: strict nonalignment and noninterference in the internal affairs of other nations. For emphasis he repeated the warning three times.[61]

In the case of the Soviet attitude toward Nigeria, the key member of the Monrovia group, a further consideration aroused special concern among Soviet policymakers: the Soviet Union's sudden anxiety over the Common Market, stirred by Great Britain's application for membership in the EEC. Elsewhere Western commentators have recounted how over 1962 Soviet fears, stimulated by the Common Market's growing attraction for members of the European Free Trade Association, sparked a vast and energetic offensive to discredit the EEC and to discourage other countries from seeking association with it.[62] Because the terms for Britain's admission to the Common Market opened the possibility of association for some members of the Commonwealth, English-speaking Africa and, in particular, Nigeria, became one front for this offensive.

The task of Soviet policy was not to persuade Nigerian leaders to reject association in the event that Britain did join, for the Nigerians

61. *Dakar-Matin* (Senegal), October 16, 1962, p. 1.

62. See Marshall D. Shulman, "The Communist States and Western Integration," *International Organization,* XVII (Summer 1963), 649–662. Khrushchev selected Modibo Keita's visit to the Soviet Union as the moment for delivering his first major public attack on the Common Market. Denouncing the Common Market as an economic front for NATO, he warned the Malian president that it reincarnated colonialism, seeking to preserve Africa as a raw-material-supplying appendage to Europe. If the timing of Khrushchev's remarks had particular significance, it was that Mali as one of the eighteen associated members of the Common Market would shortly be negotiating a new instrument of association, and the Soviet Union surely aspired to influence the position it would adopt. Negotiations for a new convention to replace the old one expiring at the end of 1962 promised to be difficult because France wished to eliminate its subsidies on the purchase of tropical products and the African countries were insisting that the development fund expand beyond what the Six were willing to offer. In these circumstances Mali, a country that publicly worried a great deal about neocolonialism, might be persuaded to harden its view toward the Common Market. If so, Keita's remarks gave no indication that Soviet hopes were well founded and, although Khrushchev dwelled at length on the dangers of the EEC, the joint Soviet-Malian communiqué contained no reference to it. (See *Pravda,* May 31, 1962, p. 2, and June 1, 1962, p. 2.) A month later, when the premier of Senegal, a country unswerving in its commitment to the EEC, was in the Soviet Union, the subject scarcely reached the public.

had repeatedly declared their unwillingness to associate with an "essentially political" organization; association with the EEC, they had said many times, would be incompatible with Nigeria's policy of nonalignment.[63] Instead Soviet leaders were trying to trade on Nigeria's alarm over Britain's prospective entry into the EEC. To some extent they succeeded. In October 1962 the Nigerian government reminded England and Europe of its commercial alternatives by lifting restrictions on the export of columbite, an additive used to harden steel in nuclear and space devices. Henceforth, columbite could be shipped to "all destinations," including the Soviet Union.[64] In July 1963 Nigeria and the Soviet Union concluded a trade agreement intended to increase trade in a number of products, specifically listing columbite.

Nevertheless, the uncertainty persisted that if Britain were to join the EEC, Nigeria might find itself involuntarily compelled by economic necessity to retreat from its opposition. Soviet spokesmen, praising Nigeria's determination to remain free of the Common Market, so often quoted Balewa's public statements opposing the EEC that it began to seem as if they were trying to convince themselves that Nigeria could resist the allure of association.[65]

Nigeria's association with the EEC represented not only a threat to whatever limited trading opportunities the Soviet Union saw in that country but, of greater importance, a danger to Soviet hopes for developing a large trade with Ghana. Nkrumah had scornfully renounced any intention of associating with the Common Market, but Nigeria's membership, because it was a competitive producer of Ghana's major exports, would have made it difficult for him to resist. For this reason the Soviet Union diligently reminded Nigerians of their determination to refuse associate status in the Common Market.

In the eyes of Soviet analysts, Nigeria enjoyed the most favorable reputation among the Monrovian states. A comparison between firsthand reports on the Lagos conference held in January 1962 and retrospective accounts of the same conference published in October 1962 reveals both the shift occuring in Soviet attitudes during the year as well as the

63. Ali A. Mazrui, "African Attitudes to the European Common Market," *International Affairs* (London), XLI (January 1963), 253.

64. Douglas G. Anglin, "Nigeria: Political Non-Alignment and Economic Alignment," *Journal of Modern African Studies*, II, no. 2 (1964), 252.

65. See E. Onan, "Nigeriya razoblachaet lovushku" (Nigeria Unmasks the Trap), *Aziya i Afrika segodnya*, no. 6 (1963), pp. 7–9.

new favor with which the Soviet press treated Nigeria by the end of 1962. Original accounts of the conference, appearing in *Komsomolskaya pravda* and *Izvestiya,* criticized the entire membership of the Monrovia group, except Ethiopia, which alone, the accounts said, "had no desire to participate in pro-imperialist groupings."[66] All others, including Nigeria, "were not free in matters of either foreign or internal policy"; all owed allegiance to old colonial masters, with whom they had collaborated in calling this conference. However, ten months later, a second look at the same conference assigned a somewhat different role to Nigeria.[67] According to the reappraisal, Nigeria had all along wanted to invite representatives of the Algerian government to the Lagos conference, but had failed in the face of opposition from the Brazzaville group. The same states had also defeated Nigeria's efforts to pass a resolution fixing 1970 as the final date for the abolition of colonialism in Africa. For its efforts, however, Nigeria now received the same rating as Ethiopia and Somalia, states said to be resisting the Paris-inspired line of the Brazzaville group and seeking "to a greater or lesser extent" unity with the Casablanca group—an argument, incidentally, which demonstrates Soviet sensitivity to efforts afoot to promote the dissolution of blocs in African affairs.

During the following months Soviet and East European writers commended, in more specific terms, the favorable direction of Nigeria's foreign policy. One commentator wrote that Nigeria recently had been following a course "which places greater emphasis than heretofore on the struggle against colonialism and on African unity."[68] Contrary to the previous "reserved" attitude displayed toward NATO, Nigeria now openly attacked the NATO powers for supporting the South African apartheid regime and the Portuguese campaign of aggression in Africa. According to the same observer, Nigeria's new trade agreement with the Soviet Union demonstrated that "ruling circles" in Nigeria—"under the pressure of popular masses"—did not wish to tie their policy only to the West. A Soviet journalist echoed similar praise, noting that Nigeria now enjoyed "increasing prestige on the continent and internationally . . . largely due to its policy of non-alignment and the stand taken by Nigerian delegations at the Geneva disarmament talks and the Addis

66. See *Mizan,* IV (February 1962), 19–20.
67. "The Monrovian Group of African States," *International Affairs,* no. 10 (1962), pp. 114–115.
68. Fred Boeticher, in *Neues Deutschland,* July 30, 1963.

Ababa summit conference."[69] He also referred enthusiastically to Nigeria's opposition to apartheid in South Africa and to popular support in Nigeria for businesslike ties with the Soviet Union.

However, neither the increasingly friendly evaluation of Nigerian foreign policy nor the decision to exchange diplomatic relations with Senegal and other members of the Brazzaville group, marked a fundamental shift in Soviet policy. For reasons already discussed, Soviet attitudes toward these countries had mellowed sufficiently to warrant experimental efforts to develop broader contacts; at the same time, improved relations with the moderate countries reflected greater readiness on the part of their leaderships to enter into direct contact with the Soviet Union. Yet these efforts scarcely heralded a major Soviet diplomatic and political offensive among the Monrovian group.

Attitudes had not changed sufficiently to prompt this kind of reversal in Soviet policy. An interesting dialogue over the merits of some varieties of African socialism appearing in Soviet journals during 1962 produced, if anything, a more critical view of leaders like Senghor, who continued to foresake scientific socialism in defending a third route to political and economic modernization.[70] Some African leaders who "sincerely favor socialism," contended one observer, were weighed down by a burden of prejudice, utopian illusions, and the muddled ideas of social reformists.[71] They seriously believed that it would be possible to have as many socialisms as there are states and that socialism could be built without following the example or drawing on the experience of the Soviet Union. Nigerian leaders, for example, interpreted basic social and economic phenomena in a fashion "very different from the scientific concept of socialism."[72] According to Soviet commentators, all three

69. Mikhail Kozlov, "Nigeria Discusses the Future," *New Times,* no. 27 (July 10, 1963), p. 16. See also L. Pribytkovsky and L. Fridman, "The Choice before Nigeria," *International Affairs,* no. 2 (1963), pp. 75–80.

70. "Sovremennaya epokha i puti razvitiya osvobodivshikhsya stran" (Paths of Development for the Liberated Countries at the Present Stage), *Mirovaya ekonomika i mezhdunarodnye otnosheniya,* no. 3 1962), pp. 20–49, and no. 5 (1962), pp. 85–108; Potekhin, "Nekotorye problemy afrikanistics," pp. 6–16; V. Kudryavtsev, "Fighting Africa's Daily Round," *International Affairs,* no. 10 (1962), pp. 51–57; G. Mirsky, "Whither the Newly Independent Countries," *International Affairs,* no. 12 (1962), pp. 23–27.

71. K. Brutents, "The October Revolution and Africa," *New Times,* no. 45 (November 7, 1962), p. 10.

72. Pribytkovsky and Fridman, "The Choice before Nigeria," p. 77.

major political parties in Nigeria defended a bogus socialism founded
on the delusion that private enterprise could be made to coexist with
public enterprise and that foreign capital should be attracted into the
country and protected against nationalization. Typical, they said, was
the pragmatic socialism of the NCNC, an "extremely ill-defined concept,"
which had "nothing in common with scientific socialism."[73] In the case
of other moderate African leaders, Soviet analysts depicted their dedication to socialism as "merely a screen for reactionary pro-imperialist activities," created to disguise their hostility toward the socialist countries.[74]

Thus shifts in Soviet behavior, produced by the fading prospects of
revolution in Africa and the weakening of divisions among African states,
did not mean that the Soviet assessment of these leaders had similarly
softened. It was the changing international environment within Africa
as well as the growing ability of Soviet leaders to judge opportunities
more accurately that made them seek improved relations with these
regimes—not progress they saw within these societies. On the contrary,
their opinion of moderate African leaders remained harshly critical.
When in December 1962 Senghor survived a physical test of power
with his prime minister, Mamadou Dia, by deposing and imprisoning
him, Kudryavtsev remarked that "the imperialists do not necessarily
have to do this dirty work themselves, since they have agents who were
carefully groomed and bred in the spirit of Western 'civilization' during
colonial rule."[75] Significantly, the reasons for this move never seemed
to be an issue; the Russians were using it as a pretext for an attack
on Senghor.[76] In the same spirit, Soviet writers dwelt—if anything, with
increasing fervor—on the corruption of the Nigerian government.
Kudryavtsev maintained that a whole stratum of government officials
provided for their own personal enrichment at the expense of the national
budget, obstructed any innovation from which they could not benefit
personally, and refused to sacrifice private interests to public welfare.[77]

73. *Ibid.*, p. 79.
74. Brutents, "The October Revolution and Africa," p. 10.
75. Kudryavtsev, "Problems of Afro-Asian Solidarity," p. 53.
76. At the time Dia lost the power struggle with Senghor, Soviet commentators
noted only Western references to Dia's greater preference for cooperative structures; apparently it seemed enough to them that Senghor had promised to follow
a policy of "political conciliation" and to fulfill agreements with the Soviet
Union. See *Pravda*, December 18, 1962, p. 3, and *Izvestiya*, December 19,
1962, p. 2.
77. Kudryavtsev, "Problems of Afro-Asian Solidarity," p. 54.

Given the fundamental reservations Soviet leaders retained toward these regimes (and, in turn, the lingering suspicion of these regimes toward the Soviet Union), it is not surprising that the economic agreements of June 1962 and June 1963 did not prove to be the entrance for a new Soviet economic offensive in this area of West Africa. In December 1962 a team of Soviet experts did carry out a feasibility study for a pump-irrigation project in Senegal's northern river region, but when the Senegalese government sent a delegation to Moscow in July 1963 to discuss the survey's conclusions, it found that little interest survived. The Soviet Union concluded no formal aid agreement with Nigeria, despite a series of public invitations extended by the premier of the Eastern Region, Michael Okpara, to participate in Nigeria's six-year development plan.[78] Soviet exports to Senegal actually declined during 1963, the first year the trade agreement was in force. Nor could the Soviet Union's initial purchases totaling $21,000 be considered a very impressive entry into the Senegalese market.[79] That the Soviet approach to this part of West Africa had not changed more was the combined result, on the one hand, of surviving ideological constraints and, on the other, of the reluctance on the part of African countries to become deeply involved with the Soviet Union. It is never easy to detect which factor accounted most for the rudimentary state of Soviet relations with moderate African states during these years.

Still, Soviet policy had entered a period of transition. After the earlier era of unspoiled optimism, events had momentarily forced upon the Soviet leaders a more realistic assessment of the African revolution. They had become convinced that progress toward socialism was not necessarily a straight-line process, and the realization that change in Africa would wind an indefinite and delayed course encouraged them to deal more seriously and more directly with states they had once largely disregarded. These first timid attempts to increase ties with countries such as Senegal and Nigeria signified that the Soviet Union was preparing to accept their relative permanence, a crucial aspect of the Soviet Union's changing conception of Africa. (In 1963 no one, least of all the Soviet leadership, could yet envisage how short and uncertain the

78. See, for example, Lagos radio (domestic service in English), 18.00 GMT, May 8, 1963.

79. *Commerce extérieur du Sénégal* (December 1963), Ministère des Finances et des Affaires Economiques, Service de la Statistique et de la Mécanographie, 1964.

life of an African regime might be. This reality awaited the events of 1965 and 1966.)

The Evolution of Theory

Along with the change occurring in the Soviet Union's relations with the Monrovian states, Soviet attitudes toward the most progressive West African states were undergoing an equally significant evolution. Despite their general disillusion with the Afro-Asian movement in this period, Soviet policymakers maintained a growing interest in developments underway in Ghana and Mali; and when circumstances within Africa stimulated a mild shift in the Soviet attitude toward the moderate states, theorists also began to modify their assessment of the militant leaderships. The two moves, however, appear unrelated, for one seemed to represent a mutation conforming to the new realities Africa imposed on Soviet policy; the second, a fragmentary hope, left over from the preceding days of optimism.

Both Guinea's partial volte-face and the favorable evolution of Ghanaian and Malian politics prompted the Soviet Union to re-examine the basis of its relationship with these countries. In trying to define the essential character of Ghana and Mali's political and economic development, Soviet analysts were inevitably compelled to raise again the issue of Nkrumah and Keita's view of socialism.

Even during the period of greatest euphoria, the Soviet Union had never acknowledged the validity of Touré's political philosophy. The optimism, though immediate and hearty, had always lacked ideological sanction.[80] Late in 1961, however, long before Soviet commentators broached the issue, British Communists confronted the problem of ideology: did Ghana really have the potential for developing along socialist lines, or was Nkrumah just another Kassim or Nasser (in disfavor at the time)? Was he no more than a bourgeois nationalist, or was he an African Castro? When one contributor to the British Communist weekly, *World News,* suggested that Nkrumah did possess some of the qualities of a revolutionary socialist and in evidence cited the Ghanaian

80. The theoretical basis for the close Soviet friendship with Guinea, Ghana, and Mali was, of course, the concept of the national democratic state; but because the Soviet Union could not accept the official ideology of these states, this theory always remained a further example of ideological temporizing.

leader's frequently expressed devotion to socialism, she roused a stern rebuke. Her critics pointed out that Nkrumah talked about the need for socialist ideas to animate his government, "but as we all know, there is socialism and socialism. President Nasser talks of socialism and attacks the working people; President Kassim talks of socialism and attacks the working people."[81] Significantly, however, the first author was given the last word, and she used it to challenge her critics: "Who would have thought a few years ago that President Castro would today be the head of a state that is building socialism?" It is possible that the same question was beginning to occur to Soviet policymakers.

If so, they made no public attempt to answer until after 1962, and then the outlines of dialogue rather than a straightforward reply appeared in the Soviet press. Three things were happening: one, the old view was changing that, because so many of its tenets conflicted with scientific socialism, African socialism had to be considered inherently reactionary. Some Soviet commentators were now finding that, on balance, the progressive features characterizing African socialism made it an essentially positive, though still not a fully acceptable, phenomenon. Second, important for the review underway among Soviet theorists, Nkrumah and Keita in this period stopped drawing distinctions between their own ideological systems and scientific socialism and began emphasizing the unity of the two. Third, as the result of the first two developments, a few Soviet spokesmen went further to accept Nkrumah and Keita at their word, granting that indeed these two leaders had selected the path of scientific socialism for their countries.

As before, the central discussions took place within the Institute of World Economics and International Relations, with Potekhin contributing key commentary from the outside. The notion that African socialism jeopardized the propagation of proletarian internationalism gave way to a more lenient view willing to grant that this theory facilitated the transition to higher forms of political and economic organization. In general, said one senior researcher at the Institute of World Economics and International Relations, the spread of socialist ideas even in their unscientific, utopian form had a positive part to play because, when the tasks of bourgeois democracy ("constituting the main content of these theories") are consistently implemented, "they objectively pave the

81. *World News,* October 21, 1961, and November 18, 1961, quoted in Radio Free Europe (Central Research Unit), Background Note no. 1747, November 19, 1961.

way for the non-capitalist development."[82] That was why, he continued, the most progressive elements in society, while criticizing the antiscientific theoretical principles underlying such programs, vigorously supported the democratic slogans written into them.

But of far greater importance than this general reassessment of African socialism, liberal Soviet academicians responded favorably to the new language used by Nkrumah and Keita in describing their ideological *commitment*. Soviet writers sooner than others outside Ghana noticed that sometime in 1962 Nkrumah dropped his former references to the special character of Ghanaian socialism and sanctioned instead a public commitment to scientific socialism as an indivisible social theory. In one of his most important articles on African socialism, Potekhin underscored Nkrumah's shift in position, which began with an espousal of African socialism as the main goal of the Convention People's Party and concluded with the 1962 CPP program based on scientific socialism.[83] According to Potekhin, Nkrumah told him in December 1962 that "there is only one socialism as a particular system of social production." In November 1963 (at a farewell gathering for a visiting delegation from the Supreme Soviet), Nkrumah reportedly remarked that Ghana had "firmly chosen the socialist path and we will build a socialist society." "The question is what kind of socialism? Only scientific socialism, of course—there is no other kind of socialism. Thus our countries, the Soviet Union and Ghana will go forward together."[84] In Mali no less than in Ghana, the dominant party had recognized scientific socialism as the party's ideological foundation and, according to Moscow radio's summary of the Sixth Congress of the Union Soudanaise, "provided a good example of what must be done in a concrete way, allowing for national peculiarities, to build a better future for all the people committed to the socialist way."[85]

Soviet writers were prepared to reassess the goals of Africa's most progressive leaders; they were not, however, prepared to go a step further and grant them credit for actually having done very much to implement them. Ready as liberals were to accept Nkrumah and Keita's professed

82. Y. Guzevaty, " 'Third Way' or Genuine Freedom?" *International Affairs* no. 4 (1963), p. 47.

83. I. I. Potekhin, "On 'African Socialism,' " *International Affairs,* no. 1 (1963), p. 78. See also K. Grishechkin, "African Prospects," *New Times,* no. 41 (October 16, 1963), pp. 7–9.

84. *Pravda,* November 6, 1963, p. 5.

85. Moscow radio (in French to Africa), 21.30 GMT, September 15, 1962.

devotion to scientific socialism, they did not yet dare to embrace their systems as genuinely socialistic. Potekhin said, "There exists in Africa an intelligentsia which has mastered the scientific principles of socialism."[86] A delegation of the Supreme Soviet traveling in Mali proclaimed that "the people of Mali, under the guidance of the Union Soudanaise Party led by President Modibo Keita, are capable of building a just socialist society."[87] A member of the Institute of World Economics and International Relations drew particular attention to the "program of social reconstruction based on socialist principles" put forward by "democratic parties and forces," such as the Union Soudanaise and the Convention People's Party.[88] But none ever admitted that Ghana or Mali was actually building socialism or, for that matter, that their policies came close to paralleling their excellent intentions. Officially Soviet leaders noted that many states, starting out along "the path of sovereign development," had declared that their countries were going to build socialism. "The Soviet people, moved by a feeling of fraternal solidarity with the peoples of Asia and Africa, well understand and fully support the strivings of the peoples of these countries to live in socialist conditions."[89] Whether they had begun the transition to this new life was another matter.

Nevertheless, judging from the evidence, the effect of this discussion was unquestionably to upgrade the definition of progress achieved in Ghana and Mali. Presumably this was why Soviet commentators excluded Guinea from studies devoted to the most progressive African states and particularly from references to the growing popularity of scientific socialism in Africa, a sign that Ghana and Mali had advanced beyond the stage attained by Guinea.[90] Moreover, the criticism sparked by the new evaluation of Nkrumah and Keita's ideologies gives a clearer idea of just how liberal this evaluation had become. Thus when Georgy

86. Potekhin, "On 'African Socialism,' " p. 75.
87. *Mizan*, V (February 1963), 18.
88. G. Starushenko, in *Pravda*, January 25, 1963, p. 3.
89. This was the report of the Soviet A-APS Committee after attending the executive committee meeting of A-APSO (Nicosia), in *Pravda*, September 14, 1963, p. 3.
90. This comment would not be valid had Guinea been completely blacklisted, for then it might appear that Ghana and Mali had not advanced, rather that Guinea's position had merely deteriorated. But, as it was, the Soviet Union was careful not to deprive Guinea publicly of the praise once reserved for it. It was, for example, still faithfully listed among the "states of national democracy."

Mirsky published some rather advanced views on the concept of national socialism in the February 1963 issue of *Mirovaya ekonomika i mezhdunarodnye otnosheniya*, two of his colleagues at the Institute of World Economics and International Relations quickly composed a rebuttal, condemning the "extremist viewpoint" that idealized such socialism.[91] "It would be incorrect," they maintained, "to call social-economic reforms, implemented in several independent national states, socialist." Such an evaluation would indicate a "fetishness for reform." They agreed that the economic mechanism created favorable objective conditions for the eventual transition to the path of noncapitalist development, but "it is by no means, *synonymous* with that path."

Mirsky, a specialist on the UAR, had concentrated his attention on reform underway in the UAR, and his enthusiasm over achievements there is what disturbed his critics most; in their estimation, the UAR under Nasser (on his way back into favor) remained of doubtful dependability. Significantly, however, they acknowledged Mali to be an exception to Mirsky's otherwise "undiscriminating" analysis of political development in progressive states. In Mali, they agreed, the ripening conditions for the transition to the noncapitalist path were most encouraging.[92]

Furthermore, as Soviet policy toward Ghana and Mali entered a transitional phase, the old theoretical formulations used by Soviet writers to describe these states began to lose precision. Descriptions of Ghana and Mali as national democratic states gradually faded from the Soviet press, replaced by rather vague references to their shifting ideological status. In Ghana, wrote Potekhin, the government "is putting through a number of measures which will place the country on non-capitalist lines of development."[93] Whether Ghana, and Mali as well, had already embarked upon the noncapitalist path—itself an ambiguous concept—or were about to embark upon that path was left unspecified, because Soviet accounts had it both ways.

Whatever theory had become or was becoming, it was evident that Soviet commentators were pleased with practical measures launched by the leaderships of these states. They praised the efforts of Mali and

91. R. Avakov and L. Stepanov, "Sotsialnye problemy natsionalno-osvoboditelnoi revolyutsii" (Social Problems of the National Liberation Revolution), *Mirovaya ekonomika i mezhdunarodnye otnosheniya*, no. 5 (1963), p. 49.
92. *Ibid.*
93. Potekhin, "On 'African Socialism,' " p. 75.

Ghana to establish state control over trade and industrial development, to develop agriculture on a collective basis, and to create a comprehensive plan for economic development. They argued that in these states the state sector had become "not only anti-imperialist, but anticapitalist as well."[94] On the third anniversary of the Ghanaian Republic, Moscow radio saluted Ghana for providing an example of "revolutionary and social transformation" watched by "millions of eyes throughout the African continent."[95] Expressing particular faith in Ghana's course, the broadcast went on: "We are firmly confident that the Republic of Ghana . . . will not go back upon the gains which put it in the foreground and will not leave the road of progress it has taken." For the first time, the Soviet media went as far as to suggest that a state like Ghana could be counted on to maintain its course.

As theory moved into a transitional phase, the strategy of Soviet policy toward the progressive states also began to show signs of noteworthy change. To Soviet leaders it seemed increasingly evident that the future of socialism in Africa depended upon the education of cadres. All of the advantages Africa possessed for making the transition to socialism— the natural place of the commune in African peasant society, the near absence of an indigenous bourgeoisie, and the expanding role of the state sector—hinged on the nature and quality of the African leadership. Whether, for example, the peasant commune would serve as a departure for the collectivization of agriculture or degenerate into a system of private land tenure was wholly a function of political leadership. The Soviet government had, of course, initiated a long-term program to develop these cadres in the universities of the Soviet Union, but this represented a grassroots investment whose return would be long delayed. The possibility of assisting with the formation of cadres at the highest level within African countries and eventually of even converting local party structures to the socialist model became an eminently more attractive proposition.

Soviet leaders began their efforts to influence African party structures directly by establishing fraternal party relations with the Union Soudanaise of Mali in September 1962. Later, the CPSU arranged similar ties with the single parties of Ghana and Guinea. Earlier, representatives

---

94. R. Avakov and R. Andreasyan, "Progressivnaya rol gosudarstvennogo sektora" (Progressive Role of the State Sector), *Kommunist,* no. 13 (September 1962), p. 93.

95. Moscow radio (in English to Africa), 15.00 GMT, July 1, 1963.

from these three ruling parties—the only three from Black Africa—had attended and addressed the Twenty-Second CPSU Congress in October 1961, special recognition of their rising status. The following April, delegates from the same three countries returned to Moscow to attend the Fourteenth Komsomol Congress, and in turn the Soviet Union dispatched representatives to their party and youth congresses. The union between the US and the CPSU, however, constituted the first formal attempt to integrate a radical African party into the world-wide socialist political community, to enroll this nonproletarian party officially in what the Soviet Union called the "world revolutionary process." For the first time the Soviet Communist party had accepted another avowedly non-Communist party on a basis of near equality or had established relations in any official sense with such a political party.

To bear fruit, though, this new arrangement required that each party come under the control of properly schooled political leaders. As might be expected, Soviet policymakers paid particular attention to the political formation of future leaders and therefore sought a strategy that would give them access to the education of these leaders. The week before Mali and the Soviet Union announced the establishment of party relations, a national seminar of the Union Soudanaise recommended that schools for cadres at the district level and a higher school for cadres at the national level be created to teach "the history and economy of the Mali Republic and Africa, the history and principles of the Party and the principles of scientific socialism without which responsible officials cannot effectively set about solving the problems of socialist construction in the country."[96] Thoroughly reported by the Soviet press, the party's decision fortified Potekhin's friendly response to Mali's announced dedication to scientific socialism.[97] A short time later the Soviet government agreed to aid in constructing a higher party school in Bamako and then offered to assist in staffing it.

In Ghana Soviet lecturers had for some time been helping with the curriculum of the Kwame Nkrumah Ideological Institute, and as a normal extension of their contribution, the Central Committee of the CPSU had invited a CPP delegation headed by Executive Secretary Nathaniel Welbeck to visit the Soviet Union to observe its system for training ideological workers.[98] They studied the party's work among the masses

96. Moscow TASS (in English to Europe), 22.18 GMT, September 8, 1962.
97. Potekhin, "On 'African Socialism,' " p. 79.
98. Pravda, July 31, 1963, p. 4.

and "the methods of effecting the party's leading role in social organizations."[99] In October 1963, a second delegation from the CPP, led this time by Kweku Akwei, the ideological secretary of the party, arrived in the Soviet Union to study the propaganda work of the CPSU. Part of the month-long study trip was spent at the Soviet Higher Party School, making them, according to Wolfgang Leonhard, the first non-Communists accorded this privilege.[100] Thus along with foreign aid and trade, education, cultural exchange, and normal diplomatic contact, the Soviet Union incorporated into its African policy an institutionalized friendship with the ruling parties of the most radical states.

Although this modification in strategy involved long-range considerations, for the Soviet Union, as with any other country, long-range considerations yielded priority in policy formation to short-term pressures. Larger considerations relate to goals and, in the case of the Soviet Union, to the hopes for the Communist millennium; immediate pressures represent the daily operational fare of policy formation. A country's internal development is of secondary importance to foreign policy and when, as has often happened in Africa, the course of one has seemed to Soviet leaders in conflict with the other they have, without exception, responded on the level of foreign policy.[101] In the case of Ghana and Mali, foreign policy and internal development tended to reinforce one another and thus explain the obvious reason for the popularity of these regimes with the Soviet government.

In general the Soviet Union could expect Ghana and Mali to support its contention that peaceful coexistence constituted the essential framework for relations with the West, for its stand on the issue of disarmament, and for its strategy in the Third World (if not always for its direct participation in Afro-Asian affairs). On specific issues Keita had called for an end to nuclear testing, the elimination of foreign bases, the implementation of the UN independence declaration, a nonaggression pact between NATO and the Warsaw Pact countries, and a peace treaty with *both* German states, each to be demilitarized.[102] Nkrumah had

99. *Pravda,* August 20, 1963, p. 3.

100. Wolfgang Leonhard. *Die Zeit,* January 10, 1963, in Joint Publications Research Service, no. 23105, February 6, 1964.

101. During this period that was true of Soviet relations with Ethiopia and, as a good deal of the remainder of this study will attempt to show, the same became true of Soviet relations with Senegal and Nigeria.

102. See Peking NCNA (in English to Europe and Asia), 01.30 GMT, July 11, 1962.

continued to advocate a German solution that would have recognized the division of Germany and put control over access to Berlin in East German hands. He condemned the Common Market as an instrument "aimed at harnessing the African countries to satisfy the profit-lust of the imperialist bloc and to prevent [Africa] from following an independent neutralist policy."[103] During the Cuban missile crisis, in contrast to Touré, Nkrumah sent a warm note to Khrushchev congratulating him for his "brave decision to dismantle the installations in Cuba which are considered offensive by the United States."[104] "I consider this," he said, "an extremely desirable first step towards the progressive liquidation of bases for firing ground-to-ground rockets situated on the territory of non-nuclear powers and a vitally important contribution to the cause of international peace." Again, unlike Touré who refused to sign the nuclear-test ban, Nkrumah strongly endorsed this agreement and reproved the Chinese for opposing it.

These common points of policy, although substantial, did not obscure the genuinely independent aspects of Ghanaian and Malian policy. On the issues that meant most to Nkrumah and Keita, obstinate Soviet behavior provoked angry censure. Nkrumah, for example, displayed particular sensitivity on the question of arms control and disarmament. On this issue, Nkrumah believed that a Third World leader could help to promote an agreement between the major powers. In his early speeches he had often raised the question of disarmament, usually by way of solutions lightly dismissing Soviet and American objections to the variety of proposals already in circulation. He seemed persuaded that on this question neither the United States nor the Soviet Union was negotiating in earnest. During the 1961 Berlin crisis, Nkrumah called the Soviet resumption of tests a "shock" and, when Khrushchev sought to escalate tension by announcing Soviet plans for detonating a sixty-megaton hydrogen bomb, he wrote the Soviet leader that this decision had "profoundly disturbed" him.[105] In a public reply Khrushchev justified Soviet action as a necessary response to Western threats occasioned by his proposals for concluding a German peace treaty.[106] Nkrumah became angriest,

103. *Ghana Today,* June 20, 1962, quoted in Rupert Emerson, "The Atlantic Community and the Emerging Countries," *International Organization,* XVII (Summer 1963), 641.

104. *Pravda,* November 2, 1962, p. 3.

105. V. Maevsky and B. Tarasov, *Pravda,* September 3, 1961, p. 4, and *Pravda,* October 27, 1961, p. 1.

106. *Ibid.*

however, in July 1962 when, less than a month after his carefully staged "World Without the Bomb" Assembly, the Soviet leadership announced its decision to resume nuclear testing. His newspapers exploded: the Soviet Union had unmasked itself on the issue of arms control as a "Jekyll and Hyde, playing the role of peacemaker and peacewrecker simultaneously."[107] Taunted the Ghanaian press, "What happened to the declaration of the recent Moscow World Peace Congress?" Those who had come to respect the peaceful aspirations of the Soviet peoples, it lamented, had received this notice with "grave disappointment." In July a year later, Ghana Radio, commenting on recent sessions of the Seventeen Nations Conference on Disarmament, offered the opinion that "the big powers, especially the United States and the USSR, do not really desire disarmament."[108]

During the early part of 1963, in a rather strange way, the Soviet Union got caught up in one of Ghana's own special problems, a problem closely related to Ghana's deteriorating African relations. The murder of Togo's President Olympio in January 1963 has already been mentioned and, in this connection, Nkrumah's hasty and provocative recognition of the new regime in Lomé. Unlike its Ghanaian ally, however, the Soviet Union circumspectly withheld recognition of the new Togolese government. The next month when a coup d'état in Iraq overthrew Kassim and the Soviet government quickly recognized his successor, the Ghanaian press commented acidly:

We sympathize with our contemporary, the Moscow *Pravda* over the resolute protest it has flung out against the mass slaughter of Communists in Iraq. The fact, however, is that Soviet recognition of the Iraqi regime even before it has been established appeared to have tied those elements hands and feet like sheep about to be led to the slaughterhouse . . . And what withheld recognition by the USSR and its European Socialist allies of the Togolese regime? Fear of risking an open quarrel with African client states like Nigeria? Wherein lies ideological purity in this, dear USSR? . . . We do not believe the absence of oil in large quantities in Togoland has anything to do with this reservation. It is clearly a case of expediency. As we said, fear of coming into open grips with the client states.[109]

107. *Guardian,* July 24, 1962, p. 7; see also *Ghanaian Times,* July 23, 1962.
108. Accra radio (domestic service in English), 13.00 GMT, June 9, 1963.
109. *Evening News* (Ghana), February 18, 1963, p. 2.

The attack reflected Nkrumah's irritation over several aspects of Soviet policy. Not only did he feel the Soviet Union had failed to uphold his interests in Togo, but he resented—and this perhaps most of all—the Soviet Union's growing rapprochement with his moderate neighbors. No doubt, too, Nkrumah identified Kassim's fate with his own position, and he could not have been happy with how easily the Soviet leadership accepted the demise of a revolutionary leader.

The Soviet Union's predicament in this case was symptomatic of the problem it confronted as relations with Ghana grew more elaborate. For as the Soviet Union was becoming more enamored of the Ghanaians, its secondary interest in broadening contacts with all African states was being undermined by Ghana's increasing isolation on the continent. The problem emerged with particular clarity at the Addis Ababa meeting in June 1963. The issue of African unity posed problems at two levels: the substance of the question itself—what kind of unity was preferable—and, second, the solution tactically wisest to support. But it must have seemed even more complicated to the Soviet leaders who, to begin with, found themselves drifting closer to a country with waning influence among the countries they wished to influence more. (Ghana's influence was waning not necessarily because of its drift toward the socialist countries; but because its influence was waning, the drift toward the socialist countries may have been accelerated.) Moreover, to make matters more difficult, the proposal of the state most popular with the Soviet Union was the plan least popular with other African states. Earlier Soviet writers had called a commitment to immediate political unity unrealistic and premature. They implied that injudicious attempts to achieve political union might in fact be counterproductive. Presumably the estimation of Soviet leaders had not changed, only the wisdom of speaking out.

What is more, Nkrumah derived his notion of African unity from pan-Africanism, a concept that the Soviet Union suspected expressed an urge toward isolation from the "progressive" currents of other continents. To a Russian, pan-Africanism represented the international counterpart of "national chauvinism." Yet the public anguish caused African leaders by the prospect of a "Balkanized" Africa, susceptible to permanent imperialist plundering, offered Soviet leaders too promising a propaganda handle to forsake. Similarly, slogans of African unity gave the Soviet Union a pretext for attacking regional groupings it disliked, such as the Afro-Malagasy Union; but, at the same time, they made it more difficult to defend approved regional groupings, such as the East African federation. To illustrate in still another instance the dilemma built into the issue of African unity: African unity constructed on an anti-imperialist and anticapitalist foundation would serve to roll back Western influence in Africa. The African Common Market, say, urged so often by Nkrumah, constituted a useful rallying point for the Soviet Union in its struggle to weaken the EEC's growing attraction for Africa.[110] But any successful effort to structure African unity would reduce the importance of the radical states by submerging them in a necessarily more moderate and conservative political structure. Any meaningful form of African unity posed once again the problem of the unacceptable lowest common denominator.

Fortunately for Soviet policymakers, Africa's inability to unite spared them the need to confront these dilemmas. Knowing that under prevailing conditions African nations could not effect a working unity on specific substantive problems—let alone set in motion a vigorous process of political integration—the Soviet Union could easily rally to the ramparts of African unity, exhorting Africa to find its strength in union and excoriating the West for thwarting efforts toward union, all without risking the potential inconveniences of growing African unity.

But the Soviet Union had at least one problem to contemplate: how was it to handle the awkward consequences that would inevitably flow from Nkrumah's increasingly radical approach to African unity? This involved not merely the delicate problem of supporting a foolish policy of a regime which, for other reasons, had stimulated profound Soviet interest; it impinged as well on Soviet efforts to foster civil relations with all types of African states. In 1962 and 1963 the problem had not yet become acute, but its future outlines could already be imagined.

In this period the pattern of African relations was changing substantially and in the case of some states, notably Ghana, so too was the basic content of policy among them. The Soviet Union responded to the first phenomenon, but ignored the second. It responded to the first by abandoning a rather sharp differentiation among African states, at once a cause and a function of the rudimentary condition of Soviet relations with the moderate states of West Africa. Henceforth the Soviet Union would gradually enlarge the focus of its African policy and seek cordial relations with a host of countries previously neglected or

110. See, for example, the review of Nkrumah's book, *Africa Must Unite,* in *International Affairs,* no. 12 (1963), p. 90.

condemned. It ignored the second because the promise Soviet leaders had begun to see in Ghana warranted a toleration of its foibles. The interval between 1961 and 1963 was distinctly a transitional period in Soviet policy, and so the progress attributed to Ghana and similar states remained tentative and carefully constrained.

Nevertheless, over the last months of this period, official attitudes were undergoing an extraordinary transformation. By December 1963 Soviet leaders stood ready to embark upon a radical departure in policy toward Africa's progressive states, a departure reflecting strikingly altered expectations for the course of socialism within those societies.

VI

*Ideological Experimentation
in Khrushchev's Last Year*

Late in 1963 Khrushchev turned from the 1961 party program to endorse "socialism of the national type." Putting aside the program's condemnation of national socialism, he publicly embraced "revolutionary democratic statesmen," who "sincerely advocate noncapitalist methods for the solution of national problems and declare their determination to build socialism."[1] "We welcome their declarations," he said, and "we fully support their measures." Although it was still not specific recognition that Ghana, Mali, and others were building socialism,[2] his statement

1. In an interview with Ghanaian, Algerian, and Burmese newsmen appearing in *Pravda*, December 22, 1963, pp. 1–2, and *Izvestiya*, December 22, 1963, pp. 1–2.

2. Indeed, at this point, Khrushchev still carefully qualified his endorsement: "The revolutionary-democratic leaders of a number of liberated countries are seeking methods and forms for the transition to a noncapitalist path of development. In the opinion of Marxist-Leninists, the national democratic state would be a suitable form for this transition for many countries." And he added that socialism "cannot be decreed, the stage of democratic transformations cannot be skipped, and measures cannot be carried out for which the necessary social-economic conditions have not been created and which are not assured the support of the masses." *Pravda*, December 22, 1963, pp. 1–2, trans. in *Current Digest of the Soviet Press*, XV (January 15, 1964), 13. These reservations would disappear several weeks later.

raised their theoretical status and for the first time gave official ideological sanction to their patterns of development. Before, Nkrumah and Keita's reforms had been considered only objectively progressive—that is, *despite* the intention and understanding of their innovators, they helped to pave the way for socialism. The difference was that, after the Khrushchev interview, these leaders were accepted as authentic socialists and therefore capable of consciously leading the way to socialism.

Coming scarcely six months after the Soviet leadership had publicly belittled the importance that China attached to the national liberation movement, Khrushchev's rather adventurous innovation was mystifying. Why, if the developing countries were declining in importance, did the Soviet leadership embark on a new course intended to upgrade the ideological standing of their regimes? Why did it sanction an ideological departure so much more suited to a moment of fervent optimism?

If, on the other hand, the discouragement had already passed and Soviet leaders were again eager to extend their interests in Africa and Asia, what had happened to revive their confidence? For, indeed, this does appear to be the case: their disenchantment had diminished. All the evidence suggests that Soviet estimations had changed in this short span of time or, at least, that Khrushchev's considerations had changed. Still the question remains—why?

Presumably the timing of the Khrushchev interview, published one week after Chou En-lai arrived in Africa, was not entirely by chance. David Morison has argued that in no circumstances could the Soviet Union concede primacy in Africa's revolutionary states to China and, therefore, to counter the impact of its "revolutionary militancy," Khrushchev was now searching for a formula with greater appeal.[3] Rather than exhorting the Africans to make the revolution, as the Chinese were doing, he was toying with the idea of telling them that they had already made the revolution and could now go forward, arm in arm, with the most advanced socialist society. Within a few weeks, in fact, this is pre-

3. See David L. Morison, "Ten Years of Soviet and Chinese Policies in Africa," *Mizan*, X (May–June 1968), 111–113. In another respect Khrushchev's December interview seemed inspired by Chou's visit: a very major portion of the Soviet leader's remarks dealt with those delicate issues which the Chinese had been emphasizing most in their relations with Africa, such as the relation of the peaceful-coexistence strategy to the national liberation struggle, the Soviet position on peaceful and armed forms of anticolonialist struggle, and the importance of economic cooperation between the socialist countries and Africa.

cisely the course that Soviet policy did take. It may also be that, with President Kennedy's assassination the month before, Soviet leaders felt that their opportunities in Africa had improved. No longer would his personal appeal be a factor in Afro-American relations. But these explanations are highly conjectural and, even if correct, clearly incomplete.

A major part of the explanation must be sought outside Black Africa, in North Africa and Cuba. From 1963 through 1964 Soviet interest in Algeria and the UAR rose steadily, reaching its highest pitch during Ben Bella's visit to the U.S.S.R. on April 25–May 6, 1964, and a week later during Khrushchev's visit to the UAR. The remarkable adjustment in ideology evident by then represented a measure of Soviet confidence in the changes taking place in these countries as well as an appeal to their ideological vanity.[4] Early in 1963 when Georgy Mirsky argued that the leaders of the UAR basically were not bourgeois but rather representatives of the progressive intelligentsia, revolutionary democrats who "understand the necessity of turning the anticolonialist revolution into an anticapitalist one," who had, indeed, made "inroads on the bases of the capitalist system of production," his colleagues remained skeptical.[5] By the fall of 1963, following a reassessment of the national liberation movement, Mirsky's formerly extravagant optimism had infected the commentary of other writers. Igor Belyaev in *Pravda,* November 26, 1963, repeated much of Mirsky's original argument, including the assertion that reforms in the UAR had "above all struck at the interests of the bourgeoisie and all capitalist elements."[6] Mirsky—vindicated by the Khrushchev interview, or at least unleashed—wrote with new verve. "Analysis of the development of the UAR shows that, dogmatist views to the contrary, in our day of a world socialist system the prospects before former colonies and semi-colonies are infinitely wider and more diversified than before."[7] On Algeria, he argued in a succeeding issue of *New Times* that because of "a socialist program at home" and

4. The subject is well covered in Uri Ra'anan, "Moscow and the 'Third World,'" *Problems of Communism,* XIV (January–February 1965), 22–31.

5. See his "Tvorcheski Marksizm i problemy natsionalno-osvoboditelnykh revolyutsi" (Creative Marxism and the Problems of National Liberation Revolutions), *Mirovaya ekonomika i mezhdunarodnye otnosheniya,* no. 2 (1963), pp. 65–66, quoted in *ibid.,* p. 25. For opposition to this view at the time, see Chapter Five.

6. I. Belyaev, *Pravda,* November 26, 1963, p. 3, quoted in *ibid.*

7. G. Mirsky, "The Changing Arab East," *New Times,* no. 2 (1964), p. 6.

"growing ties of friendship with the world's first socialist state," there was every reason to predict that this country's future would be bright.[8] The theses of the FLN program, Mirsky said, were "undoubtedly based on a Marxist analysis."

That Mirsky's theories enjoyed official sanction, perhaps that of Khrushchev himself, was evident almost from the start. The third week in December, when *Pravda* and *Izvestiya* published Khrushchev's interview with Algerian, Burmese, and Ghanaian editors, Hadj Ben Alla, a militant member of the FLN Politburo and chairman of the Algerian National Assembly, arrived in Moscow for a "visit of friendship."[9] The atmosphere surrounding his stay was particularly warm, and Soviet spokesmen were noticeably more ebullient than they had been only three months before when Houari Boumedienne, the Algerian minister of defense, had come to the Soviet Union to negotiate an agreement on economic and technical cooperation. The most striking reflection of the new direction in Soviet thought appeared in remarks that Aleksei Kosygin made at a reception for the Algerian leader. He said that the "people of the Soviet Union regard with sympathy people who are taking the path of freedom, the *path of socialism,* and who want to live secure and independent lives."[10] The enemies of Algeria label its socialist aspirations a fantasy, he said, but the Soviet Union knows that these goals are real and will be achieved. And then he reminisced that, when the Soviet Union began the process of building socialism, it stood alone among hostile armed states; the implication was that Algeria was much more fortunate to embark upon the same course with the support of a mighty socialist camp. Taken at face value, Kosygin's comments are a remarkable confession of faith in the progress of a country like Algeria, exceeding the most optimistic assessment of any of his colleagues.[11]

The communiqué signed at the close of Ben Alla's stay did not go so far, but certainly further than the one composed two months earlier for the Boumedienne visit. The Soviet government now congratulated

8. G. Mirsky, "Algeria: Yesterday, Today, Tomorrow," *New Times,* no. 17 (1964), p. 13.

9. *Pravda,* December 28, 1963, p. 1.

10. *Pravda,* December 21, 1963, p. 1; emphasis added.

11. Khrushchev, on the two occasions his remarks were published, spoke more conservatively. He acknowledged the progressive character of Algerian reform but without admitting that it had an essential socialist content. Instead he limited his endorsement to an approval of the Algerian people's "*aspiration* to build their life on socialist principles" (emphasis added). See *Pravda,* December 28, 1963, p. 1.

the FLN and President Ben Bella for "carrying out revolutionary political, economic and social transformations in the country" aimed at "overcoming the heavy consequences of colonial domination, consolidating
political and economic independence, developing the national economy
and raising the material and cultural level of life for broad masses of
the Algerian working people with a view to building socialism on an
ever firmer basis."[12] Nothing close to this kind of enthusiasm marked
the earlier communiqué; the nearest the Soviet press came to recognizing
Algeria's socialist ambitions in October was in a reference to a song
sung by Algerian children: "We, the youth, Algeria's future, will together
with Ben Bella build socialism."[13] "This song," the authors remarked
simply, "is symbolic because the President's thoughts always come back
to the well-being and happiness of the young republic's children."

After Ben Alla's visit, Soviet commentators assumed a much bolder
position. *Pravda* published an interview with him in which he emphasized
that Algeria had already taken the first steps along the socialist path.[14]
There was no qualification of his claim, no attempt to remind Soviet
readers that it expressed a commendable sentiment but an unachieved
fact. By April *Pravda*'s editors felt moved to headline an article by
their own correspondent, "Algeria's Choice Is Socialism."[15] This was
an enthusiastic account of the recent FLN congress, replete with references to the Algerian leadership's commitment to socialism. Khrushchev
chose to feature the same theme a few days later when Ben Bella arrived
in the Soviet Union to begin an official two-week visit. "It is," he said
in his greeting at the airport, "particularly pleasant for us to welcome
you to Soviet soil directly after the conclusion of the work of the [FLN]
congress which outlined concrete paths for the construction of the basis
of socialism."[16] Later at a Kremlin breakfast the Soviet premier assured
Ben Bella that the Soviet people were deeply impressed by the "determination of the Algerian people to embark upon the socialist path."[17]
Echoing Kosygin, he recalled the advantages that Algeria had in beginning this process, and then expressed his confidence that Algeria would
overcome whatever obstacles stood in the way of a successful socialist

12. *Pravda,* December 30, 1963, p. 1, trans. in *Current Digest of the Soviet
Press,* XV (January 22, 1964), 30.
13. M. Piradova and Ye. Shevelya, in *Pravda,* October 5, 1963, p. 3.
14. See N. Prozhogin, in *Pravda,* January 20, 1964, p. 4.
15. N. Prozhogin, in *Pravda,* April 23, 1964, p. 3.
16. See *Pravda,* April 26, 1964, p. 1.
17. *Pravda,* April 28, 1964, p. 1.

transition. Again, however, Khrushchev left it to one of his junior colleagues to display the full extent of Soviet expectations. When Khrushchev escorted Ben Bella to the Ukraine, Pyotr Shelest, first secretary of the Ukraine Central Committee, received him with a remarkable speech in which he explicitly announced that Algeria was "now proceeding along the socialist path."[18]

Ben Bella's visit was, in all respects, exceptional. Throughout he was addressed as comrade; on May Day Khrushchev invited him to stand at his side atop the Lenin Mausoleum for the parade; before he left, in an extraordinary gesture, the Presidium of the Supreme Soviet awarded him the decoration of "Hero of the Soviet Union." At every turn Soviet speakers praised him personally and lauded his country's progress; one even implied that Algeria had advanced beyond the uncertain status of a national democracy to begin the transition to socialism. In their joint communiqué the CPSU saluted the FLN as the rallying point for all the patriotic and democratic forces in Algeria "in the struggle for the socialist reconstruction of their state" and wished it success in strengthening Algeria's national independence and in the advance toward socialist construction.[19]

Though Khrushchev had been more restrained than Kosygin in December and Shelest now, he obviously shared—and probably sponsored—their enthusiasm. A few days later, as the celebrated guest of President Nasser and the only Soviet official speaking, he openly associated himself with the most radical view of developments in the UAR. Soon after arriving, at a youth rally he went out of his way to wish "the young citizens of the United Arab Republic, which is embarking on the path of socialist construction, great success."[20] The next day, May 11, he told the members of the UAR National Assembly that he welcomed their decision "to develop and strengthen the country, to achieve a better life for the people through socialist reconstruction."[21] "You are already moving in this direction," he said, "and you are moving successfully." To the workers at the Aswan Dam he brought his personal regards and best wishes for success in achieving socialism.[22] And in a joint communiqué issued at the end of his stay he expressed gratitude

18. *Pravda,* May 3, 1964, p. 1.
19. *Pravda,* May 7, 1964, p. 2.
20. *Pravda,* May 11, 1964, p. 1.
21. *Pravda,* May 12, 1964, p. 1.
22. *Pravda,* May 18, 1964, p. 3.

for the invitation to visit the UAR and for "the opportunity to become acquainted with the life of the working people and their successes in the struggle to improve the economy and the culture of a country embarking on the path of socialist development."[23]

As in the case of Ben Bella's visit to the Soviet Union, the Soviet leader matched his praise of the UAR's progress with generous praise of the role played by the UAR's president. Nasser too was made a "Hero of the Soviet Union." He too was referred to regularly as comrade; at one point Khrushchev said to him, your achievements give you the "right" to be called comrade.[24] This was treatment sharply in contrast with that accorded him four or five years earlier, and it underscored the basic change in the Soviet appraisal of such leaders.

By 1964, with immediate revolutionary opportunities in sub-Saharan Africa postponed, North Africa more and more became the filter and the focus of Soviet policy in all of Africa; Soviet attitudes toward radical Black African countries mirrored increasingly the Soviet reaction to Algeria and the UAR. The explanation for this is not difficult to find. Earlier when the plans of newly independent Algeria were untested and the leadership of the UAR temporarily hostile to the socialist countries, the most genuine revolutionary opportunities appeared to exist in tropical Africa. Here the most rapid alienation from Western policies and structures seemed to be taking place. Nevertheless, from the very beginning, the real Soviet stake in a country like Guinea resided in the influence its example provided the rest of sub-Saharan Africa—the area in general and more critical countries such as Nigeria and the Congo—and in the access Guinea gave the Soviet Union to these other regions. Guinea in itself never possessed great intrinsic importance for the Soviet Union.

With these options foreclosed, and the language of revolution more virulent in Algeria and the UAR, Soviet priorities shifted back to North Africa. In terms of strategic importance—population, natural wealth, location, and external political influence—these two countries were significant enough to justify exceptional attempts to foster close intergovernmental and interparty relations. Khrushchev, we can speculate, wished to rationalize the special relationship he now sought with Algeria and the UAR. Given the importance of North Africa (and commensurately the declining importance of sub-Saharan Africa), once presented with

23. *Pravda*, May 25, 1964, p. 1.
24. Associated Press report from Aswan, May 14, 1964, quoted in Ra'anan, "Moscow and the 'Third World,' " p. 27.

the defensible possibility that these regimes were committed to a major political transformation, he seized upon this prospect to bestow theoretical legitimacy on their efforts while also underwriting their ties with the Soviet Union. It may be, as Uri Ra'anan has said, that "an old man, in a hurry to offset the losses of his reign by some showy gains and pressured to prove tangibly that his approach was superior to the Chinese line, was happy to seize upon the iconoclastic theories of some bright young men who seemed to offer an easy way to success."[25]

Revisionism Applied to Mali and Ghana

Mali and Ghana fitted even more perfectly these new theoretical formulations. They lacked the strategic importance of Algeria and the UAR which had inspired Khrushchev and his supporters to undertake this distinctly "revisionist" course. But once the decision was taken to depart from doctrine in order to prod (rather than verify) the course of development in these countries, it was easy and natural to include Mali and Ghana within the new categories. They, along with Burma, became members of a group of five favored nations acknowledged in exploratory intellectual colloquia convoked during 1964 and eventually given official recognition in the statements of policymakers.

A hallmark discussion dealing with the central issues raised by this radical reassessment of national socialism took place in early 1964 and again featured important members of the Institute of World Economics and International Relations. The discussion, sponsored by the editorial board of *Mirovaya ekonomika i mezhdunarodnye otnosheniya*, involved seventeen prominent Soviet economists, historians, and journalists from all the agencies and institutes concerned with the developing countries.[26] One of the senior participants signaled the direction of the discussion when he described their dialogue as evidence that "we are mastering many new paths," adding, "It is particularly gratifying to note that the conclusions and assessments which until quite recently were shared

25. *Ibid.*, p. 30.
26. See "Sotsializm, kapitalizm, slaborazvitye strany" (Socialism, Capitalism, and the Underdeveloped Countries), *Mirovaya ekonomika i mezhdunarodnye otnosheniya,* no. 4 (1964), pp. 116–131, and no. 6 (1964), pp. 62–81. A special issue of *Mizan,* VI (November 1964), carried a translation of these discussions, and it is from this translation that the following quotations are taken unless otherwise indicated.

by a comparatively small circle of people have now begun to be shared by many."[27]

The reference was obviously to Mirsky and his allies, who like him had taken a position particularly tolerant of the political and economic forms evolved by a number of the developing countries. At the moment Mirsky was carrying his argument several steps further. Any country, he contended, whatever its level of development, "can set foot on the road to socialism."[28] "The crucially important subjective factor" hinges on whether there exists a "political leadership that accepts socialism." Having directly evoked the traditional question, "what is to be done" where the proletariat is weak, where "for one reason or another the working class is not yet prepared to lead the advance to socialism," Mirsky boldly wielded the initiative:

> The doctrinaires and dogmatists will reply: Wait. Restrict the movement to the aims of bourgeois-democratic revolution and promote capitalism in the anticipation that the working class will mature sufficiently to lead the socialist revolution. Experience, however, has shown that in our day, with the socialist world system so decisively influencing the course of world events, this long "classical" path is by no means obligatory. The national liberation revolution can immediately break out of the framework of bourgeois-democratic revolution and begin the transition to socialist revolution . . . If the conditions for proletarian leadership have not yet matured, the historic mission of breaking with capitalism can be carried out by elements close to the working class."[29]

Said Mirsky, "Nature abhors a vacuum." "Elements close to the working class," the revolutionary democrats typified by Nkrumah, Ben Bella, Keita, and Nasser and their political parties, could propel the developing countries on their way to socialism. To render the whole process recognizable to Communists who may have lacked his imagination, Mirsky proposed that "the socialist world system is performing the functions of proletarian vanguard in relation to imperialist-oppressed nations . . . by helping to provide the political, military, and economic requisites

27. *Ibid.,* p. 28.
28. G. Mirsky, "The Proletariat and National Liberation," *New Times,* no. 18 (1964), p. 8.
29. *Ibid.,* pp. 8–9.

for the continuous advance of the national liberation revolution."[30] In the spring colloquium, he contended that "reforms now being carried out in these countries are non-capitalist measures."[31] Admittedly they still did not add up to socialism but they were, according to Mirsky, "the primary stage of the transition to socialist construction."

Despite the irrefutably liberal cast to the discussion, few of his listeners were willing to go so far in ascribing to socialism of the national type qualities of genuine socialist development. However, R. M. Avakov, once Mirsky's partner and later the man who chastised him for his "undiscriminating" analysis of developments within the UAR, now, in a complete repudiation of the 1961 party program, noted a "definite transition from the ideology of nationalism to that of national-type socialism," which represented a "breaking out from the national bourgeois framework."[32] In this respect Avakov had the general support of most speakers, who now found socialism of the national type an essentially progressive phenomenon. Similarly, the discussions devoted to the role of the state sector in the developing countries, the priority of heavy industry, the position of foreign capital, and the configuration of class forces reflected a more liberal disposition on the part of Soviet spokesmen.

Although, in the comments reported, no one duplicated Mirsky's enthusiasm for compressing the stages of the transition to socialism, his arguments must have inspired significant suggestive support. This would appear to be the reason for Victor Tyagunenko's reminder to "a number of speakers" who "have voiced the idea that most of the tasks of bourgeois democratic revolutions have already been solved and that these countries are already on the threshold of socialist revolutions," to "beware of the danger of running ahead of events."[33] But the explicit support Mirsky may have received rarely emerges from the published record.

Nevertheless, the mood of the intellectuals had shifted. Gradually, under the apparent patronage of Khrushchev, Mirsky's ideas found their echo in the Soviet press and the pronouncements of party leaders. Moscow radio quoted, with no qualifiers, Modibo Keita's April pre-election speech proclaiming that the people of Mali had "taken to the road of socialism."[34] Later *Pravda*'s correspondent interpreted the Union

30. *Ibid.*, p. 9.
31. *Mizan,* November 1964, p. 16.
32. *Ibid.*, p. 17.
33. *Ibid.*, p. 29.
34. Moscow TASS (international service in English), 05.54 GMT, April 10, 1964.

Soudanaise's resounding victory in this election as proof of Mali's "overwhelming desire to build socialism."[35] "Mali," he said, "will continue to build socialism." In August Kudryavtsev entered a similar conclusion: the republics of Ghana and Mali "did not halt at the first stage" of development but "went on to remodel their life on Socialist lines."[36] In the meantime Khrushchev had paid special tribute to the achievements of the UAR, a country, he had repeated several times during his May visit, already embarked on the path of socialist construction. And, when receiving the Malian leader Madeira Keita during a September visit to the U.S.S.R., he reportedly expressed the conviction that "Mali was progressing normally in socialism."[37] In December, V. D. Solodovnikov, Potekhin's successor as director of the African Institute, provided a particularly contented comment on African socialism: "The African peoples are becoming more and more convinced that socialism is indivisible. There is no Arab or Ghanaian, Kenyan or Algerian socialism. At the same time Marxism-Leninism admits a diversity of forms for the transition of differing countries to socialism; each country brings its own special features to the construction of socialism."[38] Of course some mistakes and miscalculations were possible on this road, he conceded, "but mistakes and miscalculations are not what characterize the basic line of present-day development."

This was not so in the case of Guinea, a country conspicuously and consistently omitted from the list of five states said to be (or about to be) building socialism. Guinea, by reintroducing private control over retail trade and by reinvigorating the invitation to foreign capital, had lost prestige in Soviet eyes. During the Institute of World Economics discussions, R. A. Ulyanovsky acknowledged that in some countries "there have been periods of retrogression"—giving privileges to foreign capitalist investment, stopping nationalization, and returning nationalized property to private ownership.[39] Another participant, V. Rybakov, was more specific. In Guinea, he commented disapprovingly, the big Fria combine remained in the hands of foreign monopolies, and, still worse, the com-

35. I. Belyaev, in *Pravda*, April 21, 1964, p. 4.
36. V. Kudryavtsev, "Africa: Answer in Unity," *International Affairs*, no. 8 (1964), p. 74.
37. Bamako radio (domestic service in French), 20.15 GMT, September 5, 1964.
38. V. Solodovnikov, in *Pravda*, December 1, 1964, p. 5. Potekhin died in September 1964.
39. *Mizan*, November 1964, p. 2.

pany exploiting bauxite deposits at Boké, once a nationalized enterprise, had recently been turned over to American management.[40] Guinea constituted an exception to the general progress recorded by the most advanced African states, forfeiting any title to rank among the states said to be on or across the threshold of the socialist transition.

Reservations over Khrushchev's Revisionism

Khrushchev's program for accelerating the Third World's transformation to socialism, however, never received unanimous acceptance from either the intellectual community or, more important, from his colleagues within the party leadership. Dissenters had appeared even among the liberals taking part in the early Institute discussions. Tyagunenko's disagreement with speakers, convinced that some developing countries stood on the verge of socialist revolution, has already been noted. Others also doubted the unequivocally progressive character of socialism of the national type and, though hopeful, they did not hesitate to register reservations.[41] In another forum in September, well into the period during which Mirsky's formula pervaded the large part of commentary on the developing countries, K. Ivanov specifically questioned the measures taken by the UAR, Algeria, Burma, Ghana, "and others" against imperialism and the "home-grown" capitalist path, making it quite clear that these had not yet brought them to the socialist path of development.[42] "It is," he cautioned, "difficult to foresee what phases such development will have to pass before it becomes Socialist. Here again the position should not be simplified."

More serious for Khrushchev's ideological initiative than the restraint of some intellectuals was the evident opposition within upper echelons of the leadership. It is an important part of Ra'anan's argument that Khrushchev in his haste to prod historical forces had, in the estimation of important colleagues like Boris Ponomarev, Mikhail Suslov, and Aleksei Rumyantsev, exceeded good judgment.[43] His unjustifiable ideo-

---

40. *Ibid.*, p. 10.

41. See, for example, the speech of G. S. Akopyan in *Mizan*, November 1964, p. 24.

42. K. Ivanov, "The National-Liberation Movement and Non-Capitalist Path of Development," *International Affairs*, no. 9 (1964), p. 42.

43. Ponomarev was long the Central Committee secretary most important in shaping Soviet policy toward non-Communist regimes (and reportedly a close ally of Suslov's). Suslov, the ancient ideologue and Presidium member, was after

logical tinkering represented a further reason for removing him from power.

In February when Suslov delivered a major statement to the Central Committee on the key ideological issues in the Sino-Soviet dispute, he refrained from any mention of the progress being attributed to the revolutionary democracies elsewhere in the Soviet press.[44] Even more conspicuously, his address to the French Communist Party's Seventeenth Congress, presented in the very week of Khrushchev's visit to the UAR, completely ignored the visit and Khrushchev's remarks there—though he did in passing refer to the national liberation movement and the PCF's role in the Algerian war.[45] Nor did Ponomarev repeat any of Khrushchev's formulas in a significant comment on these subjects appearing in *Pravda* on September 29.[46] To them, apparently, Ghana, Mali, and others were not so obviously about to begin the transition to socialism.

Another straw in the wind was the failure of a number of contributors to the *World Marxist Review* to pay the slightest heed to Khrushchev's recent pronouncements. In a signed article prepared a few weeks following Khrushchev's return from Cairo, Rumyantsev carefully made no reference to his actions there, not even a reference to Nasser's status as a revolutionary democrat.[47] But he did open the pages of the *World Marxist Review* to members of the Algerian, Egyptian, and other local Communist parties, who shared few of the Soviet premier's ideas about developments in their countries.[48] Moreover, the July issue of the *World Marxist Review,* containing Rumyantsev's piece, included another curious article by Mikhail Kremnyov, which came very close to contradicting

---

Khrushchev most concerned with foreign-policy questions. Rumyantsev was editor of the *World Marxist Review;* soon after Khrushchev's removal he became editor of *Pravda.*

44. Suslov, in *Pravda,* April 3, 1964, pp. 1–8.

45. *Pravda,* May 16, 1964, p. 2.

46. *Pravda,* September 29, 1964, pp. 2–3.

47. A. Rumyantsev, "On the Basic Contradictions of the Contemporary Epoch," *World Marxist Review,* VII (July 1964), 10.

48. See Fuad Nasser and Aziz Al-Hajj, "The National Liberation Movement and the World Revolutionary Process," *World Marxist Review,* VII (March 1964), 8–14; M. Ahmadi, "Some Problems of the Algerian Revolution," *ibid.,* pp. 89–92; Khalid Bakdash, Some Problems of the National-Liberation Movement," *ibid.,* VII (August 1964), 48–56; and "Exchange of Views: Problems of the National-Liberation Movement of the Arab Peoples," *ibid.,* VII (July 1964), 74–82, and especially part 2 of the same in VII (September 1964), 51–61.

Khrushchev's assessment of the UAR.[49] Kremnyov, a correspondent for the *World Marxist Review,* had reportedly visited the UAR several months earlier and was now giving his impressions, which were far less hopeful than Khrushchev's. He wrote, for example, that although the 1962 Charter of National Action proclaimed scientific socialism the "suitable style for finding the right method leading to progress," the document "does not elaborate on the concept of 'scientific socialism.' "[50] And then in an unmatched bit of hedging he continued, "Nor does it say that it means Marxist scientific socialism." "Furthermore," he reminded the reader, "at one time the Egyptian press accentuated the differences between the 'Egyptian road to socialism' and scientific socialism as conceived and defined in Marxist-Leninist theory." As far as he was concerned, the UAR was a "striking illustration" of a newly free country striving to "embark on the non-capitalist road," a road that "may not be the shortest road to socialism."[51] After all, as he put it, "social and economic reconstruction in the United Arab Republic has its difficulties," and these difficulties are not always tackled with "due determination."

It would have been out of the question for a mere journalist to shrug off what Khrushchev had praised, to put into quotation marks those formulas he embraced, if Khrushchev was not being challenged on these points by his most important colleagues. Indeed the Soviet leader did seem to be on the defensive in a radio and television address to the nation on May 27, after his return from the UAR.[52] Though he repeated his contention that the UAR was embarking on a "journey along the road of socialist development," he confessed that this was "not a simple and easy matter." Later in the same speech, he appeared to retract even this modified version of his original formula. In referring to an upcoming congress of the Arab Socialist Union he said: *"Apparently* the decisions adopted at this congress will to a great extent determine the specific path along which the political, economic, and social life of the United Arab Republic is to develop."[53] But was his choice of words intended to show that he really did not agree? As we shall see later, it was not the only battle being fought in this speech.

49. M. Kremnyov, "The UAR—Its Progress and Its Problems," *ibid.,* VII (July 1964), 83–91.

50. *Ibid.,* p. 84.

51. *Ibid.,* p. 91.

52. *Pravda* and *Izvestiya,* May 28, 1964, pp. 1–2, trans. in *Current Digest of the Soviet Press,* XVI (June 17, 1964), 17.

53. *Ibid.,* p. 18; emphasis added.

After Khrushchev's removal, according to the press of West European Communist parties, among his alleged transgressions were journeys undertaken without consulting the Central Committee Presidium, the results of which frequently did not "accord with the interests of the Soviet Union."[54] The strongest evidence of the unpopularity of Khrushchev's ideological experimentation, however, came after his departure, when the new leadership clearly rejected the offending formulas.

The Test-Ban Treaty and the Cuban Example

There were two other considerations that may have partially accounted for Khrushchev's renewed interest in the national liberation movement, prompting him to tamper with the more restrictive formulations once applied to countries such as Mali and Ghana. First, the Soviet leadership's disappointment over the reluctance of the Afro-Asian movement to support fully the Soviet position, now under violent Chinese attack, diminished markedly after July 1963 when these countries strongly and actively endorsed the three-power test-ban treaty. Their support at this point—the Chinese were incensed by the agreement—proved to Soviet leaders that they need not de-emphasize the national liberation struggle in order to advance the struggle for peace, that both enterprises could be reconciled. In August a unanimous decision by the ministerial council of the OAU meeting in Dakar recommended that member states sign the test-ban agreement;[55] almost every African leader, with the exception of Sekou Touré, indicated hearty approval of the treaty and congratulated the three powers that had negotiated it.

Their support, moreover, was matched by the undisguised rebuff given the Chinese at the A-APSO executive committee meeting in Nicosia on September 10–12, 1963. The Chinese selected the Nicosia gathering to stage a thorough and heated attack on the test-ban agreement in the context of current Soviet policy. But most delegates, with the exception of those from Ceylon, Indonesia, Japan, North Korea, North Vietnam, and the South Vietnamese National Liberation Front, turned their backs on the Chinese and voted for a resolution reaffirming A-APSO's adherence to the principles of peaceful coexistence, the struggle for peace,

54. Unspecified selections from *L'Unità*, quoted in Ra'anan, "Moscow and the 'Third World,' " pp. 29–30.
55. See Soviet references to this action in Moscow radio (in Swahili to Zanzibar), 11.00 GMT, August 14, 1963.

plans for total and complete disarmament, and a program prohibiting nuclear weapons.[56] Moreover, they accepted a resolution commending the nations that had signed the test-ban agreement and urging the convocation of an international conference to study the problem of disarmament and the complete prohibition of nuclear tests, propositions that were anathema to the Chinese. And as further salve to a Soviet leadership still sensitive over the manhandling its forces had received at the March Moshi conference, the meeting went on to affirm the desire of the solidarity movement "to establish and develop bonds of cooperation and friendship with organizations which pursue the same objectives as our Movement whether on the international level outside the continents of Africa and Asia."[57] Soviet leaders must have been encouraged.

As a second essential part of the explanation, presumably Khrushchev found himself turning increasingly to the implications of developments within Cuba. The impact that Castro's self-proclaimed metamorphosis had on his thought cannot, of course, be measured. But it seems likely that he had Cuba in mind when he revised theories applied to Algeria, the UAR, Ghana, Mali, and Burma. After all, the single successful national conversion to Communism during Khrushchev's rule had been Cuba and this had happened not because of anything the Soviet Union had done, not even because a local Communist party existed, but because Castro had declared his revolution Communist and his country part of the socialist camp. This had occurred in 1961, however, and so Cuban events can scarcely be considered a direct catalyst for Khrushchev's 1964 experimentation with ideology. They more likely determined the extent of his vision once more recent developments elsewhere (in North Africa) had prompted him to dream. Impressed with the possibility that there lurked in the Third World other potential Castros, Khrushchev was probably trying, through ideological manipulation, to bring them forward. Apparently he hoped in the process to accelerate their commitment to more rigorous forms of socialist construction. Already institutionalized ties between the parties of these countries and the CPSU provided an instrument by which these regimes could be brought into the socialist camp. Khrushchev's modifications in theory suggest that

---

56. "Resolution and Recommendations of the Sixth Session of the Executive Committee Meeting," Afro-Asian People's Solidarity Organization, Permanent Secretariat (mimeo, n.d.), p. 4. Also see Moscow TASS (in English to Europe), 09.15 GMT, September 12, 1963, and Peking NCNA (in English to Asia and Europe), 01.30 GMT, September 24, 1963.

57. *Ibid.*, p. 30.

he added to this machinery a means for "insinuating" their political systems into that next higher stage of development. If in the years after 1958 Soviet policy had been preoccupied with finding additional "Guineas," the search in 1964 shifted to uncovering new "Cubas."

The Search for African "Cubas"

The full ramifications of Khrushchev's ideological innovations became apparent in the thesis of Jack Woodis, a British Communist and widely published African specialist. An article of his, appearing in the June 1965 issue of the *African Communist* (but prepared some time during January 1965, that is, after Khrushchev's deposition but before his policy could be gracefully invalidated), contained a remarkable extension of Khrushchev's ideas.[58] Because of its startling implications, one passage deserves to be quoted in full:

> It had previously been believed in some circles that African peoples wishing to advance to socialism would have to set up their own Communist Party, organizationally and ideologically separate from the single national party. The formation of such Communist Parties has taken place in some African countries, and may become necessary in some others. *But experience shows that in a number of African states, as the peoples drive from independence to complete their national democratic revolution and advance towards socialism, possibilities can arise which facilitate changing the class composition, character and ideology of the single, mass parties, transforming them from broadly based national parties into consciously socialist parties based on Marxism-Leninism, and increasingly led by the working people.*[59]

Thus it did not seem at all farfetched to suspect that Khrushchev too might soon admit the possibility of completing the transition to socialism in the borrowed shell of once alien institutions, skipping entirely the creation of a Communist party.

Taking the word of the *Spark* (the newspaper of CPP radicals), Woodis cited the alleged transformation of Ghana's dominant party, arguing that eventually it would become that substitute for a Communist

58. Jack Woodis, "Democracy and Africa," *African Communist,* no. 21 (April–June 1964), pp. 63–70.
59. *Ibid.,* p. 70.

party just described. In the period before independence and until recently, he maintained, the CPP existed as an "instrument of the will of all sections of the people fighting for national independence." But this phase of the struggle had closed and now Ghana's tasks were different, requiring that the nature of the party change as well. The CPP should play "its role as a vanguard party," "coordinating, mobilizing and directing the initiative of the people" in the construction of socialism.[60] As the party of national reconstruction and socialism, and no longer as the party of national independence, the function and character of the CPP had to be transformed. The "honor of membership" should be granted only to the most active, dedicated, and honest people, on the basis of their "grasp of socialist ideology, the level of political consciousness, devotion and dedication to the socialist cause."[61] A party made up mostly of white-collar workers, civil servants, and middle-class intellectuals, the *Spark* had said, could never attain socialism. So admission to the party would have to be carefully regulated, recruitment aimed at the workers, peasants, and revolutionary youth, and the entire party structure subjected to thorough ideological indoctrination, designed to prepare party members for dealing with problems in a "scientific way, in a creative and correct way."[62]

Allegedly steps to recast the character of the CPP (and in Mali, the Union Soudanaise) were already underway. Ghanaian Defense Minister Kofi Baako in March announced that socialism could not be built without socialists, insisting that all those charged with responsibilities in the various spheres of national activity be "convinced socialists."[63] The Kwame Nkrumah Ideological Institute had been in operation for more than three years, sharpening the political "consciousness" of refugees, students, and a limited number of party officials. Now Ghana's political leaders began to talk of submitting the entire political elite—party *apparatchiki,* governmental officials, leaders of "voluntary associations," and entering university students—to a process of comprehensive ideological indoctrination. Eventually even the military was to assimilate a propaganda and agitation network modeled after the Soviet Union's Main Political Administration. Nkrumaism constituted the epicenter of

60. *Ibid.,* pp. 64–65.
61. *Ibid.,* p. 65.
62. *Ibid.*
63. Accra radio (Ghana News Agency in English), 15.10 GMT, March 19, 1964.

the ideology and was said to issue from "the great foundation of scientific socialism," through Marx and Lenin to the "genius of Nkrumah who is 'enriching the socialist commonwealth' with unassailable creative thoughts."[64] Mali's leaders also set plans in motion for strengthening the ideological preparation of the party's apparatus in a higher party school, to be built by the Soviet Union.

Moreover, by 1964 Nkrumah in particular appeared determined to establish his party as the pre-eminent influence in Ghana's political life. A constitutional amendment forced upon the electorate in early 1964 declared the CPP the only legal party in that country and the acknowledged "vanguard of the people in their struggle to build a socialist society." Harshly repressive measures unleashed against every stratum of the population—in some cases for crimes no more serious than gossiping ("rumor mongering") about Nkrumah's seemingly precarious position in the wake of two assassination attempts—reflected the regime's readiness to wield power against even the smallest challenger. With the purge of Sir Arku Korsah, Ghana's chief justice, late in 1963 and the legal subordination of his successor's tenure to the whim of the president, Nkrumah had subverted the last institution holding his power in check. Meanwhile, the voice of Nkrumah's "socialist revolution," the *Spark*, vigorously praised scientific socialism, condemning with equal vigor the "spurious" and "neocolonialist" notion of African socialism. Well known in Ghana, although of debatable influence, it offered an orthodox Marxist-Leninist explanation of class relations and the struggle for economic independence. (In November 1964, Nkrumah announced his personal role in conceiving and naming the *Spark*.[65] His model had been, he said, the famous Russian underground newspaper, *Iskra*, one of Lenin's primary political instruments in the first years of Bolshevism.)

By all measurements Nkrumah's revolution fitted perfectly with new Soviet theories. He himself resembled the charismatic, somewhat mystical, and frequently unpredictable Castro, avowedly devoted to Marxism-Leninism, alienated from his Western mentors, and determined to build his country's future under socialism. The CPP was to be declared a vanguard party, incorporating the political elite and mobilizing the masses for the task of socialist construction. To infuse these cadres with a profound sense of socialism, Nkrumah had already introduced a pro-

64. Accra radio (in English to Africa), 14.45 GMT, March 18, 1964.
65. Kwame Nkrumah, *Ghanaian Times,* November 16, 1964, p. 6.

gram of formal ideological training which, according to projections, would soon be expanded to mold the minds of broad segments of Ghana's politically engaged. And in extinguishing all opposition he had ensured that no countervailing current would emerge to challenge the CPP and divert Ghana from its revolutionary course.

In addition to the close parallel between Soviet prescription and Ghana's apparent political development, Soviet optimism depended on the direct influence Soviet officials possessed within Ghana. By 1964 Soviet advisers were deeply involved in Nkrumah's security apparatus; their allies, the East Germans, had a heavy stake in his African intelligence operations; and both Soviet and East European representatives contributed important direct support to Nkrumah's chief indoctrination center at Winneba.[66] Although Soviet advisers had not penetrated the crucial agencies of control—the army and the police—their expanding role within the security apparatus opened the possibility of reaching these organizations through the back door.[67] Moreover, the fact that Nkrumah was becoming increasingly dependent on Soviet specialists for his own personal security greatly augmented Soviet influence.

Soviet involvement with his security police, beginning shortly after the Kulungugu assassination attempt in August 1962, was at first confined to the work of a single adviser, charged with the task of enlarging and training the Presidential Detail Department, the agency responsible for presidential security.[68] It seems likely, however, that contact at this level introduced Soviet officials into broader areas of national security. Soon an entire troop of security officers arrived to replace Khruschchev's single security adviser. According to one Western correspondent, in December 1963, twenty-five Russians with unspecified responsibilities appeared for the first time, took up residence in the flats reserved for Soviet airline advisers aiding Ghana Airways, and in shifts of six com-

66. After January 1964, according to Scott Thompson, a "large" group of Ghanaians were sent to the Soviet Union for a "two-year course in counterintelligence." Thompson, *Ghana's Foreign Policy,* p. 295.

67. In June 1962 a Soviet military delegation arrived in Ghana with plans for reorganizing and re-equipping the Ghanaian military forces. Apparently its program was sabotaged by the same military obstructionists who evaded Nkrumah's earlier order to send four hundred cadets to the Soviet Union for military training, ultimately sending fewer than seventy. See Moscow TASS (in English to Europe), 11.15 GMT, June 27, 1962.

68. Khrushchev had originally offered to aid Nkrumah in this area during his brief vacation in the Crimea in August 1961, but Nkrumah turned the offer down. For details see Thompson, *Ghana's Foreign Policy,* p. 184.

menced three times every twenty-four hours to visit the Castle (the seat of government).[69] Their assignment was presumably to man security arrangements at the official residence and at the state house. Shortly after Nkrumah transformed Major-General Alexander's old Presidential Guard Regiment into the President's Own Guard Regiment in . the spring of 1963, giving it responsibility for security and ceremonial functions, Soviet advisers were invited to assist with its management as well. Thus by late 1964, the Soviet Union possessed almost exclusive influence over Ghana's internal security affairs, including what after two assassination attempts had become an increasingly vital objective, the president's physical survival.

In addition, the Soviet Union had achieved extraordinary power over Nkrumah through its ambassador. The instant, direct access the Soviet ambassador had to the president's office reflected the degree of influence he wielded over Nkrumah, influence that was often applied to secure Ghana's public support for Soviet policy, despite and perhaps over ministerial opposition. (How the Soviet Union employed this exceptional leverage is something that we shall return to in the next chaper.)

As might be expected, Ghana's foreign policy (like Mali's) reinforced Soviet enthusiasm, now considerably increased by the "revolutionary implications" of domestic reform. For Ghana the period marked the removal of all but the fiction of nonalignment. Scott Thompson concludes that after the second assassination attempt against Nkrumah in January 1964: "To the extent that international issues dividing East and West were of relevance, [Ghana's] policy was designed to bring aid and comfort to one party. From an objective viewpoint, this can be non-alignment only in its most technical sense, indicating an absence of formal alliance with great powers."[70] Lloyd Garrison reported to the *New York Times* in May that, despite considerable economic ties with the West, the consensus among most diplomats in Accra was that Nkrumah had turned emotionally away from the West.[71] Later that year, another *New York Times* article contended that the "bitterest anti-American campaign to

69. Douglas Brown, *Sunday Telegraph,* March 1, 1964. I saw this article as part of an official scrapbook kept by a former member of the Ghanaian press section attached to Flagstaff House. Brown, however, may have had his dates confused. It is unlikely that Soviet advisers arrived until after the second assassination attempt in January 1964.

70. Thompson, *Ghana's Foreign Policy,* p. 300.

71. Lloyd Garrison, "Portrait of Nkrumah as Dictator," *New York Times Magazine,* May 3, 1964, p. 15.

date" had begun, in which the United States was no longer excoriated as simply neocolonialist but now as "fascist-imperialist."[72] Angered by an unbecoming American press, Nkrumah's *Evening News* wrote (and Ghana radio repeated) that "American imperialism has really shown by its dirty methods of infiltration, subversion and lying propaganda that it is the worst enemy of the African revolution today."[73] This particular article demanded an immediate stop to the "fantastic, false, shameful and rotten lies that can only come from decadent imperialists." In March, during Averell Harriman's official visit to Ghana, the *Ghanaian Times,* in a report again circulated by the state radio, underscored his cool reception and contended that this constituted evidence that the United States needed to review its African policies, which are "out of step with the aspirations and hopes of Africa."[74] Throughout the year the entire communications network regularly condemned CIA interventions in Africa, Latin America, and Southeast Asia, American aggression in Panama, and Western aggression in Stanleyville. Indeed, Ghana's leader had convinced himself (with the aid of friends) that the CIA was determined to see to his murder, and this fear no doubt intensified his hostility to American policy, perceived largely as one massive CIA operation. Characterizing the United States as the custodian of NATO, Accra radio described the alliance as the "military arm of an aggressive economic system and the instrument to be used to stop the advance of Communism."[75] On the German question, the *Ghanaian Times* (generally considered the most important newspaper during this later period) urged recognition of the GDR whose "existence is itself a factor in insuring that the greed of monopoly capital . . . the greatest contributor to world tension, is brought under control."[76] When a trade-union delegation from East Germany toured Ghana in October, Moscow radio drew attention to this particularly "noteworthy" event.[77] At a time when the ruling circles of the Western powers were attempting to boycott the GDR, said the broadcast, "a large African country like

72. *New York Times,* November 8, 1964, p. 37.
73. *Evening News,* February 4, 1964, p. 1. See also Accra radio (in English), 20.50 GMT, February 4, 1964.
74. *Ghanaian Times,* March 21, 1964, p. 2. See also Accra radio (in English to Africa), 14.45 GMT, March 21, 1964.
75. Accra radio (in English to Africa), 14.45 GMT, May 3, 1964.
76. *Ghanaian Times,* October 7, 1964, p. 2. See also Accra radio (domestic service in English), 07.00 GMT, October 7, 1964.
77. Moscow radio (domestic service in Russian), 13.00 GMT, November 1, 1964.

Ghana is establishing with the GDR not just normal relations but also cooperation through trade unions."

Mali's press and radio were equally unsympathetic with American policy positions. *L'Essor* and Radio Mali gave away nothing to their Ghanaian counterparts in attacking Western, particularly American, imperialism and neocolonialism. They may have even surpassed them in condemning the American part in the Vietnamese war. Ghana, after all, aspired to play a major international role in bringing the two sides to the conference table. Mali sublimated its hostility to no such ambitions. Minister of Interior, Information, and Tourism, Ousmane Bâ, speaking at a nineteenth anniversary reception given by the North Vietnamese embassy in September, bitterly denounced "imperialist aggression" against Vietnam and Congo-Leopoldville (Kinshasa) and voiced his government and party's support for the "fighting Vietnamese people."[78] The following month Keita, while in Peking, received a delegation from the South Vietnamese National Liberation Front and expressed his hope that in the Vietnamese struggle the lackeys of United States imperialism might "soon be wiped out."[79]

Realism and Khrushchev's Experiment

If all of these factors—the devotion of certain African leaders to scientific socialism, their efforts to transform single, mass parties into close-knit, ideologically well-heeled cadre parties, and the growing convergence of their foreign policies with Soviet policy—had persuaded Khrushchev that these countries might soon make the transition to socialism and attach themselves to the socialist camp, then he must have surprised and embarrassed Soviet embassy people who were left with the imposing task of squaring this image of radical Africa with the reality they saw daily. No one knows for sure that the Soviet embassy in Accra reported the inconsistency of Ghana's attitude toward the two Germanies—its public preference for East Germany but proportionately larger trade with West Germany, its obvious reluctance to antagonize the West Germans by recognizing the other Germany, and its greater use of West German educational facilities to which it sent the largest contingent of African

78. Peking NCNA (international service in English), 17.07 GMT, September 4, 1964.

79. Hanoi radio, VNA (international service in English), 12.54 GMT, October 8, 1964.

students (600), 200 percent more in 1964 than in 1963;[80] that Soviet representatives reported the contradiction between Nkrumah and Keita's frequent references to the socialist goal of rapidly developing the state and cooperative sectors and their continuing invitation to foreign private capital, as well as their tardiness in imposing on the private sector rigorous public regulations; that they drew attention to the dubious compatability between the frequently sworn determination of these leaders to bind tightly the bonds of economic cooperation with the socialist countries and their inability to deflect the great flow of commerce from the West or to employ more than a small portion of the credits extended by the Soviet Union. President Keita's response to Deputy Foreign Minister Malik's remarks delivered at the opening of a Soviet trade and industrial exhibition in January must have seemed typically ungracious. He warned his audience that Mali must speed its economic development "if we want to keep Africa safe from the various ideologies, if we do not want our country to be a theater of permanent help, which endangers its stability."[81] So too may the Ghanaian contention that the growth of Soviet science and technology had been possible only under socialism have appeared hypocritical alongside Nkrumah's admission that socialism in Ghana belonged to the future, after industrialization, and his recommendation that "for some time" Ghana remain a mixed economy reserving a prominent role for the private sector.[82] Did the Soviet embassy in Bamako, for example, remind Moscow that Keita, despite his public abhorrence of Western neocolonialism, often spoke solicitously of relations with France, its former colonial master? Did they report Keita's fond recollection of France's reaction to Malian independence delivered on Mali National Day, September 22, 1964, in terms that were distinctly more dulcet than those once used? "The fact that our just claims were granted us by France," he now argued, "enabled the existing friendly

80. Paris radio, AFP (in English), 20.45 GMT, March 21, 1964.
81. Bamako radio (domestic service in French), 20.15 GMT, January 22, 1964.
82. The first reference was Accra radio (domestic service in English), 07.00 GMT, October 16, 1964; the second, Nkrumah's speech to the National Assembly on the Seven-Year Plan, Accra radio (domestic service in English), 10.05 GMT, March 11, 1964. That British investors failed to respond to the opportunities theoretically created by Ghana's seven-year development plan (1963) was, as Scott Thompson has said, not out of the fear "that British concerns might be nationalized, but that Ghana's economy would deteriorate enough to render British investments worthless." For details see Thompson, *Ghana's Foreign Policy*, p. 390.

relations between France and Mali to continue."[83] Underscoring the importance Mali attached to the strengthening of this cooperation, Keita declared the great love and profound admiration that Malians had for the French. "It is also not a secret that the Mali Government considers General de Gaulle's foreign policy as one designed to maintain peace and the independence of the peoples of Africa, Asia and of Latin America."

To what extent, one wonders, did Soviet representatives in the field point up the surest sign that these societies resisted a full commitment to socialism—their overwhelming economic dependence on the West? Mali, to be sure, had shifted a considerable portion of its external commerce to the socialist countries so that by 1964 something like 30 percent of its trade flowed to the East.[84] However, Soviet policymakers must have been aware that this shift had occurred two years earlier and that trade between the East and Mali at the end of 1964 was no greater than it had been in 1962. The Soviet share of Mali's trade with the socialist countries had increased by 19 percent, but the entire increase was in imports from Mali (reflecting, in large part, a sacrifice for the Soviet Union, which purchased Mali's products without further penetrating Mali's internal markets). East Europe, on the other hand, reduced its trade with Mali by 41 percent over the same period, the vast portion of the decrease occurring in imports (indicating that the East European governments had lost interest in making the same economic sacrifice as the Soviet Union).

Moreover, Soviet trade with Mali represented the most successful phase of its economic offensive in West Africa. Less impressive was the condition of Soviet-Ghanaian economic relations. That Soviet trade with Ghana had grown by 56 percent between 1961 and 1964 and still scarcely accounted for 7 percent of Ghana's total foreign commerce demonstrated

83. Bamako radio (domestic service in French), 12.45 GMT, September 22, 1964.

84. This includes China. It is difficult to get an accurate picture of Mali's foreign trade. Soviet statistics, as indicated before, record as part of ordinary commerce goods coming in under suppliers' credits; as a result, at least the figures for Soviet *exports* to Mali are distorted. Malian statistics are not completely reliable because of the inadequacy of statistical reporting and because no consistency is maintained in the items (or categories) reported. Having stated these shortcomings, the following Soviet figures are taken from *Vneshnyaya torgovlya SSSR za 1963* (Moscow, 1964) and Malian statistics from *Statistique du commerce extérieur* (Service de la Statistique Générale et de la Comptabilité Economique Nationale Ministère du Plan et de l'Economie Rural), annual.

the Soviet Union's incapacity to move Ghana out of its old trading patterns.[85] Throughout this period the balance of trade remained decidedly against the Soviet Union. Under the swing credit of $11 million provided for by the 1961 trade agreement, the Soviet Union at the end of 1964 owed Ghana $10.6 million.[86] Soviet efforts to relieve Ghana of larger and larger portions of its burdensome, but critical, cocoa stocks went unreciprocated by Ghana's private traders, who scorned Soviet products for English goods. Year after year import licenses for Soviet-bloc exports (theoretically 30 percent of all import licenses) remained unused, compelling the Soviet Union to renege on the graduated purchasing quotas it had agreed to under the 1961 trade protocols. But it did faithfully meet obligations under the 1961 protocols to purchase a fixed portion of Ghana's cocoa in "freely convertible currency." Nor could Soviet leaders have taken heart over the opening provided by their foreign aid. With the exception of work begun on a military airstrip at Tamale, neither the number nor significance of contracts signed in 1964, under the suppliers' credits of 1960 and 1961, matched that of preceding years.[87] By the end of 1964, less than 27 percent of Soviet credits extended to Ghana had actually been drawn down.

To Soviet personnel in Ghana, Khrushchev's suggestion that Ghana was building socialism must have seemed indeed fatuous. Nkrumah's propaganda network talked of transforming the CPP into a vanguard force for guiding Ghanaian society to socialism, but anyone who visited this country could detect an opposite process of atrophy besetting the party, under the bizarre and autocratic hand of the president's irresponsible lieutenants. Ghana's leadership swore allegiance to socialism, but it had scarcely begun to squirm within the West's economic embrace. All the while it was feathering its own nest in a most vulgar capitalist manner. And toward those few so-called Marxist-Leninists within the party's ideological and propaganda apparatus, who might have been expected to provide a counterweight to the regime's shortcomings, much Soviet opinion can only be described as contemptuous. In their kindest moments Russians on the spot regarded these people as ideologically undisciplined. It seems unimaginable that such attitudes did not creep into their

85. *Annual Report on External Trade in Ghana* (December), Central Bureau of Statistics; the *Annual Report on External Trade in Ghana* shares none of the weaknesses of comparable publications in Mali and Guinea.

86. Bank of Ghana, "Report of the Board for Year Ended June 30, 1964," p. 85.

87. See *Financial Statement, 1966* (Ghana), table 9.

reports and that a generally recognizable portrayal of the African reality did not filter up to the pinnacles of political authority. One must assume, therefore, that Khrushchev was either stubbornly oblivious to the facts or was calculating an expedient intended to flush out badly needed gains for Soviet foreign policy.

The Apogee and Decline of the Chinese Threat

In 1964 Soviet diplomats were also harassed by the difficulties posed by Chou En-lai's visit to Africa. (As I have suggested earlier, Khrushchev's experimentation in ideology may have, in some measure, been a response to this new Chinese initiative in Africa.) Chou's first stop in West Africa was Ghana. He arrived on January 11 and spent the next five days laboring to create the image of a country at once fiercely hostile to any compromise with imperialism and yet tolerant of Africa's way to wage the same struggle, a foreign policy committed but disinterested. Similarly Guineans, according to reports in *Jeune Afrique,* were "extraordinarily impressed" by Chou's willingness to avoid giving unsolicited advice and making presumptuous demands.[88] And in Mali, Modibo Keita told Chou, "You have understood that we are in a hurry, and you have avoided the error of people who are attempting the conquest of space before completing the liberation of man on earth."[89] Of particular concern to the Soviet leadership, Chou was highly successful in conveying the impression that Chinese policy ran a reasoned, practical course, in dispelling the idea that China's leaders were impetuous and fanatical, in relating China's revolutionary experience to Africa, while softly but constantly drumming on the theme that the Soviet line of peaceful coexistence betrayed the national liberation movement. To perfume the air, Chou brought with him a series of new aid promises and fresh plans for employing credits already extended. Ghana was to receive additional credits totaling $20 million, and in Mali and Guinea Chou cleared the way for the rapid completion of new cigarette and match factories. In addition the Chinese premier talked generously of Chinese support for a host of other possible projects— processing plants for vegetable oils, textile mills, pencil factories, and so on.

88. Kamal Jawal, "Le neutralisme est mort," *Jeune Afrique,* March 23, 1964, p. 7.
    89. Quoted in Cooley, *East Wind over Africa,* p. 148.

Chou's trip did not pass completely unmarred by unpleasant incidents. When he stepped from the plane in Conakry, Soviet sympathizers, until discouraged by the local police, distributed anti-Chinese propanda, and when Chou launched an attack on United States policy in Panama—violating Touré's strict moratorium on polemics—his remarks suffered pointed censorship in the Guinean press and radio.[90] According to Yugoslav sources, Chou's reticence in raising the question of Ghanaian socialism provoked some cabinet members to wonder why he so carefully avoided this subject.[91] A topic that he did raise in private—the possibility of China's aiding Ghana with its most recently organized subversion camps—inspired small enthusiasm. A nervous Nkrumah declined the offer.[92] And if Chou had thought of publicly pressing China's dispute with the Soviet Union, then, to read between the lines of a later account, he was advised to hold his tongue. "It would be childish to expect that Chou En-lai came to Africa to seek support in the CPR's controversy with Russia. African leaders know that they can help in resolving these difficulties by not taking sides."[93] Nor could Chou have considered his visit to Guinea an unqualified success when early the next month Touré announced that he would travel to India to "strengthen bonds" between peoples.[94]

The upshot of Chou's African diplomatic safari was to increase the general, but diffuse, feeling of sympathy that radical African states had toward the Chinese revolution and to increase their appreciation of the central position China must occupy in any Afro-Asian coalition, without at the same time rallying new African support for Chinese policy on specific issues. The attitude of important sections of the leadership in Ghana and Guinea toward China had long been one of identification with the underdog, an international outcast—identification born not of parallel foreign policies so much as an admiration for the fervor of Chinese convictions, sympathy with the tasks China sought to fulfill, and indignation over the isolation some Western powers would impose

90. Robert A. Scalapino, "On the Trail of Chou En-lai in Africa," Memorandum RM-4061 PR, RAND Corporation, April 1964, pp. 15–16.

91. In conversations with the Yugoslav ambassador, *ibid.*, p. 20.

92. This is the conclusion of Scott Thompson after seeing transcripts of the conversations with Chou. Thompson, *Ghana's Foreign Policy*, p. 297. (Later in 1964 A. K. Barden, head of the Bureau of African Affairs, persuaded Nkrumah to make use of Chinese advisers in one such camp.)

93. Accra radio (in English to Africa), 14.15 GMT, October 25, 1964.

94. Conakry radio (domestic service in French), 20.00 GMT, February 22, 1964.

on it. When, for example, the Chinese tested their first atomic device in October 1964, Ghanaian newspapers, consistently hostile to testing by either East or West, demonstrated how this vague sense of sympathy worked. "The mitigating circumstances surrounding the China blast must not be lost sight of for it is the hostile and unreasonable half of the world, led by United States imperialism that has forced China to join the nuclear club."[95] Nevertheless, though the communiqués with each of the countries raised the issue of general and complete disarmament, none, not even that with Guinea, endorsed the Chinese position on the test-ban agreement. Speaking generally, on specific issues Ghanaian and Guinean leaders adhered to positions much closer to those of the Soviet Union.

Meanwhile, Peking's adamant pursuit of its quarrel with Moscow, regardless of forum, increased the disquiet among African leaders. Despite Africa's oft-stated desire to keep the dispute outside Afro-Asian meetings, if anything Chinese representatives intensified the shrillness of attack, until, at the sixth session of the A-APSO council, convened in Algiers during March 1964, they provoked an open rebuke from African delegates. Madame Kuo-chien led the Chinese delegation to Algiers and in her main speech delivered a savage attack on Soviet policy. She assailed Soviet support for the United Nations as a mechanism for ending colonialism, Soviet priorities emphasizing the importance of building independent national economies, Khrushchev's proposal to renounce the use of force in settling territorial disputes and boundary questions, and of course the policy of peaceful coexistence.[96] It was not merely the unwanted introduction of polemics into the conference but the nature of the attack which alienated the Africans, for these were issues on which African leaders tended to agree with the Soviet Union. Venting the remainder of her fury, Madame Kuo shouted at the Soviet delegates, "Morally you are the assassins of Patrice Lumumba." Before the stunned delegates could respond she continued, "Your expansionism and national egoism have long since made it difficult to draw a line between you, the imperialists and the colonialists, old and new." If one accepts Soviet accounts, such abuse stimulated an "impassioned and persuasive" speech by Nathaniel Welbeck, head of

95. Accra radio, Ghana News Agency (in English), 14.15 GMT, October 25, 1964.
96. For Madame Kuo Chien's speech, see Peking NCNA (international service in English), 17.33 GMT, March 23, 1964.

the Ghanaian delegation, in which he declared that "we have no right to permit anyone to split our movement and to sow mistrust on the part of some of its participants for others."[97] The day following Madame Kuo's diatribe, Welbeck proposed that at future conferences the delegation wanting to attack other delegates should turn into the secretariat its written charges so that the plenary sessions "are not disturbed by such speeches."[98] In a halfhearted attempt to balance criticism of both sides, the *Ghanaian Times* deplored the disruption caused by the exchange of invective; but blaming the Chinese for "obstinacy and extremism" while commenting on the Soviet Union's "impatience" and "justifiable repugnance" was hardly equal condemnation.[99] Thus, within weeks of Chou's goodwill mission, China, in its relentless assault on Soviet policy, had begun to dissipate the genuine sympathy that it had in Africa.

China tenaciously pressed the attack in the fall of 1964 by setting up a rival to the Hiroshima Anti-Bomb Conference, packing its membership and ramming through resolutions denouncing the test-ban treaty, Soviet revisionism, and United States imperialism. This time Chinese tactics provoked sharper censure from the Ghanaian delegate, Peter Adjei, who emphasized that "not one word spoken in the name of Africa from such a rostrum would have any legal force whatever."[100] After telling of how the Chinese "shipped in puppets" and then used the tribunal of a conference of peace partisans "for unworthy political maneuvers," Adjei assured his Soviet interviewer that "we" could not "allow an attempt to be made to conduct foul slander against the U.S.S.R. in the name of the African peoples." P. A. Curtis-Joseph, the Nigerian delegate to the rival conference, reportedly described a similar "sense of shame and outrage" at hearing "these imposters slander the Soviet Union and the world movement of peace partisans."[101]

One of the countries whose delegates did not join in the criticism of China was Mali—an indication of the stability in relations between these two countries. Throughout the early 1960s Mali's ties with China had grown steadily. By 1964 trade between the two countries, though

97. *Pravda,* April 7, 1964, p. 3.
98. Prague radio, CTK (international service in English), 09.30 GMT, March 25, 1964.
99. *Ghanaian Times,* April 6, 1964, pp. 2, 11. See also Accra radio (in English to Africa), 14.45 GMT, April 6. 1964.
100. V. Ovchinnikov, in *Pravda,* August 13, 1964, p. 3.
101. *Ibid.*

still a small portion of each country's total commerce, was twice what it had been the previous year. So rapidly was their trade expanding that within one year China would become Mali's most important socialist trading partner.[102] In 1965, when trade between Eastern Europe, the Soviet Union, and Mali had plummeted, trade with China nearly tripled and for the first time pushed China past the Soviet Union among Mali's commercial partners. In addition, the Chinese had an estimated eight hundred to a thousand technicians working on various projects throughout the country, including a well-received and well-known cigarette factory underway outside Bamako.

Economic indicators, however, scarcely convey the strong political support that some Malian leaders gave Peking. Although it should be clear by now that an African leader's sympathetic references to one or another country do not necessarily represent a clear-cut political alignment, and are sometimes not even consciously consistent, in this instance the Chinese leadership must have found many Malian comments gratifying. For example, in early 1964 Mali radio vigorously praised China's achievements over the fifteen years since it had "distinguished [itself] in the Korean conflict."[103] At the end of the year an unidentified Malian minister "responsible for problems of rural development" predicted to Le Monde's correspondent that "in five years all of Africa will be pro-Chinese and on the path of socialism."[104] After Indonesia withdrew from the United Nations, Mali was one of the few nations to support Chou En-lai's proposals for a "new, revolutionary UN" free of United States influence. (Nkrumah, in contrast, was said to have regretted Chou's proposal and even to have attempted to dissuade the Indonesians from withdrawing.[105]) Similarly Mali was one of the few governments to endorse the Chinese atomic test in the fall of 1964. While in China during November, Keita noted that the Chinese test "had made the imperialists and its [sic] lackeys tremble even more."[106] "In the face of imperialist aggression, threats and attempts at intimidation and nuclear blackmail," he said, "the People's Republic of China as well as the Afro-Asian and Latin American countries have the right, if not the obligation to strengthen

102. *Bulletin mensuel de statistique* (Mali), 1966.

103. Bamako radio (domestic service in French), 20.15 GMT, January 30, 1964.

104. George Chaffard, in *Le Monde,* December 9, 1964, p. 1.

105. Cooley, *East Wind over Africa,* p. 21, and Thompson, *Ghana's Foreign Policy,* p. 406.

106. *Peking Review,* VII (November 6, 1964), 8.

their defense capability." (Again, the Ghanaian reaction was somewhat different. Although, as noted above, some Ghanaian newspapers expressed certain sympathy for China's predicament and justified the test as a reflection of China's insecurity, Nkrumah himself voiced misgivings and dismay over the news of the test, though he "appreciated the point of view of the Chinese people in this great achievement."[107])

Briefly then, to judge from the evidence, Khrushchev sometime late in 1963 encouraged a group of liberal intellectuals to devise new theoretical formulations for the radical African states and later, over opposition from within the party leadership, embraced their "revisionist" conclusions as part of a policy adventure intended to dredge the continent for other Cuban-style conversions to socialism. The extent to which Chinese competition in Africa propelled Khrushchev toward this radical departure from doctrinal orthodoxy is difficult to determine, but little suggests that it was the decisive consideration. One must be careful in weighing the effects of the dispute, however; for though it seems true that in the months after Chou's African visit the Chinese position lost ground (except in Mali) and therefore scarcely created the urgency justifying Khrushchev's surprising initiative, at the same time Soviet leaders could not escape the ideological death hold sought by the Chinese. They were constantly in need of significant triumphs for Soviet policy. Thus in a more general way, the dispute with China may well have aroused Khrushchev's sense of plight and prompted him to embark on this strange policy experiment.

The Moderate States

Soviet theory applied to the radical states of Africa was not the only aspect of policy reflecting innovation; signs of change also appeared in the Soviet approach to the so-called moderate countries. Not surprisingly, these were still obscured by ideological considerations.[108] In the long run, from the Soviet point of view, the critical question for any African nation turned on its choice between capitalism and socialism. Soviet ideologists would admit no other. Structurally this choice de-

---

107. Accra radio (domestic service in English), 10.25 GMT, October 24, 1964.
108. The following paragraphs draw on material in Robert Legvold, "The Soviet Union and Senegal," *Mizan,* VIII (July–August 1966), 57–66.

pended on the evolution of the state sector. The distinction, however, was not simply one between those who augmented the state sector and those who stunted its emergence, for the Soviet Union now recognized the need to exploit private capital in the early stages of development and countries such as Senegal and Nigeria had long recognized the need to develop the state sector. What really mattered was who administered the system. If they were "revolutionary democrats" like Nkrumah, Keita, or Touré, progress was ensured. If they were the "bureaucratic bourgeoisie," state capitalism served only to reinforce the position of foreign monopolies. In Senegal and Nigeria, Soviet writers argued, the bureaucratic bourgeoisie, that is, politicians, bureaucrats, and professional people, had joined forces with foreign monopolies. As a consequence, foreign capital in Senegal completely controlled the centralized state bodies purchasing agricultural produce. Because they benefited from state capitalism, the imperialists encouraged its expansion and were in turn a source of enrichment for the bureaucratic bourgeoisie.

Standing outside this system were all those on whom it fed: a handful of local factory owners, low-level civil servants and office employees, "100,000" proletarians (in Senegal), and peasants, 85 percent of Senegal's population but, like peasants the world over, the inert makeweight of revolution. Soviet writers knew very well that, even by their own definitions, they did not represent a consolidated opposition. A more important element in the Senegalese political equation was the politically powerful marabouts, the traditional religious leaders in a predominantly Muslim country. This consideration inspired Majhmout Diop, the PAI's secretary-general, to make the following engaging exhortation: "The future in Senegal belongs not to a coalition of Muslims and Christians directed against the patriots, but rather, as in the past, to a firm alliance between the Marabouts and all other patriots in the struggle against the foreign exploiters and their agents."[109] If this sounds somewhat far from the Marxist-Leninist millennium, such was the condition of Senegalese politics.

But, as I have said frequently before, the ideological assessment of an African country's internal structure only partially explains Soviet foreign policy. Equally relevant is that nation's international behavior. By early 1964 Senghor could say: "I believe our relations with the Soviet Union are developing normally. There are no differences between our

109. Cheikh A. Amidou and Mamadou Dienne, "Senegal Marches Forward," *World Marxist Review*, VIII (June 1965), 39.

states which could build tension."[110] More than that, Senegal's general support for the principles of peaceful coexistence, the struggle for peace, and the hastening of decolonization now appeared to the Soviet Union sufficient basis for limited cooperation.[111] True, Senegal's leaders urged a normalization of relations with the Tshombe regime and supported a temperate response to the 1964 Congo flare-up. Yet even on these issues, despite the violence of its official position, the Soviet Union probably valued the existence of moderate voices. Elsewhere, Senegalese enthusiasm for the test-ban treaty, its part in resolving the UN financial crisis, and its endorsement of the 1964 Cairo conference of nonaligned nations drew approving comment in the Soviet press. With respect to China, the Soviet Union had the best of both worlds: the Senegalese in September 1964 broke relations with the Nationalist Chinese but remained uneager to allow Peking more representation than a few New China News Agency correspondents. Moreover, Senegal's information commissioner, Pascal Sane, admitted when asked about China's recent atomic test that his country had "some fears since China is a big country; we fear the yellow peril people talk about."[112] From the Soviet point of view, even Senegal's affiliation with the newly formed Organisation Commune Africaine et Malgache had some merit, for within this "reactionary" grouping it resisted the extreme orientation of the right-wing group led by the Ivory Coast.[113]

During 1964 Soviet-Senegalese economic relations were substantially increased. For the first time the Soviet Union took a measurable quantity of Senegalese exports. At an annual rate of less than $500,000, Soviet buying still did not amount to much in absolute terms; nevertheless it did make the Soviet Union Senegal's second most important customer for groundnuts, by far its largest export item.[114] Soviet exports to Senegal remained at a very modest level, but they too had begun

110. A. Kovalev, in *Pravda,* February 20, 1964, p. 3.

111. This was the weight of Soviet Ambassador Yerofeyev's comments on arriving in Dakar and at a press conference the following year. See *Dakar-Matin,* February 5, 1963, p. 6, and November 7, 1964, p. 5.

112. London radio, Reuters (in English), 15.22 GMT, October 28, 1964.

113. See Moscow radio (in French and English for Africa), 22.00 GMT, June 14, 1965, and TASS (Russia abroad), 12.14 GMT, February 10, 1965. It is interesting to note that the Soviets did not draw the same distinction among the French-speaking members of the AMU; see, for example, the report on the Lagos Heads of State Conference in *Komsomolskaya pravda,* January 27, 1962, p. 3, and "The Monrovia Group of African States," *International Affairs,* no. 10 (1962), pp. 114–116.

114. *Commerce extérieur du Sénégal,* first eleven months, 1965.

to increase gradually. To promote a larger trade, in 1963 the Soviet Union opened an impressive commercial council in Dakar. During Foreign Minister Doudou Thiam's 1964 visit to Moscow, the Soviet Union announced its first ($6.7 million) credit to Senegal, to finance the construction of a tuna-processing complex.[115] It was also the Soviet Union's first aid agreement with a nonrevolutionary West African regime.

On his way home, Thiam told the Paris press: "I have become convinced that the Soviet Union respects and will respect the independence and sovereignty of Senegal." Relations were stable, he said, and the two countries were developing "a fruitful cooperation without dupery or ruse."[116] Judging from Thiam's earlier invidious descriptions of the Soviet Union, his remarks were more than a polite response to a reporter's question.[117] In a sense he was publicly abandoning his previous suspicions, manifested when he welcomed the first Soviet chargé d'affaires to Senegal in October 1962. Senegalese foreign policy, he said at the time, stipulated two principles: strict nonalignment and noninterference in the internal affairs of other nations.[118] Thiam's comments in Paris more than anything else expressed Senegal's changing view of the Soviet Union.

Soviet-Senegalese economic relations followed a pattern repeated in Soviet relations with most of the other moderate states. A sudden noticeable increase in Soviet purchasing suggested that Soviet leaders had selected business as the medium for reinforcing "businesslike" political relations with these states. Although in absolute terms insignificant, trade between Nigeria, Senegal, the Ivory Coast, and the Soviet Union surged forward dramatically, demonstrating a Soviet desire for enlarged contact with the former members of the Monrovian group. Total trade with Senegal that in 1963 had barely topped $30,000 dollars the next year advanced to nearly $400,000.[119] Similarly, in the case of Nigeria, the combined total of Soviet imports and exports jumped from slightly more than $250,000 in 1963 to more than $4.6 million in 1964,[120] and even

115. The protocol was signed in Dakar in February 1965 and the first plans submitted in August 1966.

116. *Dakar-Matin,* November 4, 1964, p. 1.

117. Doudou Thiam, *La politique étrangère des états Africains* (Paris: Presses Universitaires de France, 1963), esp. pp. 42, 116, 117, 147–152.

118. See Chapter Five.

119. *Commerce extérieur du Sénégal* (1965).

120. *Nigeria Trade Summary* (December 1964), Federal Office of Statistics. Moscow radio, August 9, 1964, noted this substantial increase in trade and predicted that "within a few years it might be reckoned in tens of millions of pounds." *Mizan,* VI (September 1964), 30.

with the Ivory Coast from $7,800 in 1963 to more than $2.6 million in 1964.[121] In every instance Soviet buying constituted 90 percent or more of the increase, meaning that trade rose because of Soviet initiative. (It must be kept in mind that on the African side purchasing remained in the hands of private, uncontrolled importers and is a very imperfect reflection of official policy.)

As with Senegal, the issue of aid also influenced Soviet relations with Nigeria during this period. Throughout 1964 the Nigerian press and radio reported various invitations to the Soviet Union to assist with Nigeria's six-year plan. During the visit of a Soviet parliamentary delegation, Nigerians frequently raised the question; in April the Midwestern leader, Chief S. J. Mariere, appealed to East Europe to aid in the region's development; in May, at the time of Khrushchev's visit to the UAR, the NTUC (Nigeria's radical trade-union federation) urged that the Soviet Union give Nigeria the same kind of assistance already extended other African countries; Lagos radio pointedly praised Soviet aid to the Aswan Dam; in August a reporter asked the new Soviet ambassador, A. I. Romanov, if the Soviet Union would be willing to aid Nigeria in building the £72 million Kainji Dam; and late in the year the minister of state for the navy told Ambassador Romanov that Nigeria would welcome Soviet technical aid to the Nigerian navy. The Soviet Union, in turn, invariably indicated that it would be pleased to help and promised to do what it could, but when nothing materialized, the suspicion grew that the Soviet Union was evading a specific commitment. This, however, ran contrary to Khrushchev's increasingly active policy in the moderate states.

Appearances were misleading and the truth seems to be the reverse. Not just the Soviet Union, but the Czechs, the Poles, and other East European governments were working hard to persuade the Nigerian government to take up credits already "tentatively" offered by Czechoslovakia ($14 million), Yugoslavia ($9.1 million), and Poland ($32 million). Soviet leaders made it quite plain to the Nigerians that they too were willing to extend aid. As the content of parliamentary questioning reveals, however, the reason all these offers went unused rested with the federal Nigerian government, not the Soviet leadership, and thus a distinction must be drawn between the unofficial inclinations of different Nigerian spokesmen, even regional leaders, and the formal policy

121. *Commerce extérieur de la Côte d'Ivoire* (1964).

of the federal government. Pressed during the questioning period by labor leader Sam Bassey to explain why aid offers from the socialist countries had been turned down, the Nigerian minister of finance assured Parliament that none of these offers had in fact been rejected and that "negotiations on the terms of the offers are progressing satisfactorily."[122] His assurances must have seemed of dubious value to Polish and Czech officials who had already waited one and a half to three years for the Nigerian government to act.

In 1964 the Soviet leadership significantly enlarged previous efforts to improve its position in the moderate states, launched with the passing of the Casablanca-Monrovia groups a year and a half before. Policymakers now accepted the durability of moderate African regimes and sought to fashion an amiable working relationship with them; they had agreed in effect to encourage favorable foreign-policy modifications by supporting mechanisms within, rather than outside, the local political system. In this context, the Soviet reaction to Nigeria's unsettled December elections clearly demonstrated an unwillingness to promote revolution even in potentially revolutionary situations.

One did not have to be a Communist to be convinced that conditions in Nigeria during the 1964 national elections presented revolutionary opportunities. Before January 11, 1965 (the expiration date of the existing House of Representatives), Nigeria was to hold its first federal elections since 1959.[123] Disruption and conflict seemed inevitable. In the intervening years competition among the regions had intensified, not lessened The fundamental antagonism between North and South, particularly deepseated between the Hausa-Fulani and the Ibo, pervaded the Federation's political institutions and transformed elections into bitterly unrestrained contests to aggrandize the power of individual regions within the Federation. The acute parochialisms of Nigerian politics made ultimate leverage within the federal government essential in order to protect independent and often conflicting regional interests. For example, rather than conceiving of the Federation's economic development as an issue of integration and cooperation, by 1964 the regions were maneuvering to secure an exclusive advantage in major development

122. *House of Representatives Debates* (Nigeria), nos. 2645, 2646, October 19, 1965.

123. The best account of this period is in John P. MacKintosh, *Nigerian Government and Politics* (Evanston: Northwestern University Press, 1966), pp. 545–609.

projects, such as new power, iron and steel, and transportation facilities. They were arguing over the distribution of the East's oil revenues and continually over the allocation of patronage. The parliamentary alliance between the East's NCNC and the North's NPC had already worn thin as the Northerners, the senior partners, asserted a growing self-confidence. All sides expected the long-awaited census in 1963 to advance their national electoral positions, and when the confusing results essentially confirmed the status quo, the prospect of Eastern politicians happily complying with an election that would almost inevitably perpetuate Northern predominance became exceedingly doubtful—especially when NPC leaders strongly hinted that they intended to form the new government either with a fresh set of partners from the Western region or on their own.

The elections were scheduled for December 30, 1964, but desperate Eastern leaders and their allies from other regions—faced with an obvious electoral defeat and angered by the harassment their candidates had incurred in some districts of the North and West—called on President Azikiwe to postpone them. Otherwise they threatened a boycott. Apparently they calculated that after the dissolution of Parliament, pending valid elections, the president (an Easterner) could replace the premier.[124] Under a more sympathetic head of government, a favorable census could be prepared and elections held on more promising terms. It was a poor calculation. Their boycott succeeded only in creating a severe crisis for the Federation. Azikiwe, pulled by his loyalty to the East and pressed by both the losers and the radical labor leaders who controlled the "Lagos mob," did toy with the idea of dismissing the premier. But the strong disapproval of Nigeria's most eminent jurists, together with the refusal of military leaders to submit to the president's authority (the constitution if anything made them responsible to the premier), dissuaded him; ultimately, after several harrowing days, the United Progressive Grand Alliance conceded its rival's overwhelming triumph. During all of this, American and European observers freely predicted that Nigeria was tottering at the edge of the abyss.[125]

The Soviet Union could ponder a further factor in assessing the current condition of Nigerian politics. A massive general strike had nearly unhinged the Nigerian economy during the previous June and, in the

124. *Ibid.*, pp. 586–589.

125. See, for example, the reports of Lloyd Garrison, in *New York Times*, December 29, 1964–January 2, 1965, and *Times* (London), December 30, 1964, p. 8, December 31, 1964, p. 10, and January 2, 1965, p. 9.

process, had greatly strengthened the position of the trade unions, including the NTUC, the noisy spokesman for almost half of Nigeria's 385,000 union members. *Pravda*'s commentator maintained that "neither Nigeria nor Africa has ever known such a mass organized outburst by the workers."[126] Still, the highly flammable mixture of worker discontent and deepseated political antagonisms, brought almost to the point of combustion in the December elections, did not move Soviet leaders to urge revolutionary activity upon Nigeria's revolutionary organizations.

When Nigeria's Marxist-Leninist element, the Nigerian Socialist Workers' and Farmers' Party, proposed a tactical alliance with the United Progressive Grand Alliance, hoping through elections to improve its position, it did so with explicit Soviet approval. (The UPGA refused.) During the campaign Moscow radio strongly endorsed the NSWFP's election platform, a minimum program obviously calculated to reach a broad electoral audience—not revolutionaries.[127] The program called for fair income distribution, improved working conditions, a formal labor code, broader trade-union rights, the liquidation of peasant debts to feudal masters, peasant credits, a policy of peace, and the elimination of external influence over Nigeria's foreign policy. Moscow radio explained how suitable the NSWFP's platform was for a united democratic election bloc. And though NSWFP leaders admitted that the UPGA failed to measure up to this (it "dreaded a genuine left movement"), the alliance did advance "certain socialist slogans" and did offer a rallying point for the "antifeudalists," and therefore it did justify the NSWFP's (unreciprocated) cooperation.[128] Moreover, if a choice had to be made, the UPGA was certainly superior to the Nigerian National Alliance, composed of the NPC ("feudal aristocrats") and its Western Region partners, the Nigerian National Democratic Party ("comprador bourgeoisie").

After the elections, the sop given the UPGA—a handful of portfolios in the new "broadly based" government—created the impression that the old order had been reinstalled (only obsuring the real depths of

126. M. Zenovich, in *Pravda*, June 12, 1964, p. 4. The leadership of the NTUC kept extremely close ties with the leadership of Nigeria's Socialist Workers' and Farmers' Party, a Communist party that remained incontestably loyal to the Soviet position; leaders of the NSWFP had matured within the leadership of the NTUC and in some cases still occupied posts in both organizations.

127. Moscow radio (in English to Africa), 20.30 GMT, December 12, 1964.

128. "Nigeria after the Elections," *African Communist*, no. 21 (April–June 1965), p. 41.

the dissension). The *African Communist* described those who re-entered the coalition as leaders who "crave for government office on any terms, including capitulation to the feudalists."[129] No doubt NSWFP officials were annoyed by the compromise the UPGA made with the NNA. But it was the disastrous failure in the elections which bothered them more than the weak will of a few UPGA leaders and which, in turn, forced them to review their recent tactics. The question, of course, was whether they had been wise to support the boycott or whether they would have profited more from revolutionary action. Significantly, they concluded that "a line of action based on violence is out of the question at the present stage unless the masses become class conscious and organized, become trained and educated in class struggle."[130]

This, then, characterized Khrushchev's policy toward the countries of West Africa during his final year of command: adventure and experiment in relations with Africa's most progressive nations; tolerance and cooperation in relations with less progressive regimes. His successors accepted and enlarged the second approach. The first they repudiated.

129. *Ibid.,* p. 46.
130. *Ibid.,* p. 45.

VII

Policy after Khrushchev:
Smaller Expectations, 1965–1966

By late 1964 Black Africa no longer occupied a very large part of the
Soviet leadership's attention, and so it would be baseless to conclude
that Khrushchev's bizarre experiment in policy toward Africa's "revolutionary democracies" contributed significantly to his removal. Nevertheless
it serves to illustrate the "subjectivism" for which he was deposed. Like
so many other ventures—the fulsome promises to his own society said
to be building Communism, the impetuous and impractical educational
reform of 1958, the constant upheaval imposed on the bureaucracy and,
in 1962, on the party, the obstinate campaign to run the Chinese out
of the Communist bloc, the nerve-wracking enterprises in Berlin and
Cuba—his advances toward Africa's revolutionary states appeared foolish
and extravagant. His successors were more practical and more conservative. They doubtless suspected that he had misjudged the revolutionary
potentiality of states like Ghana and Mali and oversimplified the formidable problems involved in any genuine socialist revolution for Africa.

Their decision to abandon Khrushchev's ideological gambit was the
first notable feature of the new leadership's African policy. The shift
in emphasis and the accompanying modification of theoretical formula-

tions became apparent within six months of his dismissal. Moreover, by the time Khrushchev's successors assumed power, many of the regimes for whom his plans had been designed were plagued with serious internal problems. The troubles confronting regimes such as Nkrumah's added to the uneasiness of the new Soviet leaders and made them still more hesitant to underwrite their survival. When Nkrumah fell in February 1966, Soviet apprehensions were confirmed and the need to speak frankly of the factors that led to his defeat became self-evident; a remarkable period of reflection and candor followed. Finally, the troubles and failures of Africa's most advanced states reduced their importance to the Soviet Union. In a certain sense, Africa was assuming a fundamentally common character in the eyes of Soviet policymakers, making differentiation among African states all the more irrelevant and, consequently, the non-revolutionary states relatively more important. The result was the emergence of major new emphases in a less restricted African policy.

Revising Khrushchev's Formulas

In his haste to speed up historical processes, Khrushchev and the dialogue he sanctioned evidently offended the orthodox sensibilities of others within the Soviet leadership. Mention has already been made of the signs of resistance from some officials, such as Mikhail Suslov, Boris Ponomarev, and Aleksei Rumyantsev. Each, it may be imagined, resented Khrushchev's tamperings with ideology and remained unconvinced that any African country merited this kind of ideological endorsement.

A few months after his removal, Khrushchev's description of Mali and Ghana as states building socialism vanished and these states were said to be once again merely on the noncapitalist path, a stage short of the actual transition to socialism. When the issue of an African state's progress toward socialism arose, usually at its insistence, Soviet spokesmen politely indicated their happiness that Africans were choosing the socialist option but made apparent their estimation that no African state had yet successfully embarked upon a socialist course. They put Guinea back among the favored group, a reward for its return to the fold following the November 1964 reforms that undid the liberalizing decrees of 1963, but it was a reward that meant less now.

The revision of Khrushchev's presumptuous theoretical formulations could not be accomplished overnight, however. Had the new leadership undone instantly the theoretical underpinning of what may have seemed an unrealistic relationship with Ghana or Mali (not to mention the UAR and Algeria), it would have added to the nervousness already apparent among the beneficiaries of Khrushchev's policies. Respect for their sensibilities (and no doubt other more pressing matters such as China and party reorganization) presumably prevented Soviet leaders from turning to this issue sooner. Instead, during the first months after seizing power they tolerated, perhaps more than anything by default, intermittent ambiguous echoes of Khrushchev's ideological adventure.

One commentator, for example, discussing the course of Soviet-Malian relations emphasized the ideological affinity between the "leading forces" of these two societies. The Soviet people and the CPSU, he said, welcomed "Mali's choice in favor of socialism."[1] Vitaly Korionov, in *Za rubezhom,* credited the Union Soudanaise with being a truly revolutionary party leading the struggle for socialism in Mali.[2] An article on Ghana in the May issue of *Mirovaya ekonomika i mezhdunarodnye otnosheniya* reflected similar lingering confidence in its ability to build socialism.[3] Ghana, argued Vladimir Kondratev, because of the national democratic character of those currently in power, their commitment to the construction of socialism, the utilization of material and financial resources by the state to achieve this goal, and the undeveloped condition of capitalist relations, had produced a type of state economic activity more progressive than state capitalism. In fact it included "elements of socialist transformation." Ghana, Kondratev carefully stressed, did not yet have "a form of socialist economic organization," but nevertheless it was passing through a phase in the "creative processes leading to a socialist form of life." Even more official spokesmen betrayed a continuing commitment to old slogans, sparking open conflict with the Chinese at the A-APSO-sponsored Algiers Economic Seminar, on February 22-28, 1965. When Soviet delegates insisted on recognizing the socialist aspirations of the Afro-Asian nations, "some delegations, including some socialist delegations," who considered such a specific resolution inexpedient, were provoked to substitute a formula recognizing only the goal

1. Vladimir Kaltrev for Moscow radio (in English to Africa), 15.30 GMT, January 26, 1965.

2. Moscow TASS (in Russian for abroad), 18.39 GMT, and (in English), 20.32 GMT, February 4, 1965.

3. Vladimir Kondratev, "Gana: Vybor puti i preobrazovanie ekonomiki" (Ghana: Choice of Path and the Transformation of Its Economic Structure), *Mirovaya ekonomika i mezhdunarodnye otnosheniya,* no. 5 (1965), p. 47.

of establishing "independent national economies."[4] These people, Solodovnikov reported, denied that the building of socialism in the countries of Africa and Asia constituted a task of the first order. "We believe such a point of view erroneous, for it reflects a lack of faith in the revolutionary forces of Afro-Asian peoples and it deprives the masses of revolutionary perspective."

By June, however, unmistakable signs of change had emerged in Soviet commentary. A. A. Iskenderov in a June 4 *Pravda* article entitled, "The Developing Nations and Socialism," set the pattern by warning that "insufficient consideration of internal factors sometimes leads to obliteration of the differences between the progressiveness of one or another measure and its genuine socialist content."[5] So that in the future such confusion might be avoided, he emphasized that "social-economic measures (nationalization, agrarian reform, etc.) may be very progressive and radical, but it is well known that their implementation does not automatically lead to socialism." In the weeks that followed more restrained descriptions began to appear, such as a review of the upcoming Algiers Afro-Asian conference which pointedly underscored that Algeria, the UAR, Mali, Ghana, Guinea, and Burma had "set out on the path of noncapitalist development and have proclaimed *their goal* to be the building of a socialist society."[6] Even Mirsky now argued that progressive Asian and African states were only on the road of noncapitalist development.[7] A *Pravda* editorial was more skeptical, stating that these states were even less far along, that they were merely "making the transition to the noncapitalist path of development."[8] Indicative of the new leadership's determination to impose reason on the theoretical models applied to the developing countries, another *Pravda* writer found it "natural that the urgent need should arise for a clearer definition of all shades of contemporary socialism and that the line between proletarian and nonproletarian trends should be drawn more clearly."[9]

4. This is the report of V. Solodovnikov, "Afro-Aziatskaya solidarnost protiv kolonializma i neokolonializma" (Afro-Asian Solidarity against Colonialism and Neocolonialism), *Aziya i Afrika segodnya,* no. 5 (1965), p. 27.

5. A. Iskenderov, in *Pravda,* June 4, 1965, p. 3.

6. E. Primakov, in *Pravda,* June 12, 1965, p. 3; emphasis added.

7. In a discussion broadcast over Moscow radio (home service), 13.00 GMT, June 20, 1965.

8. *Pravda,* June 28, 1965, p. 2.

9. Moscow TASS (in Russian for abroad), 22.17 GMT, and (in English), 22.00 GMT, August 14, 1965; Fyodor Burlatsky, in *Pravda,* August 15, 1965, p. 3.

These adjustments in theory, which may appear to the outsider as so much ideological acrobatism, do nevertheless reflect important modifications in Soviet estimations. If Khrushchev, in his excitement over the turn of events in Cuba, had convinced himself that history might also leap stages in Africa, his successors were less sure. Their revised formulas reveal not only a more circumspect ideological view of Africa but, of greater significance, a more conservative political assessment. History and the process of social, political, and economic development simply could not be gainsaid. In the words of one experienced Soviet economist:

> The failures and setbacks of some African countries which have tried too rapidly to introduce measures of a socialist character show . . . that it is impossible to introduce socialism by decree, and to jump across the stages of democratic reforms and immediately find oneself in a socialist society. The advance to socialism requires planned, systematic work, and the gradual creation of the economic and social base of the new social system.[10]

Khrushchev's successors were equally reluctant to continue his casual, diffuse, sometimes prodigal economic programs in the progressive states. Within a year of his departure, they made plain their intention to weigh aid projects according to stricter criteria of feasibility, local utility, and economic return. Moreover, under the new regime's rearranged priorities it became evident that the Soviet Union's helping hand would be extended only after domestic concerns had had their turn. According to a landmark *Pravda* editorial of October 27, 1965, the people of socialist countries believed that they could best fulfill their "supreme international duty to the workers of the whole world" by focusing their energies on strengthening their own national economies. In "concentrating their main efforts on the building of socialism and Communism in their own countries," they would be preparing the "decisive condition for increasing aid to other detachments of the liberation struggle."

The genesis of this argument dates back to Khrushchev's day and bears an important relationship to the objections several of his colleagues had to his extraordinary ideological overtures to the revolutionary democ-

---

10. N. I. Gavrilov, ed., *Nezavisimye strany Afriki: Ekonomicheskie i sotsialnye problemy* (Independent African Countries: Economic and Social Problems; Moscow, 1965), quoted in *Mizan*, VII (October 1965), 6.

racies. Evidence of a marked shift in priorities began to appear in the Soviet press several weeks before Khrushchev's removal, but in a way suggesting that not all key leaders saw the change in the same light. On September 11, 1964, the theses prepared for the hundredth anniversary of the First International were printed in *Pravda*, and tucked inside was a hint of the new formula: "As V. I. Lenin foresaw, it is through their economic successes that the socialist countries exert their chief influence on the world revolution and on international development . . . the Communist and Workers' Parties of the socialist countries consider concern for the growth of the socialist economy to be their internationalist duty, their contribution to the development of the world revolutionary process."[11] Though significantly less far-reaching than the October 27 *Pravda* editorial, the reference is obviously a forerunner.

One gathers from his comments at the time that Khrushchev was not the idea's principal protagonist. He admitted that "the construction of socialism and Communism is a decisive contribution of the Soviet Union and the other socialist countries to the world liberation struggle," but he also emphasized that his country recognized its international duty as "consisting in support for the revolutionary, democratic movements of modern times."[12] Ponomarev, on the other hand, flatly stated that although the socialist countries and working people of the capitalist countries would not forget the national liberation movement, their "primary" international duty was to construct socialism and Communism.[13] The difference in viewpoint is fundamental. It was a struggle that the Soviet leader had been waging from the moment he decided to press for the early conversion of revolutionary democracies to socialism. On his return from Cairo in May 1964, Khrushchev's television report to the nation betrayed the difficulty he was having in justifying his actions in the UAR. He seemed particularly defensive about the aid commitment that he had made to this revolutionary democracy—a commitment, to make matters worse, that had been extended without first securing the agreement of the Presidium.[14] "When the Soviet Union helps the young

11. *Pravda*, September 11, 1964, p. 3. R. A. Yellon, "The Winds of Change," *Mizan*, IX (July–August 1967), pp. 163–165, deals with this question in a slightly different way.

12. *Pravda*, September 29, 1964, quoted in Yellon, "The Winds of Change," pp. 163–164.

13. *Pravda*, September 29, 1964, quoted in *ibid.*, p. 164. The reference was in his report to the hundredth anniversary meeting of the First International.

14. For Khrushchev's television speech see *Pravda* and *Izvestiya* May 28, 1964,

developing countries, giving them a portion of the wealth amassed by its own labor, then it is limiting its own possibilities for a certain period of time. But we would be poor Communists, *poor internationalists,* if we thought only of ourselves."[15] He went on at some length with the point: "Better to have a hundred friends than a hundred rubles"; the benefits to the Soviet Union would be bountiful; the Soviet Union knew its duty. Obviously there were skeptics among his colleagues, and their skepticism applied to more than a few casually granted aid promises. In the piece that Rumyantsev did for the *World Marxist Review* soon after Khrushchev's return from the UAR—the one that conspicuously ignored the Soviet leader's new formulas—an alternative was posed. " 'Capitalism can be utterly vanquished, and will be utterly vanquished,' Lenin said, 'by the fact that socialism creates a new and much higher productivity of labor.' He regarded the solution of this task as the prime internationalist duty of the victorious working class, the way in which it will exert its 'greatest influence on the international revolution.' "[16]

Khrushchev apparently did not agree. The whole point of the 1964 departures was that the Soviet Union's rapid advance toward Communism could be reconciled with a sizable commitment to the revolutionary democracies. This was perfectly consistent with his flamboyant, grandiose, and romanticized conception of the Soviet Union's capabilities as well as the opportunities open to Soviet foreign policy. Many of his colleagues doubted both. They were much more concerned with the rational and prudent introduction of economic reform within their own society and, no doubt on the advice of people like Ponomarev, saw little reason to let themselves be distracted by adventures in the radical states of Afro-Asia. If it is true that some within the Soviet leadership opposed Khrushchev's notions, then the theses of the First International centennial may have reflected a compromise of viewpoints. It was not until Khrushchev had been removed that the task of constructing socialism and Communism emerged as more than a major contribution to the world liberation struggle, as the Soviet Union's *primary* international duty. As Suslov put it shortly before the appearance of the October 27

pp. 1, 2. *Frankfurter Allgemeine Zeitung,* October 31, 1964, referring to the comments of Italian Communists, reports Khrushchev's failure to consult the Presidium; see Ra'anan, "Moscow and the 'Third World,' " p. 30.

15. *Ibid.,* emphasis added.

16. Rumyantsev, "Concerning the Basic Contradictions of Our Time," p. 3; see also Chapter Six.

Pravda editorial: "Our contribution to the cause of the international struggle of the working people of the entire world is expressed above all in the building of Communism in the U.S.S.R."[17] Khrushchev's 1964 venture had now been officially repudiated.

The thought that alternatively the Soviet Union might ease the plight of African nations either by subsidizing the price of Soviet purchases or by fixing export prices elicited very little enthusiasm. Soviet writers and diplomats were openly hostile to plans for price subsidization, and any attempt to fix export prices should not, they said, "be effected at the expense of lowering the standard of living of the population of the developed countries." Ultimately, just as it was the responsibility of the Soviet Union to devote itself first to its own problems, it also belonged to the African nation to assume the burdens of its struggle for political and economic independence. In the words of the October 27 *Pravda* editorial, "Those who can put an end to all forms of colonialism and neocolonialism, and raise the economy and culture of the young national states, are above all the peoples of these countries themselves."

However, despite its clear determination to be rid of a strategy that expected too much of revolutionary African states and that distorted the Soviet Union's own priorities, the new leadership neither could nor wanted to withdraw from these areas. As a small reminder of what continued involvement meant, one by one each of West Africa's revolutionary democracies sent delegations to Moscow during 1965 to plead for moratoriums on debt repayment and sometimes a good deal more. First the Guineans came in December 1964, then in March 1965 the Ghanaians, in June Sekou Touré himself, and in October Modibo Keita. The new Soviet leaders granted each a debt moratorium but were noticeably reluctant to give more—to Ghana relief for its seriously depleted foreign reserves, to Guinea funding for the revived Konkouré Dam, and to Mali credits for a variety of projects. The Soviet Union had a stake in these countries, but it was measured and increasingly undeceived. In early 1966 the Western diplomatic community in Bamako was astir over the recent recall of the Soviet ambassador, I. A. Melnik, and his ranking subordinates, apparently because their enthusiastic reports did not meet the criteria of a hard-headed administration that wanted careful, realistic assessments of the situation in countries like Mali.

17. *Pravda,* October 5, 1965, quoted in Yellon, "The Winds of Change," p. 165. Suslov was speaking at an ideological conference called for the thirtieth anniversary of the Seventh Comintern Congress.

Guinea's Redemption

Had the new leadership not been so determined to immunize itself against false hope, it might have been more impressed by the favorable turn of events taking place in Guinea during this same period. By late 1964 Touré had become impatient with the difficulties besetting his liberal reforms of 1963, and he was ready to reimpose strict state control over the trading system, shake up the corruption-ridden bureaucracy, and reform the party. Originally, in 1963, to dissolve the rigidities, bottlenecks, and inefficiencies that had always plagued the state trading system, Touré had announced that a large portion of retail trade would be returned to private initiative. Even diamond mining was once again to be left to private exploitation. The reforms, however, were never more than partially implemented and in February 1964, less than six months after the measure abolishing state control over internal trade had been announced, it was suddenly rescinded. What the status and organization of both external and internal trade was after this remained unclear for the next several months. The only clear thing was that corruption, smuggling, black marketeering, and currency speculation more than maintained their former scale. Then in November Touré called an extraordinary joint session of the National Assembly and the National Revolutionary Council to announce a vigorous crackdown on these abuses, the reassertion of a state monopoly over trade, and a further housecleaning within the party. He revealed plans for reducing the number of private traders from 25,000 to 5,000, introducing a far more stringent business code and accelerating the formation of agricultural cooperatives. To ready the party for its crucial role in seeing that these reforms had the necessary effect, membership was restricted to "activists who have proved themselves," specifically excluding private traders and senior officials who had been "insufficiently active."

Soviet leaders were no doubt pleased that some part of Guinea's revolution was to be redeemed, especially when one could believe that through this experience the capitalist option had been tried and exposed as a failure. It represented a small (and indirect) triumph for a regime that was soon to be besieged by setbacks in all parts of Africa. But nothing about the return of the prodigal justified truly unrestrained confidence, not on the part of leaders who viewed states like it with considerable caution. Touré, after all, had once earlier provided an indelible lesson in the unpredictability of African leaderships. As a result they had relatively little to say in the months before November as Touré fumbled with a reapplication of state control in the trading sector and improved the revolutionary tone of his pronouncements. They sat quietly, watching developments with unexpressed curiosity, waiting for a firmer indication that Touré was serious about the reinvigoration of Guinea's revolutionary option. After the measures announced in November, Soviet analysts began to acknowledge the progress they saw Guinea making once again. One of the first to comment, *Izvestiya*'s V. Midtsev, noted that a year earlier Guinea's leaders had set about to improve the supply system by permitting the expansion of private trade, but since those who took advantage of the opportunity were guided only by self-interest, this had increased the rate of smuggling and speculation while simultaneously contributing to the further disorganization of trade.[18] The recent session of the National Assembly and National Revolutionary Council, Midtsev wrote, "indicates that the PDG has decided to put an end to these unhealthy tendencies, springing from the actions of capitalist elements and running contrary to the Party's general political line." He referred to Touré's remark made during a public rally held early in November: Guinea had chosen the noncapitalist path of development. "We will not depart from this path, because this is the single path which guarantees the interests of the entire society and frees every man from the inequality characterizing the relations of men exploiting one another." Midtsev added, "Guinea is confirming its choice." Three months later *Pravda*'s correspondent expressed similar confidence. In an article entitled, "The Face of Guinea Is Changing," he summarized the reforms recently undertaken, mentioning specifically the monopolization of trade, the re-establishment of state control in important economic spheres such as diamond mining, the appointment of a special commission to battle corruption, and the improvement of party structures.[19] "The Republic of Guinea," he said, "is embarking upon a new, important stage of its independent development." Once again Soviet commentators placed Guinea in the same category as Mali, Ghana, and Africa's other most progressive states—a category, however, that by mid-1965 carried considerably less grace than before.

From Guinea's side too there were considerations that provided a sudden spur to better relations with the Soviet Union—one of the more important of which, we may assume, was Khrushchev's dismissal. Touré alone among West Africa's revolutionary leaders had experienced what

18. V. Midtsev, in *Izvestiya*, November 24, 1964, p. 2.
19. N. Prozhogin, in *Pravda*, February 16, 1965, p. 3.

he believed to be direct Soviet interference in his country's affairs, and quite likely he found it easier to deal with another leadership. In October Guinea's press included none of the guarded lamentations over Khrushchev's "retirement" appearing in the Ghanaian and Malian newspapers. The high-level Guinea delegation that went to the Soviet Union a month after Khrushchev's departure was particularly well received. Its members, Ismael Touré, Keita N'Famara, and Leon Maka, had talks with Kosygin, Podgorny, Mikoyan, Ponomarev, Semen Skachkov, Chairman of the State Committee on Foreign Economic Relations, and Deputy Foreign Minister Malik, all of which, according to the Soviet press, underscored the "unity of views between the Union of Soviet Socialist Republics and the Republic of Guinea on many international questions."[20] On November 27, two days before the arrival of this delegation and a week after the November reforms, Khrushchev's ambassador to Guinea, Dmitry Degtyar, was replaced by Alexis Voronin. The following July Sekou Touré returned to the Soviet Union for the first time since 1960.[21]

In Moscow Touré's performance was mildly reminiscent of the former cordial support he had lent Soviet foreign policy in the first years following independence—in any case a more honest reflection of his general attitude on international questions than his off-and-on flirtation with the United States. His view of American intervention in South Vietnam and aggression against North Vietnam, racial discrimination in Rhodesia, the need to strengthen the United Nations, and the situation in South Africa and the Congo closely paralleled the current position of the Soviet leadership—but, as indicated, this support was scarcely cause for notice. On the other hand, it may have been significant that he endorsed the struggle for general and complete disarmament (after his opposition to the test-ban treaty) and supported the decision to hold the Second Afro-Asian Conference, a decision strongly opposed by the Chinese.[22]

Harmony at this level, however, told less about the essential nature of Soviet-Guinean relations than the reception Soviet leaders gave Touré's program for economic development. He had revived plans for

20. They were sent to the Soviet Union to negotiate a debt moratorium on credits secured in 1959 and 1960.

21. *Le Monde*, July 28, 1965, p. 3, gave much of the credit for Touré's decision to accept the Soviet invitation to Ambassador Voronin.

22. In April 1964 at the Djakarta preparatory meeting for this conference, the Guinean foreign minister had supported Chinese efforts to exclude the Soviet Union, an issue on which the Chinese lost and which prompted them to oppose holding the conference at all. See Chapter Five.

building a single large Konkouré River development project, a massive undertaking that involved at a minimum an outlay of $250 million, and from all the evidence he expected the Soviet Union to help in a major way. His expectations were not so farfetched as it may seem, at least in one sense. Much earlier, in another era, the Soviet Union had officially declared its willingness to aid with the development of the Konkouré River, and in 1960–61 others (American diplomats, for example) perpetuated the rumor that the Soviet Union was seriously interested in giving Guinea the great dam.[23] Belatedly Touré sought to test the strength of the Soviet commitment.

Although the Soviet leadership probably did not reject his proposal outright, they quite clearly did not accept an obligation to undertake a second Aswan Dam in West Africa—not during a period of economic retrenchment. More likely, the Soviet leadership promised him, as it had promised Nkrumah, to explore the feasibility of the dam—that is, to conduct preliminary technical surveys. (This much they began before the end of 1965.) Touré, however, announced to the world on his return home that the Soviet Union would build the Konkouré Dam, along with a hydroelectric station and aluminum factory.[24] His diplomats were left with the task of persuading doubters that the Soviet Union had in fact agreed to undertake so huge a project. In the meantime the Soviet press remained absolutely silent; articles on Guinea often mentioned Touré's visit but never, in any context, the Konkouré Dam. In Conakry the Soviet ambassador informed Western diplomats that the Soviet Union had in fact agreed to no such thing. Eventually the Soviet Union supplied the Guinean fishing fleet with ten new trawlers, but this was something less than a major dam.

Guinea's recovery of revolutionary momentum or, at least, its return to a more progressive course evoked noticeable satisfaction in the Soviet press. "Not so long ago," remarked Nikolai Gavrilov, "the bourgeois press . . . was trumpeting wherever possible that Guinea had slipped onto the capitalist path of development, that it had become 'disillusioned' with socialist economic methods. Today such reasoning is rather rare."[25]

---

23. See Morrow, *First Ambassador to Guinea,* p. 244, and Attwood, *The Reds and the Blacks,* p. 37.

24. See report of Guinean radio announcement in *Le Monde,* August 10, 1965, p. 5, and Touré's opening speech to the National Council of the Revolution, August 13, 1965, summarized in *Mizan,* VII (October 1965), 25.

25. N. Gavrilov, "Gvineya—'Gosudarstvo-pioner' " (Guinea—"Pioneer State"), *Aziya i Afrika segodnya,* no. 11 (1965), p. 23.

Triumphantly he concluded, "the 'pioneer state' has not turned from the noncapitalist path." Everyone knew now, though, that this kind of enthusiasm had narrow limits.

Ghana: The Cornerstone of Relations with West Africa

Whatever happiness Guinea's deflection back onto the path of progress brought the Soviet leadership, it was not enough to prompt another elaborate commitment to this country: first, Soviet leaders must have kept in mind how capricious and unreliable Guinea's leadership could be; second, it was simply not in character with the new regime's general outlook. However reassuring, Guinea's return to revolution could not have been expected to stimulate a major departure in the Soviet approach to West Africa.

Insofar as a cynosure of Soviet policy existed in sub-Saharan Africa, it remained Ghana. Relations with this country more than any other embodied the immensely complicated mixture of frustrations and satisfactions, obstacles and access, reservations and hope, that was coming to characterize so much of Soviet contact with radical Africa. Because, despite Ghana's peculiarly heavy economic dependence on the West and the megalomania of its leader, Soviet-Ghanaian relations tell so much about the specific nature of Soviet involvement in the revolutionary democracies, they deserve to be recalled in some detail.

At the roots of Soviet policy toward Ghana was the tension between the new regime's determined restraint in relations with the Third World, including Ghana, and its huge stake in many of these countries, not least Ghana. For very practical reasons, Soviet policymakers would have found it difficult to extricate themselves from their important involvement in Ghanaian affairs. In Ghana, however, special reasons existed for wanting to trim the Soviet commitment and to hedge Soviet investments.

At a moment when Khrushchev's successors chose to turn their energies inward and to accentuate the struggle to put their own economy in order, Ghana's regime was slipping dizzily toward economic disaster. Even to survive it required emergency aid from somewhere. Unabashed, Nkrumah beseeched a host of Western states (states denounced daily in his press for neocolonialism) to extend his government loans reportedly approaching $3.5 billion.[26] From the United States alone he is said to

26. *New York Times,* April 14, 1965, pp. 1, 8.

have requested $200 million. When he had no luck in Washington or London or Bonn, he then appealed to the International Monetary Fund. Before rejecting his request, the IMF and the World Bank submitted a report suggesting that efforts to shift a substantial portion of Ghana's trade toward Eastern countries under clearing agreements and the reckless quest for short-term suppliers' credits had seriously jeopardized Ghana's national economy.

Pressed by heavy debts, exhausted foreign exchange reserves, disastrously depressed export prices (cocoa), and shrinking commercial opportunities in the West, Nkrumah needed desperately to secure hard currency from the outside. As might be expected, the Ghanaian president also turned for assistance to the Soviet Union. No one in the Second African Section of the Soviet Foreign Ministry could have doubted the certain disaster facing Ghana unless it soon secured financial relief.

Given the advanced stage of economic deterioration in Ghana, the Soviet Union's response provides interesting evidence of the limits set on its involvement in Black Africa's revolutionary states. In early 1965 when Western powers were being canvassed for aid, Foreign Minister Kojo Botsio flew to Moscow to do three things: arrange for a debt moratorium, persuade the Soviet Union to increase its cocoa purchases (at subsidized prices), and talk the Soviet leadership out of hard currency. The first two requests Soviet leaders agreed to consider and eventually they acceded to both. But they refused to draw on their own modest foreign exchange reserves to bail Nkrumah out of his predicament.[27] Their refusal, though hardly surprising, indicates how far the new leaders would go in supporting such regimes: they had considered Khrushchev's search for African Cubas and, after weighing the economic cost, had concluded that they could not afford a similar involvement in Africa.

Their response, in this case, reflected more than mere reluctance to share scarce foreign exchange reserves. In general, Soviet leaders looked unfavorably upon Nkrumah's economic priorities, particularly his passion for large and uneconomic development schemes. Soviet engineers, in mid-1965, specifically reported their reservations over the $100 million Bui Dam he wanted the Soviet Union to build. They were supported by the Ghanaian Ministry of Fuel and Power and, in at least one cabinet meeting, by Kojo Botsio. The president, however, announced that the surveys had proved the dam to be feasible and preparatory work would

27. From interviews with members of the Ghanaian ministries of trade, foreign affairs, and industries in July 1966.

soon be underway. During the period of the IMF and World Bank evaluation mentioned earlier, a Soviet economic adviser assigned to Nkrumah's secretariat similarly advised against the continuing overextension of the nation's economy. On a different occasion the same adviser approached an official of the Ministry of Finance and urged him to insert into his recommendations conservative proposals that the Russian hesitated to make himself.[28] Nor is there any reason to doubt an experienced Soviet diplomat, interviewed in Accra, who reported (after Nkrumah's removal) that his government had long considered many of Nkrumah's pet projects, such as Ghana Airways and "Job 600"—the massive complex built for the 1965 OAU conference—premature and impractical, and that they had tried to convince him of the value of productive industries directed toward the local market and drawing on local resources, such as cocoa-processing plants, a shoe factory, and a gold refinery. (They were successful in the last instance.) Former Foreign Minister Kojo Botsio has testified that in 1965 a team of Soviet experts surveyed Ghana's economy and "recommended putting more energy and resources into productive enterprises and less on social and other projects. This was practically ignored."[29] It is characteristic of Soviet policy during this period that a Soviet writer urged Ghana to exploit Western aid, turning if necessary to multilateral aid sources.[30] He specifically cited the $39 million Ghana saved on its Volta River hydroelectric station by "making use of the competition between private foreign companies."

Thus the Soviet Union's unwillingness to save Nkrumah's regime from financial collapse cannot be attributed solely to a shift in the new regime's economic priorities. The conditions of Ghana's economy influenced their judgment as well, for they were determined to avoid a heavy commitment if Nkrumah should fail to surmount the crisis.[31] The withdrawal of Soviet experts from the state farms, for example, may have been an attempt to escape from a project in economic trouble.[32]

28. Personal interview, August 1968.

29. Interview with Botsio, July 29, 1966, CFL-B in Thompson, *Ghana's Foreign Policy,* p. 401.

30. L. Fedorov, "Put nezavisimoi Gany" (The Path of Independent Ghana), *Aziya i Afrika segodnya,* no. 11 (1965), p. 18.

31. Soviet diplomats maintained (after Nkrumah's overthrow) that they were convinced the English would come to his aid.

32. According to an invoice in the office of the State Farms Corporation, the number of Soviet engineers, economists, agronomists, and so on, attached to the four Soviet state farms declined from 42 in 1964 to 20 by the end of 1965.

Nkrumah's economic difficulties were not, however, the only liabilities Soviet leaders saw. Day by day his isolation among African leaders was growing and, in equal measure, at home his political power was becoming increasingly unsteady. After the Cairo OAU conference late in 1964, Nkrumah stood unmistakably ostracized, spurned on the issue of African unity. By now his obsession with schemes to create political unity in Africa was driving him to wage subversive warfare against those states he judged responsible for the failure of proposals that had collapsed of their own weight. Each passing week made Ghana more useless to the Soviet Union as a lever of influence on the remainder of Africa. At home two assassination attempts represented only the most obvious form of discontent, which permeated the entire society from the military to market women to university students. Nor could Soviet leaders have been oblivious to the fact that, with the notable exception of Minister of Finance Amoako-Atta and Minister of Defense Baako, most of the remaining ministers and the great portion of the administrative apparatus disapproved of the Osagyefo's economic orientation and seized every opportunity to subvert his efforts to draw Ghana closer to the socialist countries.

Along with these shortcomings, Soviet leaders were apparently fretting over Nkrumah's attempts to institutionalize a personality cult, accompanying an extraordinary indulgence of personal power. The Soviet reaction to the official hagiolotry Nkrumah encouraged never appeared publicly, but it is easy to imagine their feelings in the most notorious instances. What would the new leadership, which held strong opinions on the question of personality cults, have said about a party resolution (September 1965) declaring that the monolithic foundation of the party's organizational might and philosophy could be expressed in the fusion of the party's ideology with the personality of the founder of the ideology himself?[33] A week later an editorial in the *Evening News* stressed the resolution's practical importance, underscoring the need "to express the ideology of the CPP in the personality cult because all comrades realized that in our situation the people need a charismatic leadership, a beacon light to look up to in their development."[34] At one point Soviet readers

---

33. *Communist Influence in Nkrumah's Ghana* (London, May 1966), pp. 16–17. The resolution was the result of a presidential conference convoked on September 28, 1965, at his lodge in Aburi, attended by Central Committee members, cabinet ministers, and "party activists."

34. *Evening News*, October 2, 1965.

must have winced when the editorial attributed the same historical role to Nkrumah in Africa as Lenin's in the Soviet Union and Mao's in China, and they must have felt uncomfortable when the editorial concluded that a "lack of charismatic leadership and the correct use of nationalistic feeling of the people" had "killed many a political organization which started off a Marxist-Leninist organization."

Ambassador Rodionov never said so explicitly, but to Botsio his uneasiness and concern were clear.[35] The most that Soviet representatives could do was to warn the Ghanaians against the overconcentration of power within the party. The Soviet team in Ghana in 1965 "recommended a democratization of the top branches of the party machine," but to no avail. Rodionov frequently talked of this problem with Botsio, with similar lack of effect. From the Soviet point of view it was the distortions in party organization which seemed the most endangering—distasteful as the personality cult may have been. They feared justifiably that the entire process had significantly sapped the vitality of the party organization and now threatened to undermine its utility as a revolutionary instrument.

All of these drawbacks—the dilapidated condition of Ghana's economy in the context of Soviet economic retrenchment, the alienation of Nkrumah's own people from his leadership, the opposition his pan-African aspirations aroused among fellow leaders, and the decay of party institutions in the face of a tasteless and oppressive crusade to reinforce the president's vanity—explain in large part the ambivalence of the Soviet position in Ghana. Such considerations naturally prompted serious reservations that would have generated a cautious approach toward Ghana if other aspects of the Soviet-Ghanaian relationship had not offset them.

One can doubt that Soviet writers sincerely believed that Ghana's 1963 seven-year plan mapped the highway to socialism as they once reported; one hundred state farms, the gradually projected transformation of small peasant holdings into larger cooperatives, or the comparatively greater (though minuscule) growth of the proletariat in the state than in the private sector could not really constitute persuasive evidence of Ghana's advance along the noncapitalist path.[36] Still, it is very likely that the Russians preserved a sturdy confidence in their own ability to influence Ghana's development, based in part on Nkrumah's evident

35. Thompson, *Ghana's Foreign Policy*, p. 401.
36. Fedorov, "Put nezavisimoi Gany," p. 17.

susceptibility to revolutionary organization and their own unique presence in Ghana. Soon after Touré announced the transformation of the PDG into a narrow cadre party, Nkrumah, in an address to the nation on the eve of Ghana's national day (March 6, 1965), declared the need "to scrutinize party membership. As a vanguard organization of our people, the Convention Peoples Party must review its existing membership, regulate the inflow of new members and raise the ideological levels of its membership."[37] The February 1966 issue of the *World Marxist Review* published an article by Kofi Batsaa, the *Spark*'s editor, which repeated a theme long voiced by his group: The "task is now to transform the [CPP] into a vanguard party, leading and organizing the masses on the basis of common ideology—scientific socialism, Marxism-Leninism applied to African conditions."[38]

But it was in areas other than party organization that Nkrumah was preparing to introduce his most significant reforms, reforms that, if implemented, would have almost surely revolutionized Ghana's political system. The most important of these concerned the military and began in July 1965, when Nkrumah removed the President's Own Guard Regiment (POGR) from the army command and placed it under his direct authority. At the same time, he transferred defense affairs from the defense portfolio to a special secretariat within the presidential office. The POGR's new status foreshadowed its eventual ascendence over the remainder of the military, until this time free of Soviet influence. Soviet advisers were deeply involved in training and equipping the POGR. At Shai Hills, the training camp for POGR detachments, a dozen Soviet military advisers were already reportedly engaged in the active preparation of a potential alternative command; similarly, Soviet KGB officers at the same location had undertaken to provide small-arms training for the Presidential Detail Department, the civilian security organization. It may have been mere coincidence that at the time of the July defense reorganization the Soviet Union signed a secret protocol with a representative of the president's office, granting Ghana 803,000 rubles in military equipment.[39] Protagonists of the agreement steadfastly maintained that

37. Accra radio (domestic service in English), 18.15 GMT, March 5, 1965.

38. Kofi Batsaa, "Ghana's Road," *World Marxist Review,* IX (February 1966), 24.

39. Photostat of a letter from Soviet Ambassador Rodionov to E. K. Otoo, office of the president of Ghana, July 26, 1965, containing the agreement and an appendix listing the types and quantity of arms and ammunition to be delivered.

its merchandise was intended to arm members of Nkrumah's subversion camps. Others noticed that 76mm ZIS-3 guns, 82mm mortars, and 12.7 mm antiaircraft machine guns (DShK) were inappropriate for small-band guerrilla activity and concluded that these arms were intended to serve elements closer to Ghana's own political arena. Members of the military, indeed, were convinced that most of this equipment was destined for a network of secret arms dumps outside the control of the regular military.

Two fragments of evidence tend to support their suspicions: first, when members of the military command raided the secret arms dumps following the February coup d'état, they discovered large quantities of Russian-manufactured arms and ammunition. (The regular army was trained to use British, not Russian, equipment.) Second, the secret military agreement specified that Soviet organizations, if necessary, would send Soviet instructors to assist "Ghanaian specialists in mastering the special equipment." Yet the "freedom fighters" being trained in Nkrumah's subversion camps were not Ghanaians, but refugees from other African countries. Moreover, by 1964 the Soviet Union had made it clear to Nkrumah that it was unwilling to participate in efforts to train subversives to be deployed against other African governments. According to an official Ghanaian publication, these ammunition and arms depots were unknown to the Ghanaian armed forces until the day of the coup d'état.[40] The military command "believed that the arms and ammunitions at the dumps were to be used by Nkrumah's private army."

In addition, Soviet advisers were helping to prepare major modifications in a number of other Ghanaian institutions. By 1965 Nkrumah had a full-time Soviet economic adviser attached to his own secretariat. At the University of Ghana one of the Soviet members of the faculty of law, A. N. Talalayev, had drawn up plans for revamping the university's organization that included the addition of new courses on Marxism-Leninism, the appointment of Soviet instructors to handle courses in the history of socialism, the placement of a CPP secretary in the pro-vice-chancellor's office, and the introduction of representatives from the recently installed branch of the CPP into the university council, giving them control over appointments and tenure. Furthermore, by the end of 1965, plans were afoot to revamp the organization of Ghana's economy. According to at least one version, state corporations were to

40. *Ghana Today* (Information Department of the Ministry of External Affairs), April 6, 1966, p. 5.

be placed under the supervision of people with proper ideological training, a shift that would lead to the sweeping nationalization of other
major enterprises.[41]

Prospective changes of this sort promised to augment Soviet influence
in Ghana and, eventually, to give Soviet representatives leverage in deciding the direction of Ghana's "revolution." In the meantime the Soviet
Union was making excellent use of the influence it already possessed.
For firsthand observers the most remarkable aspect of Soviet-Ghanaian
relations in this period was unquestionably the unusual, inordinate influence that the Soviet ambassador wielded over Nkrumah. In discussing
this era, not a single high-level observer, whether American, European,
or Ghanaian, fails to mention the direct access to and power over
Nkrumah which Rodionov enjoyed. A former Ghanaian foreign minister
recounted in an interview the experience, repeated more than once,
of seeing the Soviet ambassador enter Flagstaff House and walk past
him directly into the president's office as he waited patiently for an
appointment. An official of the Cocoa Marketing Board recalled the
reprimand he received from the president after the Soviet ambassador
had complained that his agency was resisting the sale of cocoa to the
Soviet Union on a schedule preferred by the Soviet Union. Scarcely
a Ghanaian official was not touched personally by the ambassador's intervention in some affair concerning his sphere of responsibility. Aside from
the Osagyefo himself, no other person's picture appeared in the Ghanaian
press so often as Rodionov's; here he was welcoming a delegation from
the Supreme Soviet, there he was aiding with the dedication of a Soviet-
built aid project or the opening of a new Soviet trade exposition. Even
when one discounts the amount of newsprint purchased by the Soviet
embassy, the attention the ambassador received remains a fair measure
of his influence in the two years before Nkrumah's removal.

Rodionov applied his influence in varied fashion. Frequently he acted
only to remove an impediment that Ghanaian bureaucrats had placed
on a commercial arrangement between the two countries. If the military
balked at buying Soviet equipment, the ambassador would report to
the president that these "Sandhurst-trained officers are turned against

41. Interview with B. D. G. Folson, chairman of the department of political
science, University of Ghana (Legon), July 26, 1966. He was describing a document given him by Willy Abrams, pro-vice-chancellor of the university, Nkrumah's
brilliant confidant and sometime ghost writer. (Nkrumah was the university's
chancellor.)

anti-imperialist forces," and orders would come down from Flagstaff House to buy; if the university refused to hire Soviet professors, the ambassador would intervene to insist that "real socialists" be allowed to teach socialism; if orders for expensive and inefficient or inappropriate tractors declined, the ambassador would call the president to complain about pro-capitalist civil servants and, after formal pressure from the president's office, the Farmers' Council would make new purchases. On other occasions Rodionov would protest local Chinese activity or the seating arrangement at a diplomatic reception.

Beyond such housewifery, Rodionov employed his influence to solicit Nkrumah's specific support on issues important to Soviet policy elsewhere. When, for example, Ghana's representative to the United Nations (and General Assembly president), Alex Quaison-Sackey, spoke out sharply against the failure of any party to pay the expenses of the UN Congo operation, he first received a polite rebuke from the Soviet representative, Nikolai Fedorenko, and then swiftly, following Rodionov's intervention, a reprimand and new instructions from Flagstaff House.[42] In another case, after the Soviet ambassador had, as he mentioned to an officer of the Ghanaian Ministry of External Affairs, spoken with "Number One," Nkrumah launched a series of angry attacks on the MLF, denouncing the pact as a violation of the partial test-ban agreement and a threat to world peace.[43] The attacks coming in early 1965 corresponded with a quickening Soviet campaign against the sputtering plan to form the MLF. In the same period Rodionov again applied his influence to determine the scheduling of the Fourth A-APSO Conference planned for Winneba (Ghana) in May 1965. Early in the year participants in the conference's organizational committee, with an eye to the Second Bandung Conference scheduled for the same period in Algiers and the OAU conference to be held in Accra a matter of months later, persuaded Nkrumah to postpone the Winneba conference. The Soviet Union, on the other hand, was eager to press its advantage over the Chinese and wanted the conference to open on schedule. Rodionov called on the president and within hours the organizational committee received instructions to reactivate its planning.[44] It seems likely that, in addition to

42. Interview with Alex Quaison-Sackey, July 22, 1966.
43. Nkrumah's sudden concern over the MLF first appeared in his speech delivered at the opening of Parliament, reported in the *Ghanaian Times,* January 13, 1965, p. 1.
44. Interviews with members of the foreign ministry and the Winneba organizational committee, July 18, 1966.

swaying Nkrumah's judgment on a number of specific issues occupying the attention of Soviet policymakers, Rodionov seized his advantage to push the Soviet line in general.

Soviet interest in Ghana, inspired in part by Rodionov's ability to influence the president, also stemmed from the special facilities they had been able to develop there. At Tamale Nkrumah had permitted Soviet technicians to begin construction on a major military airfield designed to accommodate jet planes, even though the Ghanaian air force possessed few jet aircraft. When Soviet leaders signed contracts to undertake this project in November 1964, perhaps the thought had crossed their minds that facilities of this kind would have been useful in 1962 during the Cuban missile crisis, or since at that time they did exist in Guinea, the thought may have been that the investment would have been more wisely made in Ghana.

Similarly, Soviet involvement in Ghana's security affairs yielded intelligence on other African countries that the Soviet Union could never otherwise have collected. For example, when in 1965 the Bureau of African Affairs formulated highly secret plans to create an intelligence network to infiltrate the presidential offices of every major African nation, Soviet security officers had access to these plans and presumably expected to benefit from the information to be gathered.[45] Although the East Germans won the contract to train Ghanaian espionage agents, the bill for facilities used by agents working in the Star Hotel, one of the three major hotels bugged for the Accra OAU conference in October 1965, was presented against "Andreyev and Nikolai."[46] The espionage equipment employed in training programs was of Soviet manufacture. And after the February 1966 coup d'état, when representatives of the new leadership visited the atomic reactor being installed by twenty-seven Soviet technicians, they were surprised to discover nearby a previously unknown monitoring station.[47]

All of these benefits were in addition to the comfort Soviet leaders derived from Ghana's increasingly churlish attitude toward the United States and its European allies. The tempo at which Nkrumah and his press assailed Western imperialism and neocolonialism accelerated steadily over 1964 and in 1965 reached something of a climax with the dis-

---

45. These plans, included in a "top secret" document undated and unauthored and probably unknown to the MEA, were never implemented.

46. Photostat of invoice totaling 136.80 cedis (Ghanaian currency).

47. *Communist Influence in Nkrumah's Ghana*, pp. 34–35.

tribution of Nkrumah's book, *Neo-Colonialism, the Last Stage of Imperialism,* to delegates attending the Accra OAU conference. At the Winneba A-APSO conference in May, Nkrumah had characterized American intervention in the Dominican Republic as a potential "symbol of a new stage in open and undisguised aggression by imperialists against a national government,"[48] and earlier, at the March OAU council of ministers' meeting in Nairobi, Foreign Minister Botsio had deplored United States military aid to the Congo, used, he said, to bomb Uganda and neighboring Congo Brazzaville while serving American efforts to "neocolonialize" the Congo.[49] But in *Neo-Colonialism* Nkrumah (and the book's authors) leveled his most extensive and intemperate denunciation of United States foreign policy. Nkrumah charged that as the nation foremost among neocolonialists the United States sought to "achieve colonialism . . . while preaching independence."[50] According to him, the IMF, the IBRD, and the ICFTU all served American imperialism, and when these instruments proved insufficient, the United States developed additional vehicles for securing its colonialist aims, such as the Peace Corps, the USIA, the AID, and even Hollywood. In the case of the latter, in order to contribute to the "incessant barrage of anti-socialist propaganda," Hollywood chose as its hero "the policeman, the gumshoe, the Federal agent—in a word, the CIA type," consistently portraying the "trade union man, the revolutionary, or the man of dark skin . . . as the villain." Evangelism, the Businessman Corps, Operation Crossroads, "slick, clever expensive magazines," and Moral Re-Armament collectively emerged from this furious, flailing attack as an immense American conspiracy directed against the revolutionary forces of the world.

However, what probably pleased the Soviet Union more than Nkrumah's noisy assault on Western policy was his mounting irritation with the Chinese, who doggedly insisted on reviling the Soviet government, even if by doing so they disrupted Nkrumah's carefully staged show at Winneba. Several weeks before the Fourth A-APSO Conference was scheduled to open, as one Ghanaian official later told me, Nkrumah summoned both the Soviet and the Chinese ambassadors to his office and demanded a moratorium on polemics at Winneba. In his opening

48. *Times* (London), May 12, 1965, p. 9. The fact that Nkrumah permitted the conference to be held in his country had a decisive impact on the attitude of American diplomats; see Thompson, *Ghana's Foreign Policy,* p. 408.

49. *Ghanaian Times,* March 8, 1965, p. 12.

50. Kwame Nkrumah, *Neo-Colonialism: The Last Stage of Imperialism* (London: Thomas Nelson and Sons, 1965), pp. 239–248.

speech to the conference, Nkrumah softly echoed the warning, adding that the delegates were there "to wage war against a system, not a race."[51] Thus when the Chinese press and radio maintained the intensity of their attack on Soviet policy and Chinese delegates continued to lobby against the Soviet position at the conference, he did little to suppress his disgust in the company of advisers. This may partially explain Nkrumah's curt reminder to the Chinese during the Indian-Pakistani war in the fall—a conflict the Chinese were seeking to exploit with threats of intervention—that the Colombo agreement (which Ghana had helped to frame) required China to notify other parties concerned of any action taken on the border.

By the time of the second Kashmir war, however, the Chinese had already unleashed Nkrumah's fury by embracing the deposers of Ben Bella. The June coup d'état had greatly distressed Nkrumah. Among African leaders these two men were, in his view, brothers. Moreover, Nkrumah was probably inclined to see Ben Bella's removal from the perspective of his own political insecurity. As for China, its immediate endorsement of Colonel Boumedienne's new regime can be explained only within the context of the Sino-Soviet dispute. Little other than the negative satisfaction given the Chinese by the fall of a Soviet ally can account for their willingness, even eagerness, to take up with a leader who was much less of a "revolutionary socialist" than Ben Bella. *France nouvelle,* the weekly of the French Communist Party, claimed that China's rapid recognition of the new Algerian regime demonstrated just how far the Chinese Communists were prepared to go in their "anti-Sovietism."[52] Responding for the Chinese, the Albanians asserted that Moscow and Belgrade were not interested in the Algerian revolution, only in one man, "their hero."[53] It happened that Nkrumah shared the same hero, and he could not forgive the Chinese for so warmly receiving his political assassins.[54]

For all the advantages Ghana offered, Soviet leaders were willing to pay a price. (That their price had definite limits, we have already seen.) But Nkrumah came to the Soviet leadership in much the manner of a Ghanaian sidewalk vendor selling python skins and Ashanti dolls

51. *Times,* May 12, 1965, p. 9.
52. *France nouvelle,* July 1, 1965.
53. *Zeri i Popullit,* July 10, 1965, in RFE Research Report, July 14, 1965.
54. Since someone, presumably Soviet agents, had given Nkrumah an intelligence report implicating the Chinese in the coup, his fears of the Chinese were accentuated. See Thompson, *Ghana's Foreign Policy,* p. 406.

to tourists: demanding an absurd reward, hoping for a modest return, and willing to accept a great deal less. Unlike his more humble counterpart, Nkrumah habitually turned up only the low offer, and with the new Soviet leadership this would certainly continue. Botsio in the spring of 1965 cleared the way both for a three-year debt moratorium and for a new cocoa-purchasing agreement, negotiated in November by Finance Minister Amoako-Atta, one of the advocates of stronger trading ties with the Soviet Union.[55] An agreement to buy cocoa, however, even with convertible currency, hardly constituted the financial relief Ghana required at this stage, and Nkrumah, unless he remained exceptionally undiscerning, must have realized that his Soviet allies were for the moment unwilling to offer the massive assistance needed by Ghana's economy.

In any case, trade with the Soviet Union brought special difficulties that by 1965 were obvious even to many Ghanaians outside the foreign-policy and administrative bureaucracies. An editorial in the *Ghanaian Times* on July 26, 1965, had some sharp things to say about the circumstances of trade with the socialist countries. Both the socialist and the developing countries had agreed that the cause of depressed world market prices for raw materials stemmed "from the desire of the imperialist nations to exploit the primary producers." "But there is a fundamental contradiction between the acceptance of this thesis and the present attitude whereby the socialist country also pays the same price which the Western countries, because of their desire to exploit, have contrived to pay. This contradiction may not be deliberate but its existence is not healthy by any means."[56] Many Ghanaians viewed this "contradiction" not only as deliberate but as the mildest form of socialist exploitation. Privately they often expressed the opinion that the Soviet Union, more than the capitalist countries, took advantage of depressed market prices to buy cocoa. Unlike trade agreements with the Soviet Union, arrangements with capitalist countries permitted Ghana to withhold cocoa from sale during periods of particularly depressed prices. Moreover,

55. Interview with member of Ghanaian Ministry of Trade, July 15, 1966. See also "Cocoa Creeps Back," *West Africa,* no. 2534 (December 25, 1965), p. 1454. In the agreement the Soviet Union consented to purchase 150,000 tons of cocoa beans during 1966 and 1967, a 50 percent increase over buying in 1964 and 1965, at partially subsidized prices, 20 percent to be paid in freely convertible currency. The Soviet Union may also have agreed to increase purchases after 1970 to 120,000 tons annually.

56. *Ghanaian Times,* July 26, 1965, p. 6.

the cocoa the Soviet Union did buy, according to many of these people, frequently reappeared on the world market. (This is not, however, an established fact.)

Another indication of the Soviet leadership's reluctance to provide Nkrumah unlimited support related to Nkrumah's subversion camps. Frustrated by the almost universal rejection of his schemes to form a political pan-African movement and blaming his more conservative neighbors, Nkrumah eventually persuaded himself that the obstacles they created could only be removed by overthrowing their governments. For this purpose he reactivated a number of the subversion camps administered by the Bureau of African Affairs and began training so-called freedom fighters, refugees from the Ivory Coast, Niger, and Cameroun. Chou En-lai, during his visit to Ghana in January 1964, offered Nkrumah assistance with the camps but, at that time, the Ghanaian leader declined. Later in the year, A. K. Barden, the bureau's director, persuaded Nkrumah (perhaps after the fact) to accept Chinese participation. In an October 1964 memorandum Barden reported to the president that he had had the opportunity to take the six Chinese "instructors" to Obenemase (the camp with heaviest Chinese involvement) in order to acquaint them "with the general surroundings of this camp, buildings, terrain, etc., and to give their expert recommendations as to whether the camp was an ideal place for the type of training envisaged by the President . . . the training of potential guerilla officer cadets."[57] After the 1966 coup d'état, Barden testified before the investigating Apaloo Commission that the Soviet Union also helped to train subversives, but apparently he had in mind the single Soviet officer who, on a limited number of occasions in the early months of 1964, had demonstrated Soviet weaponry at the Half-Assini Camp.

The Soviet Union's refusal to participate directly in Nkrumah's camps is important, explicit evidence of its reluctance to get involved in this kind of "revolutionary activity." After 1962 the Soviet leadership had appeared to abandon guerrilla warfare as a significant means of pursuing its interests in Africa. But it is one thing to say generally:

At the same time, in the solution of revolutionary tasks the socialist countries cannot replace other detachments of the liberation struggle . . . They cannot replace the peoples of the young national states in the solution of the tasks of the national liberation movement

57. Photostat of memorandum from Barden to Nkrumah, October 13, 1964.

. . . This would be to force their will on other peoples, which is alien to the very nature of Marxism-Leninism. To this it must be added that such actions might lead to the unleashing of world thermonuclear war, with all its very grave consequences for all peoples.[58]

And it is another thing to bear witness to abstinence by denying material support for the dubious, but nevertheless revolutionary, projects of an allied African leader—particularly when the Chinese stood at the sidelines eagerly awaiting a chance to make good on the Soviet Union's default. With the exception of the minor involvement just noted, not a single observer, not even Ghanaian officials convinced of Soviet espionage and intentions to infiltrate the regular military, has tried to implicate the Soviet Union in the activity of the subversion camps.

Extending Khrushchev's Approach to the Moderate States

No doubt one of the major considerations motivating Soviet leaders to reject the specific revolutionary option of the camps derived from the raucous commotion Nkrumah's plans had stirred among his neighbors. By the fall of 1964, the subversion camps were an open secret, as enraged leaders in the Ivory Coast, Niger, and Upper Volta bitterly condemned Ghana's attempts to sabotage their governments. The November 1964 trial of Sawaba insurgents had directly implicated Ghana in their training.[59] With the arrival of Chinese instructors in this period, West African leaders decided the threat deserved joint counteraction and in February, at the desert capital of Nouakchott, they met to create a new regional organization, the Organisation Commune Africaine et Malgache (OCAM). Though they advanced a variety of reasons for banding together in a revival of the old Union Afro-Malgache, a chief reason was the threat posed by Nkrumah and, behind Nkrumah, by the Chinese. Their public statement "energetically [condemned] the action of certain states, notably Ghana, which welcomes agents of subversion and organizes training camps on their national territory."[60] In the

58. *Pravda,* October 27, 1965, p. 3.
59. *Le Niger,* November 23, 1964. For a thorough account of relations between Ghana and its West African neighbors see Thompson, *Ghana's Foreign Policy,* pp. 365–386.
60. *Le Monde,* February 14, 1965, p. 4. For a full account of this conference see Victor D. DuBois, "The Search for Unity in French-Speaking Black Africa," part 1, *American Universities Field Staff Report Service,* West Africa Series VIII, no. 3 (1965).

ensuing months OCAM members re-emphasized their intention to boycott the Accra OAU summit conference scheduled for October because
Nkrumah had persisted in his program to subvert their governments.
Addressing the OAU foreign ministers' meeting in Lagos (July 10–13,
1965), the Niger foreign minister, Amadou Mayaki, provided a detailed
report of activity, including Chinese participation, in what he referred
to as the "training and death camps in Ghana." The conference agreed
that until these programs ceased and foreign elements were expelled,
the OAU conference was seriously endangered. Botsio, as head of the
Ghanaian delegation, agreed to a compromise formula promising that
his government would "send away from its territory before the conference
all those persons whose presence is considered undesirable to countries
of their choice and to forbid the formation of any political groups whose
aims are to oppose any member state of the OAU."[61] But Nkrumah
had not authorized Botsio's concessions and he was reluctant to keep
the agreement. Whatever his position, the Soviet leadership clearly understood that any support for the camps would undermine its increasing
efforts to stabilize and expand relations with the moderate states.

Given its priorities, China willingly paid the price of alienation among
these states. Its activity in the Congo, Burundi, and particularly Ghana
had moved Ivory Coast officials to identify the "peril threatening Africa
today" as "yellow-tainted Peking Communism." They had warned
against the danger of substituting Chinese domination for other, more
historic forms of foreign domination.[62] Niger's president, Hamani Diori,
had charged that the recent "attack by commandos of the opposition
Sawaba party was organized, financed, and led by Communist China
and the weapons used were bought with Chinese money deposited in
banks at Brussels, Geneva and Accra."[63] But the Chinese, because they
focused their energies on particular areas of Africa—the Congo, East
Africa, and colonial Africa—and placed a primary emphasis on political
revolution, accepted the hostility of countries like the Ivory Coast, Niger,
and Malagasy as a normal and tolerable consequence.

Soviet policy, which now more than ever struggled against confining
relations to the radical African states, had a considerably broader range.

61. Thompson, *Ghana's Foreign Policy*, p. 381.

62. Paris AFP (in French), 17.30 GMT, January 8, 1965. In addition, see
summary of Houphouet-Boigny's January 23 speech reported in "News in Brief,"
Africa Report, X (March 1965), 36–37.

63. "News in Brief," *Africa Report*, p. 38. Also see *Le Monde*, August 6,
1965, p. 5.

It accented the economic rather than the political struggle, and it sub-scribed to a long-term, gradual evolution toward socialism rather than violent revolution. By 1965 Soviet African policy differed substantially from China's, and as a result the Soviet Union responded differently to the revolutionary opportunity Ghana presented. Soviet leaders declined to undertake the training of freedom fighters because it threatened to undermine their objectives elsewhere on the continent; Chinese leaders happily accepted the responsibility precisely because it corresponded with their objectives elsewhere on the continent.

The contrasting effects of each country's policies emerged sharply from Houphouet-Boigny's speech to the Fourth Congress of the PDCI in Sep-tember 1965. He announced, on the one hand, that his government would no longer refuse to establish relations with the countries of the East, especially with the Soviet Union and Yugoslavia, countries which, he maintained, would not exploit diplomatic relations to interfere in the internal affairs of the Ivory Coast, which would agree to respect Ivory Coast institutions, and which would not support or encourage sub-version in his country.[64] "It seems that Russia, preoccupied by the task of raising the welfare of its people and wisened by its failures on our continent, has renounced any intention of dominating Africa through the imposition of its doctrines." "In contrast," Houphouet continued, "we exclude the eventuality of any diplomatic relations with the China of Peking, whose criminal policy rests on permanent revolution by sub-version . . . on the physical suppression of leaders who do not share its ideological conceptions for the conduct of affairs." Houphouet's dis-crimination reflected the comparative opportunity costs of Soviet and Chinese policy.

One of the subversion camps the Soviet Union had cautiously avoided opened at Teshi late in 1964, about the time Nigeria was caught up in the tension of national elections. Its trainees were Nigerian refugees, and the fact that the Soviet Union refused to become involved in their preparation reinforced the impression that Moscow was hesitant to use a tumultuous political situation to press for revolutionary advance. Rather than further unravel the Federation's frail political fibers by encouraging the NSWFP to adopt revolutionary tactics, Soviet commen-tators publicly expressed concern over Nigeria's precarious political condi-tion. In both the December federal elections and the August 1965 West-

64. *IVᵉCongrès PDCI-RDA,* Ministère de l'Information (mimeo) September 23–25, 1965, p. 17.

ern elections, they condemned those who sought to "whip up intertribal hatred" in order to subvert the elections. Though they rejected the frontrunning Nigerian National Alliance as a bloc "composed of the feudal elements of the North with the bourgeoisie of the south of the country, linked with foreign monopolies," they nevertheless recognized elections as the only legitimate arena for political competition.[65] In the last chapter it was noted that, when the NNA achieved its inevitable triumph and the leaders of the opposing United Progressive Grand Alliance (supported by the NSWFP) made their equally inevitable compromise with the victors, this too Soviet writers accepted with only perfunctory criticism.

Wahab Goodluck, vice-president of the NSWFP, surely understated the problem with Nigerian politics when he wrote in *Pravda* (October 4, 1964) that "there are no textbooks to give ready-made solutions for the work of Marxist-Leninist parties in Africa." Soviet leaders certainly had none. Increasingly their policy was marked by three not altogether consistent characteristics. First, the Soviet leadership was beginning to realize that Nigeria had greater potentiality for explosive internal change than any other Black African country. Another reaction would have been surprising, for no firsthand observer could remain complacent in the face of the mounting tempest of tribal friction and economic discontent threatening Nigeria. Stunned by the magnitude and force of the spontaneous general strike in the summer of 1964, the Soviet Union suddenly perceived the long-term importance of economic pressures in this largest sub-Saharan country. The rate of unemployment in Lagos, Black Africa's most populous metropolitan center, unknown but variously estimated to comprise between 25 and 45 percent of the adult urban population, promised to generate irrepressible political fission. As British diplomats nervously contemplated the prospect of 60 percent of those completing secondary school in 1965 failing to find suitable jobs or being unable to go on to higher educational institutions, Soviet writers dwelt increasingly on the surge of working-class solidarity and the emergence of "a most bitter and implacable [class] struggle."[66] One Soviet author pointedly recalled recent events in Dahomey, Togo, and Congo (Braz-

65. Moscow radio (in English for Africa), 22.30 GMT, November 11, 1965; see also Moscow (in English for Africa), 18.30 GMT, August 6, 1965.

66. Moscow radio (home service), 10.30 GMT, November 22, 1965. See two articles by V. Korovikov, in *Pravda,* August 21, 1965, p. 3, and August 24, 1965, p. 5; and Moscow radio (in English for Africa), 21.00 GMT, November 18, 1965.

zaville) which "demonstrated how effective the intervention of the unem-
ployed in the political struggle can be if they receive leadership from
opposition parties or trade unions" (in Nigeria's case, from the NSWFP
and the NTUC).[67]

The other two characteristics of the Soviet attitude incorporated, on
the surface at least, contradictory impulses. On the one hand, Soviet
analysts rejected the new government that was dominated, they contended, by the "feudal party of the North." Members of the UPGA
who joined the new cabinet were depicted as reactionaries intent on
sharing power, whatever the price in shattered principles. According
to one Soviet commentator, the presence in the cabinet of Minister of
Finance Okotie-Eboh, a "representative of the right wing of the NCNC,
confirms the conclusion about the strengthening of the position of reaction in the government."[68] Nor did the refusal of Wachuku, the former
foreign minister so often castigated by the Soviet press for "supporting
the American-Belgian intervention in the Congo" (Stanleyville), imply
any desire on the part of the new government to alter its foreign policy.
To complete the appraisal, Soviet observers argued that more than four
years after political independence, Nigeria not only remained economically dependent on the capitalist world but it actually was "growing
increasingly dependent thanks to the 'open door' policy, which promotes
domination by foreign capital."[69] Thus at one level the new Soviet regime
found it no easier to embrace Nigeria's political system and its program
for economic development than Khrushchev had.

At the same time, short-term interests prompted Soviet leaders to
enlarge contact with a wider spectrum of African states, and Nigeria,
as one of the most important, represented an obvious target of Soviet
attention. The approach remained essentially economic. In June Soviet
officials received a trade delegation from Nigeria's Produce Marketing
Company promoting the sale of Nigerian agricultural products. The
next month an official delegation from the Nigerian Ministry of Trade
came to persuade Soviet officials to buy larger quantities of Nigerian
cocoa. Although the published record fails to indicate whether the Soviet
Union consented to these appeals, a subsequent article in *Aziya i Afrika
segodnya* characterized the July mission as a success and noted that

67. V. Iordansky, "Pyat let politicheskoi zakalki" (Five Years of Political Tem-
pering), *Aziya i Afrika segodnya*, no. 8 (1965), p. 22.
68. Leonid Fedorov for Moscow radio (home service), 15.30 GMT, January
14, 1965.
69. Moscow radio (in English for Africa), 20.30 GMT, June 3, 1965.

the previous year, when Nigeria was unable to find markets for its agricultural products, the Soviet Union had made a substantial purchase of cocoa.[70] In 1965 Soviet trade with Nigeria, though still only a small portion of each country's total trade, was nearly twice the previous year's total—Khrushchev's last year and the year of the Soviet Union's first significant entry into the Nigerian market.[71] However, because the Nigerian government lacked the authority to control the buying practices of private importers, Soviet leaders could not have expected exports to Nigeria to rise substantially, and hence the prospects for a vastly expanded trade remained dim. Soviet-Nigerian trade was more important as a token of the Soviet desire to increase political contact with this crucial member of the moderate group.

The Soviet Union's new leaders had accepted Khrushchev's efforts to increase connections with the nonrevolutionary states. Unlike his policy toward the revolutionary democracies, they found this aspect of policy realistic and perfectly in tune with Soviet interests. Under their auspices Khrushchev's initiatives were not only continued but, in two interesting respects, developed further. First, they sought to establish diplomatic relations with the last and most reactionary category of African state—the Ivory Coast and Upper Volta. Second, they presided over what by 1966 had become a remarkable turnabout in Soviet descriptions of the moderate states.

Efforts to establish diplomatic relations with the Ivory Coast began to blossom after Houphouet opened the way at the Fourth Congress of the PDCI. Progress toward the establishment of relations was momentarily interrupted by the Ghanaian coup: Houphouet apparently had not liked the revelation of the full range of Soviet activity in this neighboring country. But these second thoughts proved short-lived, and in August 1966 he welcomed V. I. Yerofeyev, the Soviet ambassador to Senegal, who came to help celebrate the sixth anniversary of Ivory Coast independence. While he was there, the Ivory Coast's official press agency let it be known that the Ivory Coast "might next establish diplomatic relations with the Soviet Union."[72] For his part, Ambassador Yerofeyev

70. Geivandov, "Pervoe pyatiletie Nigerii" (Nigeria: The First Five Years), *Aziya i Afrika segodnya,* no. 10 (1965), p. 27.

71. Nigerian Trade Summary, Federal Office of Statistics, December, 1965. Figures are for the first nine months.

72. *A(gence) I(voirienne) de P(resse) Information* (mimeo), August 4, 1966. p. 3.

worked to reinforce the image of a circumspect regime willing to co-operate modestly with any nation regardless of its political system. In his speeches he discreetly praised the Ivory Coast's economic progress and noted its important role in international, as well as African, affairs. On his departure, the ambassador predicted that relations would soon be established between the two countries.[73] And in January 1967 they were. The next month the Soviet press announced the establishment of diplomatic relations with Upper Volta, another of the West African regimes once despised by Soviet writers.

The second feature of the new leadership's policy in moderate African states is more interesting. Ever since Khrushchev had successfully begun relations with these states in 1962, public evaluation of their regimes had grown less and less critical. By 1966, under Khrushchev's successors, attitudes were strikingly different from Soviet commentary published early in the 1960s. Compare, for example, an early assessment of Senegal's four-year plan with a comment made in 1966. Shortly after the plan's introduction in 1961, one Soviet observer had predicted that the "collaborators of colonialism" would find it difficult to generate any enthusiasm for a plan that in effect meant giving foreign monopolies control over Senegal's economy.[74] Five years later the Soviet Union commended the Senegalese government for "building up the national economy on the basis of a four-year plan" and for "beginning agrarian reform" in the face of colonialism's difficult heritage.[75] Soviet comments on the occasion of Senegal's sixth-anniversary celebrations, in April 1966, were also unlike things said several years earlier. Solodovnikov dropped by a commemorative soirée held in Moscow's House of Friendship and spoke of the great interest of the Soviet people in Senegal. A TASS commentator noted that Senegal's foreign policy of "positive neutrality" had earned it great prestige.[76] Similar praise gently reverberated throughout the Soviet press. *Sovetskaya Rossiya* said the country had made great advances in six years. *Trud* stressed the independence of Senegalese foreign policy and its cooperation with the Soviet Union.[77] Later in the year, *Pravda*'s special correspondent, Igor Belyaev, visited Dakar and wrote a warm report of his impressions.[78] After the long Pan Ameri-

73. *Dakar-Matin,* August 11, 1966, p. 1.
74. S. Zykov, in *Izvestiya,* May 24, 1961, p. 5.
75. Moscow TASS (in English), 16.15 GMT, April 2, 1966.
76. Moscow TASS (in English), 12.15 GMT, April 2, 1966.
77. Moscow TASS (in English), 08.15 GMT, April 3, 1966.
78. I. Belyaev, in *Pravda,* December 19, 1966, p. 5.

can flight up the coast, how wonderful to arrive in this "most beautiful West African city" where, he said, "I again felt I was in real Africa." He described the growing sense of Africanism among the Senegalese, the confidence that theirs was a "genuine African country" with a significant role to play in Africa. He praised the leadership's earnest efforts to strengthen the country's national economy and to improve the lot of the peasant. He spoke enthusiastically of the desire to learn more about the Soviet Union, of the Russian-language programs, and of official interest in expanding cultural ties between the two countries. "Senegal, which is strengthening its independence," he concluded, "can undoubtedly make a large positive contribution to the anti-imperialist struggle" in Africa and beyond.

Equally striking was the Soviet Union's participation in Senegal's 1966 World Festival of Negro Arts. Earlier Potekhin had rejected Senghor's notions of "negritude" as an "unhappy term" that excluded certain African peoples and substituted the idea of "unity between the negroid peoples of Africa and America's Negroes."[79] In many ways the festival symbolized what Potekhin had disparaged, and yet no one publicized the event more abundantly or more favorably than the Soviet press.[80] Professor Olderogge, an eminent Soviet Africanist, and another Soviet academician joined the colloquium on Negro arts. Yevgeny Yevtushenko came to honor the festival with his poetry (read after the festival's close) and Yevgeny Dolmatovsky, a conservative member of the Union of Soviet Writers, tagged along, apparently to watch Yevtushenko. Soviet authorities rented the passenger liner *Rossiya* to Senegal to serve as a floating hotel for the festival's guests.

In some ways, however, the most impressive evidence of the Soviet leadership's desire to improve its image in Senegal comes from the way it handled relations with the Parti Africain de l'Indépendance. No longer did the Soviet press rush to defend this "fraternal" ally when the regime clamped down on its members. In June 1965 when a captured PAI commando group was brought to justice, after an abortive attempt to subvert civil installations in eastern Senegal, the Soviet media made scarcely a murmur. This was in marked contrast to the angry denunciations that had followed the 1960 trial of PAI militants.[81] Nor did a

79. Potekhin, *Afrika smotrit v budushchee*, p, 78.
80. See the entire issue of *Aziya i Afrika segodnya*, no. 12 (1965); Moscow TASS (in English), 13.18 GMT, April 25, 1966; Moscow TASS (in English), 05.54 GMT, April 21, 1966; and *Pravda*, May 13, 1966. p. 4.
81. See S. Volk, "Sudilishche v Senegale" (Trial in Senegal), *Aziya i Afrika segodnya*, no. 8 (1961), p. 54.

further trial of PAI members in March 1966 attract attention. In February 1966 when students at the University of Dakar staged protest demonstrations over Nkrumah's removal, again the Soviet press had no comment. Senegalese officials were a little irritated when the Soviet Union invited the PAI to the Twenty-Third Party Congress and gave Majhmout Diop an international platform, but even this was done in a way designed to give the least possible offense. In welcoming the foreign delegations to the congress, Brezhnev had carefully placed the PAI among the "national democratic and left socialist parties," not among the more significant "fraternal Communist parties" from Morocco, Tunisia, and South Africa. Brezhnev's gesture was apparently noticed by the Senegalese.[82] Subsequently the Soviet press displayed considerable interest in a rapprochement that would remove the ban on the PAI and lead to its collaboration with Senghor's Union Progressiste Sénégalaise.[83]

In a country like Senegal the reasons for the Soviet Union's new tolerance stemmed, in part, from those specific material advantages that came with closer bilateral ties. Each year Dakar, one of West Africa's most important ports, serviced an increasing number of Soviet trawlers. In 1965 the port fees paid by the Soviet Union exceeded its total trade with Senegal. By the aid agreement of 1964 Soviet trawlers were given access to storage and freezing facilities and, as a result, could be expected to use the port even more frequently. Dakar also stands at the feeder end of the railway to Bamako, a vital conduit for Soviet products being shipped into Mali. Finally, in July 1965, Soviet and Senegalese officials initialed an agreement opening Yoff Airport to Aeroflot and Sheremetyeva to Air Afrique.[84] For Aeroflot, Dakar was potentially an important leg on its flights to both Latin America and other Black African countries. Because the Soviet Union clearly had no desire to become heavily committed to the Senegalese, the rising level of trade and aid could be considered "rent" on these airport, railway, and port facilities.

82. The irritation of Senegalese officials over the invitation was related to me in interviews I had in Dakar in 1966. François Zuccarelli mentions the ranking given the PAI in his "Un parti politique africain: l'Union Progressiste Sénégalaise" (unpubl. diss., University of Dakar, 1968), p. 91. In 1966 Zuccarelli was an extremely able *conseiller technique* in the Senegalese interior ministry. For more information see Foltz, "The Parti Africain de l'Indépendance," pp. 11–12.

83. See Majhmout Diop's interview for *France nouvelle*, printed in *Aziya i Afrika segodnya*, no. 8 (1967), pp. 36–37.

84. The Soviet Union announced the beginning of service between Moscow and Dakar in December 1968. See *New Times*, no. 48 (December 4, 1968), back cover.

More fundamentally, however, there was a second consideration that probably serves better to explain the evolution of Soviet behavior: one must look up from the narrower problem of Soviet relations with moderate African states to see what had happened to Soviet perceptions of Africa over six years. By 1966 that initial flush of optimism characterizing early Soviet involvement in independent Africa was far in the past, the revolutionary sequel had elongated, and Soviet expectations had been considerably moderated. This evolution, which had so much to do with relations between the Soviet Union and the former members of the Monrovia group, paradoxically depended most on the Soviet Union's response to the so-called progressive countries. As the conviction grew that the course of events in Africa was erratic—in Soviet terms, characterized by "zigzags" along the path to socialism—the more tolerable were relations with the moderate states. Long before the year of the colonels, beginning with Touré's vacillations in 1961, the Soviet Union had learned that in Africa tomorrow is another day. The target of today's broadsides may turn out to be tomorrow's collaborator, and this makes any sharp differentiation among African states impractical. Revolutionary advance may suddenly degenerate into creeping capitalism. Overnight a revolutionary democrat may be replaced. In this way, disappointments and doubts had prompted the Soviet Union to broaden its policy in Africa—this before it became apparent that life was to grow even more difficult.

West Africa's Military Coups

The new Soviet regime had scarcely settled in, when serious trouble began to beset its closest African friends. Without any warning in June 1965, military officers in Algeria deposed Ben Bella, one of the Soviet Union's most promising African allies. In less dramatic fashion, Kenya, whose careful nonalignment had once evoked Soviet enthusiasm, began to waver and then, unmistakably in the spring of 1965, to shift its course. Difficulties occurred first in April when twenty-nine Kenyan students fled the Soviet Union, complaining angrily about the brutality and race prejudice they had encountered among Russian citizens. Later that month the Kenyan government turned back a shipload of Soviet arms and a military mission of seventeen technical advisers arranged by Kenya's pro-Soviet vice-president, Oginga Odinga. A few weeks later it announced the closing of Lumumba Institute, built by the Soviet

Union at Odinga's instigation at a cost of $2 million. From this point on, Odinga's position in Kenya's power structure, the linchpin of Soviet-Kenyan relations, gradually deteriorated. In the course of his defeat, first within the party and then within the government, Odinga's Soviet and Chinese benefactors came under strident attack; by the early months of 1966 the Soviet press had little reason to disguise its irritation over the course of events in Kenya.

But it is in Ghana that the Soviet Union suffered its most stunning setback. On February 24, 1966, Moscow home radio reported that the military had overthrown Nkrumah while he was out of the country. (It did not indicate that he was in Peking on a Vietnam peace mission wanted by no one but him.) "Here is a message just received from London. A military coup took place in Ghana today. The army has seized power. Kwame Nkrumah, President of the Republic, who is on a trip abroad, has been deposed; Ministers have been dismissed; and Parliament and the People's Convention Party, the ruling party, have been dissolved."[85] It did not take great skill to see that the forces which had toppled Nkrumah were committed to a course of action running counter to Soviet interests. Even to the most obtuse it was apparent that this was not going to be, like the Algerian coup, merely a momentary disruption in the pattern of Soviet-Ghanaian cooperation. Ghana's National Liberation Council (NLC) represented a thorough break with the recent past. From the moment the president's loyal security guard surrendered to the army and police, Ghana's new rulers set about dismantling Nkrumah's political establishment and reorienting his foreign policy. They expelled a host of Soviet advisers, spread across Ghana from the Tamale airfield to the University of Ghana, from Shai Hills to the Kwame Nkrumah Ideological Institute, and from Flagstaff House to the Tema seaport. Within a week of the coup d'état, the new regime had sent all 620 Soviet technicians and teachers packing. Their ouster removed nearly the entire staff of Ghana's medical school (25), one third of all the qualified secondary educators in mathematics and science (125), 54 advisers attached to the Ministry of Defense, 200 workers at the Tamale airbase, 47 geologists, the staff of four state farms, 27 technicians completing atomic-research facilities and technicians aiding with a variety of other projects such as a fish-processing complex, a concrete panel factory, and so on. All of these projects, including the atomic-research center, were simply shut down. On March 1 Lieutenant-

85. Moscow radio (home service), 09.00 GMT, February 24, 1966.

General Joseph Ankrah, the chairman of the NLC, announced the cancellation of all Aeroflot flights to Ghana, ostensibly because Aeroflot had flown Nkrumah from Peking to Moscow the day before. A few hours later the NLC expelled the East German trade mission and ordered the Soviet embassy to reduce its staff from 67 to 18.[86] Amid this turmoil a rumor that eleven Soviet security officers had been killed during the siege of Flagstaff House circulated freely in diplomatic circles and at the marketplace.[87]

Now Soviet leaders confronted the immediate decision of how to handle the arrival of Ghana's deposed leader in Moscow. The coup had negated the point of Nkrumah's Vietnamese peace mission and transformed his journey into a desperate search for assistance in re-establishing his power. When Peking refused to intervene directly, he went on to Moscow. There the Ghanaian embassy announced that, as far as it was concerned, Nkrumah was now only an ordinary Ghanaian citizen and no one would be sent to the airport to meet the former president. Around the world Ghanaian embassies quickly removed the enlarged pictures of Nkrumah and declared their loyalty to the new government. Observers waited to see whether the Soviet government would give Nkrumah full honors, including a greeting by President Podgorny, send a lower-level delegation, or ignore him altogether. The Soviet leadership sent Foreign Minister Gromyko to the airport and, after a day of presumably evading any firm response to Nkrumah's pleas, placed him on a secret flight to Guinea where Touré awaited his sometime friend with military honors and a presidential appointment.

In Accra the NLC had already begun mending Ghana's badly mangled relations with neighboring countries and restoring its withered economic ties with Western capitals. On March 12, Ankrah promised the diplomatic corps that Ghana would "scrupulously respect the sovereignty and territorial integrity of all states," and he assured countries that had suffered from the "illegal activities of the deposed regime that the NLC will not allow Ghana to be used as a base for subversive activities against any independent African state."[88] Missions crisscrossed the west coast, carrying to countries against which Nkrumah had plotted the

86. *New York Times,* March 3, 1966, p. 1.

87. Although by July 1966 both Ghanaian and Soviet officials denied the rumor, Western diplomats remained firmly convinced that eleven security advisers had in fact been taken out of Flagstaff House and summarily shot by angry army officers. Without more explicit evidence, however, I am personally skeptical.

88. Accra radio (domestic service in English), 13.00 GMT, March 12, 1966.

same message of goodwill and initiating the first steps toward normal relations. While Ankrah was reassuring the diplomatic corps, E. N. Omaboe, chairman of the NLC's economic committee, was making an "impassioned appeal" to all foreign businessmen in Ghana to retain their pending transfers of profits and reinvest these in the country as a "mark of support for the NLC."[89] In response to petitions directed abroad, Western governments had indicated an early willingness to assist the new regime. Both the United States and the United Nations stepped forward with immediate promises of aid—in the American case, food denied the former government in November 1965.[90] A few days later, five members of a seven-man IMF staff mission arrived in Accra for consultations, and Ghana's new high commissioner to the United Kingdom prepared to depart for London, following the resumption of relations severed two months earlier over the Rhodesia issue.

The Soviet leadership could hardly be expected to welcome a regime that had turned its back on the socialist countries and was now seeking to resurrect old ties with the capitalist states of the West. Its immediate reaction, however, was relatively restrained; in a style well developed during previous moments of difficulty, the Soviet press confined its reporting to the commentary of the foreign press. Thus *Pravda, Izvestiya,* and Moscow radio recounted the joy and satisfaction other news media attributed to Western leaders at the news of Nkrumah's fall.[91] The innuendo, of course, was that Western leaders were happy because the new regime would be amenable to their foreign policies and influence. Moscow radio carried Guinea's more explicit accusation that "the Ghana coup is another act of aggression against African freedom, unity, and progress," reaffirming the fact that "imperialist forces, with the aid of traitors of the homeland in their pay, are now methodically pursuing in Africa a broad plan of reconquest."[92]

Soon, though, Soviet commentators abandoned this facade of foreign criticism and began casting their own stones. Whether naively or decep-

89. *Ibid.*

90. *Le Monde,* March 17, 1966, p. 6.

91. See *Izvestiya,* March 2, 1966, p. 1; *Pravda,* February 25, 1966, p. 5; *Izvestiya,* March 3, 1966, p. 1; and Moscow radio (home service), 09.00 GMT, February 26, 1966. One illustration of the indirection in Soviet reporting is amusing. *Pravda,* March 3, 1966, p. 1, carried a TASS report that Nkrumah had arrived in Conakry, based on a Reuter report filed from Dakar, in turn drawn from monitorings of the Guinean radio, although it was Aeroflot that had flown him to Guinea.

92. Moscow radio (home service), 13.00 GMT, February 27, 1966.

tively, the Soviet press and radio accepted the story of Khow Amihiya, an expatriate Ghanaian living in London, who passed himself off as the head of a so-called revolutionary council and claimed that his organization had planned the coup with the assistance of British intelligence and the CIA.[93] Moscow radio reported that Amihiya's account clearly indicated American and British complicity in the overthrow of Ghana's president.[94] When Amihiya returned to Ghana, where he was promptly arrested by an irate NLC, one Soviet writer drew the conclusion that a power struggle had begun between the leaders of the plot.[95]

Overlaying this crude and simplistic explanation of the Ghanaian coup were the more complicated issues raised by shrewder analysts. Though they did not deny the existence of an imperialist conspiracy, the obvious ease with which the new regime seized power required some explanation (as did, one assumes, the coup's obvious popularity). It was true, Kudryavtsev wrote in the first authoritative commentary on the coup d'état, that the progressive character of Ghana's former president supplied imperialists with sufficient reason for wishing his removal.[96] Kwame Nkrumah's government had carried out a number of radical social and economic reforms, was building a strong state sector, and gradually "ridding the country of capitalist monopolies." It had acted as a consistent advocate of African unity, of the earliest possible liberation of the whole of Africa from colonialism, and it had demanded the abolition of the racist regime in Southern Rhodesia. In international affairs, his regime had pursued an anti-imperialist and anticolonialist policy. For all these reasons Ghana naturally came to represent a "mote in the eye of the imperialists who had been sharpening their claws for a long time on this progressive African country."

Yet, Kudryavtsev admitted, unresolved problems had made it easier for local reaction and foreign imperialism to execute the conspiracy. The difficulty was that the masses had had too little share either in governing or in the fruits of independence. A Polish commentator remarked that, since the real opposition to Nkrumah had been in London, the coup could not be interpreted as primarily an internal affair.[97] He

93. See Victor Sidenko, "Le Ghana et les imperialistes," *Temps nouveaux,* no. 10 (March 9, 1966), pp. 14–16.

94. Moscow radio (in English for Africa), 14.30 GMT, March 2, 1966.

95. Sidenko, "Le Ghana et les imperialistes," p. 14.

96. V. Kudryavtsev, in *Izvestiya,* March 6, 1966, p. 3.

97. "The Monitoring Report" (BBC), Second Series EE/2104/i, 09.00 GMT, March 3, 1966, 09.00 GMT, March 4, 1966.

too, however, recognized that the situation in Ghana had been deteriorating and ascribed some of the difficulty to the personality cult that had grown up around the Ghanaian leader. On March 15, a Radio Moscow commentator revised the charge of collaboration between foreign imperialists and local forces: "It is difficult to judge with certainty yet about imperialist participation in the Ghana coup, but it is well known that the coup was welcomed with unconcealed joy by the rulers in Britain and the USA."[98] He also acknowledged "the economic difficulties experienced by Ghana, particularly in recent years," but blamed them on the "deliberate policy" of Western monopolies of driving down the price of cocoa.

As has often been the case, the substance of Soviet diplomatic activity during the first weeks after the coup never wholly reflected the critical reports of the press. Unquestionably the overthrow of Nkrumah distressed Soviet policymakers but, given the nature of the Soviet Union's nonrevolutionary involvement in sub-Saharan Africa and its stake in stable, businesslike relations with a broad segment of African states, there remained few alternatives other than stoic acceptance. Obviously these events could not easily be reversed and to lament too loudly, let alone to try and undo the coup's results, would surely have compounded the failure of Soviet policy. Thus, although unhappy, Soviet leaders felt compelled to prevent illwill from erupting into open antagonism. For example, they believed it important to undermine rumors that eleven Soviet advisers had been killed during the fighting at Flagstaff House: involvement of this kind would make other African states nervous, and a disclosure of this kind would magnify tension between the two countries.[99] Similarly, the Soviet media carefully deleted from their coverage of Nkrumah's speeches and radio broadcasts to Ghana his exhortations to the Ghanaian people to rise up against the "military clique" and overthrow their "illegal" regime. In his second address to the Ghanaian people, Nkrumah specifically urged the masses to revolt, to "overthrow these irresponsible army and police traitors and adventurers."[100] Moscow radio ambiguously

98. Farid Seyful-Mulyukov for Moscow radio (home service), 18.00 GMT, March 15, 1966.

99. "The Monitoring Report" (BBC), SU/2106/i-(TASS); and Moscow radio (in English for Africa), 21.30 GMT, March 9, 1966. TASS termed the rumors, particularly those of Reuters, "a fabrication from beginning to end." See *Pravda* and *Izvestiya*, March 8, 1966, p. 4.

100. Conakry radio (domestic service in English), 20.00 GMT, March 13, 1966.

described this speech as a "call for an active struggle to preserve the gains of independence," adding only that Nkrumah had declared that Ghanaians "should not lose their trust in the future."[101] Moreover, it seems likely that Soviet leaders ducked responsibility for organizing Nkrumah's reconquest of power and even shied away from any major involvement with the contingent of Ghanaian security guards accompanying him into exile.[102] Here, though, Soviet leaders had difficulty in persuading the new Ghanaian leadership of their innocence. In the first months after the coup, the feeling spread among Ghanaian officials that the Soviet Union was supplying matériel to a secret camp for saboteurs in Guinea. Following the delivery of two Antonov-24s to Conakry in early March and later the conclusion of an arms sale to Mali, the Ghanaian press hinted that this equipment was intended for a secret Soviet subversion camp in Guinea. Not surprisingly the Soviet press denied this accusation, but then added: "The Soviet Government used to maintain friendly relations with the Government of Ghana, and it strives to do so now. The Soviet people have sincere friendly feelings for the Ghanaians. They maintain that the slanderous allegations in Ghana's newspapers concerning the menace which is said to be represented by Soviet weapons contradict the attitude of most Ghanaians to the Soviet Union."[103]

Further evidence of the desire to control tension emerged from the circumstances in which the Soviet Union extended recognition to the new government. The Soviet Union gave its recognition on March 17, despite the expulsion of twenty additional Russians, including top embassy officials, on the previous day for alleged espionage activity. The Chinese, in contrast, refused to extend recognition and, after Chinese officials had been sent home, addressed a violent note of protest to the Ghanaian government. Their note accused the new government of repeated lies intended to "vilify and calumniate" China and blamed Ghanaian authorities "for the deterioration in relations between the two countries."[104] A similar protest submitted by the Soviet government was far milder in tone, referring in its sharpest sections to the "defamatory inventions of some circles."[105] Ultimately China was unable to reconcile

101. *Pravda,* March 15, 1966, p. 5. See also Moscow radio (home service), 18.00 GMT, March 15, 1966.

102. Many of them had just finished a two-year course in the Soviet Union.

103. Moscow radio (in English for Africa), 20.30 GMT, July 2, 1966.

104. *Le Monde,* April 3–4, 1966, p. 4.

105. *Le Monde,* April 5, 1966, p. 7.

itself to the new regime and on November 5, 1966, at Ghana's request closed its embassy.

Nigeria and the Military Coups

By the time Ghana's army and police seized power in February, the intrusion of the military into African politics was becoming a commonplace. Already military coups d'état had occurred in the Congo, Dahomey, the Central African Republic, Upper Volta, and, most significantly, Nigeria; like a contagion the phenomenon swept on across the continent, destroying regimes debilitated by internal political quarrels, economic difficulties, or simply failure to overcome the restraints of traditional relationships and antagonisms. Soviet writers said (*before* the events in Ghana) that the coups reflected the "growing dissatisfaction of the broad popular masses" with corrupt leaderships more concerned with serving foreign monopolies than with improving the economic condition of the nation. But since these writers were as startled and baffled as anyone by the sudden and virulent rash of military revolts, their immediate reaction may have been less well considered than was characteristic in the years after Khrushchev. Sensing the mounting restlessness of the masses, an analysis would commonly begin, the army intervened to prevent "popular dissatisfaction [from destroying] the legal framework and [from forcing the military] along with the corrupt clique . . . to fall by the political wayside."[106]

There was a certain timid optimism in this analysis. "The latest military coups have occurred in countries in which the economic situation is little different from that prevailing under former colonial conditions."[107] Soviet writers, looking for the encouraging aspects of the military's new role, concluded that countries turning toward capitalism had become the logical victims because, after all, their leaders used power to serve themselves and "to block social and economic transformations." Rather than risk being struck down by the vengeful masses, the army "stepped in to save the ruling clique, even though this meant sacrificing some of its members."[108] The military, Soviet writers decided, is "the last organized force of the ruling class."

106. V. Kudryavtsev, in *Izvestiya*, January 15, 1966, p. 2.
107. *Ibid.*
108. Boris Paveltsev, "The Military Coups in Africa," *New Times,* no. 4 (January 26, 1966), p. 13.

Hence the ambivalence in the Soviet response. Presumably the destruction of antiprogressive regimes was pleasing, but how should their military successors be regarded? With reservations apparently, for seen by one Soviet observer they were still products of European colonial armies, taken from their societies' "ruling element," trained and molded by British or French officers, and now the last force capable of saving order in the face of popular discontent.[109] "That is not to say that the army cannot play a revolutionary role," this same observer wrote: "Many officers are sincere patriots and democrats." But there were those groups within the army "closely connected with the former colonial bosses," and the intentions of the new military leaderships were still too unclear to allow a judgment. Before February 22, Soviet commentary was vague, somewhat hopeful because unprogressive regimes had been destroyed but carefully qualified by a wary assessment of the military leaderships now in power.

Of the military coups the most important was the one carried out by young Nigerian officers in the early morning of January 15. It removed a regime enervated by corruption and internal discord. Had the military not intervened, it seemed almost certain that Balewa's government would disintegrate under the growing pressure of regional antagonisms. To the young officers, the politicians appeared too fat and comfortable and too interested in bickering to act decisively to prevent this from happening. The officers were determined to drive off the politicians, to close down their parties and undermine the forces fostering regional divisiveness. If the politicians resisted, as it was expected they would, they were to be physically eliminated. Then a unitary state could be instituted, tribalism and corruption eliminated, and the problems of economic development attacked frontally without the encumbrance of regional competition.

When the coup came, its executors—a handful of predominantly Ibo officers led by Major Chukwuma Nziogwu—fanned out to the four regions and within a few hours murdered, in some cases according to plan, in others apparently unintentionally, the premiers of the North and the West and Prime Minister Balewa. The Eastern premier, Michael Okpara, escaped, reinforcing the misleading impression that the coup was primarily intended to strengthen the Ibos against the Northerners. Thus almost in a single blow the old political order had been annihilated, the power of the reactionary North seemingly broken, and a fresh start

109. *Ibid.*, pp. 11, 13.

prepared. No one applauded more than Soviet commentators. They were delighted to see a regime destroyed which they considered thoroughly subservient to British and American interests, corrupt and unwilling to embark upon a substantial reform of its country's administrative and economic structures. They wrote that "the success of the coup has demonstrated the precariousness and unpopularity of the former regime, which had been pictured by Western propaganda as a 'model of democracy,' and 'governmental wisdom' for the rest of Africa."[110] Here was a ready theme for the Soviet Union's own propaganda, and its exponents gloated on it: the West's "showcase" in Black Africa had collapsed, ruined by its own corruption and reckless tolerance of foreign exploitation. Moscow radio picked up the description that Tunji Otegbeye, the general secretary of NSWFP, applied to the old leaders as "thorough agents of neo-colonialism" who enriched themselves while "the masses of the people were subjected to abject poverty," who turned the economy over to foreign imperialists, and who restricted contact with the socialist countries.[111] (Never mind that Soviet analysis had been somewhat less candid before their removal.)

But as events developed, those originally behind the coup lost control during its execution and eventually wound up in prison. In Lagos, in the confusion, the permanent secretaries and what remained of the senior ranks within the military turned over power to General Johnson Aguiyi-Ironsi, commander-in-chief of Nigeria's armed forces. Although an Ibo, Ironsi had not been a part of the original plot and, in fact, was evidently to be among those assassinated. All of this took place so swiftly that we only have reflections after the event, but these suggest that Soviet observers had warmly welcomed the first phase of the coup and grudgingly accepted the defeat of what they called the "patriotically minded" younger officer corps by "the senior command of the Nigerian army, linked to the old government and under the political influence of the feudal North."[112] "The coup has turned out to be a 'compromise' coup, to a certain extent. This evidently explains the rather calm attitude toward the coup and toward the physical elimination of the political leaders of the North . . . on the part of Britain."

Still, at a minimum, the revolt had been directed "primarily against

110. V. Korovikov, *Pravda,* January 22, 1966, p. 4.
111. Moscow radio (in English for Africa), 19.30 GMT, March 28, 1966. See also L. Fedorov, "Nigeriya do perevorota i posle" (Nigeria, Before and After the Revolt), *Aziya i Afrika segodnya,* no. 6 (1966), pp. 48–50.
112. V. Kudryavtsev, in *Izvestiya,* March 6, 1966, p. 3.

the reactionary feudal clique in northern Nigeria whose rule . . . weighed heavily on other regions and held back Nigeria's development as an independent state."[113] This could only be considered a step forward. Thus, more because of what had been before than because of what came after, the first Nigerian coup aroused expectations that the Ghanaian coup five weeks later would smother. Perhaps now a campaign could be launched cleansing the government of massive corruption and nepotism. Undeniably the need to do away with corruption offered Soviet spokesmen a convenient handle for attacking administrators they considered too partial to Western influence, but to say this does not contradict their sincere repugnance for unrestrained public graft in a country where economic deficiencies were immense.

The prospect of "good government," however, excited Soviet observers less than the possibility that Nigeria's new government would reduce its dependence on Western investment. Expatriate enterprise, a protected private sector, and the six-year plan drafted by the IBRD proved, in the view of Soviet observers, the former government's commitment to the capitalist path and thus vassalage to Western imperialism. Soviet commentators hoped that the advent of military rule would change this. "It will take some time to revise the six-year plan to the interests of Nigeria," one noted, "but the first steps to rectify the position seem to have been taken."[114] At least General Ironsi had declared his government's intention "to promote national economic development" under a clear-cut program of four five-year plans, and planned development usually implied restraints on private and foreign investment.

At this point Soviet commentators could also be enthusiastic about the new military government's plans to suppress tribalism and the forces aggravating tension between regions, particularly between the East and the North. An important reason for the original coup had been to prevent these forces from tearing the Federation apart, and that purpose had been embraced by those who ultimately came to power. They recognized that no political party commanded national loyalty, that the bureaucracy was politically impotent and leaderless, and thus that the military remained the only institution capable of controlling these divisive tendencies. From the Soviet perspective this meant inevitably destroying the autonomy of the dominant Northern Region—the area whose "feudal"

113. *Ibid.*
114. Ivan Sergeyev for Moscow radio (in English for Africa), 20.30 GMT, June 14, 1966.

and reactionary character had long distorted Nigeria's foreign policy and impeded progressive economic change. However presented, the struggle against sectionalism struck most severely at the North's sources of power and, therefore, had the Soviet Union's complete sympathy. Even when the military regime dissolved all political parties and tribal organizations, including the NSWFP (May 24), Soviet writers did not flinch; they accepted this decision as unavoidable in the circumstances. If the regime argued that suppression of parties contributed to the stifling of tribal quarrels and sectionalism, they were not prepared to make an issue of it. For the effort to build national unity, the promise of stability, and perhaps even for the new government's public assurance of nonalignment, the Soviet Union announced: "On balance, the progressive forces of the country support the new regime and hope that, beyond replacing former leaders, it will promote real changes in Nigerian policy, liberating it from the yoke of neocolonialism."[115]

Ironsi's government now proclaimed the abolition of federal divisions and the establishment of a unitary state, a madcap measure. Instantly the enraged emirs reacted, the Northern Region began to seethe, and the simmering loathing of the Ibo erupted in bloody violence. By challenging the basic independence of the Northern rulers, the military regime had overspent its effective political power and, in the process, set in motion a chain of events ending in its own destruction. Apparently Soviet analysts saw this no more clearly than General Ironsi and his colleagues. Their commentary in this phase contains none of the warnings against a precipitous assault on Nigeria's powerful traditional structures found in later accounts, only vacant and irrelevant homilies about neocolonial intrigues—such as Valentin Korovikov's reference to the "sinister flames of intertribal strife" fanned by British residents (including the British high commissioner) anxious to encourage "secessionist elements in Nigeria."[116] One need not question the convictions behind this assessment to wonder how a correspondent with years of experience in Africa could see matters so simply. Another commentator offered the equally useless observation that Nigeria's troubles "made trade-union solidarity difficult to achieve."[117] As Nigeria slipped toward national tragedy, one

115. Victor Nilov, "Le nouveau regime au Nigeria," *Temps nouveaux,* no. 24 (June 15, 1966), p. 23.
116. V. Korovikov, in *Pravda,* June 14, 1966, p. 3.
117. Vladimir Dunayev for Moscow radio (home service), 18.30 GMT, June 2, 1966.

could hardly but feel the frustration and bewilderment of Soviet analysts trying to find an appropriate ideological explanation for what was about to happen.

On July 29, when the end came for Ironsi and his military regime, and Nigeria approached total chaos amid the carnage of an anti-Ibo pogrom within the army and in the Ibo communities of the North, Soviet observers expressed distinct misgivings. The intramilitary coup against Ibo officers was being exploited by power groups opposed to a strong central government and a unitary state. "This must be definitely regarded as a step backwards in the political development," Moscow radio commented.[118] Nigeria, another observer noted, ran the risk of succumbing to forces eager to reintroduce "the old feudal structure" and Northern domination or of dissolving into a number of small, Balkanized states.[119] The more rigid and unimaginative analysts blamed the second coup on Western imperialism, accusing capitalist countries of doing in Africa what the United States had done countless times in the Central American banana republics.[120] "Whether they will succeed in perpetrating this plot against the people of Africa," one commentator concluded, "will depend on the activity and consciousness of the social forces and their resistance to the schemes of reaction and imperialism."[121]

But life was not so uncomplicated—not even in the shadowy, bewitched world of neocolonialist intrigue—and Soviet observers knew in the inner reaches of their consciousness that some more subtle accounting of the factors behind the coups would have to be produced. The military coup d'état that Soviet commentary originally seemed to consider cosmic retribution imposed upon the unreconstructed capitalist countries of Africa turned out to be the affliction of Africa's most revolutionary states as well—an affliction whose causes were far more profound than the meddling of Western intelligence agencies. Soviet analysis now proceeded a step further to examine the basic difficulties confronting African nations, particularly the most progressive.

118. Moscow radio (in English for Africa), 14.30 GMT, September 12, 1966.
119. Moscow radio (in English for Africa), 20.30 GMT, and (in Hausa), 17.30 GMT, August 3, 1966.
120. Vladimir Dunayev for Moscow radio (home service), 17.00 GMT, August 6, 1966.
121. *Ibid.*

VIII

The New Realism, 1967–1968

"Why," wondered *Izvestiya*'s commentator Vladimir Kudryavtsev, "have the organizers of the military coups in Africa been able to bring them off with relative ease?"[1] Why, since this must have concerned Soviet leaders more, had progressive, even revolutionary, regimes become the victims of military revolts? Kudryavtsev's answer was perfectly straight forward. These regimes had been overthrown because of their own inadequacies—as he said, because the soil was exceedingly fertile for military coups d'état.[2] They had failed to see all that was wrong with their policies, to understand the barriers that traditional habits and structures put in the way of social transformation, and to grasp the artificial quality of the revolution they proclaimed. It had not helped, of course, that

1. Kudryavtsev, in *Izvestiya*, March 6, 1966, p. 3. Kudryavtsev was by this time the Soviet Union's most significant political commentator on Africa. As much as anyone, he had assumed this part of Potekhin's role. He had long experience as a correspondent for *Izvestiya* in West Africa and had gone on to be a chief commentator for *Izvestiya* in Moscow. In addition, he served as an adviser to the foreign ministry and on the Foreign Affairs Commission of the Council of Nationalities, a group chaired by Boris Ponomarev.
2. Kudryavtsev quoted Algeria's *Actualités* to this effect, in ibid.

their Soviet benefactors had been only marginally more astute. As one Soviet writer put it: "The effective achievements of the national liberation movement on the continent, the establishment, in a few years, of dozens of new national states tended to create the erroneous impression that the struggle was almost at an end, that the way to liberation was easy and that the forces of imperialism were played out."[3] This was, he admitted, false optimism. Instead, it had to be confessed that the path to progress was painfully hazardous, filled with treacherous obstacles, and subject to untimely delays. "As the African revolution gains in depth, the internal weaknesses and objective difficulties in the liberation movement on the continent become increasingly evident." Much as history's ally hated to admit it, events were not, as it had once been thought, aiding the revolutionary process in Africa.

Implicitly Soviet writers were acknowledging that not merely had they overlooked some of the special problems endemic in African society, but that their whole sense of revolutionary momentum was somehow awry. Not too long ago they had divided coups d'état into progressive and reactionary categories: in one case irrepressible revolutionary forces had erupted to seize power; in the second, foreign interests had intervened as a last desperate measure to reinforce the doomed forces of local reaction. But that was clearly wrong. The Ghanaian coup and the July coup in Nigeria proved that in fact the weakest forces in Africa were revolutionary and the strongest were traditional with no need of direct imperialist intervention. When subsequently Soviet analysts talked about the "internal weaknesses" and "objective difficulties" in Africa's liberation movement, their shift in perceptions was apparent. In the words of one writer, "the extreme backwardness of social relations, the ill-defined social differentiation, the political backwardness of the peasants who are the main force behind the movement but the majority of whom are still under the sway of tribal and other prejudices" make revolution exceedingly difficult.[4] Traditional factors, it turned out, were decisive in African politics.

General Ironsi had underestimated the durability of such factors and was destroyed. It came too late, but Soviet commentators now pointed out that in contemporary Africa "the question of the state system cannot be resolved without taking stock of specific conditions, such as the ex-

3. K. Brutents, "African Revolution: Gains and Problems," *International Affairs*, no. 1 (1967), p. 21.
4. *Ibid.*

istence of tribes and the virtual absence of an established nation."[5] With a blithe expertise he did not show before the event (the article was entitled, "Africa as It Is"), Kudryavtsev treated the demise of Ironsi's military government as more or less an inevitable consequence. "No wonder that the sharp transition from a federal to a unitary system evoked a stormy reaction on the part of tribal leaders and the feudal aristocracy, resulting ultimately in a new coup." Ironsi had failed both to attack the economic privileges of the "feudal and tribal aristocracy" and to give the "broad popular masses" a feeling of the benefits to be realized through a unitary state, thereby leaving them an easy mark for the "reaction" seeking to develop opposition to an "objectively progressive course."[6] But his more serious failing (like that of Soviet observers) remained his basic insensitivity to the lethal power retained by traditional leaders.

Could not the same be said of Nkrumah? Had he not also overlooked the perils of tolerating traditional structures? Kudryavtsev seemed to think so:

> The gradual elimination of intertribal differences, naturally, is inconceivable without a resolute offensive against the positions of the feudal and tribal aristocracy, which at the present stage of the national-democratic revolution is joining ranks with neocolonialism, unwilling to lose its privileges. Attempts at compromise solutions to this highly important problem have led only to defeat for progressive forces.[7]

In Guinea, the cantonal chieftaincy had been eliminated before independence, permitting the unhindered implementation of "fundamental social and economic transformations." In Ghana, the chiefs survived to play an "active role in the military coup." Nkrumah's error was to indulge traditional elements, Ironsi's to provoke them, without annihilating them. Both overestimated the susceptibility of these forces to their power.

But Ghana was different from Nigeria—first, because the impact of traditional factors was less conspicuous (there was no tribal war for instance); second, because, as one of Africa's vanguard states, its fate

5. V. Kudryavtsev, in *Izvestiya,* August 30, 1966, p. 2.
6. *Ibid.* See also Moscow radio (home service), 16.30 GMT, August 8, 1966.
7. *Ibid.*

concerned the Soviet Union more. For the sake of other revolutionary leaderships, the circumstances that wrecked Nkrumah's regime deserved careful elaboration. Soviet commentators set about their task with remarkable candor.

Nkrumah had made mistakes. He had overextended Ghana's economy with "too large scale of industrial construction" and with too many different projects, leading to "breakdowns in planned schedules for the completion of work."[8] He had imported ultramodern farm machinery that turned out to be not only expensive but inappropriate. This was as close as Soviet writers came to saying that Nkrumah's adolescent ambitions had made him eschew more modest and prosaic measures for the more ostentatious and ego-gratifying. In his preoccupation with status symbols he failed to give the masses, particularly the peasantry, a "feeling of the tangible, material fruits of national independence."[9] In his self-deceived and arrogant monopolization of power, he had neglected to involve the masses in political and state activity.

If the lessons were not sufficiently evident to Keita, Touré, and others like them, two Soviet commentators drew the point with special clarity.[10] The first concern of progressive leaderships at the present stage of the national liberation movement is the rapid augmentation of productive forces in order to raise the living standard of the people. Unless this is done, they predicted, experience has shown that the critical "intermediate social strata" will be alienated. By demanding greater sacrifices, with a view to extending state control over secondary and petty trading, industry, resources, and transportation when the means and cadres are lacking, revolutionary democrats only generate dissatisfaction and undermine their essential alliance with the middle-range social strata. African leaders should be wary of launching radical social and economic reforms if these jeopardize the political stability of a progressive regime. Their principal focus must be on raising the material level of life within their societies.

In the fall of 1966 the editorial boards of *Problems of Peace and Socialism* and of the Egyptian journal *At Talia* called a conference in Cairo to discuss the problems plaguing the African revolution. Originally scheduled to be held in Ghana under the joint sponsorship of

8. Vl. Iordansky, in *Izvestiya*, February 24, 1967, p. 2.
9. V. Kudryavtsev, in *Izvestiya*, March 6, 1966, p. 3.
10. See A. Iskenderov and G. Starushenko, in *Pravda*, August 14, 1966, p. 4.

the *Spark* and *Problems of Peace and Socialism,* the Cairo Seminar, as it was called, took on a different and more urgent complexion when the February coup made these plans impossible. Throughout the conference's discussions the implications of Nkrumah's overthrow clearly weighed on the minds of the seventy delegates from "revolutionary parties and progressive organizations."[11] (The paper that Mrs. W. E. B. DuBois read for Nkrumah, written from his Conakry exile, must have been a further awkward reminder of what had happened in Ghana.) How much Soviet attitudes had shifted under the pressure of these events soon became evident from the remarks of the chief Soviet delegate, Alexander Sobolev, executive secretary of *Problems of Peace and Socialism.*

Never before had Soviet analysis reflected such constrained expectations, sensitivity to local problems, and pragmatism in designing solutions. On the important question of agricultural reform, where earlier Soviet spokesmen had urged swift, harsh, and orthodox modifications, Sobolev accepted a formula advising the gradual modernization of agriculture, if necessary by means not entirely along socialist lines. "The essence of the agrarian reform in these countries [tropical Africa] consists primarily in raising the rural economy to the level of modern production and a gradual advance towards cooperative farming."[12] The trouble with producers' cooperatives—in the past the Soviet Union's minimal program for agricultural reform—was that they were "up against not a few technical and economic difficulties (shortage of technicians, scientists, administrative and political personnel, shortage of agricultural machinery and implements)."[13] Sobolev's discussion group warned that because some African countries had disregarded these difficulties and had

---

11. The participants were representatives of "advanced" ruling parties—Idrissa Diarra and Madeira Keita from Mali's Union Soudanaise, Fedialah Keita from Guinea's Parti Démocratique de Guinée, and others from the Tanzanian African National Union and the Algerian National Liberation Front. There were delegates from the Sudanese Communist Party, Sawaba, the Moroccan Communist Party, and the Parti Africain de l'Indépendance (Majhmout Diop). They were joined by progressive organizations from the Portuguese and Spanish colonial territories. See J. Sharif and V. Shelepin, "The Seminar in Cairo," *World Marxist Review,* IX (December 1966), 43. Shelepin was a member of the editorial board of the *World Marxist Review* and attended the Seminar. (We shall encounter him again.)

12. "At the Cairo Seminar," *World Marxist Review,* X (February 1967), 20.

13. *Ibid.*

proceeded hastily to establish producer cooperatives, "many proved ineffective with the result that output dropped." The Soviet delegate's attitude toward the local private sector, once considered an obstacle to essential reform which should be eliminated as quickly as possible, reflected similar moderation: "It is often maintained that the emergence and especially the development of a private capitalist sector should be opposed. Only time, the experience of each country, can provide the final answer. Everything depends on circumstances, but as I see it one cannot always categorically deny the need to draw on private initiative."[14] Similarly refashioned were his views on the related question of the dependence of many African nations on the capitalist world. While economic ties with the socialist countries were preferable because they contributed more to progressive development, he recognized that it would be "hard to imagine the African countries being able to isolate themselves from the capitalist world." Many of these concessions had previously been suggested, at least in part, but not since the MEiMO discussions of May 1964 had so full and pointed an exploration of such themes paralleled official attitudes.[15]

Several months before the Cairo Seminar, Soviet commentators had begun to ponder the question that bothered them most: Why had the dominant party failed to help revolutionary democrats "to overcome their personal shortcomings or correct their policies?"[16] Once they had seen the folly of staking a policy on the tenure of a given leader, Soviet leaders could admit the incompetence and personal eccentricities of someone like Nkrumah, but they had never fully abandoned their faith in the advance of structural reform in these societies, particularly of the party. Despite its obvious shortcomings, the single-party system represented the primary means of safeguarding progressive change in revolutionary African states. So why had these parties, the CPP in this case, fallen so far short of expectations? And—a more sobering consideration—if the party turned out to be unreliable, on what institution, on what group, on what circumstance could Marxist-Leninists count in the future? The issue of the party's structure and role, therefore, became the focal point of the discussion. Attitudes emerging from this discussion

14. Alexander Sobolev, "Some Problems of Social Progress," *World Marxist Review,* X (January 1967), 13.

15. See my Note on Methodology.

16. N. Gavrilov, "Africa: Classes, Parties and Politics," *International Affairs,* no. 7 (1966), p. 42.

came to dominate the Soviet Union's broader approach to revolutionary African states—an approach that took on the growing appearance of neo-orthodoxy.

In Khrushchev's day Soviet writers had made considerable commotion over the necessity of transforming the dominant party from a mass movement generated by the struggle for independence into a closely organized, elite party capable of providing the society with decisive leadership. If the socialist revolution was to be reproduced in places like Guinea, Mali, and Ghana, then the mechanism for its reproduction had to be created. This meant trimming and reshaping such parties as the PDG, US, and CPP until only the most dedicated and well-trained socialists remained members. Khrushchev and the commentators he blessed, to take them at their word, eventually let themselves believe that these parties had indeed started to make the essential changes. His successors never fully shared this confidence—though they certainly considered the party issue crucial—and when the Ghanaian coup occurred they were better prepared to acknowledge frankly the deficiencies of an organization like the CPP. Again the elements of their analysis were not entirely new, but to translate them from a rather abstract case for remodeling the party into a critical and precise admission of what the party had not done added a further dimension to the analysis and, more significantly, revealed the total loss of illusion about the problems faced by revolutionary democrats.

The revolutionary democrats should have anticipated the tribulations that would come from perpetuating the party as a conglomeration of different social and political groups. Soviet writers asked: What but conflict could be expected from a party of "workers, peasants, progressive intellectuals and also members of the national bourgeoisie and bureaucrats?"[17] Interests so disparate led inevitably to a struggle within the party over ways of development. In Ghana's case the original contest between the CPP and the opposition United Party (banned in 1964) had re-emerged within the CPP itself. As a consequence, the "bureaucratic" bourgeoisie's resistance to Nkrumah's program had continued within the sanctuary of the ruling party. (Few would quarrel with Soviet analysis on this point.) And ultimately, according to the Soviet assessment, the bourgeois stratum *within* the CPP had played an instrumental role in overthrowing Nkrumah's regime (this extension of the argument

17. *Ibid.*, p. 40.

is plausible only in a figurative sense, unless the phrase "bourgeois stratum" referred to Ghana's army and police).

If the analysis had stopped here it would have fallen into the category of "I told you so" and would have revealed very little that was new in Soviet attitudes. The mass party had long been identified as an evil to be dispensed with as quickly as possible, and because party leaders had failed to engineer the transformation to a vanguard party soon enough, they had paid a high penalty. Soviet writers could say, we anticipated this state of affairs and, to revolutionary democrats, we warned you. But circumstances were not so simple. There was more to party leaders' dereliction than merely allowing petty-bourgeois bureaucrats to thrive within the party. Their own conduct contributed significantly to the ultimate disaster. At first Soviet analysts did not criticize them directly, but when one writer noted that in Upper Volta circumstances "hindered the democratic election of the leadership even at the party's grass roots," few readers could have been misled.[18] Again it was a question of finding the proper fit. Why would a Soviet commentator be interested in making a case of Upper Volta in these terms: "Party secretaries were frequently appointed from the top on the strength of personal trust. In some places, the party leaders selected their subordinates from among their friends and relatives."[19] In truth what really mattered was that *Ghanaian* leaders had managed their party badly. They had been stupidly oblivious of the shallow base of their power and cavalier in executing the functions of a ruling party, including the crucial one of recruitment. Lutfi El Kholi, editor of *At Talia,* spoke more candidly when he told the Cairo Seminar: "The party [the CPP] had overestimated its possibilities, judging its strength by the fact that it was the ruling party, and not by the actual influence of its organizations and its activists on the masses, the real source of strength. It remained a ship floating on the surface of society, comprising a group of revolutionary intellectuals and town dwellers."[20] Sobolev must have nodded in agreement.

If we examine the more conventionally ideological aspects of the discussion, its conservative thrust is easily perceived. Much of the specific criticism of a regime such as Nkrumah's recalls in modified form the traditional Soviet view of African leaders. Seen in this way, Soviet atti-

18. *Ibid.,* p. 43.
19. *Ibid.*
20. Lutfi El Kholi, "The Current Phase of the Anti-Imperialist Struggle," *World Marxist Review,* X (January 1967), 4–5.

tudes were assuming a neo-orthodox quality, whose implications were seminal not only for the solutions policymakers would recommend to revolutionary democrats but for the general expectations they would retain for Africa. The reader, as he goes through the next pages, may be struck by how much Soviet policy was coming back full circle to its starting point ten years before—and this would hardly be a mirage. On the other hand, the path traveled was like a circular ramp, leaving policy in the end at another level from its beginning and making it impossible for the circle ever to close. Despite the similarities of contemporary Soviet themes with those of a decade ago, in essential respects there could be no return to that era of tender innocence when Soviet leaders first discovered the Dark Continent (as they then called it). Thus, the revived notion of class struggle now referred to a process quite different from that which Soviet writers had thought they were describing in the earlier period; the renewed doubts about Africa's progressive leaders had a different basis because they derived from genuine frustrations, not suspicions in the abstract; and the solutions offered came in an entirely different spirit, one stripped of idealism.

In grasping for a satisfactory explanation of the unsavory new trends in Africa, Soviet writers would normally begin by emphasizing that the successful struggle for political independence had led to an intensification of conflict within African societies, in their phrase, to a "rapid sharpening of contradictions." Almost immediately the unity of the broad national liberation movement had dissipated and a disruptive struggle had begun between reactionary and progressive elements over the direction these societies were to take—in effect, over the choice between socialism and capitalism. In recent years, Soviet writers argued, antiprogressive elements—feudal lords, "the big and small, particularly comprador, bourgeoisie," and "international imperialism"—had become particularly active. They had seized the offensive and were viciously battling against more progressive socioeconomic reforms. For Soviet writers to dust off the old notion of class struggle in Africa and advance it so emphatically at this point was a significant departure from their recent commentary. And so was the courage they found to remind African leaders that their confidence in the essential harmony among African classes had been misplaced.[21] A few years before Soviet commentators had apparently accepted the argument of Nyerere, Touré, Keita, and others that the

21. V. Solodovnikov, "Beacon of Revolutionary Africa," *International Affairs,* no. 12 (1967), p. 23.

overwhelming predominance of the peasantry, together with the undeveloped state of the proletariat and the still weaker condition of the
national bourgeoisie, rendered the idea of class conflict insignificant.
The turnabout implied by the return to the idea of class struggle had
its match only in the turnabout of Touré, Keita, and others, who also
began to talk about the intensifying conflict between classes within their
societies.

Or so it seemed. In fact, Soviet writers (and African leaders) had
in mind quite a different conception of class struggle from what the
term usually conveys. No one was arguing that African society had
suddenly begun to crystallize into well-formed classes—bourgeois and proletarian. Soviet specialists knew, as well as anyone, that "class relations"
in Africa were scarcely more differentiated than before. But they had
come to see that the politically active groups in any African country
form a comparatively small part of the total society, and it was in this
smaller arena that the clash of classes was said to be growing. They
were contending, in effect, that the masses were not for the moment
crucial to the political process (except insofar as their passivity permitted
the early ouster of revolutionary regimes). Illiterate and semiliterate
peasants could not be expected to respond to the exhortations of a political party that they could not comprehend and, too often, even reach.
This left politics to the urban middle class, civil servants, the rural elite,
trade unionists, politicians, university students, and, recently, army officers. It stretched matters to consider these groups "classes," but there
was something to the notion that the bureaucratic bourgeoisie, "profiteer-
ing middlemen," "plantation owners," traditional leaders, and professional military officers were frustrating the ambitions of Africa's most
revolutionary leaders. In countries like Ghana, this class struggle had
flourished *within* the dominant party.

The problem ran far deeper than the vexing and somewhat baffling
challenge these unreconstructed elements posed for a truly revolutionary
transformation of society. That of course was trouble enough. But a
more distressing feature of Africa's current trials inhered in the suspicion
that the radical leaders on whom the Soviet Union had wagered were
not up to the challenge. More and more it became evident that revolutionary democrats suffered character flaws making them vulnerable to
opposition forces. Profound as the structural defects of the African revolution were, the more immediate problem turned out to be essentially one

of personnel. Along with a neo-orthodox but—in contrast to the earlier period—basically pessimistic assessment of political phenomena at work within Africa, some of the same reservations Soviet observers had once exhibited toward Africa's most progressive leaders now reappeared.

Once again the knowledge returned implacably that these people were "petty bourgeois" and subject to all the frailties of that estate. "The petty-bourgeois origin of the revolutionary democrats," two Soviet writers reminded themselves, "answers many questions connected with the home and foreign policies of countries developing the non-capitalist way."[22] It explained, for example, why revolutionary democratic ideologists so often mixed "more or less important elements of Socialism . . . with petty-bourgeois and utopian ideas."[23] Africa's revolutionary democrats were being defrocked and sent back to the old position they occupied when they still maintained a commitment to African socialism. "What is characteristic of them is their inconsistent adoption of scientific Socialism and their vacillation between proletarian and bourgeois ideologies . . . [They], for example, rejected capitalism as a social system, but left a loophole by recognizing the possibility of permanent co-existence of a state and private sector."[24] To be sure, N. I. Gavrilov, the author of this criticism, never specifically referred to Nkrumah or even to revolutionary democrats—he spoke of "men belonging to so-called intermediate, non-proletarian sections of African society, representing the military or civilian intelligentsia"—but who else had ever pretended to adopt scientific socialism as an ideology in whole or in part? Moreover, Soviet commentators had worse to say about revolutionary democrats when there was absolutely no ambiguity about the reference. Their descriptions often make them appear impetuous and slightly puerile, inclined to undertake radical economic measures without sufficient preparation, and too worried about their revolutionary image. One important analyst, R. A. Ulyanovsky, remarked that too often these "national democrats" (the use of this classification seems in itself a rebuke) acted "hastily and unwisely," for example, in nationalizing retail trade, services, and

22. G. Kim and A. Kaufman, "Non-Capitalist Development: Achievements and Difficulties," *International Affairs*, no. 12 (1967), p. 73. Kim was a department chief within the Institute of the Peoples of Asia. He had long been a conservative spokesman on questions dealing with the developing countries. Kaufman was a "senior scientific worker" in the same institute.

23. *Ibid.*, p. 72

24. Gavrilov, "Africa: Classes, Parties and Politics," p. 40.

small industry.[25] (Perhaps Soviet writers had this all straight in their own minds, but the outsider begins to wonder who was guilty of greater inconsistency, the revolutionary democrat supposedly incapable of adhering to a thoroughgoing revolutionary program or Soviet commentators who accused him, on the one hand, of compromising with the private sector—the need for which they themselves had acknowledged before and after the Cairo Seminar—and, on the other, of nationalizing some sections of the economy too rapidly.) Soviet commentators clearly meant to say that poor economic management was more than Nkrumah's aberration alone; that it was a malady prevalent among revolutionary democrats generally. Much of Guinea's current difficulty, for example, allegedly owed to the fact that most investment "was not initially channeled into production."[26] Instead, as Soviet commentary tactfully put it, capital had been utilized to show the people that "independence spelled a better life for them," that is, to build hotels, stadiums, and the like.

Pressing the case against Ghana (and presumably other revolutionary democracies), Ulyanovsky underscored the traps into which the regime's grandiose scheming had led, notably bureaucratism at the top levels of authority and the failure to secure mass support or participation.[27] As a result the economic situation became complicated and the lot of the masses worsened. Too often, said another commentator, progressive African states pioneered in the development of democratic institutions but, in practice, fell into the habit of using authoritarian methods.[28] An interesting admonishment coming from a Soviet source: there was in these countries "a tendency toward authoritarianism, toward resolving

25. R. Ulyanovsky, "Nauchny sotsializm i osvobodivshiesya strany" (Scientific Socialism and the Liberated Countries), *Kommunist,* no. 4 (March 1968), p. 104. Ulyanovsky was usually identified as a deputy director of the Institute of the Peoples of Asia or as a member of the editorial board of *Narody Azii i Afriki.* His more significant position, however, was as a deputy chairman of the international section of the Central Committee Secretariat immediately under Boris Ponomarev. Moreover, he was writing in the principal ideological organ of the Central Committee.

26. Vladimir Shelepin et al., "Guinea's Tenth Year of Independence," *World Marxist Review,* X (December 1967), 17. Shelepin was a member of the editorial board of *Problems of Peace and Socialism.* He had attended the Cairo Seminar and more recently the Eighth Congress of the Guinean PDG. By 1968 he was becoming one of the more authoritative commentators on Africa.

27. Ulyanovsky, "Nauchny sotsializm i osvobodivshiesya strany," p. 104.

28. K. Brutents, "O revolyutsionnoi demokratii" (On Revolutionary Democracy), *Mirovaya ekonomika i mezhdunarodnye otnosheniya,* no. 3 (1968), p. 19. The Armenian, Karen Brutents, long a major Soviet commentator on Africa, had also attended the Cairo Seminar.

important problems exclusively at the top by administrative methods," ignoring the activity and initiative of the masses.[29]

All of this left Soviet policymakers with a serious problem. One would have to be exceedingly cynical to assume that they had lost their faith in the eventual triumph of socialism in Africa; but because revolutionary democrats had proved ineffectual, the transition promised to be far more problematic than they had once anticipated. Moreover, sorry as they were as revolutionary socialists, Africa's progressive leaders remained the Soviet leadership's only hope. No responsible foreign-ministry official could have contemplated a policy based on the emergence of genuine African Communist parties. In the short run, whatever progress Africa would make would still be under the leadership of men like Keita and Touré. If this prospect roused modest enthusiasm among Soviet policy-makers, then it might only be expected that in the full range of Soviet foreign policy Africa would become less important than other areas— South Asia, the Middle East, and even Latin America. It requires no more than a brief scanning of Soviet periodicals, including those devoted to Afro-Asia, to see how definitely this did happen.

Noting that the comparative significance of Africa diminished swiftly after 1966, however, does not aid us in understanding that part of policy which remained. Even though Africa figured less in Soviet dreams, policymakers had not yet escaped the burden of formulating some kind of policy. In Africa's most advanced nations, to be constructive, policy had to offer some solution for the failures of revolutionary democratic regimes. In Africa in general, if policy was to reflect Soviet interests it would have to establish those areas in which a stake was most worth-while preserving. The logic of the changing Soviet reaction to Africa did not guarantee that these priority areas would continue to be the revolutionary states; but this portion of the story must wait for later telling. First the strategy Soviet analysts urged upon Africa's surviving revolutionary leaders deserves attention. Being the active response generated by a hardnosed examination of radical Africa's problems, it naturally had the same neo-orthodox quality as the other part of the discussion.

Soviet experts would not like to admit that they were grappling with the unyielding problems of *political* modernization, even less that Western political scientists had already properly identified the task as one of discovering the means by which a "mobilization system" is created

29. *Ibid.*, p. 24.

in more than name only.[30] Though Russians from Lenin on have been political manipulators without peer (the Stalinist system was history's most perfect mobilization system), the mythology has it that economics leads politics and therefore that the need to transform political structures cannot be deemed equal or, as in the Soviet experience, preliminary to the transformation of the economic system.[31] Nevertheless, in this instance, Soviet analysts sought a pre-eminently political solution to the central challenge confronting regimes such as the Malian and the Guinean: how to mobilize human and material resources more effectively to break the restraints of the old society and its concomitant economic backwardness while guaranteeing a secure and steady development toward socialism. The real problem, it turned out, was not to convert African leaders to socialism; however imperfectly, several had chosen the socialist option. Rather it was to make the socialist option viable—to institutionalize the mobilization system. Whether or not Soviet analysts couched the issue in these terms, they recognized it as an essentially political enterprise: "There is still a definite disproportion between steps to create the new socio-economic basis and the relative slowness in providing the political superstructure, organizing the masses and democratizing home political life."[32] The failure of modern political structures to reach beyond a narrow portion of society, the difference between the revolution proclaimed and the revolution prosecuted, had forced Soviet observers to retreat several steps and focus on ways for giving the progressive single-party system not merely declared, but substantive, legitimacy.

How were revolutionary democrats to establish their modern institutions in traditional societies? The times would not allow Soviet theorists to advise, "Emulate Stalin." But how else could constraining structures be demolished and the masses conscripted to accomplish what they never would do voluntarily? Bukharin in Africa would have been an even greater disaster than he was in the Soviet Union. Yet, as Soviet observers were compelled to confess to themselves, in Africa "life" had not produced Stalins, and Stalinism ineptly practiced was unproductive, even

30. David E. Apter, *The Politics of Modernization* (Chicago: University of Chicago Press, 1965), pp. 357–390.

31. Some might be troubled by an oversimplification that ignores the implications of contributions such as Stalin's "Regarding Marxism in Linguistics," a useful discussion of which is found in Zbigniew K. Brzezinski, *The Soviet Bloc: Unity and Conflict*, rev. ed. (Cambridge: Harvard University Press, 1967), pp. 105–107.

32. Kim and Kaufman, "Non-Capitalist Development," p. 73.

suicidal. Understanding, therefore, the remoteness from Mali or Guinea of the terror-enforced beehive state, Soviet analysts had to accept more marginal measures for enhancing the power of the dominant party.

These depended on the party's ability to touch the masses and rally them behind its goals. In the words of one writer:

> The state must be led by a well-organized party closely allied with the people and relying on their activity. It must not be a revolutionary intellectuals club . . . It must work among the masses and know how to organize them. It must not confine its activity to the capital, but, in view of the peasants' role in the African countries, must be especially active in the countryside.[33]

But this begged the question. How was the party to work among the masses and organize them? How was it to become the ally of the people? Any African leader looking to these writers for an answer must have returned to his problems perturbed. He had been told that "the policy of the party and the state must be clear to the masses" (again, the matter of disdaining the masses: "Progressive changes are lasting when there are not only decrees from above, but also active support from the masses").[34] He did not have to be overly shrewd to perceive that Soviet commentators were saying more than to improve his communication with the masses—that they meant as well to clarify policy within the party itself. This led directly to the point about purifying the party's ideology—achieved, one can almost fill in the blank, by purifying the party's membership. Or was it the other way around? Their argument, that if the masses were to be drawn into "economic and state construction, mass organizations must be quickly set up and strengthened," clearly depended on the leadership's prior success in refashioning the party.[35] Otherwise what point was there to creating a network of auxiliary ("mass") organizations to radiate the party's influence? Before the party could become "the backbone of society" and "the people's leader and educator," it would have to overcome its own internal division and do away with party appointments made on the basis of personal ties.[36] But how, the revolutionary democrat must have muttered to himself,

34. *Ibid.*, p. 30.
33. Brutents, "African Revolution," pp. 27–28.
35. Kim and Kaufman, "Non-Capitalist Development," p. 73.
36. Gavrilov, "Africa: Classes, Parties and Politics," p. 43.

was all this to be accomplished? What good African progressive would quarrel with advice like this: "Sound economic development, profitable operation of enterprises in the state sector, effective state control over foreign capital, the use of private enterprise within reasonable limits and real improvement of the condition of the peasants and the workers are what the ruling party and the state must concentrate on."[37] At this level Soviet counsel seemed distinctly beside the point.

Mali and the Lessons of the Ghanaian Coup

No country in Black Africa reacted more swiftly or (eventually) more thoroughly to the lessons of Nkrumah's fall than Mali. Therefore the way Soviet spokesmen treated it provides some measure of how seriously they, in fact, believed revolutionary democrats were capable of counteracting the forces that had destroyed Nkrumah. Mali's ruling party, Soviet writers had warned, like the CPP was a victim of internal struggle between reactionaries and those who had firmly "rejected the capitalist way."[38] It would have been awkward for Soviet writers to identify openly the reactionaries they had in mind—presumably men like Jean-Marie Koné, minister of state for planning and economic and financial coordination, Mahamane Alassane Haidara, president of the National Assembly, and Louis Nègre, governor of the Bank of Mali, whose less than total commitment to the "socialist option" was well known. Koné and Haidara were both members of the party's powerful Politburo and Soviet fortunes would scarcely have been advanced by attacking either. From the Soviet point of view, however, their presence in the highest circles of leadership gave concrete form to the competing tendencies within the ruling party. As long as they and their sympathizers within the party and armed forces and among the *fonctionnaires* and traditional leaders remained influential, Mali ran the same risks that had eventually toppled Nkrumah.

But in one important respect Mali was very unlike Ghana. Its socialists, especially those with power, exhibited fewer traits of megalomania, irresponsibility, and opportunism than Ghana's socialists. Mali had its equivalent of Kofi Batsaa, Kweku Akwei, and Kojo Addison in Mamadou Gologo, minister for information and tourism, his lieutenant, Bakary Traoré, Moussa Keita, high commissioner of youth and sports, and a

37. Brutents, "African Revolution," p. 28.
38. Gavrilov, "Africa: Classes, Parties and Politics," pp. 40–41.

sizable number of other promiscuously carefree, halfbaked radicals, but none carried real weight in politics at the center. Socialists that mattered, those in the Politburo like Madeira Keita, minister of justice, Ousmane Bâ, minister-delegate for foreign affairs, and Seydou Badian Kouyaté, development minister, represented far more hardheaded, dedicated, and sensible leaders, the kind that in another context Soviet analysts have described as the "sober men." Furthermore, President Keita was as much of a contrast to Nkrumah as one could imagine—unpretentious, prudent, honest, willing to share power, and committed to a forthright but reasonable socialist transition. For example, he confessed to an interviewer from *Jeune Afrique* in May 1966 that Mali had made some mistakes "in the methods used up to now, especially in the organization of the peasantry"; that the collectives had been too much emphasized and too little appeal made to the peasant's natural interests; that the targets for the state enterprises had not always been carefully conceived (he was later to promise that unprofitable state enterprises would be closed); and that improved productivity must become the principal goal of economic management.[39] His willingness to face problems squarely no doubt impressed Soviet leaders. They must also have valued his personal humility and determination to avoid the "trap" of the personality cult, as he termed it in this interview. The most important thing, he said, was "team work" and "collegial leadership."[40]

Soviet writers were quick to pick out Mali as a country that understood the implications of Nkrumah's failure. In an article published soon after the Ghanaian coup, *Pravda*'s West African correspondent, Fyodor Tarasov, emphasized the party's efforts to reduce the threat of counter-revolution.[41] These included the recent creation of a Comité National de Défense de la Révolution (CNDR), endowed "with full power to defend and consolidate the gains of the people."[42] Second, the party had seized the initiative in the economic battle, which was now "the basic element in the struggle against imperialism." It planned to implement such critical measures as "the introduction of a policy of economy, the reduction of government expenditures, the rationalization of the

39. "Modibo Keita parle," *Jeune Afrique,* no. 280 (May 8, 1966), p. 10. See also Keita's speech to the National Assembly reported in *L'Essor* (weekly), July 18, 1966, p. 2.

40. *Ibid.,* p. 11.

41. F. Tarasov, in *Pravda,* March 24, 1966, p. 5. The article was broadcast on Moscow radio (in English for Africa), 14.30 GMT, March 24, 1966.

42. The CNDR, however, would not become significant until the next year.

management of state and public enterprises . . . the extension of the socialist form of organization in the country."[43] This, of course, current Soviet literature insisted upon, just as it urged that the party be careful not to isolate itself from the masses. (Tarasov's article was entitled "To Rely on the Masses.") He made a special point of trade-union leader Mamadou Samady Sissoko's plea "to place greater trust in the masses, to make them feel their role in the defense and consolidation of the gains of the revolution." And he praised efforts "to raise sharply the quality of political and ideological work among the people," in particular the branch meetings and economic conferences being held across the country to explain recent events in Africa, to celebrate the achievements of a free Mali Republic, and to involve the masses in the country's economic advance.

Much as Soviet commentators may have genuinely believed that Mali's leaders deserved special notice, in the context of the Soviet Union's general attitude toward revolutionary democrats and of the immense problems confronting these leaders, the specific credit paid them possesses a distinctly stylized quality. In other words, since it seems likely that Soviet observers appreciated Mali's increasingly serious economic plight and since, moreover, they would be expected to view in their own way the implications of the Politburo's mottled composition, Tarasov's praise can be either of two things: one, largely reflexive (a reflection of the tendency to treat old friends kindly and assure Soviet readers that old friends were doing well) or second, and more likely, a prod fashioned from the regime's own best standards. Soviet observers knew that not only were rather awesome problems working against Mali's success in all those areas they praised, but indeed that many in Mali's leadership rejected essential parts of their explanation for what was wrong and how to go about correcting it. Despite his adherence to scientific socialism as an indivisible faith, Modibo had never really moved very far from belief in the fundamental distinctiveness of Malian socialism. In the *Jeune Afrique* interview he reaffirmed his country's intention to regard scientific socialism in a critical spirit—to take from it those values enriching Mali's "positive realities." "We Malians," he said, "have never blindly accepted a ready-made idea, whatever its source."[44]

The Malians, however, regarded the designation "scientific socialism" as both a token of their commitment and a measure of their success

43. Tarasov, in *Pravda*, March 24, 1966.
44. "Modibo Keita parle," pp. 8–9.

(presumably they wished to underscore the distinction between their program and that of African socialists like Senghor). Thus when Khrushchev's successors demoted all revolutionary democracies to the "noncapitalist path" and averred that only the emergence of strong vanguard parties would change their mind, they were publicly challenged by the Malians. It happened at the Cairo Seminar in October 1966. Idrissa Diarra, the political secretary of the Union Soudanaise, deliberately tossed aside Sobolev's formulations: the US considers that "there is no qualitative distinction between the non-capitalist and the socialist ways. But socialist development is a stage by stage process."[45] What is more, he continued, there can be no question but that a mass party, "that is, a party with a national rather than a class following," can carry out the tasks of building socialism.[46] The fundamental difference between the Malian and Soviet positions could scarcely have been more obtrusive. The South African Communist party's *African Communist* admitted that Sobolev's formulation of the noncapitalist path "did not meet with unanimous approval among the participants in the Seminar."[47] And even a Soviet participant ruefully confessed that another standpoint on the vanguard party "was expressed by representatives of the Sudanese Union, who believe . . . a mass party relying, naturally, on scientific Socialism, could lead the revolutionary struggle."[48]

Perhaps Soviet leaders consoled themselves with the thought that some within the Malian Politburo held a more rigorous view of socialism, one closer to their own. Madeira Keita, Seydou Badian Kouyaté, and Ousmane Bâ had the reputation of urging more far-reaching changes, particularly in the countryside, and of preferring a vanguard party roughly along the lines suggested by Soviet writers. Keita, especially, had emphasized the need to improve ideological work within the party. Their views would become increasingly important a few months later in August 1967, after a major upheaval of the Union Soudanaise eclipsed Diarra and the party moderates. Because the ascendence of the more militant members of the Politburo obviously affected Soviet attitudes toward Mali, the events leading up to the reorganization need to be reviewed. One of the most significant of these was Mali's re-entry into the franc zone.

45. Idrissa Diarra, "The Mass Party and Socialist Construction," *World Marxist Review*, X (January 1967), 15.
46. *Ibid.,* p. 14.
47. *The African Communist,* no. 28 (first quarter 1967), p. 37.
48. Brutents, "African Revolution," p. 27.

Throughout 1966 signs pointed to the resumption of the monetary talks with France so abruptly interrupted in June 1965. Economic pressures had long been building to abandon the independent Malian franc and to seek re-entry into the French-supported Union Monétaire Ouest-Africaine. Inconvertibility, the absence of a disciplined monetary policy, and consequent inflation had seriously distorted Mali's cost and price structure, jeopardized its trading position (particularly in agricultural exports), encouraged smuggling, and accentuated its balance-of-payments problem. By 1966 IMF statistics showed that Mali's external debt exceeded $140 million and that its internal debt was nearing $8 million, a figure beyond the nearly $45 million owed by state enterprises.[49] So Malian leaders had excellent reasons for wishing to arrange a return to the franc zone, and their remarks during 1966 suggested that soon, when conditions favored successful negotiations, talks would resume.[50] On December 18, 1966, the last day of his first visit to Senegal since the Mali Federation split apart, President Keita announced their imminent resumption. One month later Jean-Marie Koné and Louis Nègre (recently promoted to minister of finance) arrived in Paris and the following month, on February 15, signed an agreement providing for Mali's ultimate re-entry into the UMOA. The agreement stipulated several conditions for Mali's acceptance back into the West African monetary group—the first of which required stringent measures to put Mali's financial house in order, to curb inflation, reduce government expeditures, and facilitate inter-African trade.

The hardships that would follow devaluation (the French were to insist on a 50 percent devaluation) and a harshly austere budget were not the only results of a return to the franc zone with possible political importance. Another, which surely interested the Soviet Union, was the effect the agreement would have on both the state enterprises and the state trading monopoly. If the French demanded that Keita make good his promise to eliminate unprofitable state enterprises—and rumors at the time indicated that they did—or if they sought privileges for French importers, not to mention leverage over economic agreements reached with Communist states, then Mali's socialist option would be endangered. Presumably the inclusion of financial experts within a Soviet parliamentary delegation

---

49. "Les accords financiers Franco-Maliens," *Afrique contemporaine,* no. 30 (March–April 1967), p. 8.

50. See, for example, "Modibo Keita parle," p. 10, and Keita's remarks on June 11, 1966, noted in *Africa Report,* XI (October 1966), 52.

headed by S. O. Pritytsky, which was sent to Mali in March, had something to do with these rumors.[51] The Soviet Union no doubt appreciated the wisdom of this monetary realignment but, at the same time, it would want to preserve as much freedom as possible for Mali to continue on the noncapitalist path.

If not every Malian leader shared the Soviet concern, Modibo Keita did. Angered by the indiscreet relish with which people like Jean-Marie Koné received the accord, conscious of the opposition the accord had aroused among sections of the youth, and particularly apprehensive that an increasingly effete party might falter under the pressures of economic reform, Keita decided to embark upon a wholesale reconstruction of the Union Soudanaise and its leadership. He chose the Sixth Week of Youth early in July to declare a sudden acceleration in the Malian revolution, subsequently designated "Year One of the Revolution." A few weeks later, as a taste of things to come, Idrissa Diarra's younger brother, Oumar Bara Diarra, was dismissed for malfeasance, which reportedly included giving special housing preference to his mistress, using state vehicles to transport private commerce, and securing a ghost-written thesis for his mistress' daughter, a student at the Ecole Nationale d'Administration. On August 22 the Politburo was disbanded, and government and party power was placed in the previously dormant twelve-man Comité National de Défense de la Révolution (CNDR). In making the announcement, Keita talked about the "unnatural" condition of the Politburo, its "lack of cohesion," and its harmful divisions.[52] Neither Jean-Marie Koné nor Idrissa Diarra were a part of the new leadership. Keita was later to say that party leaders excluded from the CNDR represented potential counterrevolutionaries.[53]

The removal of Koné and Diarra vastly strengthened the position of the more militant elements. Madeira Keita emerged as the second most influential Malian leader; the president and Madeira and his two allies, Ousmane Bâ and youth leader Gabou Diawara, now formed a formidable inner power circle. The revolution would be deferred no longer. The CNDR began at once to dismantle Diarra's party apparatus and to establish in its place a more tightly organized, well-heeled struc-

51. Interview in Bamako, July 26, 1968.

52. See "What's Happening in Mali," *West Africa*, no. 2622 (September 2, 1967), p. 1135.

53. See his remarks on September 22, 1967, the seventh anniversary of Malian independence, noted in *Africa Report*, XII (November 1967), 46.

ture. Comités Locaux de Défense de la Révolution were deployed to carry out the formal assault on regional party organizations, and everywhere youthful militants were mobilized to wage war on "counterrevolutionaries, opportunists, demagogues, pseudo-socialists, and all those who in one way or another engage in fraud, smuggling, and speculation . . . in a word, all those whose daily conduct is in conflict with the socialist option."[54] On November 25, 1967, thousands had assembled in the Soviet-built stadium (soon to become Stade Modibo Keita) to hear Gabou Diawara read off a list of 177 ministers and officials accused of illegally owning taxis. "L'Opération taxis," as the purge was called, represented an integral part of the "active phase" of the Malian revolution, a description supplied by President Keita himself.[55] The president's own speech for the occasion contained more than a faint echo of Soviet arguments: during a period when "international imperialism was becoming more and more aggressive," the party's primary task consists of fighting "degenerate cadres, bourgeois elements, and all other reactionaries." For this reason, he said, a "class alliance" of youth, workers, the popular army, and women has been formed to "defend at all costs our socialist option."[56]

Everything said and done affirmed the Malian leadership's serious intention to reinforce the authority of the party and to safeguard, indeed speed up, Mali's socialist course. Soviet diplomats had attended the October 1967 dedication of the Ecole Supérieure du Parti, a higher party school built with Soviet assistance to improve ideological work within the party. In February these same diplomats could read in L'Essor of the leadership's decision to dispatch properly schooled militants down to the lowest levels of party authority.[57] As described by the editorialist, these cadres were to be "equipped with solid political and ideological training . . . wholeheartedly committed to the socialist option" and possessed of "compassion for the masses." In May Madeira Keita held an "ideological conference" at the Ecole Normale Supérieure and underscored the need to transform the Front National into a genuine vanguard force.[58] And at the end of the month, the Premier Séminaire National sur la Coopération en Milieu Rural announced a "veritable revolution

54. See the editorial in L'Essor, February 3, 1968, p. 1.
55. See L'Essor (weekly), December 4, 1967, p. 3.
56. Ibid. The same issue of L'Essor published an article emphasizing the growing class struggle in progressive African countries.
57. Editorial, L'Essor, February 3, 1968, p. 1.
58. L'Essor (weekly), May 13, 1968, p. 2.

in the countryside." Its objective was to "liquidate the vestiges of feudal and capitalist production," to rid the peasant masses of outmoded ideas and traditions, and to arm them instead with socialist ideology.[59] To carry out this "profound cultural and ideological revolution," the CNDR substituted Comités Révolutionnaires de Base for the old village councils. These were to be party agencies, carefully staffed and given full administrative power. They were ulitmately to be under the authority of Gabou Diawara.

No other Black African country had matched Mali's efforts to give firm footing to its revolution. The determination of its leaders to make the socialist option work, their spirit of sacrifice and strenuous commitment to transforming primitive structures and habits, must have encouraged Soviet observers. And their satisfaction was presumably reinforced by the temperance that Malian leaders demonstrated in implementing reform. Care was being taken not to undermine lasting change by moving forward too impatiently. In the same conference during which Madeira Keita advocated the strengthening of the vanguard party, he had strongly rebuked hot-headed students who criticized the Franco-Malian accords and complained of the slow pace of economic transformation.[60] L'Essor reminded these youth of President Keita's earlier warning against sectarianism and left-wing extremism.[61] (It also trotted out, as many others have before, Lenin's pamphlet, Left-Wing Communism: An Infantile Disorder.) And so was the radical language of the Séminaire sur la Coopération en Milieu Rural balanced with a suitable quote from Lenin, in which he recommended that smallholders be bargained with and not coerced. "One can (and must) transform them, re-educate them, but only by a very long, slow and careful organizational effort."[62]

In the circumstances it is hard to imagine what more any African regime could have done to satisfy Soviet expectations. That, in turn, Soviet commentators responded so languidly indicates how deeply they doubted the strength of the revolutionary democrat and what little they expected of revolutionary action. In June, before the "active phase" of the Mali revolution, Tarasov wrote an article that opened with the usual obeisance to the determination of Mali's leaders and masses to strengthen their independence, surmount the difficulties standing in the

59. See L'Essor (weekly), June 3, 1968, pp. 1, 3–5.
60. See ibid., May 13, 1968, p. 2.
61. Ibid., May 20, 1968, p. 2.
62. Ibid., June 3, 1968, p. 4.

way of a socialist transformation, and frustrate imperialist ambitions.[63] It was bravely entitled "Independence Is Not for Sale." More interesting, however, was the gloom and obvious nervousness beneath its optimistic veneer. Tarasov tried to fix blame on imperialist propaganda for making invidious comparisons and lacking faith: always the imperialist emphasizes the negative aspects of life along the noncapitalist path, "the inadequacies of development in these countries," "the 'failure' of their methods," and "their inevitable 'collapse.'" He protested too much. As he himself admitted, Mali had undertaken to accomplish something in which no other African society had yet succeeded—to transform an extremely backward country into a leading socialist state. For a country "hundreds of kilometers from the sea, deprived of significant mineral reserves, with a population nine tenths peasant . . . where at the moment of independence not a single capitalist enterprise existed," the task would not be easy. Moreover, he confessed that Mali was "experiencing a difficult period," and the "contradictions in the process are great." Three months later, after the events of July and August, Tarasov wrote more confidently of "the successes of the Malian people," as *Pravda* entitled this article.[64] "This past summer," he reported, "was marked by heightened political activity on the part of Mali's working masses." Their demands for "A Single Party—the Union Soudanaise–RDA! One Choice—Socialism! No Responsible Posts for Those Who Oppose the People's Choice!" had led the party leadership to dissolve the Politburo and launch a campaign against "internal reaction." Tarasov repeated the old warnings about the difficulties facing those who chose an independent path of development and again described the particular limitations Mali suffered. But he praised the CNDR for "fearlessly revealing past mistakes" and making efforts to normalize party activity. With some relief, it seemed, he concluded that Mali had resolutely taken the road forward, preserved its nonalignment, and survived unharmed the "disruptive acts of internal and external reaction."

Perhaps mere survival was a commendable feat in Soviet eyes at this point but, understandably, not one generating much enthusiasm. Ritual required that Mali and other revolutionary Black African states be paid the respect due people with the right sentiments (and courtesy required that regimes so often helpful on foreign policy issues be rewarded). But the frailty of their power discouraged the Soviet Union from giving

63. F. Tarasov, in *Pravda,* June 9, 1967, p. 5.
64. *Ibid.* September 22, 1967, p. 5.

them a more generous spiritual and material commitment and, once stripped of their teleological value, these few nations could not keep Soviet policymakers from seeing their interests increasingly in a broader African context. Rarely any longer did *Pravda* or *Izvestiya* devote space to the triumphs of Africa's most advanced states. In July and August 1968, during Modibo Keita's month-long vacation in the Soviet Union (where he was eventually joined by Ousmane Bâ and Gabou Diawara), the Soviet press scarcely noted his presence. A few years earlier a similar visit would have produced several lengthy articles celebrating his country's promise. A few years earlier a Soviet diplomat in Bamako would never have been so amused by my efforts to make the case for Malian socialism as one was in August 1968, not out of cynicism but because he knew how shallow revolutions—socialist or otherwise—were in Africa.

As if to confirm Soviet reservations, on November 19, 1968, a military coup d'état drove Modibo Keita's regime from power. His had proved no more indestructible than regimes that did less to incorporate the lessons of Nkrumah's failure. The young officers who plotted the coup (the principal conspirator, Moussa Traoré, was only a lieutenant in the army) made it somewhat easier for the Soviet Union to accept events gracefully by promising to salvage the best part of Modibo's revolution and by reaffirming Mali's interest in excellent relations with the socialist countries.[65] The repudiation of the previous course, therefore, was less emphatic than in Ghana. Nevertheless, no one could fail to understand that the coup meant a fundamental change in the direction of Malian politics. The new regime's first act was to disband the CNDR, the *milice populaire,* and the *comités de vigilance,* and then a few days later to suspend the Union Soudanaise and a series of party auxiliaries such as the Union Nationale des Travailleurs Maliens, the Conseil National de la Jeunesse, and the Organisation des Femmes Maliennes. On November 22, it launched an appeal to "all foreign capitals and private investors" to aid Mali's economic and social development and assured investors

65. See, for example, the reports of statements by Moussa Traoré and other spokesmen for the new military regime in *Le Monde,* November 23, 1968, p. 12, and November 24–25, 1968, p. 14; and Pierre Biarnes, in *Le Monde,* November 27, 1968, p. 14. For other details see Justin Vieyra, "Le 'coup' de Bamako," *Jeune Afrique,* no. 412 (November 25, 1968), pp. 26–29; Justin Vieyra, "Le Mali après le coup d'état," *Jeune Afrique,* no. 413 (December 12, 1968), pp. 32–35; Pierre Biarnes, "Mali: Fin d'un régime," *Le Mois en Afrique,* no. 36 (December 1968), pp. 2–9; and "Le coup d'état militaire," *Afrique contemporaine,* no. 41 (January–February 1969), pp. 14–17.

they would receive "all guarantees."[66] It promised to reorganize the state sector and save only those enterprises which were economically viable. It provided assurances that the private sector would not be tampered with. And it decided to liquidate the collective farms, transfer the land to those who worked it, and permit those who produced to sell their products freely.[67] In constituting the new government, the Comité Militaire de Libération Nationale, as it called itself, carefully excluded militant members of the former government (many of whom were under lock and key) and gave the two most important civilian posts to Louis Nègre (finance) and Jean-Marie Koné (foreign affairs). On his first trip to Paris after the coup, Koné told the Association des Journalistes d'Outre-mer that the young officers had acted to end the "radicalization of the Marxist regime" of Modibo Keita. [68]

Moreover, even if one agrees that the manner in which Mali's revolutionary democracy was dismantled offended Soviet observers less than in Ghana's case, by the same token Mali's was an eminently more defensible revolutionary democracy. The Soviet Union could rationalize Nkrumah's failure as the product of his own excesses, vanity, and ineptness; the same could not be said of Keita. It seems inappropriate, therefore, that it was left to the *Washington Post* to deplore his overthrow: "The fall of Modibo Keita, the man who persuaded France to grant Mali independence and then became its President, is a matter for heavy regret. He was a tough, dedicated, honest leader, not just a nationalist but a skilled politician and an able administrator. Few African states can boast leaders of his stature."[69] No comparable statement appeared in the Soviet press.

Soviet newspapers did not repeat the bulletin of Mali radio announcing the demise of Modibo Keita's "dictatorial regime" or the public attacks on the former president and his "lackeys," but in all other respects Soviet reports were neutral and matter-of-fact.[70] Though extremely brief, they

66. *Le Monde,* November 24–25, 1968, p. 14.
67. *Le Monde,* November 23, 1968, p. 12.
68. *Le Monde,* December 12, 1968, p. 5.
69. Editorial, *Washington Post,* November 24, 1968, p. B6. There were other similar expressions of regret in the nonsocialist press: see Philippe DeCraene, *Le Monde,* November 21, 1968, p. 10; and Bechir Ben Yahmed, "Un 'coup' pas comme les autres," *Jeune Afrique,* no. 412 (November 25, 1968), p. 25.
70. See especially *Pravda,* November 20, 1968, p. 5, November 23, 1968, p. 5, November 24, 1968, p. 5, and November 27, 1968, p. 5; and *Izvestiya,* November 21, 1968, p. 3, November 24, 1968, p. 3, November 27, 1968, p. 1, and December 3, 1968, p. 3.

recounted the military revolt, the arrest of Keita and his colleagues, the formation of the Comité Militaire de Libération Nationale, the dissolution of the previous regime's governing institutions, and the announcement of the new leadership's program. Perhaps Soviet policymakers preferred to give Mali's new rulers the benefit of the doubt and therefore consciously sought to create the impression that they would wait for a clearer indication of intentions. Thus, for example, TASS drew attention to Traoré's promise to preserve the state sector in those areas "which correspond to the people's interests."[71] A few days later TASS featured the new head of government Yoro Diakité's affirmation of nonalignment as Mali's fundamental policy and the struggle against "imperialism, colonialism, and neocolonialism in all its forms" as its unchanging commitment.[72] Even Kudryavtsev, in the first analysis of the coup, made note of an official spokesman's reassurance to rebellious students: "If the people choose socialism the army will not raise any obstacles."[73] He too mentioned Diakité's reference to Mali's policy of nonalignment and, in general, he too refused to judge the new regime. For example, he raised the issue of the coup's basis by referring to the "various reasons" foreign observers had advanced for the downfall of Modibo Keita's government, and then neither summarized these nor supplied any of his own. He avoided all speculation about the new leadership's political orientation (their "political views are practically unknown") and disposed of the question of the probable fate of Keita's "socialist line" by saying simply, "there are . . . too few facts to draw any well-grounded conclusions." Some socialist countries, such as Cuba, did not think so, however. Their press condemned the coup and rejected the new military government.[74] Moreover, Western commentators unanimously agreed that the new military government would be more moderate than its predecessor, more receptive to French influence, and less enamored of the socialist countries.[75] Therefore the extraordinary restraint of Soviet commentary raises important questions: Did Soviet reserve simply reflect the lessons learned at the time of the Ghanaian

71. *Pravda,* November 23, 1968, p. 5.

72. *Pravda,* November 27, 1968, p. 5.

73. V. Kudryavtsev, "After the Coup in Mali," *New Times,* no. 49 (December 11, 1968), p. 7.

74. Reference to the Cuban opposition is in *West Africa,* no. 2692 (January 4, 1969), p. 24. Interestingly enough, the Chinese did not even mention the coup.

75. See Pierre Biarnes, in *Le Monde,* November 22, 1968, p. 9.

coup? Was it simply that French neocolonialism seemed at this point more tolerable than Anglo-American neocolonialism? Or, still in the same category, was it simply that the deposers of Keita appeared more palatable than the deposers of Nkrumah? Or, in a more fundamental sense, had the fate of this revolutionary democracy—because it was without other attractions—come to weigh relatively little in the Soviet scheme of things?

The Nonrevolutionary States

Since 1966 Soviet officials had indulged a growing sense of impatience with Africa's progressive states, concealed, if at all, as a forebearing skepticism toward their revolutionary programs. At one level the frustration Soviet leaders must have felt over the weaknesses of their closest African allies caused them to shift the focus of Soviet African policy, emphasizing less the nature of the regime than the intrinsic importance of the country. This development, emerging clearly in the course of the Nigerian civil war, will be discussed at length later. At another level, however, the unrealized hopes of Soviet leaders for Africa's revolutionary states further diminished the importance of this entire area. And when Black Africa in general lost importance for Soviet officials, the pressures to preserve an amiable tolerance of the less significant of the less revolutionary states also declined. By 1967 one could, in a few minutes' conversation with Soviet diplomats, discover that statements made in the Soviet press disguised a persisting but good-natured distaste for regimes such as those in Senegal, the Ivory Coast, and Liberia. The policy of pursuing civil and businesslike relations with these countries still led Soviet writers to suppress sharply critical opinions, but in part because Africa as a whole could be taken more casually and because this policy had produced poorer results than Soviet policymakers may have expected, Soviet spokesmen privately expressed less complimentary feelings.

Officially the Soviet Union stood ready to improve diplomatic and economic relations with any independent African state (there would be no quibbling over the term, independent). As part of the bargain Soviet writers had tacitly agreed to soften their criticism of leaderships such as Senegal's and the Ivory Coast's. In turn, these leaderships were expected to attest to the objectivity of Soviet involvement in Africa and stand aside as cultural and economic contacts grew.

It worked like this: anyone vaguely familiar with the history of Soviet African policy knew that the Ivory Coast epitomized the most reactionary kind of state; it had made no pretense of being nonaligned; it had openly affirmed its commitment to capitalism and unabashedly recruited foreign investment; and it had long cast a suspicious eye on the activity of Communist states in Africa. But Soviet authorities had decided several years earlier that their country's interests would be better served by avoiding candid (inflammatory) comment on Ivory Coast policy, foreign or domestic. This become even more apparent once the two governments established diplomatic relations in January 1967.

How much less annoying this concession would have been, however, had the Ivory Coast been less a triumph for capitalism. The extraordinary economic progress of the Ivory Coast (all the more disagreeable because of Ghana's and Mali's difficulties) caught Soviet writers moderating their views toward a state whose system was not only repugnant but enormously successful. Thus Soviet commentators confronted the double-edged task of strengthening Soviet–Ivory Coast relations in a modest way without condoning the Ivory Coast model while, at the same time, detracting from Ivory Coast success without damaging recently established ties. The result was a curiously compromised analysis, which achieved only part of its objective.

Soviet commentators conceded that the Ivory Coast enjoyed a high level of economic activity, but resorted to the most oblique language in describing it. "I shall not burden the reader with the figures," one wrote.[76] He preferred to make the point more suggestively: "Airlines flying planes to Abidjan have no lack of bookings, the hotels are always full-up, ships arrive in port one after the other. In the cities new buildings are constantly rising up. Loads of freight, commercial delegations, financiers, businessmen are for ever arriving and departing. In short, an endless commercial merrygoround." No doubt this was a more painless way to present the Ivory Coast's "economic miracle," as he admitted it was called, than to cite the figures. Still, Soviet accounts labored so conspicuously to minimize the significance of Ivory Coast economic growth that even the laziest reader could see that something special was occurring there. He was, however, assured that Ivory Coast growth

76. V. Katin, "Travel Notes from the Ivory Coast," *New Times,* no. 11 (March 20, 1968), p. 27. See also B. Pilyatskin, in *Izvestiya,* February 1, 1968, p. 4, and February 8, 1968, p. 5.

had been achieved by throwing open the doors to foreign capital, with all its attendant evils. Neocolonialism, warned an *Izvestiya* correspondent, moved into a country stealthily and benignly until, without local leaders ever perceiving the danger, it could "undermine the foundations of independence and subordinate the national economy to foreign dictates"[77] Meanwhile, the argument continued, the capitalist countries sought to keep the Ivory Coast's economy monocultural, forcing the country to import foodstuffs and textiles that it should itself be producing—not to mention leaving the country to the mercy of price fluctuations in world markets they controlled. They plundered the country's natural wealth, returning a trifling 8 percent of their profits to the state—"involuntarily [bringing] to mind the loin cloths with which the colonialists used to pay native labor fifty years ago."[78] The average Ivoirien was said to be as impoverished as ever—only a "small privileged section" profited. The old problems of education and health care persisted, for "economic growth is not accompanied by social progress, by all-round development."[79] Despite the impressive advance the national economy seemed to be making, somehow the masses were not sharing in its bounty; their schools, hospitals, and general living standards had been neglected by foreign investors who, the implication was, dominated the Ivoirien system.

Nevertheless Soviet writers made their points without vilifying the Ivory Coast's leadership. No one any longer called President Houphouet-Boigny a "troubadour of neocolonialism" or a "Black African capitalist." All the bombast had been removed from Soviet comment; even the wrathful predictions of some awful end awaiting these lackeys of imperialism had mellowed into a "Time will show where its present course will lead."[80] As Vladimir Katin concluded in another article, "the Soviet Union recently established diplomatic and trade relations with the Ivory Coast. Many here [in the Ivory Coast] express the hope that contacts between our countries will develop and grow stronger."[81]

The Ivoiriens, however, were not letting Soviet writers off so easily. In August 1966, J. Kessé, apparently a member of *Fraternité-Matin*'s Paris bureau, responded to an article in the May 1966 issue of *Mirovaya*

77. Pilyatskin, in *Izvestiya*, February 1, 1968, p. 4.
78. Katin, "Travel Notes from the Ivory Coast," p. 28.
79. *Ibid*. Katin makes the same point in *Pravda*, February 14, 1968, p. 4.
80. *Ibid*.
81. Katin, in *Pravda*, February 14, 1968.

ekonomika i mezhdunarodnye otnosheniya.[82] "Your article," he said in his letter to the editor of the Soviet journal, though "serious, well-researched, and on the whole favorable to our country, contains . . . certain confusions and errors to which we direct your attention."[83] For example, the article contends that the Ivory Coast's method of development preserved the monocultural character of its economy, when in fact the percentage of Ivory Coast exports made up of cocoa and coffee had steadily diminished from 89 percent in 1952–1956 to 53 percent in 1965 (a better record, he pointed out, than the UAR's). Similarly the percentage of industrial exports had increased from 1 percent in 1958—59 to 12.5 percent in 1964—progress, Kessé could not resist adding, achieved while the export of manufactured goods in other underdeveloped countries calling themselves "socialist," such as Guinea, had stagnated or even regressed. And so the letter went, on down through the list, refuting each of the Soviet Union's standard charges and, whenever the chance came, making the unfavorable comparison with Guinea. Year by year the Ivory Coast raised its food production, permitting it to cut rice imports from 11 percent of the food imports in 1960 to 6.8 percent in 1970—in contrast to "socialist Guinea," with similar soil and climatic conditions, which imported four times as much rice as in 1962.[84] Kessé even gibed the Soviet Union for charging high prices on chocolate products, despite the decline in world market prices, and as a result narrowing its own domestic cocoa market. Finally, presumably with tongue in cheek, he asked that these corrections be communicated to MEiMO readers. There is no record that they ever were.

Yet Kessé's letter was a far cry from the bitter broadsides Ivoiriens once leveled against the Soviet Union and so in a sense represents a victory for Soviet policy toward the moderates. It may even have been

82. A. Anatolev, "V interesakh mestnoi burzhuazii (In the Interests of the Local Bourgeoisie), *Mirovaya ekonomika i mezhdunarodnye otnosheniya,* no. 5 (1966), pp. 102–104.

83. See *Fraternité-Matin* (Abidjan), August 3, 1966, p. 7.

84. Touré wanted no part of this comparison and instead was making one of his own. "The noncapitalist approach is that of a concrete and complete democracy. You will note that I have seldom used the work 'socialism,' whereas some African governments which claim to be socialist have done nothing to create democratic, popular, and progressive institutions . . . Now this mere claim of socialism has made certain European socialist states consider these African governments as being ahead of the Guinean regime." Touré's interview with *Nouvelle revue internationale,* as reported on Conakry radio (domestic service in French), 20.00 GMT, March 5, 1967.

that Soviet officials savored it as something of a triumph, since other returns were slow to come. Set beside the sluggish, though proper, relationship with Senegal, this much change represented real progress.

Having come this far, though, Soviet-Ivory Coast relations were presumably expected to level off and settle into the pattern of Soviet relations with countries like Senegal—not a very enlivening prospect.[85] The Cairo Seminar had said that in states such as the Ivory Coast, Senegal, and the Malagasy Republic "capitalist tendencies of development have even strengthened."[86] A look at the statistics of Soviet-Senegalese trade certainly does not contradict this assessment. In the four years after 1964 Senegalese imports from the Soviet Union had increased by scarcely more than $175,000 and exports from $315,000 in 1964 to $1.2 million in 1967.[87] The Soviet Union finally had authorization to sell books in a small bookshop in Dakar's Medina, and Soviet teachers could come

85. As it turned out, the Soviet Union was denied even this success. Though it is beyond the period of this book, the Ivory Coast's decision to sever relations with the Soviet Union on May 30, 1969, ought to be noted. On May 22 the Ivory Coast ambassador and first counselor in Moscow were recalled. The same day a critical dispatch allegedly filed by Novosti's Dakar correspondent was protested by National Assembly president Philippe Yacé. The Soviet Union maintained that it was a forgery and, when the break came, that it was used as a pretext. See A. Rovnov, in *Komsomolskaya pravda*, July 2, 1969, p. 3. Before these incidents a student strike had disrupted the University of Abidjan, and Yacé had accused "certain foreigners" of leading Ivory Coast students astray. See *Le Monde*, June 1–2, 1969, p. 1. Given Houphouet-Boigny's edginess about Communist presence in Abidjan and the contacts Ivory Coast students in Paris had with French Communists, these disturbances were sufficient to explain his decision to oust the Soviet mission. The Soviet Union had never been able to gain the confidence of the Ivoiriens. The March 1, 1968, *Fraternité-Matin* devoted its entire front and back pages to a sarcastic rejoinder to Vladimir Katin's February 14 article in *Pravda*. Though Katin's assessment seemed a reflection of the Soviet Union's growing moderation, Ivory Coast officials obviously did not think it sufficiently moderate and, with this flourish, made known their dissatisfaction. From March 1968 until the break in May 1969, I can find no further comment on the Ivory Coast in the Soviet press. Whether the Novosti report was in fact a forgery does not really matter. (The Soviet argument is persuasive.) It is more significant that the Soviet Union went to considerable trouble to repudiate a document that was no more hostile to the Ivory Coast regime than many bona fide articles appearing a few years earlier. The Soviet Union seemed genuinely surprised and disappointed by the Ivory Coast's action. Even then it avoided explicit criticism of the Ivory Coast leadership and placed blame "wholly with the [unspecified] enemies of peace, friendship, and mutual understanding among nations." Rovnov, *Komsomolskaya pravda*, July 2, 1969, p. 3.

86. *Zarya Vostoka* (Georgian), March 31, 1967, pp. 2–3, in FPIR 0355/67, March 31, 1967.

87. See *Commerce extérieur* (Senegal), December for each of these years.

from time to time to lecture at the University of Dakar. Senghor had specifically exempted the Soviet Union from his angry attack on outsiders who, he said, had abetted leaders of the Dakar disturbances in May, and Soviet diplomats were delighted with this modest sign of affection.[88] On the other hand, Senegal had decided not to go ahead with the tuna-processing plant envisaged in the 1964 Soviet aid agreement and in December 1967 settled on ten refrigerated fishing vessels instead, utilizing slightly more than one half of the $6.7 million credit. The planning for the fish plant had been far along, and when Senegalese officials indicated they preferred to let a French subsidiary use the site, the reasons were all too obvious.

In short, Soviet leaders must have found their relationship with these countries, though in small ways useful, rather dull, and when things went sour, as they had with Ghana, the restraints were lifted and Soviet commentators spoke their minds. Admittedly Ghana's National Liberation Council was not quite the same as the Senegalese regime; it had overthrown a progressive African leader and reversed foreign and domestic policies that appealed to the Soviet Union. As a country that had once known the way and strayed, it naturally evoked a level of hostility that more innocent heathens did not, and Soviet writers therefore condemned it in a way they would not have other states: "It is symptomatic that, in taking the country's economy in hand, the U.S. imperialists and their Western partners are trying at the same time to transform Ghana, which quite recently was in the vanguard of fighters in the African anti-imperialist, anticolonial front, into an instrument of their policy in the continent."[89] In October 1966 a *Pravda* correspondent reported that a so-called Council of Struggle against Communism in Africa had been formed in Accra and then commented that this new organization constituted advance payment for Western aid, the remainder of which included breaking relations "with Cuba and certain other socialist countries" and establishing relations "with the Chiang Kai-shek clique."[90] A month later, the Soviet press complained that individuals and newspapers in Ghana were carrying out a slanderous campaign against the Soviet Union by accusing it of interfering in

88. See his speech to the nation in *Dakar-Matin,* June 1, 1968, p. 4. Soviet diplomats indicated their satisfaction over this favorable reference in interviews in Dakar in July 1968.
89. K. Geivandov, in *Pravda,* November 14, 1967, p. 5.
90. Victor Maevsky, in *Pravda,* October 5, 1966, p. 5.

Ghana's internal affairs and those of other African countries. "A number of Ghanaians are eager to join their puny, malevolent voices to the anti-Soviet campaign of the imperialists."[91] Valentin Korovikov, *Pravda*'s West African correspondent, filed a report soon after in which he implied that Ghana's military rulers were encouraging the chiefs to regain their old power over local government, the upper chamber of the new parliament, and the law courts, and even to seek a return of crown lands.[92] To this Soviet writers added that Ghana's new rulers had accentuated unemployment and slowed the rate of economic activity by abandoning a wide range of state projects and by denationalizing the state sector of the economy; that they had promised to liberalize trade restrictions and permit the free withdrawal of profits from the country; that they had drastically curtailed expenditures on all social needs, including education and medical services; and that they had taken to defending the interests of South Africa, Malawi, and other reactionary African regimes.

Since the Ghanaians gave as good as they got, Soviet-Ghanaian relations remained constantly in a petulant state. Early in March 1967 Police Chief John Harlley charged the Soviet Union with trying to smuggle arms and explosives into Ghana on the freighter *Ristna*. *Pravda* called his accusation "crude fabrication" and "hostile slander"—similar to the "fantastic fabrication" a year earlier that Soviet authorities were transporting tanks to Guinea across the Sahara for use against Ghana.[93] In June, the Ghanaians expelled Korovikov and a Novosti agent named Aleksei Kazantsev, after a search of Kazantsev's residence reportedly uncovered "documents relating to the dissemination of propaganda against the Ghanaian government."[94] The Soviet Union retaliated by accusing Ghana's leaders of "serving the Western powers more and more openly, hoping to maintain [themselves] in power with their help."[95] This regime, it said, "takes pride in its animosity toward the Soviet Union and other socialist countries." A few months later Soviet authorities were again angered when sixteen young Ghanaian doctors trained in the Soviet Union received instructions to return to medical school, after tests revealed their preparation to be inadequate. Finally, a scurrilous piece

91. Yu. Tsaplin, in *Izvestiya*, November 4, 1966, p. 2.

92. V. Korovikov, in *Pravda*, November 30, 1966, p. 5.

93. *Pravda*, March 8, 1967, p. 5. Harlley was a key member of the NLC and the member responsible for foreign affairs.

94. Accra radio (domestic service in English), 06.00 GMT, June 10, 1967. See also *Times* (London), June 7, 1967, p. 5.

95. *Pravda*, June 8, 1967, p. 3.

in the *Ghanaian Times,* describing Russians as the political assassins of history, provoked the Soviet ambassador to go directly to Harlley and threaten to close the Soviet embassy immediately if something were not done to repudiate the insult. The next day the front page of the *Ghanaian Times* published a small item dissociating the Ghanaian government from the article.[96]

In the circumstances, it is hardly surprising that negotiations between the two sides over unsettled economic questions, such as debt repayment, unfinished aid projects, and the 1961 trade agreement, did not go smoothly. Some time in 1966 Ghana's Ministry of Trade had prepared a memorandum recommending that a review of all trade agreements with the socialist countries be undertaken "with a view to removing their harmful effects on the economy."[97] It concluded that "in the main, the continued operation of these agreements will not be in the interest of Ghana and it is proposed that consideration should be given to the renewal of these agreements for a further period of one year only during which time, arrangements could be made to settle our debts with these countries on the clearing accounts both by an exchange of goods and by currency." In November Ghanaian officials indicated that they wished to renegotiate the trade and payments agreement signed with the Soviet Union in 1961. As it had been written, however, the five-year agreement would automatically be renewed unless one of the parties notified the other of its desire to change matters six months before the agreement's expiration date (December 1966). In the confusion after the coup, officials had neglected to act swiftly enough (some said they confused the notification period on the Soviet agreement with the much shorter period provided for by the agreements with East European countries), and now the Soviet Union insisted that the agreement was in force for another five years.

Soviet officials maintained their "rigid" attitude, as a Ghanaian aide-mémoire called it, even after the NLC had cooled down and taken a

96. The offending article was "Maestros of Murder," *Ghanaian Times,* July 17, 1968, p. 7. At one point it alleged, "indeed Brezhnev and Kosygin themselves rose, in the Ukraine and Leningrad respectively, on a ladder of corpses." My information about the Soviet ambassador's action was gathered in Ghana in August 1968. For the Ghanaian government's response, see *Ghanaian Times,* July 18, 1968, p. 1.

97. "Renewal of the Bilateral Trade [Agreements] with Socialist Countries of Eastern Europe, USSR and China," memorandum by Ministry of Trade (mimeo, n.d.).

longer look at Soviet-Ghanaian relations, particularly at several nearly completed Soviet aid projects.[98] These included a gold refinery at Tarkwa, a fish-processing plant in Tema, and a cement-paneling factory in Accra. In part because there seemed no point in depriving Ghana of these facilities and in part because the regime wanted to try again to persuade Soviet leaders to renegotiate the trade agreement, in March 1967 it sent E. N. Omaboe, at the time chairman of the NLC's economic committee, to Moscow. Moscow radio contended that public pressure had forced the NLC to reconsider its relations with the Soviet Union.[99]

Soviet officials, however, were not about to reconsider their position on outstanding economic issues. They rejected any effort to raise the question of the trade agreement and, according to Ghanaian sources, would talk only about the annual protocol by which it would be implemented.[100] (Ghana had to settle for this nonbinding instrument as the best available. One was signed the next month, containing, as before, a clause prohibiting resale of commerce on the world market.) When Omaboe pressed them to ease the repayment schedule on the suppliers' credits, they were adamant: an obligation was an obligation. Only on the question of completing aid projects did they show any flexibility. Moscow radio reported that the Ghanaian government had "requested the Soviet government to return its fishery experts" and it had responded favorably.[101]

But that month Harlley had assailed the Soviet Union for trying to smuggle arms into Ghana, and this, combined with the uneasiness caused by an attempted coup in April, interrupted both the arrival of Soviet experts and more generally the drift toward a gradual normalization of relations.[102] Matters were not helped by the Russians' refusal to upgrade their embassy to the ambassadorial level. In October 1967, as he was leaving for Canada, Lieutenant-General Ankrah (chairman of

98. Interview with an officer of the Ghanaian Ministry of Trade, in Accra, August 7, 1968.

99. Moscow radio (in Hausa to Africa), 18.30 GMT, March 27, 1967.

100. Interview with an officer of the Ghanaian Ministry of Trade, in Accra, August 7, 1968.

101. Moscow radio (in Hausa to Africa), 18.30 GMT, March 27, 1967.

102. The Russians, however, were careful never to let relations deteriorate so far that they lost their presence in Ghana. Even during the exchange over the *Ristna* the Soviet Union avoided provoking the NLC to a more serious response. *Pravda* assured it that "the Soviet Union following its invariable policy of friendship and all-round cooperation with the states of Africa on the basis of equality, strict respect for sovereignty, and noninterference in their internal affairs . . . has for its part expressed its willingness to maintain and develop interstate relations with the Republic of Ghana." *Pravda,* March 8, 1967, p. 5.

the NLC) curtly informed the Soviet chargé d'affaires: "If by the time I come back from Canada, you have no ambassador here, I'll recall our man in Moscow." Within a few weeks the Soviet government had posted Vasily Safronchuk to Ghana as its new ambassador. Eventually, in May 1968, the two sides reached an agreement to have Soviet experts come to Ghana to see about renewing work on the uncompleted projects. A twelve-man delegation arrived early in June and spent a month touring projects and discussing various aspects of Soviet-Ghanaian economic relations.[103] Two months later Omaboe returned to Moscow to work out the final arrangements for the resumption of project construction and, in addition, for the repayment of debts contracted by the previous regime.

Nigeria's Civil War

Soviet relations with few African countries matched the turbulence and, at times, rancor of those with Ghana. This stemmed in part from the deep resentment Ghana's military leaders nursed because of the role Soviet officials had played in Nkrumah's regime. Partly it stemmed from the new leadership's nervousness over Nkrumah's presence just up the coast in Guinea and their fear that Soviet authorities might give him enough material help to be troublesome. From the other side, Soviet leaders could hardly have been expected to accept graciously the radical reversal of Ghana's socialist course and the eager pursuit of Western economic support. But this probably would not have stirred the energetic criticism it did, had there not been the other constant irritants—the seizure of Soviet ships, the harrassment of Soviet-trained Ghanaian students, the insults of the press. Toward other less provocative states, Soviet comment seldom became seriously uncomplimentary. Still, much of the Soviet condemnation of Ghana applied equally to states like Senegal and the Ivory Coast. When Soviet writers denounced Ghana for trying to reattract foreign investment, for liberalizing import restrictions, for imposing conservative monetary policies, and for seeking to develop the private sector, it is hard to believe that only Ghana came to mind. In these other cases, Soviet spokesmen (except, in private, diplomats and journalists) apparently suppressed their feelings in order to secure the limited benefits of cooperation with such countries. (Even toward Ghana, rather than jeopardize the carefully constructed image of a re-

103. See "The Russians Are Back," *West Africa*, no. 2665 (June 29, 1968), p. 752.

strained, uncapricious leadership or risk being cut off from Ghana in the future, Soviet writers had managed to control their tempers.)

On the surface at least, the pragmatism of Soviet policy toward moderate African states (as opposed to the neo-orthodox viewpoint directed to the revolutionary states) persisted. In no case was this clearer than in the relationship forged between Nigeria and the Soviet Union after the second coup in 1966. The steps by which the Soviet Union lost its aversion to Nigeria's new military government, shifted to an openly sympathetic attitude, and finally firmly rallied to its side in the war against secessionist Biafra are an overwhelming demonstration of Soviet readiness to adjust to the exigencies of policy. When the stakes were sufficiently alluring, Soviet policymakers showed themselves to be the purest of pragmatists. The more important point, however, is that the stakes of the involvement in a country like Nigeria were becoming so great, reflecting a crucial shift in the emphasis of Soviet policy in Black Africa.

The Soviet Union had not liked the July coup. It brought to power people who Soviet analysts at first suspected spoke for the "feudal" North, and they anticipated a swift re-creation of the old situation, including the revival of a foreign policy largely unsympathetic to Soviet interests. An early *Pravda* release on the coup was headlined "Alarming Situation"; other accounts drew dark references to the revenge Northern leaders had plotted and now exacted for the January events.[104] Few people, however, knew precisely what had happened in the hours between July 29 and August 1 (certainly the Soviet embassy did not rank among the best informed in Lagos). And by the middle of the week it became clear that the Northern officers who, with the prodding of Northern politicians, had launched the coup had been unable to establish their predominance. The new head of state, Colonel Yakubu Gowon, though a Northerner, was not among the coup's original planners nor was he from the Hausa tribe, the dominant tribe of the North and the group most aggrieved by the January revolt. He came from the Angas, a minority non-Moslem tribe concentrated in the southern part of the Northern region, and he was conspicuously a compromise candidate, acceptable to the North and yet also in a position to deal with the Ibos.

At this point, soon after the coup, Soviet commentary became more

104. *Pravda*, August 2, 1966, p. 1; see Moscow radio (in English for Africa), 20.30 GMT, August 3, 1966.

ambivalent. Gowon obviously ruled at the sufferance of Northern officers and their collaborators among the politicians and bureaucrats. His first act had been to abolish Ironsi's recently announced unitary state and to reinstitute the Federation. Korovikov noted that "the Northern emirs were clearly pleased with the course of events, for on the very first day Gowon had declared the impossibility of creating a centralized, unitary state in Nigeria."[105] But, continued Korovikov, Gowon understood that a complete capitulation to the North would accentuate the Federation's problems by pushing the frightened and angered Ibos close to secession. It was therefore noteworthy that Gowon in his first speech as Nigeria's new head of state "had not criticized, but had praised Ironsi, had called for a stop to intertribal conflict, and had come out for the unity of the country, albeit in the form of a federation." He was genuinely determined to reconcile the Ibos to the change in power, as far as Korovikov was concerned, and his release of Michael Okpara, the former prime minister of the Eastern Region, provided evidence of his good faith. Soviet observers were even more encouraged by the decision to free Chief Awolowo, imprisoned since his 1963 conviction for plotting to overthrow the former Balewa government. Korovikov called his release "an important step toward averting the exacerbation of intertribal quarreling," but presumably Soviet leaders were also delighted that a man whose political positions had inspired their confidence in 1960–61 would again be taking an active part in Nigerian politics. By August 6, Moscow radio was already calling attention to Gowon's reported "far-reaching plans for Awolowo"; it is possible, speculated the broadcaster, that Awolowo will be "the first civilian in the government, or even become head of it."[106]

In the ensuing weeks Soviet accounts grew increasingly sympathetic to Gowon's government, giving the definite impression by the end of September that the new leadership had the Soviet Union's basic support. Nothing, of course, served better to establish the new regime's credentials than evidence of its independence from the reactionary leaders of the North. Soviet writers did even better. By mid-September they had detected opposition on the part of the "feudal Hausa leadership" to Gowon's government.[107] Because the overthrow of Ironsi had not "restored

105. V. Korovikov, in *Pravda*, August 20, 1966, p. 3.
106. Vladimir Dunayev for Moscow radio (home service), 17.00 GMT, August 6, 1966.
107. V. Midtsev, in *Izvestiya*, September 20, 1966, p. 2.

their privileged position in the Federation," these reactionary forces were supposedly turning away from the new government. Who was to say that they might not even try to overthrow Gowon's regime, so unsatisfied were they with the few concessions he had given them?[108] With opponents like this, even the most dubious parts of Gowon's program deserved special consideration. Soviet commentators, for example, began to search for ways to justify his repudiation of the unitary state and commitment to federation—a relic of colonialism long the target of Soviet critics. They found the explanation in the circumstances created by the first officers' revolt. "The last military coup aggravated intertribal and interregional relations to such an extent that a split was imminent and several independent states with little vitality might have emerged. With the danger of this split in view you must admit objectively that the return to federalism helped keep Nigeria a more or less single entity."[109] Admittedly for good reason, many people regarded "the return to the old federal system as a step backwards"; nevertheless "progressive forces in Nigeria do not dismiss the idea of federal structure out of hand," provided it was "founded on the basis of equality between all areas."[110] In other words, if federalism eliminated the advantage possessed by the North under the old arrangement, then it might not be so bad. There was always the risk that Gowon would be unable or ultimately unwilling to challenge Northern leaders on this point, but Soviet commentators were apparently heartened in September by the pressure Midwestern leaders were exerting to have the Federation divided into a large number of states, a proposal strongly supported by Awolowo.[111]

Unfortunately, the widespread bloody revenge unleashed against Ibo officers and civilians in the weeks before and during the July coup made it increasingly unlikely that Easterners would accept any solution that did not concede virtual autonomy to the individual regions. To protect themselves against further retaliation from other members of the Federation, the Ibos demanded the creation of a loose confederation, leaving

108. *Ibid.*

109. Leon Leonov for Moscow radio (in English for Africa), 20.30 GMT, September 2, 1966.

110. *Ibid.*, and Moscow radio (in English for Africa), 14.30 GMT, September 12, 1966.

111. See, among others, "Opting for Federation?" *West Africa*, no. 2573 (September 24, 1966), p. 1079. Soviet observers commented on both the position of leaders from the Midwestern Region and Awolowo's interest in a federation of many states. See Leonov's commentary for Moscow radio and Midtsev, in *Izvestiya* September 20, 1966.

only essential common services to the central government. (For the same reasons they refused to consider weakening their position within their own region by accepting its further division, as the Midwest and Awolowo wanted.) By the time an interregional conference met in mid-September to consider reshaping the Nigerian constitution, sentiment in the East strongly favored secession and Eastern leaders, responding to these pressures, were showing little willingness to compromise their demands for regionally based army commands and the allocation of considerably more power to each of the four regions. If their demands were not satisfied, they openly threatened to leave the Federation.

Soviet policymakers were now confronted with extremely hard decisions. Up to this point Soviet commentators had argued that the North, not the East, presented the gravest threat to the survival of the Federation. It was there that all the "centrifugal tendencies" were supposedly compressed. Commenting on the July coup, one analyst recalled Ironsi's commitment to a unitary state and concluded: "The emirs' only hope was to take the North out of Nigeria and they held this as a threat over the Ironsi government. This makes it clear that the forces of disruption are concentrated in northern Nigeria and not in the East."[112] Soviet analysts knew perfectly well that from the moment of the July coup the East's leader, Lieutenant-Colonel Odumegwu Ojukwu, had expressed the strongest reservations over his region's continued association with federal Nigeria but, until the confrontation of regional delegations at the Lagos constitutional conference in mid-September, they had chosen to play down the significance of the East's discontent. Watching this conference slide helplessly into deadlock, Soviet observers must have realized the moment for choosing sides was approaching. A short-lived agreement between the Northern and Eastern delegations on the desirability of preserving a loose federation based on existing regions came apart when Northern representatives suddenly announced their support for a scheme to carve a number of states from the four regions. This was something Midwestern representatives, led by Awolowo's old ally, Chief Anthony Enahoro, had been urgently seeking. Awolowo, at the conference as a member of the Western delegation, gave it his strong backing, and when the Northerners threw their weight behind the proposal, the East refused further cooperation. No doubt Eni Njoku and others in the Eastern delegation were fearful that separate states for

112. Leon Leonov for Moscow radio (in English for Africa), 20.30 GMT, August 14, 1966.

Eastern minorities, like the Ijaw and Ibibio, would seriously compromise their region's power. Moreover, they suspected that the ambitious Awolowo was using the scheme to advance his own interests in the Calabar–Ogoja–Rivers area, an oil-rich coastal section of the East dominated by the Action Group under Awolowo's close friend, E. O. Eyo. In any case, a little more than a week after the conference opened, it had become hopelessly tangled; on September 24 it adjourned for a brief period, partially under the pressure of renewed violence in the North, and when it reopened in early October the Easterners were no longer present. Though the conference continued fitfully over the next month and a half, they never returned.

Unhappy as Soviet commentators were with what they apparently considered Eastern intransigence, they were still too eager to preserve their neutrality to criticize Eastern leaders directly. Instead they let their criticism be inferred. Ojukwu, for threatening secession, was ranged among the elements opposing Gowon's regime—a category also filled by the reactionary leaders of the North. In contrast, Soviet writers warmly praised Awolowo's viewpoint and clearly associated it with Gowon's regime.[113] By now no doubt they were growing increasingly confident that a number of progressive political leaders close to Awolowo, disintegration. An early report filed by Korovikov from Accra began given major responsibilities by the regime. Not only did chiefs Enahoro and Awolowo play central roles in the conference, their counterparts from the North were progressive men like Joseph Tarka, the former leader of the United Middle Belt Congress and an ally of the Action Group, and Alhaji Aminu Kano, the only Hausa among the Northerners and a well-known leader of the socialist Northern Elements Progressive Union, a party opposed to the NPC and strongly attracted to Nasser's regime. One can imagine the fascination with which Soviet policymakers viewed the advance of these leaders after the July coup.

Unfortunately the North's traditional leaders were not equally enthusiastic about their new role and apparently reacted with dismay to their readiness to accept the division of the North—so much so that they deliberately instigated further violence against the hundreds of thousands of Ibos remaining within their reach. There had been trouble in a number of Northern cities between September 18 and 24, leading to many Ibo deaths. (Tarka's delegation had just swung around to sup-

113. See Midtsev, in *Izvestiya*, September 20, 1966.

porting the possibility of creating more states from the four regions.) But on September 29, while the Lagos conference was adjourned, the disorder intensified significantly when soldiers mutinied and executed twenty-five Ibos aboard an aircraft at Kano. In the next few weeks thousands and thousands of Ibos lost their lives or were cruelly maimed by the angry mobs that rampaged through many of the towns in the North. The point of no return was now passed. Ojukwu refused to send delegates to the constitutional conference until Northern troops stationed in Lagos and the Western region were returned to the North, and he flatly denied that any larger agreement could be reached until a settlement had been arranged, adequately compensating Easterners for the loss of life and property. Given the mood of both Northern and Eastern leaders, it was highly unlikely that these demands would be met or a compromise found which would preserve Nigeria intact; from this hour Eastern Nigeria lumbered inexorably toward secession.

The savage bloodletting in the North appeared to give Soviet leaders serious second thoughts. Not only were they uncomfortable about the misery befalling the Northern Ibos, now a terrorized mass fleeing to the sanctuary of the East; they seemed to have grown suddenly fearful that indeed the entire Federation was rapidly approaching the point of disintegration. An early report filed by Korovikov from Accra began by emphasizing the murderous storm in which the Ibo of the North had been caught.[114] Significantly the article avoided any reference, and therefore any invidious reference, to Ojukwu and his colleagues. It also expressed distinct reservations over plans to create a larger number of Nigerian states. In the crucial dispute over Nigeria's destiny as a united state, "the Nigerian public realizes that, with a weak federal government, limited means and massive unresolved problems, the strife between ten autonomous regions could spread still further than under the old regime, destroyed in January." For the next several weeks the Soviet press was silent, or almost so. Either it confined itself to brief factual reports or published strikingly contrived noncommital accounts.[115] One of the few direct references to the effect the bloodshed would have on the Eastern leadership's attitude toward the continuation of the Federation bitterly condemned Northern leaders.[116] "The fact that [the outbreak of violence]

114. V. Korovikov, in *Pravda,* October 4, 1966, p. 3.
115. See, for example, K. Geivandov, in *Pravda,* October 21, 1966, p. 5.
116. V. Iordansky, "Trying Times for Nigeria," *New Times,* no. 46 (November 16, 1966), p. 18.

occurred at one and the same time in towns a long way apart" proved to this writer that it was "deliberately engineered." And since it happened "just as the constitutional conference in Lagos was nearing successful conclusion," the motivation behind it seemed transparent. (It is interesting that a Soviet writer would choose to see the already floundering conference as moving toward success.) "After long discussion and heated debates, the Eastern Region had agreed to maintain the federation. The riots were clearly intended to make the Eastern Region leaders reverse this decision." No doubt Soviet leaders were stunned and appalled by the carnage let loose on the Ibo, but it was not something for which they blamed Gowon. He had not wanted the violence and was now caught in the middle. They apparently trusted his commitment to saving the Federation and, though sympathetic to the plight of the Ibo, expected him to make sacrifices also in order to preserve this larger goal. They, like others, seized upon the Aburi (Ghana) meeting of the four military governors and Gowon early in January to justify their lingering hopes that a reconciliation might still be effected. Significantly, even after Ojukwu and the others resumed the quarrel, this time over what had been agreed to at Aburi, Soviet commentators persisted in treating dialogue as a realistic means to a solution. On Feburary 25 Ojukwu threatened to initiate unilateral measures if by March 31 steps had not been taken toward fulfilling the Aburi decisions (which, he was correct in saying, included the reorganization of the army into area commands and the restoration of major executive and legislative power to *all* regional military governors acting through the Supreme Military Council). Yet, as late as March 8, *Pravda* commentator Igor Belyaev affirmed that "the meeting at Aburi . . . showed that it was possible to find the basis for the continuation of dialogue between eastern Nigeria and the other parts of the country."[117]

Throughout the weeks from the beginning of the October pogrom to the final failure of the Aburi agreement, the Soviet Union maintained a neutral position—one that urged concessions to relieve the apprehensions of the Easterners but that firmly supported Gowon's efforts to keep "Nigeria one." In the end, there could be no doubt that the Soviet Union favored Gowon, for the irreducible premise (as perhaps opposed to objective) of Soviet policy was to preserve the Federation. If and when the East actually moved toward secession, it would lose Soviet

117. Igor Belyaev, in *Pravda*, March 8, 1967, p. 5.

support. This remained the unchanging implication of the backing Soviet commentators had given Gowon as early as September, backing repeated in November when he indicated an intention to create eight to fourteen states within a strong federal system.[118] Eastern leaders understood his statement to be a rejection of confederation and a threat to use force to preserve Nigeria, an idea so objectionable to them that they apparently contemplated immediate secession and were dissuaded only by Awolowo's equally strong objection to a highly centralized federal structure. The Soviet press, however, received Gowon's plans favorably, calling them a "realistic approach to the country's complicated problems and . . . a basis for a political settlement."[119] In early 1967 the Soviet Union added further quiet support by sending a five-man team of economists, metallurgists, and engineers to Nigeria to undertake an extensive feasibility study for a long-planned major iron and steel industry.[120] A few weeks earlier, on January 16, Abdul Aziz Atta, the permanent secretary of the Ministry of Finance, had announced that Nigeria was now ready to accept loan offers from the socialist countries, including the Soviet Union.[121] On January 26, the two countries initialed an agreement clearing the way for air service between Moscow and Lagos.[122]

The open question, then, was how long Soviet sympathy for the Easterners could be reconciled with its underlying commitment to Gowon's government. At what point in the growing confrontation between Ojukwu and the federal military regime would the Soviet leadership move from behind its publicly affected neutrality to reject the Eastern government? Through the early part of March Soviet writers carefully refrained from condemning Ojukwu and his colleagues directly. They confined their criticism to vaguely identified secessionist forces in the Eastern Region, before whom Ojukwu came off as quite possibly the unwilling victim. Apparently they had not given up hope that he might still be cajoled into resisting these forces. In mid-March, however, their view

118. "Gowon's Solution," *West Africa*, no. 2583 (December 3, 1966); p. 1405.
119. See V. Sidenko, "Program for Nigeria," *New Times*, no. 51 (December 21, 1966), p. 20.
120. See Alhaji Lateef Teniola, in *Nigerian Review*, September 1967. The delegation was headed by Victor Bileko, a metallurgist, and during the month it was in Nigeria (February 2–March 3) it visited iron-ore or potential energy sites in all four regions.
121. *Le Monde*, January 18, 1967, p. 6.
122. Moscow (in Hausa to Africa), 17.30 GMT, January 27, 1967. See also press release from the Federal Ministry of Information (Lagos), no. F 2606 (mimeo), November 18, 1967.

changed sharply. On March 13, Ojukwu called a press conference for a hundred foreign journalists and diplomats, at which he announced the Eastern Region's firm intention to "decentralize" Nigeria by March 31. He had in mind greater regional control of a number of spheres previously handled by the federal government, including revenue allocation, a decision that he emphasized should not be construed as secression. Yuri Kharlanov, a commentator for *Pravda,* referred to this press conference specifically and said that "in the last several days the political situation in Nigeria has again become seriously aggravated."[123] He ventured—citing the *Morning Post* of Nigeria—that Ojukwu's press conference was a ploy "to get in advance Anglo-American support for the separatist republic of 'Biafra.'" Further on in his comment he drew the comparison between the Congo and Nigeria, identifying the East with Katanga. It is, of course speculation, but it appears that during this period, perhaps after the March 13 press conference, Soviet observers realized that the situation in Nigeria had become desperately serious and that indeed the East would soon secede.

If the faded prospects of conciliation were not evident then, they became so a few days later, on March 17, when the federal military regime published a decree implementing its interpretation of the Aburi principles. Since it resurrected sections of the old constitution permitting three of the four regions to act against a fourth during a state of emergency, Ojukwu vehemently denounced the decree. On March 21 Kudryavtsev strongly endorsed Gowon's position.[124] He credited him with striving to preserve the country's unity by means of a federation divided into a number of units in which no single nationality or tribe would dominate. "It is in this spirit," he said, "that Gowon and his adherents interpret the decisions of the confererce of Nigerian leaders held in Aburi." In contrast, Ojukwu would turn Nigeria into a virtual confederation—"a step backward" even when measured against the old state system. If he did so, Gowon's regime intended "to take resolute measures to preserve the integrity of the country." The attack on Ojukwu now became explicit. In pursuing tribal separatism, he was using American imperialists and, in turn, being used by them. "Recent occurrences fully confirm this transformation of the leaders of the Eastern Region into a tool of the foreign monopolies." Already, Kudryavtsev warned, efforts were underway to generate a favorable press in the United States and mold

123. Yuri Kharlanov, in *Pravda,* March 15, 1967, p. 5.
124. V. Kudryavtsev, in *Pravda,* March 21, 1967, p. 5.

American public opinion to support the East's "just cause." "In Nigeria a tragedy is being performed, one in which the leading characters are the separatists from Enugu and their foreign patrons, who are dreaming aloud of getting their hands on the country's riches." The Soviet Union had openly chosen sides. On March 28 the two countries signed an agreement promoting cultural cooperation, the vehicle employed four months later in negotiating an arms deal. The chief Nigerian spokesman was Edwin Ogbu, permanent secretary of the Ministry of Foreign Affairs and the man who eventually cleared the way for the arms negotiation.

By now events in Nigeria were rapidly moving toward a climax. On March 31 the Eastern Region government issued orders that all revenue collected for the federal government in its region must after April 1 be paid to its treasury, a move that Gowon denounced as "illegal and unconstitutional." He promised the severest counteraction. On April 18, the Eastern government assumed control over the branch offices of a number of federal agencies, including the Electric Corporation of Nigeria, the Nigerian Broadcasting Corporation, and the Nigerian Coal Company. The week before, the Central Bank had blocked the transfer of foreign currencies to the Eastern Region, and now Gowon's regime warned that further steps toward secession would lead to the creation of a separate Calabar–Ogoja–Rivers state. Late in April a last effort to revive the constitutional conference collapsed when Awolowo, Lateef Jakande (the Lagos representative), and Sir Ibrahim Kashim (the leader of the Northern delegation) withdrew—Awolowo because of the continued presence of Northern troops in the Western Region and because of the futility of proceeding without the Easterners.[125] Several weeks later, Ojukwu rejected the compromise proposed by a National Reconciliation Committee, and on May 27 the Eastern consultative assembly mandated Ojukwu to declare Biafran independence as soon as "practicable." Gowon responded by creating the long-contemplated twelve-state federation, and on May 30 Ojukwu took the East out of the Federation.

In the aftermath of Biafran secession, the Soviet press returned to its previous neutrality. *Pravda*'s first report blamed the "ruling circles" of

125. At the time (April 25) Awolowo said that, although some of the demands of Eastern Nigeria were "excessive, within the context of a Nigerian union most of such demands are not only well founded, but are designed for a smooth and healthy association amongst the various national units of Nigeria." "Nigeria: Leaders Resign," *West Africa*, no. 2605 (May 6, 1967), p. 609. Significantly, the Soviet press ignored Awolowo's intervention.

the United States and Great Britain for the trouble.[126] The nearest
it came to betraying bias occurred in a single reference to the central
government's efforts to meet Ibo demands for greater regional control
"in economic and political spheres." But Ojukwu was not criticized for
refusing to take up Lagos' offer. Two weeks later, Korovikov went to
even greater lengths to avoid taking sides.[127] Again Ojukwu and Eastern
separatists escaped any mention, and again the entire responsibility for
the crisis was assigned to Western interests, particularly to American
oil companies. (They were so deeply involved, Korovikov said, because
the recent "six-day war" in the Middle East had jeopardized their stake
in the Arab states.) If anything, an allusion to the suffering of the
Ibo in the North invited sympathy for their predicament. With the ut-
most moderation he concluded: "The course of the Nigerian crisis has
shown that Nigerian unity can be restored only on the basis of a decisive
democratization of the life of the country, of true equality for all its
peoples, and of a broad program of economic development, assuring
fifty-five million Nigerians work and bread." The Soviet Union was,
of course, behaving very much in accord with the general reluctance
of the major powers to become embroiled in the Nigerian conflict. Moreover, in these same days the Soviet leadership was reeling under the
impact of the disastrous Middle Eastern war and, before defining its
position in a new crisis region, no doubt wished to make a very careful
reading of the situation.

Even after civil war began in early July, the Soviet press was careful
not to manifest an obvious bias. Reports on the course of the war used
the brief bulletins filed by Western wire services, usually Reuters. No
major commentary, not even a bylined report, appeared in *Pravda* or
Izvestiya during July. By focusing on the successes of federal military
forces while largely ignoring the counterclaims of Biafran radio, the
Soviet press did give some indication of its preferences.[128] Yet, on balance, Soviet leaders clearly wished to avoid a strong public commitment
to the federal government and, whatever suspicions were concerning
Soviet preferences, these had not destroyed hopes among Biafran leaders
that the Soviet Union would remain effectively neutral. Late in July

126. *Pravda,* May 31, 1967, p. 5.

127. V. Korovikov, in *Pravda,* June 16, 1967, p. 5.

128. See, for example, *Pravda,* July 9, 1967, p. 5; *Pravda,* July 12, 1967,
p. 5; *Pravda,* July 17, 1967, p. 5; *Izvestiya,* July 18, 1967, p. 3; and *Izvestiya,*
August 1, 1967, p. 2.

Biafran radio still thought it plausible to appeal for Soviet neutrality, although by this time the Soviet government was very near to abandoning it.

> Gowon wants to tarnish the image of the Soviet Union in Africa by dragging it into a foreign war . . . There is no basis for meaningful association between the progressive socialist government of the Soviet Union and the reactionary clique of renegades in power in Lagos. Gowon only wants to make a mockery of the progressive foreign policy of Moscow by dragging the Soviet government into a scandalous marriage of convenience with Nigeria.[129]

Behind the scenes, however, the Soviet Union moved cautiously to secure its interests in Lagos. In the third week after Biafran secession, Ogbu arrived in Moscow, ostensibly to inspect the Nigerian mission but more likely to solicit possible Soviet aid in building up the federal government's military, particularly air, capability. At the moment, Gowon's emissaries were beseeching a number of governments to supply Nigeria's forces with aircraft and other "offensive" weaponry but, with the exception of Moscow, to little avail. Early in July the British formally rejected Gowon's request for aircraft. On July 29 Ogbu returned to Moscow, where he was joined by Chief Enahoro, and though all sides protested that the visit was only to sign the cultural agreement arranged in Lagos in March, they were in fact negotiating the sale of Soviet and Czech aircraft. In mid-August Soviet MiG 17s and Czech L-29 Delphin trainers began arriving in Kano airport, together with Soviet technicians to assemble, test, and later maintain them.[130]

129. Enugu radio, July 30, 1967, quoted in Arthur Jay Klinghoffer, "Why the Soviets Chose Sides," *Africa Report,* XIII (February 1968), 48.

130. The deal was, as Chief Enahoro announced on August 26, "on a strictly commercial and cash basis" and covered the price of from fifteen to twenty MiG 17s and a half dozen L-29 Delphins. The number of Soviet technicians was something under two hundred, and most of them left after assembling the aircraft. The MiGs were flown primarily by Egyptian pilots. Later other Soviet equipment arrived, including three patrol boats. The arms deal was reported by a number of sources. See Benjamin Welles, in *New York Times,* August 22, 1967, p. 7; Alfred Friendly, in *New York Times,* August 27, 1967, p. 15; *Africa Report,* XII (October 1967), 54–55; "Arms for Lagos," *West Africa,* no. 2620 (August 19, 1967), p. 1093; "Nigeria War Diary," *West Africa,* no. 2621 (August 26, 1967), p. 1099; and Hugh Hanning, "Lessons from the Arms Race," *Africa Report,* XIII (February 1968), 45. The estimates vary, however, and I have used a range that seems to be a common denominator.

A few days before the federal government launched military action against secessionist Biafra, Tunji Otegbeye appealed for a peaceful resolution of this "burning national question."[131] He deplored the "very unfortunate trend" in opinion toward crushing the rebellion by force. Once war had begun, though, and particularly after the East had linked up with a bold offensive in the Midwest Region during the first part of August, Otegbeye's party completely shifted its position. An article in *Advance* late in August exhorted, "Total war! Total destruction must be the vow of the Nigerian army . . . Crush the vandal Ojukwu."[132] Later in the war, the NSWFP was to lose all of its mercy and press vigorously for an invasion of the shrunken Ibo heartland.[133] Presumably the Soviet attitude toward a military solution of the problem went through roughly similar stages. Whatever unspoken reservations existed before war began, once Soviet leaders had agreed to come to the aid of the federal regime late in July, the Soviet press never wavered in its support for the military effort. Well-timed backing in a number of areas reflected Moscow's increasingly serious attempt to win the favor of Nigeria's current (and future) leaders. In October, for example, Premier Kosygin sent Major-General Gowon a formal message assuring him of Soviet support for the "unity and territorial integrity of Nigeria."[134] Two weeks later Ambassador Romanov reaffirmed his government's readiness to aid Nigeria with its industrial development. It was at about this time that both the Americans and British were showing a reluctance to go ahead with new projects until the future of Nigeria became clearer, and the Nigerian press made excellent use of Romanov's reference to the long-standing aid offer and his willingness "to initiate action . . . as soon as the Federal Military Government is able to determine the projects to be financed."[135] In February 1968 R. K. Fedorinov, a counselor from the Soviet Foreign Ministry, told a press conference in Kaduna of his government's readiness to help suppress the rebellion—

131. Tunji Otegbeye, "Progressives of Nigeria Unite," *Advance,* July 2–8, 1967, p. 5.
132. Rilewa, "On with Total War," *Advance,* August 20–26, 1967, p. 5.
133. See *Advance,* August 11–17, 1968, p. 1.
134. *Le Monde,* October 18, 1967, p. 5; see also Lagos radio (in English to Europe), 07.00 GMT, October 17, 1967.
135. Press release, Federal Ministry of Information (Lagos), no. F 2480 (mimeo), November 2, 1967. Romanov had just been to see Commissioner for Trade and Industries Shettima Ali Monguno.

support repeated by Romanov during a two-day visit to the Midwest later the same month.[136] Thus when Western capitals had resisted selling arms to the federal government, the Soviet Union had promptly filled the void; when the United States and Great Britain had manifested reluctance to undertake new aid projects in Nigeria until the turmoil stopped, Soviet officials had pointedly assured the Nigerians that the Soviet Union stood ready to assist in any way possible. When others, such as the United States, had kept themselves aloof from the struggle, the Soviet Union had underscored its undivided commitment to the federal government.[137]

How strangely ironic that the Soviet Union should be allied with political leaders thought—at least initially—to belong to Nigeria's most reactionary forces and even now whose character remained ambiguous at best, allied against the people whom Soviet commentators had always considered the most progressive and sympathetic. For more than a decade Soviet leaders had looked upon the Easterner and his political organizations as the most hopeful among Nigerians, and the Northerner (admittedly an undifferentiated designation that almost invariably meant the "feudal" Hausa emirs) as the most retrograde. When now the Soviet government enlisted in the struggle against Biafra, it was hard to keep one's memory from returning to the early pre-independence comparison between Azikiwe's NCNC and Awolowo's Action Group (that party of "feudal, marionette princes of Yorubaland") or the "reactionary" Northern People's Congress; to the hopes Soviet leaders had placed on the NCNC's membership in the first coalition government; and when these were not fully met, to the faith they had preserved in the young malcontents within the party who demanded a more progressive direction. Of the four regions, the East had most consistently urged expanded contacts with the Soviet Union and East Europe, had most often expressed interest in Soviet aid, and in fact had unilaterally negotiated the first Soviet suppliers' credit *without* the federal govern-

136. See *New Nigerian* (Kaduna), February 9, 1968, and Benin radio (domestic service in English), 14.30 GMT, February 28, 1968.

137. At a press conference on August 26, 1967, Chief Enahoro said: "Friends who desert you in your hour of need deserve that much less friendship afterward . . . When you're in difficulties, those who come to your rescue naturally have a claim to your gratitude." See Friendly, in *New York Times*, August 27, 1967.

ment's approval.[138] If before July 29 the Soviet Union had preferred any region in the Federation, it was the East.

Soviet commentators could, of course, argue that the position of the East's leadership had changed fundamentally: that however much Ojukwu may have been the spiritual heir of Azikiwe, Okpara, and Ironsi, his purpose was basically different. Though perhaps understandable, the East's decision to secede broke a long-held commitment to the Federation and Soviet commentators had never approved separatist tendencies in Nigeria. At the same time they could argue, as many others did, that after two military coups Northern power had been seriously damaged and Northern political society transformed. A number of non-Soviet foreign observers took the position that the division of the North and the ascendance of the minority tribes had deprived the emirs of their former authority in the region.[139] Kudryavtsev picked up this argument in November to debunk the idea that the East was "allegedly combating the dominance of the feudal North."[140] This was nonsense, he said, because "socially, the North is heterogeneous, and numerically the feudal elements constitute an insignificant stratum there."

> The national-liberation movement in the North of the country, as elsewhere, has given rise to progressive forces that favor a unified Nigeria whose policy will take into account the specific features of each nationality, not for the sake of their separation, but with the aim of the gradual liquidation of tribalism in the interests of strengthening the independence of all Nigeria.

But Kudryavtsev wrote this in November when the argument was easier to make and long after the Soviet Union had decided to aid the federal government. In August no Soviet writer justified his government's choice

138. During a November 1965 visit to Nigeria, N. S. Khmelev, vice-president of Moscow University's medical school, referred to an agreement between his government and the government of *Eastern Nigeria* to build a medical school in that region. This was the Enugu teaching hospital on which the Soviet Union was still negotiating in May 1967. See press release, Federal Ministry of Information (Lagos), no. F 2012 (mimeo), November 5, 1965.

139. See Colin Legum, in *The Observer*, August 13, 1967, p. 2; "Keeping Nigeria One," *West Africa*, no. 2611 (June 17, 1967), pp. 1–2; and a three-part study, "Creating the States," *West Africa*, no. 2635 (December 2, 1967), p. 1537, and subsequent issues.

140. V. Kudryavtsev, in *Izvestiya*, November 17, 1967, p. 2, trans. in *Current Digest of the Soviet Press*, XIX (December 6, 1967), 17.

in these terms. At the time they could only suspect that the Northern political structure was changing.

Other, more practical considerations provided better reason for supporting the federal government. First, like many other observers, the Russians concluded that the war would be over quickly and this time they wanted to be on a winning side. Early reports emphasizing the easy, swift victories of federal troops reflected this confidence, as did the attention given Enahoro's prediction in August that the war would end within three months.[141] Second, the reluctance of the United States and Great Britain to supply the Federal Military Government with the arms it sought gave the Soviet Union an irresistible opportunity to improve its position in Lagos. Third, Soviet leaders probably believed quite genuinely that Western, particularly American, influence would grow in a break-away Biafra. From the earliest discussion of Eastern secession, Soviet writers had attributed the primary impetus for the dissolution of the Federation to American and British oil interests.[142] Finally, Soviet leaders were no doubt keenly aware that most African leaders condemned Biafran secession and would be critical of any great power which lent it support.

Nigeria, of course, was one of sub-Saharan Africa's most important states, and the unsettled condition of its politics encouraged the Soviet Union to devote special efforts toward strengthening its position there. But Soviet policy was based on more than Nigeria's uncertain political future. The chance always existed that, if the military government were to step down or fly apart, its successor might be radically different; but for the moment Soviet leaders were presumably more impressed by the increasing influence of Nigeria's most progressive leaders in the *present* regime. A few days after Biafran secession, the military leadership added a number of civilians to the federal executive council, several of whom were assumed to be more sympathetic to the Soviet Union than their predecessors.[143] Awolowo was named vice-chairman of the new cabinet and commissioner of finance; his close ally in the old Action

---

141. *Izvestiya,* August 23, 1967, p. 2. Enahoro's comment was reported in "Enahoro: Encore trois mois de guerre," *Jeune Afrique,* no. 346 (August 27, 1967), p. 11.

142. Almost every article that raised the issue made this point, but see particularly Victor Sidenko, "Oil War in Nigeria," *New Times,* no. 11 (March 15, 1967), pp. 20–21.

143. Korovikov, in *Pravda,* June 15, 1967, in this otherwise noncommittal article made special mention of this change.

Group, Anthony Enahoro, became commissioner of information and labor; Joseph Tarka, the leader of the UMBC and another of Awolowo's allies, assumed control over the transportation ministry; the head of the NEPU, Alhaji Aminu Kano, was given communications, and his fellow NEPU leader, Femi Okunnu, works and housing; finally the new commissioner of education, Wenike Briggs, a non-Ibo Easterner, was like the rest, a man who appealed to the Soviet Union. All of these leaders maintained more or less "advanced" views; all could be expected to support a more genuinely nonaligned policy and greater contact with the Soviet Union. Indeed, a few months later, Okunnu "expressed the hope that the relations between Nigeria and the Soviet Union which had considerably improved within the past four to five months would generate into something bigger to the mutual benefit of both countries."[144] During the same press conference he appealed to Ambassador Romanov to use his "good offices to secure Russian aid" for the reconstruction of war-damaged bridges and roads. Almost simultaneously, Kano, speaking in the North, indicated a readiness to bid for Soviet assistance in developing Nigeria's communication programs.[145] In December, Briggs opened a Soviet book exhibit in Lagos by commenting that "the present interest by the Soviet people in Nigeria had placed them further ahead than any other country of the world."[146]

Many of these leaders were close to the leadership of the radical Nigerian Trade Union Congress, and often took part in its activity. The NTUC, in turn, was closely affiliated with the NSWFP; it shared much of the same leadership and, at least in theory, a good deal of the same funding; by this route Tunji Otegbeye, the Soviet Union's most conspicuous Nigerian contact, gained his entry into the highest political circles. No one pretended that Otegbeye, a prosperous medical doctor with a growing number of offices in the Lagos area, was himself a major political figure, but he was no doubt an important, if somewhat dubious, source of information for the Soviet Union. In terms of influence Soviet leaders were probably more impressed with the new role the regime has assigned to Samuel Grace Ikoku, Nkrumah's bright and militant confidant. Ikoku had been under arrest since his expulsion from Ghana

144. See press release, Federal Ministry of Information (Lagos) no. F 2542 (mimeo), November 10, 1967, and Lagos (international service in English), 21.00 GMT, November 11, 1967.

145. See *Advance,* November 12–18, 1967, p. 1.

146. Press release, Federal Ministry of Information (Lagos), no. F 2826 (mimeo), December 16, 1967.

in 1966, but after his release late in 1967 this talented, ambitious young Ibo, another of Awolowo's alleged collaborators in the 1963 conspiracy trial and an avowed Marxist, soon found special, though unpublic, responsibilities, including an occasional mission abroad.[147] Soviet officials were not so foolish as to believe that these men were the only ones who counted in Lagos or, even to the extent of their importance, that they intended to be the Soviet Union's friends exclusively. Nevertheless, the more their influence grew—and given the chaotic and decentralized state of Nigeria's political leadership, who could say what the limits to their influence would be?—the more Nigeria's domestic and external orientation was likely to shift. It was not pure naiveté that prompted Soviet interest in Otegbeye's call for a "united front of progressives" coming from the banned Nigerian Youth Congress, NEPU, UMBC, Action Group, and NCNC.[148]

Soviet leaders no doubt found their involvement on the side of the federal forces easier because people like Kano, Tarka, and Okunnu were in the government; but it would be carrying the point too far to assume that their presence was decisive. The Soviet leadership responded to more pragmatic considerations, such as the effect the civil war would have on its relations with other African countries, the advantages Western nations would obtain in an independent Biafra, and the opportunity created for Soviet policy by the Anglo-American refusal to give the federal government every source of support. As long as the regime was willing to deal with the Soviet Union, its general character remained a secondary issue. This, then, is the crucial implication of the commitment: the federal government captured the Soviet interest because it controlled one of Black Africa's most important countries, not because it was one of Black Africa's most progressive regimes. In Africa, the Soviet Union was beginning to focus attention on key countries *irrespective* of regime. Before, the Russians had concentrated on the progressive states of Africa because they believed revolutionary forces to be sweeping the continent. Later when these revolutionary forces turned out to be weaker than anticipated, the Soviet leadership made peace with less progressive regimes and intensified its involvement with a wider range of countries. Now again Soviet leaders were restricting the scope of their African policy. Quite unlike the earlier experience, however, and precisely because of the failure

147. Interviews in Lagos, August 1968.
148. Otegbeye, "Progressives of Nigeria Unite," p. 5. In interviews in August 1968, Soviet diplomats in Lagos raised the possibility.

of revolutionary democracy (the surrogate for the unrealized spontaneous revolutionary process), Soviet policy chose to emphasize states more because of their intrinsic importance than because of their revolutionary merit. On a continent of diminishing significance, where revolution remained too improbable to be worth pursuing for its own value, the Soviet stake shrank to only the larger and more vital countries. Nigeria came closest to representing the India of a large portion of Black Africa. And, as in India's case a dozen years earlier, the Soviet Union's willingness to contribute significantly to its economic development reflected the evolution of policy. In November 1968 the Nigerian government announced that the Soviet Union had agreed to extend a $140 million credit, primarily to build the iron and steel project (as in India) under study by Soviet experts since February 1967.[149] While the status of this offer was subsequently clouded, it would be a striking measure of the change in Soviet policy toward Black Africa if the first "Aswan Dam" below the Sahara were to be constructed in Nigeria, and not in one of the few remaining revolutionary democracies.[150]

149. See Alfred Friendly, in *New York Times,* November 22, 1968, p. 1.
150. The agreement was obviously negotiated before the fall of Keita's revolutionary democratic regime.

IX

Conclusion

More than a decade has passed since the Soviet Union launched itself into the affairs of Africa, time enough to reveal a distinct evolution in perceptions of this continent and of the opportunity it offers Soviet policy. One of the clearest reflections of this evolution is the contrast between the objectives of contemporary Soviet policy in West Africa and those formed at the outset. No outsider, of course, can know with certainty precisely what ends the Soviet Union pursues in any country, whether Nigeria or the United States, but they are not so obscure as to be beyond conjecture. By cautiously extrapolating from the commentary contained in the Soviet press as well as from the specific actions of Soviet leaders, it is possible to reconstruct tentatively the goals that Soviet policy was originally designed to achieve.

It does not oversimplify the difference between Soviet goals at either end of this ten-year period to say that the thoroughgoing optimism once motivating Soviet ambitions had disappeared by late 1967. When, in 1958, the Soviet Union opened an ambitious diplomatic and economic offensive in Guinea, it acted out of the conviction that events there heavily favored Soviet interests. Even if Guinea were not soon to become a Communist state or an extension of the socialist camp, the anti-Western orientation of its foreign policy and the radical course of its internal development strengthened what Soviet writers began calling "the world revolutionary process." In terms of strategy, the phrase referred to a triple alliance of the socialist countries, the proletariat of the developed capitalist nations, and progressive elements within the Third World. It was based on the assumption that the emerging countries were rejecting the capitalist alternative and following another, more progressive path of development; that they had been profoundly alienated from the West and now felt seriously imperiled by the forces of neocolonialism; and that increasingly they would close ranks with the socialist countries. For the moment it mattered little that these countries were not Communist. They promised to reinforce the interest of Soviet policy and, equally important, to damage the influence of Western powers in this new promising arena of East-West competition. The search for other bellwethers like Guinea became the primary objective of Soviet policy.

Although it has been beyond the scope of this study, the first opportunity the Soviet Union found to extend its strategy to another part of Africa occurred in 1960 in the Congo. Here, in far more fluid circumstances than Guinea, the Soviet Union discovered another attractive revolutionary candidate in Patrice Lumumba, the premier of the new Congolese government. Quite likely, even had the Katanga secession not taken place, Soviet leaders would have been drawn to the Lumumba government as a leadership willing to develop extensive ties with socialist countries. As it was, they responded unhesitatingly to Lumumba's request for assistance. The transport lorries and Ilyushin aircraft they gave him had less to do with a Communist attempt to "take over" the Congo than with an effort to build relations with a government that the Soviet Union hoped to influence in the future.

There was however, more to Soviet optimism than the confidence that the process of decolonization was yielding new governments hostile to Western Europe and its American ally, inclined to support many aspects of Soviet policy and, as a result, governments subject to Soviet influence. The notion that the Soviet Union could supplant predominant Western influence in sub-Saharan Africa, in retrospect, appears also to have depended on the more fundamental, though inexplicit, belief that the African revolution portended the early arrival of the socialist revolution. Rather than interpret the anti-Western fulminations of Africa's angry young leaders as the product of exaggerated nationalism, Soviet observers seemingly took them at face value; that is, as reliable evidence that these leaders had fully rejected capitalism. Their emphatic repudiation of capitalism, combined with the pressures of modernization and the rudimentary development of entrenched classes, evidently convinced the Soviet leadership that Africa represented unusually propitious soil for socialism. This is not to say that in these first years the Soviet Union accepted the definition of socialism provided by African leaders. It was simply that many factors seemed to them to create *objectively* favorable conditions for the emergence of genuine socialism.

If this optimism stemmed not simply from a momentarily hopeful shift of events but from the conviction that the long-term momentum of events favored the Soviet Union, then current policy had a double dimension: first, it was intended to achieve immediate, specific objectives—perhaps to rally support against a Western action threatening Soviet interests in the Middle East (Lebanon, 1958), for a Soviet initiative in Europe (Berlin, 1961), or for measures calculated to undermine the Western position in Africa (Congo, 1960–61). Second, however, Soviet policymakers had to consider broader consequences. Foreign policy, in theory, is supposed to be framed in accord with a country's anticipated interests over time, but in practice it seldom pays much attention to carefully structured distant goals. If it is true that Soviet policy possessed a longer-term perspective, this may have been due less to the superiority of Soviet planning than to a belief that the future had suddenly come into view. To illustrate, Soviet leaders in their economic offensive could not separate the short-term desire to reward a visiting African chief of state who supported the general Soviet position on important international issues (or to generate the good will conducive to such support) from the long-run imperative of reinforcing a natural drift toward socialism. A fish-processing complex in Ghana or a cement factory in Guinea must have been considered not only a means for building stronger friendships but as a measure to expand the state sector and speed the transition to socialism. Nonproductive aid projects, such as a hotel in Conakry and a sports complex in Bamako (in any case there were many fewer than frequently assumed), were intended to ingratiate Soviet leaders with African governments, not merely to secure momentary favors but permanent influence. As a result of Soviet optimism, long-range considerations intruded more than they might otherwise have on the daily task of policy formation.

The United States also allocated aid for the purpose of investing in the future development of West African countries. But to judge from the spirit of the times, it felt pressed to do so primarily because of the "Communist challenge," seen as an ambitious program to subvert the independence of these new nations. American leaders may not have been so convinced as their Soviet counterparts that natural forces in several West African countries (Guinea, Ghana, and Mali) were moving inexorably away from capitalism. They had, however, persuaded themselves that many of these countries remained vulnerable to Communist intrigue. States already judged too close to the Communist position were denied aid (as in the case of Guinea before 1961), or aid that had been promised encountered serious obstacles in implementation (as in the case of the Volta project in Ghana, 1960–61). American pessimism just as surely as Soviet optimism—aroused by the same concern, the apparent success of the Soviet Union in West Africa—distorted the foreign policies of both nations. The expected flowering of Soviet-African relations imposed itself constantly on early Soviet policy; and the inability of the United States to judge its long-term interests in West Africa except in relation to the Soviet Union dominated American policy. Both operational codes were faulty. Certainly developments in West Africa, whether in radical or moderate states, warranted neither the Soviet Union's preoccupation with questionable expectations nor the United States' failure to assesss thoroughly its larger interests.

If this emphasis on the early preoccupation of Soviet leaders with Africa's revolutionary potential appears to contradict a persistent theme of this book—that from the very beginning the Soviet Union has generally sacrificed considerations of the socialist revolution in Africa to the immediate interests of Soviet foreign policy—the contradiction is more apparent than real. To say that Soviet perceptions were, at the outset, heavily colored by revolutionary expectations is not of course equivalent to saying that an overriding priority of early Soviet policy was promoting the socialist revolution. When support for a socialist transformation suited the immediate objectives of foreign policy, then the support came easily. When pressing for socialist reform jeopardized the short-term interests of Soviet foreign policy, Soviet leaders refused to make the effort. Nevertheless, from 1959 to 1962 the anticipation that conditions in several West African countries favored progress toward socialism had a direct bearing on short-term policy formation. Thus the Soviet Union undertook a sizable economic offensive in Guinea, joined Ghana, Guinea, and Mali in assailing the developmental pattern of less revolutionary countries, and urged on the most radical states stilted Marxian prescriptions for their further development.

By 1968 the Soviet Union had long since been disabused of its revolutionary vision of Africa. Beginning with the murder of Lumumba and culminating in the downfall of Nkrumah, the African reality heavily imposed itself on the minds of Soviet policymakers. Policy was no longer shaped by the happy conviction that developments in Africa favored Soviet interests and ultimately the emergence of socialism. Africa's advance to socialism, once considered a relatively straight-line course, now appeared strewn with hazards and marked by retreats. As the revolutionary sequence was elongated and Soviet expectations moderated, long-range considerations played less a part in determining Soviet policy; the anticipation of easy, far-reaching gains ceased to condition short-term policy formulation.

To a large extent, the decline of revolutionary potentialities in Guinea, Ghana, and Mali altered a major commitment of Soviet policy. When it became apparent that these countries did not necessarily represent the vanguard of the African revolution or, when they did, that their development did not necessarily correspond to Soviet aspirations, much of the compulsion for treating them specially disappeared. Africa in general, rather than particular countries, became the focus of Soviet policy; differentiation in the Soviet approach now represented less of a response to fundamental differences among African states than an acknowledgment that diversity in Africa persisted. The Soviet Union, of course, still preferred certain West African countries to others, but these preferences no longer constituted the vital consideration for Soviet policy in this area. It was not so much that contrasts in internal and external conditions and politics among West African states had diminished, but that Soviet leaders were more inclined to see these contrasts as marginal and, for the first time, as secondary to common characteristics that made variations in the intractability of African politics only a matter of degree. So, little reason existed for preserving a highly differentiated African policy and even less for making a heavy commitment to the revolutionary development of particular West African countries. On the other hand, shifting priorities and the residual need to stabilize their position in Africa prompted Soviet leaders to increase contacts with a wide stratum of African states and to put these contacts on a distinctly moderate basis. Still later, after the obvious failure of Africa's revolutionary democrats and the equally obvious loss of interest on the part of Soviet leaders in most of Black Africa, Soviet policy began to restrict its attention to inherently important countries, without worrying about the character of any given regime.

Two other contrasts between early and recent Soviet objectives also need to be mentioned. Whether the question was one of cooperating with a state whose economic and social structure exemplified reaction but whose international behavior roughly paralleled Soviet interests (Ethiopia) or one of sacrificing fraternal allies (PAI) to strengthen relations with a moderate government (Senegal), Soviet policymakers maintained a constant commitment to the immediate requirements of foreign policy. If this scheme of priorities changed between 1958 and 1968, it was only to stress further the pre-eminence of short-run policy interests. Diminished expectations of a major social and economic transformation in West Africa, the shift in focus from sub-Sahara to North Africa, the Middle East, and Latin America, and the concentration on domestic priorities, all guaranteed that more than ever Soviet African policy would be geared toward reinforcing immediate interests. For the same reasons, however, West Africa mattered less in the support it gave Soviet policy—particularly when by 1968 Soviet policymakers could expect considerable sympathy from a wide range of countries in other parts of the world. On major international issues, such as Vietnam, a European settlement, the Kashmir dispute, and the Middle East, support for the Soviet position came from a variety of quarters, not least of which was West Europe. No longer did Soviet policymakers confront the necessity of rallying African spokesmen among the nonaligned nations (as it had in 1961 at Belgrade) or earlier within the United Nations (1960–61, over the Congo crisis).

In the same way, whatever impetus the Chinese challenge to Soviet world revolutionary leadership may have originally provided for the Soviet entrance into West Africa, this, after 1965, largely disappeared. Strong as the attraction of West Africa may have been for Soviet policy in 1958–59, the opportunity was taken, in part, because of China's unmistakable intention to replace the Soviet Union as the mentor of these nations, indeed, of the entire Afro-Asian national liberation movement. Soviet leaders responded to the challenge for two reasons. First, the ascendance of a disaffected China within the national liberation movement not only threatened the traditional Soviet role as the center of the world's revolutionary forces, but it also strengthened tendencies toward polycentrism within the socialist camp. Second, they responded to the challenge because it seemed well founded: Africa appeared susceptible to the revolutionary exhortations of the Chinese.

By 1966, however, the challenge was no longer plausible, at least not in West Africa. Chinese foreign policy in India, Vietnam, Indonesia, and Algeria, as well as Chinese activity within the Afro-Asian solidarity movement, had been effectively repudiated by the most revolutionary and anti-imperialist regimes. Even among Marxist-Leninist parties those factions that split from the PAI and NSWFP, overtly to defend the principles of the Chinese revolution, very quickly expired.[1] After the Chinese leadership launched its cultural revolution in 1966, the effects of Peking's policy, if detectable at all, had become unproductive. Most African leaderships were repelled by developments within China and frightened by their external implications. Early in 1967 the New China News Agency complained that "modern revisionists and imperialists and reactionaries of all countries" were "falsely accusing China of 'exporting' the cultural revolution, engaging in 'subversive activities,' wanting to purify the revolution of Africa."[2] After reaffirming China's adherence to its "five principles" of noninterference, the NCNA continued, "it is up to the people of the countries concerned to organize themselves to wage revolutionary struggles." African leaders, however, were not reassured and when, in May 1968, following major disturbances in his capital, Senghor needed

1. Some time in the spring of 1965 a group of malcontents from the PAI under the leadership of Samba N'Diaye, a teacher in the Kaolack lycée, formed the Parti Communiste Sénégalais (PCS). The avowed purpose of the new party was to "struggle against deviations . . . to denounce and combat openly modern revisionism which at the moment constitutes the principal danger menacing the International Communist movement." *Manifeste du Parti Communiste Sénégalais,* May 1, 1965 (typed copy). The PCS never got off the ground. In Nigeria in the previous August the trade-union leader Michael Imoudu announced the creation of the Nigerian Labour Party (NLP) or Marxist-Leninist Party of All Nigerian Toilers. "Nigerian Left's Dissensions," *African Review* (October 1964), pp. 16–18. The precise reasons for this group's formation are difficult to disentangle but it appears that Imoudu, defeated earlier in a power struggle within the Nigerian Trade Union Congress, was challenging the NSWFP, a party patronized by the NTUC leadership. Imoudu attacked the NSWFP as being bourgeois and contended that only the NLP preserved the principles of scientific socialism. Since the NSWFP clearly enjoyed the support of the Soviet Union, the NLP inevitably assumed positions contrary to the Soviet line. Moreover, one of the NLP's allies, the inactive Nigerian Communist Party, had long maintained its adherence to the Chinese view. Origins and orientations notwithstanding, the NLP, like the PCS, never really was able to establish itself as a viable party.

2. Responding to articles in the *Daily Nation* (Kenya), March 13, 1967, and the *East African Standard,* March 14, 1967, in Peking NCNA (international service in English), 15.16 GMT March 23, 1967.

a scapegoat, the Chinese were obvious candidates. After blaming Chinese sympathizers (and exempting the Soviet Union) for his troubles, the Senegalese president expelled the only Communist Chinese ever allowed to reside in his country, four representatives of the NCNA.[3] Even China's oldest African friends reacted impatiently to some of the more bizarre manifestations of the cultural revolution. In November 1966, a thirty-four-member delegation led by one Wan Tao-han turned up in Mali and at once began a comprehensive purge of the Chinese mission.[4] It departed in January with Ambassador Ma Tse-ching in tow, leaving a military officer, Lieutenant-Colonel Liu Ho-lin, as chargé. Liu promptly proved his revolutionary mettle by publicly abusing the Soviet ambassador at the dedication of a North Korean aid project. Modibo Keita had gone to some lengths to persuade Cameroun President Ahmadou Ahidjo, his guest at the time, to accompany him (Cameroun did not recognize North Korea), and the startled Malian president was visibly displeased at the outburst. Within the Afro-Asian People's Solidarity Organization, China's prestige had declined so seriously that when its representatives walked out of the Nicosia council meeting in February 1967, following a decision to change the site of the Fifth A-APSO Conference from Peking to Algiers, the only African delegates to join them were from the South West African National Union, the Bechuanaland People's Party, the Basutoland Congress Party, the Swaziland Progressive Party, and the Pan-African Congress of Azania.[5]

Thus circumstances influencing Soviet policy toward West Africa changed considerably in the course of a decade. By 1968 no longer did the energizing optimism that characterized the Soviet debut in Guinea remain a factor in Soviet perceptions; no longer did Soviet foreign policy depend in any significant way on the alignment of West African states; and no longer did the challenge thrown down by the Chinese seriously threaten what interests the Soviet Union retained in this area.

Though it is true that Soviet policy in Africa primarily depends on short-term considerations, ultimately this area diminished in importance because its internal revolution faltered. However much Soviet leaders act according to the immediate requirements of policy, at some point

3. See "The Whale and the Minnows?" *West Africa*, no. 2671 (August 10, 1968), p. 915; also, Senghor's speech to the nation reported in *Dakar-Matin*, June 1, 1968, p. 4.

4. Interviews in Bamako, August 1968.

5. "China: A Revolution for Export," *Mizan*, IX (March–April 1967), 84.

they must confront the general question of the socialist revolution in Africa. Constantly Soviet analysts have had to take stock of the prospects for socialism's advance on what has been, theoretically, one of the important fronts of the national liberation struggle. To a Soviet theorist assessing circumstances that favor or impede a smooth transition to socialism, the vital issue is inevitably the role assumed by the working class. Traditionally, it has been assumed that in order to achieve socialism the working class (or those who speak for the working class) must occupy a "leading role" in the decision-making structures of the political system. In Africa, with no working class to speak of, the Soviet theorist's essential problem has been to predict progress toward socialism without the immediate emergence of an aroused and organized proletariat. How he has worked his way around the weakness of the African working class provides the most meaningful framework for analyzing the evolution of Soviet expectations for the rapid social and political transformation of West African nations.

From the beginning of the Soviet involvement in this part of Black Africa, the lack of a true working class prevented Soviet leaders from encouraging the formation of local Communist parties.[6] The weakness

6. I have been unable to find any evidence in West Africa for the conclusion drawn by Richard Lowenthal and Alexander Dallin that in different periods Soviet policy was intent on promoting the formation of local Communist parties. Lowenthal has argued that from 1959 to 1961 the Soviet Union stimulated the organization of local Communist parties in sub-Saharan Africa in order to apply direct pressure on national bourgeois leaders. He repeats the argument most recently in his "Russia, the One-Party System and the Third World," *Survey*, no. 58 (January 1966), p. 45. Dallin arrives at a similar conclusion but for another period, 1962–63, in "Soviet Political Activity," Brzezinski, ed., *Africa and the Communist World*, pp. 40–41. In both cases the evidence assembled is sparse and, in the instance of one West African country, doubtful. Lowenthal's assertion that the Soviet Union had sought to create a Communist organization of sorts in Guinea in the fall of 1961 is a misreading of activity, which at the most represented indiscriminate meddling by Soviet representatives intended only to influence the course of events surrounding the teacher-student strike, not to build up structures that would challenge Touré's leadership and own party. The only two parties in West Africa with a Marxist-Leninist orientation (the PAI and the NSWFP) emerged either before or after the phases during which it was allegedly Soviet policy to encourage their formation, and in both cases they appeared with post-facto Soviet support, not upon Soviet instigation. Also, during the period 1959–1961, and particularly 1962–63, attempts to create new Communist parties would have run directly counter to the objectives of Soviet policy. For this reason, Soviet spokesmen apparently discouraged the organization of formal Communist parties in countries such as Ghana. (See Chapter Two.)

of the working class denied indigenous Communist parties the necessary basis for organization, and because the working class remained undeveloped, the Soviet Union had no alternative but to address its policies to the "national bourgeoisie." To complete the circle, because the Soviet Union sought to influence the bourgeoisie, it dared not antagonize this group by simultaneously sponsoring the formation of local Communist parties. In other areas where the prospects of local Communists seemed better, perhaps where Communist parties had already appeared, Soviet leaders could justify both enterprises, acting as the benefactor of Communist cadres while dealing with the national bourgeoisie. It was for these other areas—Algeria, the UAR, India, Indonesia—that the theory of "national democracy" was most suited. The concept had been designed primarily to extend the compromise between local Communist parties and the national bourgeoisie into the post-independence period. In West Africa, except as an aspiration, such a compromise bore no resemblance to reality. Applied to West Africa, the theory of national democracy became a rationalization for developing strong ties with nationalist bourgeois regimes, unguarded by the presence of a local Communist organization.

Still Soviet analysts felt constrained to fit West Africa into the old formulas as best they could. Thus West Africa had to be portrayed as undergoing basic transformations that conformed to conventional notions about class structure and conflict. In 1960 a combined lack of sophistication about the nature of African society and a first flush of excitement prompted Soviet commentators to present tropical Africa as an area where "new social forces," (working class, national bourgeoisie, and intelligentsia) were surging forth, pushing aside traditional, tribal structures. Admittedly the working class was small, without cohesion, and held back by the large number of part-time laborers who returned frequently to their life in the village. Similarly it was recognized that the bourgeoisie had been stunted by the overshadowing presence of expatriate capitalists. But the mere fact that Soviet writers marched these symbols to and fro, shadows of an imaginary reality—discussing the sharpening clash of economic classes, calculating the large increment to a minuscule proletariat—revealed the major adjustment they had yet to make. Ten years later Soviet theorists worried less about contriving a conventional Marxian class analysis as a basis for their studies of sub-Saharan Africa. It is worth repeating Alexander Sobolev's comments at the Cairo Seminar: "Significant features of class relations in the

African countries are extreme immobility of the social processes, slow rate of social differentiation, absence of clearly defined class boundaries, numerous transitional social groups, uneven development of these groups and their interpenetration."[7] Not only was this assessment very similar to one that a Western Africanist might have made, it could very well have served as the retort to Soviet descriptions of African class structures ten years earlier.

The language of ideology notwithstanding, the main issue of these early years centered on the reconciliation between the Soviet Union and national bourgeois leaders. The idea of reconciliation should convey more than a sense of tactical compromise, that practice of cultivating a momentarily friendly atmosphere in order to advance current Soviet interests; it refers to the far more fundamental process by which Soviet leaders arrived at an understanding of the *nature* of their relationship with these new nonproletarian nationalists. As the evolution of Soviet experience in Africa would have it, this relationship was to become more than the primary focus of Soviet policy; it was to become the primary object, the factor determining Soviet hopes for socialism in sub-Saharan Africa. The relationship between the Soviet government and national bourgeois leaders, no mere alliance with the more "revolutionary" workers and peasants, constituted the very essence of the Soviet involvement in Africa.

Initially the Russians' attitude toward West Africa's revolutionary nationalists was one of reserved optimism. Their optimism stemmed largely from the faith Soviet leaders placed in the forces engulfing African politics during the early phases of independence; such forces would provide basic stimulation for the progressive behavior of the national bourgeoisie and would act as a constraint should the bourgeoisie waver. The dynamics of the national liberation struggle, as viewed by Soviet policymakers between 1958 and 1961, warranted a substantial psychological as well as economic and political commitment on the part of the Soviet Union, and the only feasible channel through which this commitment could be made was the national bourgeois leadership of these young states.

At the same time, Soviet optimism was tempered by a natural mistrust of this group. Only a few years earlier Soviet analysts had argued that it represented an unreliable, indeed treacherous, political force, and it

7. Alexander Sobolev, "Some Problems of Social Progress," *World Marxist Review*, X (January 1967), 10.

seems unlikely that Soviet leaders, simply because their assessment of external political factors had changed, now placed full confidence in the attitudes and intentions of national bourgeois leaders such as Touré, Nkrumah, and Keita. The Soviet Union's strong distaste for all forms of African socialism, including theirs, served as a reminder of its previous views. As their ideology, the socialism of these bourgeois nationalists embodied the subjective factor conditioning their political behavior. When the Soviet Union condemned African socialism (implicitly in the case of radical leaders), it was simultaneously rejecting their system of values, thereby circumscribing the Soviet commitment to the revolution they proclaimed.

Eventually under the pressure of setbacks in Guinea, the Congo, and within the Afro-Asian movement, the Soviet Union found it difficult to sustain the same confidence in the natural momentum of events. The dynamics of the struggle for independence were not, it turned out, independent of the will of those who led the struggle. By 1962 Soviet leaders could see that, if Africa was to move forward toward political and economic revolution, the transition would have to be carefully guided. That is, natural processes would not lead to socialism without considerable direction from some internal group. Obviously the only one sufficiently cohesive and influential to exert leadership in West Africa was the national bourgeoisie, but the question remained whether the national bourgeoisie could be persuaded to lead in the proper direction. If not, then the Soviet leadership had to convince itself that the national bourgeoisie already represented a dependable mechanism for transforming society.

To judge from the evolution of Soviet theoretical comment, during 1963 and 1964 Soviet leaders satisfied themselves that certain representatives of the national bourgeoisie, the revolutionary democrats, could indeed be trusted to bring their societies the entire distance to socialism. They conceded, in effect, that several regimes, such as those in Ghana and Mali, knew the way to socialism and had already adopted programs carrying them toward this goal. Khrushchev and his intellectual allies had dreamed up the possibility that these countries would "build socialism" without the emergence of a Communist party or, at least, until the time a Communist party did emerge. To accept this prospect, however, Soviet leaders first had to embrace the values of the revolutionary democrats. Specifically they had to accept the brand of socialism advocated by Nkrumah and Keita as the genuine thing. This kind of ideological sanction Khrushchev extended to Ghana and Mali in 1964, and to give theory a measure of life he set about reinforcing the institutional link between the leading force in Soviet politics (the CPSU) and the leading force in these two countries (their single-party systems). Fraternal party relations were established; party representatives expanded their participation in the congresses of the other; and a steady exchange of party delegations took place. The Soviet Union developed a particular interest in cadre education within these African parties, encouraging party leaders to study the techniques of party organization and agitation perfected by the CPSU and to avail themselves of Soviet assistance in constructing and operating their own higher party schools.

The shift in the way Soviet leaders envisioned Africa's transition to socialism was fundamental. They, principally Khrushchev and the liberals within the Institute of World Economics and International Relations, substituted faith in subjective forces—until then regarded as a potential obstacle to socialist transformation—for their previous conviction that objective conditions favored the advent of socialism.

Certain events of 1965 and 1966 proved to Khrushchev's successors that the second assumption was no more realistic than the first. The erratic development of African politics, and particularly the coups d'état in Algeria and Ghana, convinced Soviet leaders—who, in any case, had doubted the justification for Khrushchev's actions while he still ruled—that neither the natural evolution of events nor the leadership of the revolutionary democrats portended an imminent progression toward socialism. Once again the assumptions of Soviet African policy were to change. Policy became less optimistic on both counts and was modified to reflect considerably restrained expectations. No longer could Soviet commentators sustain their uncomplicated, though imaginative, approach to the tasks facing Africa's vanguard states. Nkrumah's failure, in particular, underscored the absurdity of endorsing the ill-fitting application of Marxism-Leninism in the African milieu. If something was to be salvaged from the dreams of Africa's revolutionary leaders, both the Africans and the Russians would have to stop deceiving themselves with foolish assumptions about the success of revolutionary parties with their revolutionary programs. When it seemed that Soviet analysts had come back by 1968 to urging orthodox solutions, in fact they were only saying that at last African revolutionaries must see, this time they must really see, how indispensable it is to create a healthy, well-disciplined, dedicated party, to purify ideology, to make a full commitment to destroying the old society, and to fight consistently and patiently for socialist development. They were done with letting these leaders think that their Soviet friends took them at their word. But, at the same time, when Soviet analysts wrote of the need to transform the single party into a genuine vanguard party adhering to a purer form of scientific socialism, they kept sharply in mind the enormous impediments to basic change and the compromise that had to be made with reality. Swift and wholesale reform, however laudable, could destroy its authors, thereby undermining further reform and maybe even turning the society over to reactionary elements. There was, above all else, nothing sanctimonious about the neo-orthodoxy; its essence was the demand that Africa's revolutionaries make a serious and thorough commitment to their socialist aspirations. (The Soviet Union, of course, still retained the right to evaluate the quality of their socialism.)

But since Soviet leaders now doubted that Black Africa's revolutionaries were capable of making this kind of commitment, they found it difficult to sustain a major interest in the area. Midnight had struck and revolutionary democrats were again bourgeois nationalists, petty-bourgeois nationalists. The Soviet Union's infatuation with Africa, that wild peasant romance of the early sixties, had long since vanished, and now even its memory was to be erased. Matured Soviet relationships in Black African were suave and aloof, unemotional, and, most of all, less and less endogamous. For the moment this area had been pushed back to the periphery of Soviet concern. And unless circumstances changed radically, Africa would likely remain of secondary interest. Having lost its potential as a major arena of East-West competition, the primary challenge it now posed was in raising the efficiency of local political and economic organizations, in overcoming the restraints of tradition, and in generating the capital needed to industralize. The Soviet Union faced this challenge with the same limitations (and the same lack of enthusiasm) as other developed countries.

Note on Methodology
Bibliography
Index

Note on Methodology

Any Sovietologist who is honest with himself recognizes that his study of current Soviet policy is conjecture based largely on the Soviet press and that this conjecture is only from time to time reinforced by evidence of specific diplomatic activity. Since he does not have access to the diplomatic record on both sides—and only rarely on one side (and then in part)—his is largely an exercise in reconstructing the plausible. If he is careful, perceptive, and blessed with considerable luck, he may come very close to uncovering not merely Soviet attitudes toward another state or set of states, but the character of their relationship which conditions diplomatic and economic activity. Even then, however, one must remember that for a government dealing with the Soviet Union—particularly an African government that has not developed the Kremlinological skills of the U.S. State Department—the nature of Soviet policy comes across essentially in its diplomatic form; in official conversations with Soviet leaders and diplomats. A study that focuses on the evolution of Soviet attitudes, verified as far as possible by the record of diplomatic and political activity, will seem odd to the African leader who has dealt with the Soviet government. And even if he accepts the analysis after the fact, the student of Soviet foreign policy must remember that, at the time, the African was responding almost exclusively to the deeds of Soviet leaders and their official representatives.

There is another point to be made on the question of methodology. Students of Soviet policy should recognize the increasingly dubious character of attempts to identify "official" Soviet attitudes—that is, the attitudes of policymakers within the appropriate Central Committee Secretariat section and within the foreign ministry. Elizabeth Valkenier has demonstrated the growing free play of ideas permitted Soviet researchers and, therefore, the risks involved in considering an article from *Narody Azii i Afriki* or *Mirovaya ekonomika i mezhdunarodnye otnosheniya* as a perfect reflection of the mind of policymakers. (See Elizabeth Kridl Valkenier, "Recent Trends in Soviet Research on the Developing Countries," *World Politics, XX* [July 1968], 644–659.) The Soviet researcher's approach to a variety of problems, including economic development, social structure, and population, is surprisingly independent, advanced, and susceptible to the relatively open and freewheeling criticism of colleagues. Without arguing the indefensible proposition that academics and journalists enjoy autonomy, their work had by 1967 become increasingly difficult to use as an accurate measure of the prevailing attitude in Ponomarev's section of the Secretariat.

This is not to say that contrasting views and a dialogue among different commentators had emerged for the first time. Conflicting points of view among Soviet experts were long a feature of Soviet publications, but previously it was easier to establish who had the sympathy of the politicians—such as, for example, the liberals within MEiMO in 1964. Thus it may be significant that one heard less from the staff of MEiMO in 1966 and 1967. Since 1965, it seems to me that anyone interested in policy must pay closer attention to the links between commentators and official circles. Wherever possible, I have tried to disentangle these relationships in the last section of the book. As a general observation, I found myself relying more and more on the essentially nonacademic analyst, a man like Kudryavtsev, or on the academic with responsibilities closer to policy formulation—a man like Ulyanovsky or Solodovnikov. Those in the last category, more often than not, turned out to be generalists, basically concerned with current political problems, rather than specialists with comprehensive area training and a preference for more rigorous scholarship. In short, the work of a publicist who has an impact on policy was not likely to reflect a careful and regular reading of *Africa Report, Le Monde, Présence africaine,* or UN studies, let alone primary sources. To put the point another way (and allowing for the obvious flaws in the illustration), the problem of someone examining Soviet policy in this area is not totally dissimilar to that of the Soviet specialist interested in the official American assessment of Soviet involvement in Africa who has been handed this book and a hypothetical *Foreign Affairs* article on the same subject by G. Mennen Williams, Joseph Palmer, or David Newsom.

Bibliography

The principal sources used in this book are Soviet and African newspapers, journals, and radio broadcasts. From the Soviet side the most
important of these journals is *Mirovaya ekonomika i mezhdunarodnye
otnosheniya*, the major theoretical publication of the Institute of World
Economics and International Relations. Although concerned with a wide
range of international issues, this journal has repeatedly carried authoritative summaries of theoretical innovations bearing on Soviet-African relations, very often generated by discussions within the sponsoring Institute
itself. *Pravda* and *Izvestiya* provide important accounts of diplomatic
exchanges and, frequently, pace-setting articles and editorials. The elaboration of these themes and their application to specific African countries
is delegated to more specialized journals: the popular monthly, *Aziya
i Afrika segodnya* (before mid-1961 *Sovremenny Vostok*), and the more
scholarly bimonthly, *Narody Azii i Afriki* (earlier *Problemy vostokovedeniya*). Another useful publication, reflecting not only various Soviet
viewpoints but other often divergent interests within the socialist camp
and among Marxist parties, is the *World Marxist Review* (the English
translation of *Problemy mira i sotsializma*). An excellent survey of this
literature, along with an analysis of Soviet attitudes toward the Third

World, appears bimonthly in *Mizan* (London). The Soviets publish an extremely useful bibliography of Soviet and Western materials on Africa in the monthly *Novaya sovetskaya i inostrannaya literatura po stranam Azii i Afriki* (New Soviet and Foreign Literature on Asian and African Countries). The *Afro-Asian Bulletin,* the monthly journal of the permanent secretariat of the Afro-Asian People's Solidarity Organization, gives news of that organization; Chinese materials are available in *Survey of the China Mainland Press.*

For the African perspective, local newspapers are indispensable: in Ghana, the *Ghanaian Times* and *Evening News;* in Guinea, *Horoya;* in Mali, *L'Essor;* in the Ivory Coast, *Fraternité-Matin;* in Senegal, *Dakar-Matin, L'Unité Africaine,* and for the PAI, *La Lutte* and *Momsarev;* in Nigeria, the *West African Pilot,* the *Daily Times,* and for the NSWFP, *Advance.*

Western journals and newspapers such as *West Africa, Africa Report, Le Monde,* the London *Times, New York Times, The Economist* (Intelligence Unit Reports), *Jeune Afrique,* and *Le Mois en Afrique* include valuable analysis of developments related to Soviet-African relations.

In addition the following Soviet monographs, statistical accounts, and secondary sources have been of use:

Official Publications

Annual Report on External Trade in Ghana (annual, December). Central Bureau of Statistics, Accra.

Commerce extérieur du Sénégal (annual). Ministère des Finances et des Affaires Economiques—Service de la Statistique et de la Mécanographie.

1961 Ghana Treaty Series, VI, October 19–December 20. Ministry of Foreign Affairs (1962). Pages 59–61.

Statistique du commerce extérieur du Mali (annual). Service de la Statistique Générale and de la Comptabilité Economique Nationale-Ministère du Plan et de l'Economie Rural, Bamako.

Vneshnyaya torgovlya Soyuza SSR (*External Trade of the USSR;* annual). Moscow.

Books

Aleksandrovskaya, L. *Gana.* Moscow, 1965.

——— and V. Rybakov. *Africa's Economic Problems.* Moscow: Novosti Press, n.d.

Alexander, H. T. *African Tightrope.* London: Pall Mall Press, 1965.

Ameillon, B. *La Guinée, bilan d'une indépendance.* Paris: François Maspero, 1954.

Apter, David E. *The Gold Coast in Transition.* Princeton: Princeton University Press, 1955.

Attwood, William. *The Reds and the Blacks.* New York: Harper and Row, 1967.

Avakov, R., and others. *National Liberation Movement: Vital Problems.* Moscow: Novosti Press, 1965.

Barnett, Donald L., and Karami Njama. *Mau Mau from Within.* New York: Monthly Review Press, 1966.

Brzezinski, Zbigniew, ed. *Africa and the Communist World.* Stanford: Stanford University Press, 1963.

Chaffard, Georges. *Les carnets secrets de la décolonisation.* Paris: Calmann-Lévy, 1967.

Cooley, John K. *East Wind over Africa.* New York: Walker and Company, 1965.

Dallin, Alexander, ed. *Diversity in International Communism.* New York: Columbia University Press, 1963.

Datlin, S., and others. *Imperialisticheskaya borba za Afriku i osvoboditelnoe dvizhenie narodov* (Imperialist Struggle for Africa and the People's Liberation Movement). Moscow, 1951.

Dementyev, Y. P. *Respublika Mali.* Moscow, 1962.

Draper, Theodore. *American Communism and Soviet Russia.* New York: Viking Press, 1960.

Firsov, A. A. *Ekonomicheskie problemy Gvineskoi Respubliki* (The Economic Problems of the Guinean Republic). Moscow, 1965.

Fokeyev, G. V. *Oni ne khotyat ukhodit* (They Do Not Want to Leave). Moscow, 1965.

Foltz, William J. *From West Africa to the Mali Federation.* New Haven: Yale University Press, 1965.

Friedland, William H., and Carl G. Rosberg, Jr., eds. *African Socialism.* Stanford: Stanford University Press, 1964.

Gavrilov, N. I., ed. *Nezavisimye Strany Afriki: Ekonomicheskie i sotsialnye problemy* (The Independent Countries of Africa: Economic and Social Problems). Moscow, 1965.

Goncharov, L. V., ed. *Ekonomika Afriki* (The Economics of Africa). Moscow, 1965.

Griffith, William E. *The Sino-Soviet Rift.* Cambridge: MIT Press, 1964.

Hamrell, Sven, and Carl Gosta Widstrand. *The Soviet Bloc, China and Africa.* Uppsala: Alinguist and Wiksell Bokforlag, 1964.

Hooker, James R. *Black Revolutionary: George Padmore's Path from Communism to Pan-Africanism.* London: Pall Mall Press, 1967.

Hoskyns, Catherine. *The Congo since Independence: January, 1960–December, 1961.* London: Oxford University Press, 1965.

Iskenderov, A. A., ed. *Rabochi klass stran Azii i Afriki* (The Working Class of Asian and African Countries). Moscow, 1964.

Johns, Sheridan Waite, III. "Marxism-Leninism in a Multi-Racial Environment: The Origins and Early History of the Communist Party of South Africa, 1914–1932." Unpubl. diss., Harvard University, 1965.

Kanet, Roger Edward. "The Soviet Union and Sub-Saharan Africa: Communist Policy toward Africa, 1917–1965." Unpubl. diss., Princeton University, 1966.

Kashin, Yu. *Senegal.* Moscow, 1965.

Kolarz, Walter. *Communism and Colonialism.* New York: St. Martin's Press, 1964.

Kotovskiy, G. G., ed. *Sotsialno-ekonomicheskie posledstviya agrarnykh reform i sotsialnaya struktura derevni v razvivayushchikhsya stranakh Azii i Afriki* (Socio-Economic Effects of Agrarian Reforms and Social Structure of the Village in the Developing Countries of Asia and Africa). Moscow, 1966.

Lessing, Pieter. *Africa's Red Harvest.* New York: John Day, 1962.

London, Kurt, ed. *New Nations in a Divided World.* New York: Frederick A. Praeger, 1963.

Lyubimov, N. N., ed. *Afrika v mirovoi ekonomike i politike* (Africa in World Economics and Politics). Moscow, 1965.

MacKintosh, J. M. *Strategy and Tactics of Soviet Foreign Policy.* London: Oxford University Press, 1963.

MacKintosh, John P. *Nigerian Government and Politics.* Evanston: Northwestern University Press, 1966.

Milon, René. *Marxisme, communisme et socialisme africaine.* Paris, 1962.

Morgenthau, Ruth Shachter. *Political Parties in French-Speaking West Africa.* London: Oxford University Press, 1964.

Morison, David. *The USSR and Africa.* London: Oxford University Press, 1964.

Morrow, John H. *First American Ambassador to Guinea.* New Brunswick: Rutgers University Press, 1968.

Nkrumah, Kwame. *I Speak of Freedom.* New York: Frederick A. Praeger. 1961.

——— *Neo-Colonialism: The Last Stage of Imperialism.* London: Thomas Nelson and Sons, 1965.

O'Brien, Conor Cruise. *To Katanga and Back.* London: Hutchinson and Co., 1962.

Olderogge, D. A., and I. I. Potekhin, eds. *Narody Afriki* (The Peoples of Africa). Moscow, 1954.

Padmore, George. *Pan-Africanism or Communism?* New York: Roy Publishers, 1955.

Phillips, Claude S., Jr. *The Development of Nigerian Foreign Policy.* Evanston: Northwestern University Press, 1964.

Potekhin, Ivan I. *Gana segodnya* (Ghana Today). Moscow, 1959.

———— *Afrika smotrit v budushchee* (Africa Looks to the Future). Moscow, 1960.

Ra'anan, Uri. *Arming the Third World: Case Studies in Soviet Foreign Policy.* Cambridge: MIT Press, 1969.

Rosberg, Carl G., Jr., and John Nottingham. *The Myth of "Mau Mau" Nationalism in Kenya.* New York: Frederick A. Praeger, 1966.

Schlesinger, Arthur M., Jr. *A Thousand Days.* Boston: Houghton-Mifflin Co., 1965.

Shelnov, A. K. *Senegal: Ekonomika i vneshnyaya torgovlya* (Senegal: Economic Structure and External Trade). Moscow, 1963.

Sivolobov, A. M. *Natsionalnee osvoboditelnoe dvizhenie v Afrike* (The National Liberation Movement in Africa). Moscow, 1961.

Sklar, Richard L. *Nigerian Political Parties.* Princeton: Princeton University Press, 1963.

Snyder, Frank Gregory. *One-Party Government in Mali.* New Haven: Yale University Press, 1965.

SSSR i strany Afriki: 1946–1962 (The USSR and the Countries of Africa). 2 vols., Moscow, 1963.

Thiam, Doudou. *La Politique étrangère des états africains.* Paris: Presses Universitaires de France, 1963.

Thompson, W. Scott. *Ghana's Foreign Policy, 1957–1966: Diplomacy, Ideology, and the New State.* Princeton: Princeton University Press, 1969.

Thornton, Thomas Perry, ed. *The Third World in Soviet Perspective.* Princeton: Princeton University Press, 1964.

Touré, Sekou. *L'Action politique du Parti Démocratique de Guinée pour l'émancipation africaine.* Conakry, 1958.

Tuzmukhamedov, R. A. *Organizatsiya Afrikanskogo edinstva* (Organization of African Unity). Moscow, 1964.

Tyagunenko, V. L. *Problemy sovremennykh natsionalno-osvoboditelnykh revolyutsi* (Problems of Contemporary National Liberation Revolutions). Moscow, 1966.

Vasileva, V. Ya., I. M. Lemin and V. A. Maslennikov, eds. *Imperialisticheskaya borba za Afriku i osvoboditelnoe dvizhenie narodov* (Imperialist Struggle for Africa and the People's Liberation Movement). Moscow, 1953.

Verin, V. P. *Prezidentskie respubliki v Afrike* (Presidential Republics in Africa). Moscow, 1962.

Vlasov, A. V. *Nigeriya: Ekonomika i vneshnyaya torgovlya* (Nigeria: Economic Structure and External Trade). Moscow, 1965.

Zagoria, Donald S. *The Sino-Soviet Conflict, 1956–1961.* Princeton: Princeton University Press, 1962.

Zolberg, Aristide R. *One-Party Government in the Ivory Coast.* Princeton: Princeton University Press, 1964.

Articles

Adie, W. A. C. "China, Russia and the Third World." *China Quarterly,* no. 11 (July–September 1962), pp. 200–213.

Alexandre, Pierre. "Nationalism, Communism and the Uncommitted Nations: Marxism and African Cultural Traditions." *Survey,* no. 43 (August 1962), pp. 65–78.

Anglin, Douglas G. "Nigeria: Political Non-Alignment and Economic Alignment." *Journal of Modern African Studies,* II (July 1964), 247–263.

Ansprenger, Franz. "Nationalism, Communism and the Uncommitted Nations: African Profiles." *Survey,* no. 43 (August 1962), pp. 73–90.

Bell, M. J. V. "Military Assistance to Independent African States." *Adelphi Papers,* no. 15 (December 1964).

Bird, Christopher. "Scholarship and Propaganda." *Problems of Communism,* XI (March–April 1962), 32–37.

Carlisle, Donald S. "The Changing Soviet Perception of the Developing Process in the Afro-Asian World." *Midwest Journal of Political Science,* VIII (November 1964), 385–407.

——— "Stalin's Postwar Foreign Policy and the National Liberation Movement." *Review of Politics,* XXVII (July 1965), 334–363.

Carnett, George S., and Morris H. Crawford. "The Scope and Distribution of Soviet Economic Aid," in U.S. Congress, Joint Economic Committee. *Dimensions of Soviet Economic Power.* 87th Congress, 2nd session. Washington: U.S. Government Printing Office, 1962. Pages 461–474.

"Eastern Europe Overseas: Africa." *East Europe,* X (August 1961), 8–12.

Emerson, Rupert. "The Atlantic Community and the Emerging Countries." *International Organization,* XVII (Summer 1963), 628–648.

Foltz, William J. "The Parti Africain de l'Indépendance: The Dilemmas of a Communist Movement in West Africa." Forthcoming.

Garrison, Lloyd. "Portrait of Nkrumah as Dictator." *New York Times Magazine,* May 3, 1964, pp. 15ff.

Goldman, Marshall I. "A Balance Sheet of Soviet Foreign Aid." *Foreign Affairs,* XLIII (January 1965), 349–360.

Griffith, William E. "Africa." *Survey,* no. 54 (January 1965), pp. 168–187.

Grundy, Kenneth W. "Marxism-Leninism and African Underdevelopment." *International Journal,* XVII (Summer 1962), 300–304.

———— "Nkrumah's Theory of Underdevelopment: An Analysis of Recurrent Themes." *World Politics,* XV (April 1963), 438–454.

"Guinea after Five Years" *The World Today,* XX (March 1964), 113–121.

Herman, Leon M. "The Political Goals of Soviet Foreign Aid," in U.S. Congress, Joint Economic Committee. *Dimensions of Soviet Economic Power.* 87th Congress, 2nd session. Washington: U.S. Government Printing Office, 1962. Pages 477–485.

Hinterhoff, E. "Soviet Military Aid and Its Implications," *Fifteen Nations,* February–March 1962, pp. 79–87.

"Influence-Buying in West Africa." *East Europe,* XIII (July 1964), 2–8.

Ismaguilova, R., and I. Yastrebova. "Cinq siècles de relations avec le continent africain." *Le Mois en Afrique,* no. 15 (March 1967), pp. 53–63.

Keita, Modibo. "The Foreign Policy of Mali." *International Affairs,* XXXVII (October 1961), 432–439.

Klinghoffer, Arthur Jay. "Why the Soviets Chose Sides." *Africa Report,* XIII (February 1968), 47–49.

Kolarz, Walter. "The West African Scene." *Problems of Communism,* X (November–December 1961), 15–24.

———— "The Impact of Communism on West Africa." *International Affairs,* XXXVIII (April 1962), 156–169.

Labedz, Leopold. "The USSR and the Developing Countries," in Leopold Labedz and Walter Laqueur, eds., *Polycentrism.* New York: Frederick A. Praeger, 1962. Pages 153–160.

Laqueur, Walter Z. "Communism and Nationalism in Tropical Africa." *Foreign Affairs,* XXXIX (July 1961), 610–621.

———— "Towards National Democracy: Soviet Doctrine and the New Countries." *Survey,* no. 37 (July–September 1961), pp. 3–11.

Legum, Colin. "Socialism in Ghana: A Political Interpretation," in Wil-

liam H. Friedland and Carl J. Rosberg, Jr., eds., *African Socialism.*
Stanford: Stanford University Press, 1964. Pages 131–161.

Legvold, Robert. "The Soviet Union and Senegal." *Mizan,* VIII
(July–August 1966), 161–170.

———— "Lignes de force de la diplomatie soviétique en Afrique." *Le
Mois en Afrique,* no. 15 (March 1967), pp. 30–52.

London, Kurt, "The Role of China." *Problems of Communism,* XI
(July–August 1962), 22–27.

Lowenthal, Richard. "Russia, the One-Party System, and the Third
World." *Survey,* no. 58 (January 1966), pp. 43–68.

MacKintosh, John P. "Nigeria since Independence." *The World Today,*
XX (August 1964), 328–337.

Markov, Walter. "Mouvement national et classes sociales dans le Tiers-
Monde." *Cahiers internationaux,* no. 117 (March-April 1961), pp.
47–64.

Marin, Y. "Soviet Policy in Africa." *Bulletin of the Institute for the
Study of the USSR,* XI (June 1964), 17–21.

Montias, John M. "The Soviet Model and the Underdeveloped Areas,"
in Nicholas Spulber, ed., *Study of the Soviet Economy.* Bloom-
ington: Indiana University Press, 1961. Pages 57–82.

Morison, David L. "Communism in Africa: Moscow's First Steps." *Problems of Communism,* X (November–December 1961), 8–15.

Mosely, Philip E. "Soviet Policy in the Developing Countries." *Foreign
Affairs,* XLIII (October 1964), 87–98.

Nkrumah, Kwame. "The Movement for Colonial Freedom." *Phylon,*
XVI (fourth quarter 1955), 397–409.

Nove, Alec. "The Soviet Model and Under-Developed Countries." *International Affairs,* XXXVII (January 1961), 29–38.

Nutter, G. Warren. "Soviet Economic Policies Toward Afro-Asian Countries," in Kurt London, ed., *New Nations in a Divided World.*
New York: Frederick A. Praeger, 1963. Pages 193–204.

Pistrak, Lazar. "Soviet Views on Africa." *Problems of Communism,* XI
(March–April 1962), 24–31.

Ra'anan, Uri. "Moscow and the 'Third World.' " *Problems of Communism,* XIV (January–February 1965), 22–31.

Scalapino, Robert A. "Sino-Soviet Competition in Africa." *Foreign
Affairs,* XLI (July 1964), 640–654.

———— "On the Trail of Chou En-lai in Africa." Memorandum
RM-4061 PR, RAND Corporation. April 1964.

Schapiro, Leonard. "The Soviet Dream of Africa." *Encounter,* XXIV
(February 1965), 49–53.

Schatten, Fritz. "Polycentrism–Africa: Nationalism and Communism." *Survey,* no. 42 (June 1962), pp. 148–159.

Shinn, William, Jr. "The 'National-Democratic State,' a Communist Program for Less-Developed Areas." *World Politics,* XV (April 1963), 377–388.

Shulman, Marshall D. "The Communist States and Western Integration." *International Organization,* XVII (Summer 1963), 649–662.

Stolte, Stefan C. "Africa Between Two Power Blocs." *Bulletin of the Institute for the Study of the USSR,* VIII (May 1965), 32–39.

Thornton, Thomas Perry. "Peking, Moscow and the Under-Developed Areas." *World Politics,* XII (July 1961), 491–504.

Yakobson, Sergius. "Russia and Africa," in Ivo J. Lederer, ed., *Russian Foreign Policy.* New Haven: Yale University Press, 1962. Pages 453–488.

Yellon, R. A. "The Winds of Change." *Mizan,* IX (March–August 1967), 51–57, 155–173.

Zagoria, Donald S. "Sino-Soviet Friction in Underdeveloped Areas." *Problems of Communism,* X (March–April 1961), 1–12.

Index

Aborigines' Rights Protection Society, 18

Abrams, Willy, 246

Action Group: and appeal for "united front of progressives," 329; criticizes Nigerian foreign policy (1961), 109; early Soviet assessment of, 27; on relations with USSR, 94–95

Adam, Assi Camille, 86

Adamafio, Tawia, 132, 134

Addison, Kojo, 48, 290

Adoula, Cyrille, 137

Adjei, Ako, 138n

Adjei, Peter, 216

Aeroflot, 261, 264

Afghanistan, 6, 41

African Institute (of Soviet Academy of Sciences), 38

African socialism: condemned by *Spark*, 205; of moderate states, 171–72; 1961 party program condemns, 114; of radical states appraised (1962–63), 174–78

African unity: Casablanca-Monrovian interest in, 147; movement toward, 164–65; and Nkrumah, 184–85

African worker: and class struggle, 339; and decolonization, 22–23; and national democratic state, 113; in revolution, 29

Afrique Occidentale Française (AOF), 68

AOF-Confédération Générale du Travail, 61

Afro-Asian Conference, First (1955). *See* Bandung conference

Afro-Asian Conference, Second (1965), 154, 237

Afro-Asian Journalists' Conference, 154

Afro-Asian movement: Chinese position in, declines, 337; Soviet role in, 153–55; support for test-ban treaty, 201

Afro-Asian People's Solidarity Organization: second conference (Conakry, 1960), 69, 74, 82, 83, 84–85; third conference (Moshi, 1963), 149, 153, 154–55, 202; fourth conference (Winneba, 1965), 247, 249–50; fifth conference site changed from Peking to Algiers, 338; Algiers council (1964), 215–16; Algiers

Soviet Policy in West Africa   *Robert Legvold*

Harvard University Press, Cambridge, Massachusetts, 1970

TO MY MOTHER AND FATHER

.

Preface

This is a study of Soviet foreign policy in six West African countries: Guinea, Ghana, the Ivory Coast, Mali, Nigeria, and Senegal. These six countries represent in their differing foreign and domestic attitudes the full spectrum of countries the Soviet Union has dealt with in Black Africa. They were all in the first wave of colonies to achieve independence between 1957 and 1960 and, therefore, of the former African colonies they have had the longest involvement with the Soviet Union. They, as Russian eyes have viewed Africa, span a range from the most progressive of nations to the most reactionary. Each, in its own right, has had an interesting relationship with the Soviet Union that adds something to a general appreciation of Soviet relations with Black Africa. Together they have supplied illustrations of every problem Black Africa poses for an outsider's foreign policy: from hypersensitive nationalism to, what Soviet theorists are not far wrong in calling, neocolonial dependence; from relative internal stability to fundamental instability; from military coups d'état to civil war. Other countries—Ethiopia, Congo (Kinshasa), and Somalia are obvious examples—would have been equally significant subjects for a study of Soviet policy in sub-Saharan Africa, but their distance from the most important West African countries (no study of Soviet policy in Black Africa could exclude policy in Ghana and Nigeria) would have made field research far more difficult. The countries selected are conveniently in a single region, a region that in one further respect offers a useful basis of comparison: it contains both former French and former British colonies.

When I began this study several years ago my interest was in Soviet policy in the Third World, and the area of policy that fascinated me most was Black Africa. A number of studies had already surveyed Soviet involvement in this area, and it seemed to me that the next step toward understanding Soviet policy in sub-Sahara was an intensive study of Soviet relations with particular African countries. Since Soviet policy in no single African country encompasses all of the features of Soviet policy in Black Africa, it seemed equally important to look at several countries, and automatically my method became comparative. Throughout this book I have tried to compare Soviet policy in different countries or categories of countries, to compare policy over time, and to compare theory with practice. I wanted to build the comparison around answers to several basic questions: How has the Soviet Union coped with the problems and opportunities that this very special part of the Third World has created? How have its perceptions of Black Africa evolved over the last decade? Has policy shifted correspondingly with changes in these perceptions? Thus, although Soviet relations with any country or group of countries are of intrinsic interest, this study of Soviet relations with specific countries is intended as an illustration of more general phenomena; by the same token, its title does not mean to imply that these six countries are the only countries that matter in West Africa.

Every author thanks those who have helped him in preparing his book, but few can be acknowledging a debt so large as mine, or a debt owed to so many. There are those who cannot be named because they are officials of their government—Soviet, American, French, British, German, Ghanaian, Guinean, Malian, Ivory Coast, Senegalese, and Nigerian. I hope some of them will have a chance to see this book and that they will find in it a fair reflection of their patient efforts to improve my understanding of the real world of diplomacy and politics. Also I am most grateful to the generous agencies that made travel to Africa, the Soviet Union, and England possible and to their administrators who extended this aid so efficiently and pleasantly. The Ford Foundation through its Foreign Area Fellowship Program enabled me to spend thirteen months in England, the Soviet Union, and (eight of the thirteen months) West Africa during 1965–66. The American Philosophical Society and the Tufts Faculty Research Fund supported a return trip to West Africa in the summer of 1968, where I collected information for the last chapters. I wish to express appreciation to the staffs of a number of institutions that made available basic materials: the Edwin

Ginn Library of the Fletcher School of Law and Diplomacy, the Russian Research Center and Widener Library of Harvard University, the Center for International Studies of MIT, the African Studies Library of Boston University, Chatham House, the Institute for Strategic Studies (London), the Institut Français d'Afrique Noire in Dakar, the African Studies Institute of the University of Ghana, and the University of Lagos. A number of people gave me guidance early in my research and I want to acknowledge their kindness: Leopold Labedz, Alexander Dallin, William E. Griffith, Mary Holdsworth, Sheridan Waite Johns, Walter Laqueur, and Tibor Szamuely.

A major part of my debt is to friends and colleagues who graciously agreed to read and comment on the manuscript at various stages of its development: David Albright, David Morison, Waldemar Nielsen, Professors William J. Foltz and Charles B. McLane. Professors Rupert Emerson and Ruth S. Morgenthau made many useful suggestions for improving the manuscript. Three other people I must mention especially. The first is Professor Uri Ra'anan, always my teacher and now also my colleague, who was pulled into this project at its formulation and who throughout the next four years provided frequent advice and stimulation. The second is Professor W. Scott Thompson, whose influence is only partially reflected in the footnotes and who has been an exceptionally unselfish source of ideas, information, and friendship from our first meeting in Ghana to the present. And the third is Professor Marshall D. Shulman, who directed this study when it was a dissertation and who has been my teacher, mentor, and benefactor in countless ways. Finally, I must thank those who helped with the formal preparation of the manuscript: a superb typist, Mrs. Stanley Krauz; for aiding with footnotes, Joseph Restuccia, Timothy Weiskel, and Mrs. Herbert Sawyer; and Joyce Lebowitz, a remarkably accomplished editor.

Most authors, particularly young authors, also thank their wives and children for enduring the agony of a book's preparation. My agony was negligible and theirs, I am assured, was tolerable; so, while I am deeply grateful that Gloria and Nancy were with me throughout the adventure, I know that rather than receive gratitude from me they would prefer to join in expressing appreciation to all those individuals and institutions that made the adventure possible.

R.H.L.
Woburn, Massachusetts, October, 1969

Contents

A-APSO   Afro-Asian People's Solidarity Organization
AFP   Agence France Presse
CMLN   Comité Militaire de Libération Nationale (Mali)
CNDR   Comité National de Défense de la Révolution (Mali)
CRB   Comités Révolutionnaires de Base (Mali)
CECEC   Committee for Economic Cooperation with the Eastern Countries
   (Ghana)
CPSU   Communist Party of the Soviet Union
GGT   Confédération Générale du Travail (France)
CPP   Convention People's Party (Ghana)
FLN   Front de Libération Nationale (Algeria)
GEC   Groupes d'Etudes Communistes
IBRD   International Bank for Reconstruction and Development
ICFTC   International Confederation of Free Trade Unions
IMF   International Monetary Fund
KCA   Kikuyu Central Association (Kenya)
MEiMO   Mirovaya ekonomika i mezhdunarodnye otnosheniya
MLF   Multilateral (Nuclear) Force
NASSO   National Association of Socialist Students Organization (Ghana)
NCNC   National Convention of Nigerian Citizens
NLC   National Liberation Council (Ghana)
NCNA   New China News Agency
NLP   Nigerian Labour Party
NNA   Nigerian National Alliance
NNDP   Nigerian National Democratic Party
NSWFP   Nigerian Socialist Workers' and Farmers Party
NTUC   Nigerian Trade Union Congress
NEPU   Northern Elements Progressive Union (Nigeria)
NPC   Northern People's Congress (Nigeria)
OCAM   Organisation Commune Africaine et Malgache
OAU   Organization of African Unity
PAI   Parti Africain de l'Indépendance (Senegal)
PCF   Parti Communiste Français
PCS   Parti Communiste Sénégalais
PDG   Parti Démocratique de Guinée
POGR   President's Own Guard Regiment (Ghana)
RFE   Radio Free Europe
RDA   Rassemblement Démocratique Africain
SCMP   Survey of the China Mainland Press
UMOA   Union Monétaire Ouest-Africaine
US   Union Soudanaise (Mali)
UMBC   United Middle Belt Congress (Nigeria)
UPGA   United Progressive Grand Alliance (Nigeria)
WANG   West African National Congress (Ghana)
WFDY   World Federation of Democratic Youth
WFTU   World Federation of Trade Unions
WPC   World Peace Council